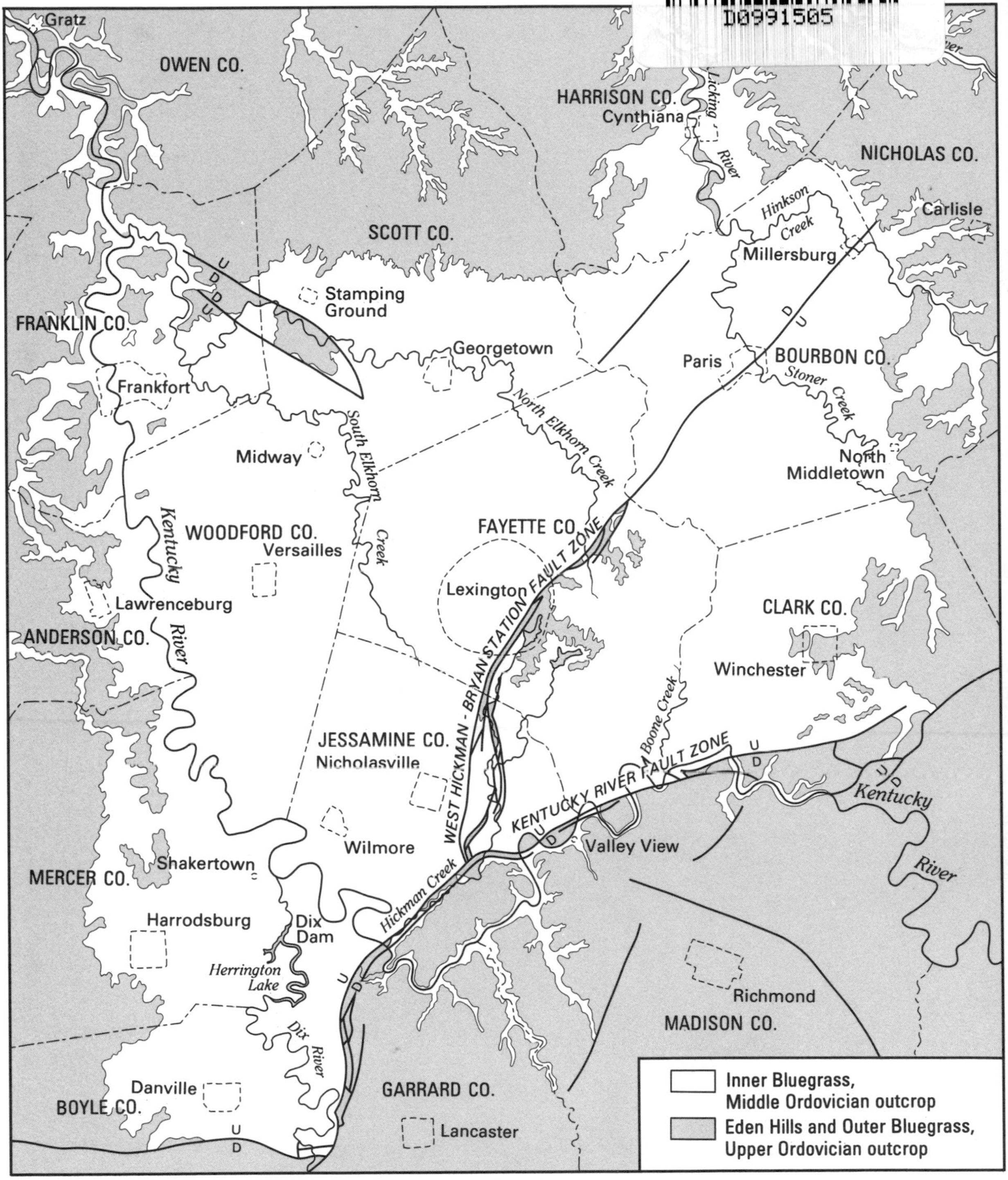
Gratz
OWEN CO.
HARRISON CO.
Cynthiana
Licking River
NICHOLAS CO.
Hinkson Creek
Carlisle
SCOTT CO.
Millersburg
Stamping Ground
FRANKLIN CO.
Georgetown
Paris
BOURBON CO.
Stoner Creek
Frankfort
North Elkhorn Creek
South Elkhorn Creek
Midway
North Middletown
Kentucky River
WOODFORD CO.
Versailles
FAYETTE CO.
Lexington
CLARK CO.
Lawrenceburg
ANDERSON CO.
WEST HICKMAN - BRYAN STATION FAULT ZONE
Winchester
Boone Creek
JESSAMINE CO.
Nicholasville
KENTUCKY RIVER FAULT ZONE
Wilmore
Valley View
Shakertown
MERCER CO.
Hickman Creek
Harrodsburg
Dix Dam
Herrington Lake
Dix River
Richmond
MADISON CO.
Danville
BOYLE CO.
GARRARD CO.
Lancaster
U
D
Inner Bluegrass, Middle Ordovician outcrop
Eden Hills and Outer Bluegrass, Upper Ordovician outcrop

THE INNER BLUEGRASS OF KENTUCKY

Bluegrass Land & Life

Land Character, Plants, and Animals of the Inner Bluegrass Region of Kentucky

Past, Present, and Future

MARY E. WHARTON
and
ROGER W. BARBOUR

THE UNIVERSITY PRESS OF KENTUCKY

Publication of this book was assisted by a grant
from the Land and Nature Trust of the Bluegrass.

Scholarly publisher for the Commonwealth,
serving Bellarmine College, Berea College, Centre
College of Kentucky, Eastern Kentucky University,
The Filson Club, Georgetown College, Kentucky
Historical Society, Kentucky State University,
Morehead State University, Murray State University,
Northern Kentucky University, Transylvania University,
University of Kentucky, University of Louisville,
and Western Kentucky University.

Editorial and Sales Offices: Lexington, Kentucky 40508-4008

Library of Congress Cataloging-in-Publication Data

Wharton, Mary E., 1912-
Bluegrass land and life : land character, plants, and animals of the Inner Bluegrass region of Kentucky, past, present, and future / Mary E. Wharton and Roger W. Barbour.

p. cm.
Includes bibliographical references.
ISBN 0-8131-1688-0
1. Natural history—Kentucky. I. Barbour, Roger William, 1919-
II. Title.
QH105.K4W43 1991
508.769—dc20 90-36745

This book is printed on acid-free paper meeting
the requirements of the American National Standard
for Permanence of Paper for Printed Library Materials.
♾

To the memory of

FRANK T. MCFARLAND
who introduced me to the flora of the Kentucky River country

B.B. MCINTEER
who kindled my interest in the unique presettlement ecosystems
of the Bluegrass

ARTHUR C. MCFARLAN
who initiated my fascination with Kentucky geology

All more than fifty years ago

—Mary E. Wharton

With sincere appreciation for the efforts of

GRACE CROSTHWAITE
for acquainting me with the world of books

WM. J. HAMILTON
for guiding me through graduate school

E.L. PALMER
for introducing me to many of the wonders of the out-of-doors

—Roger W. Barbour

Contents

List of Maps, Figure, and Tables	ix
Foreword by John O. Simonds	xi
Acknowledgments	xiii
Introduction	1
Part I. Geology and Environmental History	
1. Geological Background	5
2. Presettlement Vegetation	19
3. Presettlement Animal Life	33
4. Early Modification of the Presettlement Ecosystems	40
Part II. Habitats and Natural Community Organization	
5. Plant Communities	51
6. Vertebrate Animal Habitats	62
7. Present Status of Vertebrates	74
Part III. Annotated Lists	
Vascular Plants	79
Vertebrate Animals	159
Part IV. The Future of the Bluegrass	
8. The Bluegrass Region of Tomorrow in Light of Present Trends	207
Appendixes	
A. Glossary of Geologic Terms	227
B. The Geologic Time Scale	227
C. Plant Communities and Succession	229
Bibliography	230
Index of Species	237
General Index	255

Illustrations follow pages 18 and 50

Maps

1. The Inner Bluegrass of Kentucky — Front endsheet
2. Kentucky River and West Hickman–Bryan Station Fault Zones — Back endsheet
3. Generalized Geologic Map of Kentucky — 6
4. Physiographic Diagram of Kentucky — 7
5. The Inner Bluegrass in Relation to Surrounding Areas — 9
6. Outcrop Area of the High Bridge Group — 10
7. Abandoned Meanders of Boone Creek — 14
8. Courses of the Kentucky River, Dix River, and Elkhorn Creek — 16
9. Some Military Land Grants that Determined Road Patterns — 43
10. Overlapping Claims in the Bluegrass — 44
11. Counties of the Inner Bluegrass — 80

Figure

1. Structure Section — 8

Tables

1. Diameters of Selected Large Trees in a Harrison County Woodland Pasture — 29
2. Diameters and Estimated Ages of Bur Oaks on a Former Farm in Fayette County — 30
3. Mammalian Species Found in Welch Cave — 35
4. Composition of Canopy, Maple-Ash-Oak Forests, on Mesic Cliffs of the Kentucky River — 54
5. Composition of Forest Canopy, Kentucky River Cliffs, from Xeric to Slightly Mesic — 55
6. Comparison between Canopy Species on Opposite Cliffs of Creek — 56
7. Importance Value of Tree Species in Four Relic Savanna-Woodlands — 60
8. Population Growth in Selected Bluegrass Counties — 207

Foreword

JOHN O. SIMONDS

Bluegrass Land and Life, by Drs. Mary E. Wharton and Roger W. Barbour, is a timely and informative examination of the ecology of this world-renowned region of Kentucky. This new book by two distinguished scientists describes in an engaging way the transition of this unique terrain from early geologic time to the brink of the twenty-first century.

The whole of the Bluegrass landscape is now, as always in its long history, undergoing change. The ancient past saw the gradual evolution from seas, with their shelled animals and mineral deposits, to savanna-woodlands, rich with the big game animals cherished by several Indian tribes. More recent centuries have witnessed the transition to cultivated agricultural lands unsurpassed for the abundance of their yields and the richness of their pasturage. In the world of the horse, particularly, the word Bluegrass has become synonymous with "quality unexcelled."

Today the Bluegrass region is threatened by the all-too-common American phenomenon of urbanization out of control. One can only hope that the evolution of the next decades will be guided by wise land planning of the highest order. In this process the best of the region's natural, scenic, and historic resources must be defined and protected. Existing towns and cities should be restudied, circumscribed, enhanced, and revitalized within an interconnected openspace framework.

The process is complex. Multi-modal systems of transportation and energy transmission must be pre-planned together to cause as little disruption as possible and to provide much more efficient means of interconnection and movement. Urban sprawl must be stemmed and eradicated. Pollution in all its insidious forms must be outlawed. In sum, the new land use patterns must be devised in harmony with the natural systems of soil, water, topography, and the "want-to-be" of the land. The region can then take its evolving form within the green matrix of protected farmland and forest, as in England, Scandinavia, Switzerland, and Germany.

The basis for such comprehensive landscape and transportation planning must be a fuller understanding of the land and its physical "givens." It is in this regard especially that this book will make a significant contribution. Just when this knowledge is most urgently needed, we are presented with a highly readable compendium of the essential facts by scientists of impeccable credentials.

Here is a book that can make a difference. While in recent years it has seemed to some that the beloved Bluegrass countryside might fade into history, this book is hearteningly reassuring. It instills a comprehension of the immense cultural and economic wealth at stake, and it should foster a determination both to preserve and to advance the Bluegrass tradition.

Dr. Mary Wharton is a wise, patient, and singularly knowledgeable botanist, ecologist, and geologist. Dr. Roger Barbour is a widely known zoologist and wildlife photographer. Both have been leaders in efforts to preserve the Bluegrass region, and they have collaborated on two previous books. Now they have compiled a truly remarkable scientific and cultural sourcebook. There are few to compare with it in America, none before in the Bluegrass region. It will long serve as the definitive reference for all who seek a richer and deeper understanding of Bluegrass land and the life it supports—animal, plant, and human.

Mr. Simonds is a nationally known landscape architect, environmental planner, and writer who lives in Pittsburgh, Pennsylvania.

Acknowledgments

The authors are grateful to Johnnie B. Varner for the inclusion of his many unpublished collections of plant species in the Inner Bluegrass, and to him and to William S. Bryant for data on the composition of certain forests. Julian Campbell, Max Medley, Hal Bryan, Steve Rice, William E. Blackburn, and Elwood Carr also permitted us to use some of their collection data. Bettye Lee Mastin graciously shared with us some of her research relating to her book *Lexington 1779*. Doris Westerman, Albert G. Westerman, and John MacGregor served as consultants on amphibian and reptile distribution and life histories. Wayne Davis was consultant on bird and mammalian species.

Contributions toward publication of this book came from the Land and Nature Trust of the Bluegrass, which recognized its importance in fostering understanding and appreciation of the natural assets of the Bluegrass Region—flora, fauna, land, and environmental history—as prerequisite to intelligent planning in the region. The organization therefore offered to underwrite the cost of publishing color plates and sought contributions from individuals.

Contributors of one page or more of color plates:

John R. Cooke
Winifred W. Haggart
Mrs. A.B. Hancock, Jr.
Charles J. Isbell
Walter W. May
Dr. Wally Montgomery
Mr. and Mrs. A.C. Newbery
Matthew Tierney
Dr. Woodford Van Meter
Mrs. William Wichman
Mr. and Mrs. Kenneth V.L. Miller

Contributors of a portion of a page of color plates:

Richard Bean
Jessica A. Bell
Mrs. Luther Caldwell
Anne Campbell
Mrs. Ben Chandler
Sam Clay
Mrs. Richard Crutcher
Dr. W.A. Doyle
Mr. and Mrs. William Floyd
Dr. John Fox
Joseph C. Graves, Jr.
Dr. J.D. Hasbrouck
Victor Heerman
Sally Hinkle
Mrs. Brereton Jones
Lars la Cour
Mary Lee Mahin
Gloria Martin
Muir Meadow
Mrs. William Patterson
Mrs. Bruce Poundstone
Jacqueline Purdy
Geggy Ryen
Dr. and Mrs. Edward Ray
Rose Shrimpton
R.H. Swigert
Clara Wieland
Mr. and Mrs. Fred Wachs, Jr.
Catharine W. Wilson
J.R. Wilson, Jr.
Carolyn Murray-Wooley

Introduction

"BLUEGRASS KENTUCKY is more than a region which can be definitely located by a geologist or a geographer upon a soulless map," writes historian Thomas D. Clark. "It is not alone a matter of geographical tangibility, but it is likewise a state of mind . . . and a satisfactory way of life" (1942, 109). This intangible quality is the human fruition of a unique physical environment that has produced exceptional conditions for plant and animal life through countless ages.

Although all sections of the Bluegrass region have many characteristics in common, the Inner Bluegrass (about 30 percent of the whole) is a more distinct entity, unique in the character of its land, its native vegetation, and its indigenous animals—our considerations in the following pages. The Bluegrass way of life is a natural result.

Explorers here in the mid-1700s were startled by the aspect of land, vegetation, and wildlife so different from anything previously encountered in the New World. News of this rich and verdant wonderland abounding in animal life spread quickly along the Eastern Seaboard. In 1769 Daniel Boone, after journeying through a mountain wilderness, first viewed the Bluegrass section "from the top of an eminence . . . and saw with pleasure the beautiful level of Kentucke." This land he "esteemed a second paradise" (Filson 1784, 51, 56).

With the Piedmont and Tidewater soils of the Eastern Seaboard eroding and becoming depleted, the peopling of Kentucky that began in the 1770s was rapid, sometimes ten thousand arriving in a single year. Within fifteen years the population of what is now Kentucky reached 73,677, according to the 1790 census. As migration to Kentucky was rapid, so too was the destruction of the region's vegetation and animal life. Since the Bluegrass was the first section of Kentucky to be settled, it was also the first to have its original vegetation destroyed or modified and its indigenous large mammals—bison, elk, and deer—decimated. Nevertheless, many native plant and animal species remain to this day.

One of our most distinguished botanists has described the Inner Bluegrass section as "the most anomalous vegetation area of eastern United States" (Braun 1950, 124). The anomaly lies not in endemism (i.e., species found nowhere else) but in unexpected plant communities and species distribution. The resulting ecology fostered a pattern of land use which began early in the settlement and which subsequently flourished in the production of high-quality livestock, especially the Thoroughbred horse, in which the area has held preeminence for a century and a half. This was no accident; the two facts are related. The patterns of human culture that developed in the Inner Bluegrass were influenced not only by the propensities of its people but by its vegetation, its physiography and climate, and its underlying geology.

Unfortunately there were no botanists or zoologists among the early explorers and surveyors to provide a detailed scientific account of the virgin life, although we have some general descriptions from laymen. A few botanists, such as André and François Michaux, did visit Kentucky in the early days but were more concerned with individual plant species than with a regional floristic emphasis or community ecology.

In the late 1940s, Mary E. Wharton began looking into existing indications of the structure of presettlement vegetation in the Inner Bluegrass, reading pioneers' descriptions and adding to her personal library books containing early accounts as they became available through rare book dealers. At that time she suggested to one of her undergraduate students, Ursula Davidson, who was beginning her graduate study at the University of Kentucky, that she choose as research for her thesis the original vegetation of Fayette County.

Through the 1950s Mary Wharton did field work toward "A Flora of the Inner Bluegrass." After purchasing land for a Bluegrass nature sanctuary, she traced the history of that land back to its first owner in the 1780s and realized the botanical significance of early land records. Hence in the next few years she read hundreds of the earliest surveys and deeds, all of which mention trees and many of which mention cane. She then recalled that a neighbor, the late Judge Samuel M. Wilson, an attorney and a historian, had years before uncovered a court case of 1805 based on the presence of bluegrass here when white settlers arrived.

In recent years, as more and more natural features of the Inner Bluegrass have become threatened by urban growth and development, interest in Bluegrass plant ecology and the study of its uniqueness have fortunately increased. William S. Bryant, William H. Martin, and Johnnie B. Varner have collaborated with Mary Wharton, as well as working independently, on this subject. In 1980 Julian J.N. Campbell completed a doctoral dissertation at the University of Kentucky on "Present and Presettlement Forest Conditions in the Inner Bluegrass of Kentucky," and in 1985 he issued a report entitled "The Land of Cane and Clover."

On September 1, 1950, when Roger W. Barbour joined the zoology faculty at the University of Kentucky, surprisingly little was known of the fauna of the Inner Bluegrass. Over the years he and his students spent thousands of hours on research in the region. Many Master of Science and several Doctor of Philosophy degrees dealt in whole or in part with various aspects of the distribution and life history of various species of terrestrial vertebrates in the Inner Bluegrass.

This book ties together the long threads of our studies of Bluegrass land and life—threads sometimes interrupted by publications pertaining to the entire state: *A Guide to the Wildflowers and Ferns of Kentucky* and *Trees and Shrubs of Kentucky*, on both of which we collaborated; *Amphibians and Reptiles of Kentucky*

(RWB), *Kentucky Birds* (RWB et al.), *Mammals of Kentucky* (RWB and Wayne H. Davis), and *The Horse World of the Bluegrass* (MEW et al.).

Roger Barbour wrote the chapters on contemporary vertebrates and the account of ancient animal remains in Welch Cave. Mary Wharton is responsible for the remainder of the book and drew the base maps used to create the endpapers by placing together the geologic quadrangle maps involved and greatly reducing the composite.

Part I of the present book presents an overview of the Inner Bluegrass region. Following a background picture of its geology, we examine early records of the original vegetation and wildlife and note the significance of the species of 200- to 400-year-old trees remaining, as we seek an explanation for the anomaly of vegetation and associated animals. Also we show human modification or extermination of natural ecosystems. Part II presents an analysis of existing plant communities and an account of vertebrate animal habitats. Part III comprises annotated lists of species known to occur at present in the Inner Bluegrass: first the vascular plants, then the vertebrate animals. Part IV looks at the possible future of the region in light of present trends.

Part I
Geology and Environmental History

1. *Geological Background*

NATURE'S ENDOWMENT of beauty and fertility in the Inner Bluegrass has a background of many millions of years. It results from a combination of rock type, geological structure, and geological history that accounts for the gently rolling, rich, and fertile upland into which the Kentucky River has cut a spectacular gorge. Geology is fundamental in determining all aspects of life. The type of rock and the regional topography it creates, together with climate, determine what vegetation will flourish, how much animal life the land will support, and whether a human community established there will be rich or poor.

The Inner Bluegrass is a portion of the Bluegrass Section[1] of the Interior Low Plateaus Province of eastern United States, according to Fenneman's physiographic classification (1938). Fenneman's Bluegrass Section includes the Inner Bluegrass, the Outer Bluegrass, and the intervening Eden Hills.

STRUCTURAL GEOLOGY, STRATIGRAPHY, AND SOILS

The Inner Bluegrass region encompasses approximately 2,400 square miles, occurring in portions of fourteen counties (Davis 1927). Its occurrence is determined by the outcrop of Middle Ordovician limestones deposited about 400 million years ago, the oldest in the state.[2] These limestones appear here and not elsewhere because the area is situated on the Jessamine Dome of the Cincinnati Arch, or Geanticline, which is the main axis of the uplift between northwest Alabama and Lake Erie. The dome has been beveled by erosion through long geologic ages, exposing the oldest strata at the point of greatest uplift. From the center of the dome, the beds dip gently away in all directions. Hence in a somewhat concentric pattern successively younger rock is encountered as one moves outward in any direction (Fig. 1, Structure Section).

The Inner Bluegrass is immediately surrounded by the "Eden shale belt" or

1. The term "Section," when capitalized, denotes a specific physiographic classification, whereas when lowercased it merely indicates an area. Likewise, "region" refers to an area, while "Region" denotes a specific classification, physiographic or vegetational.

2. See Appendix A, "Glossary of Geological Terms," and Appendix B, "Geologic Time Scale," pages 227-28.

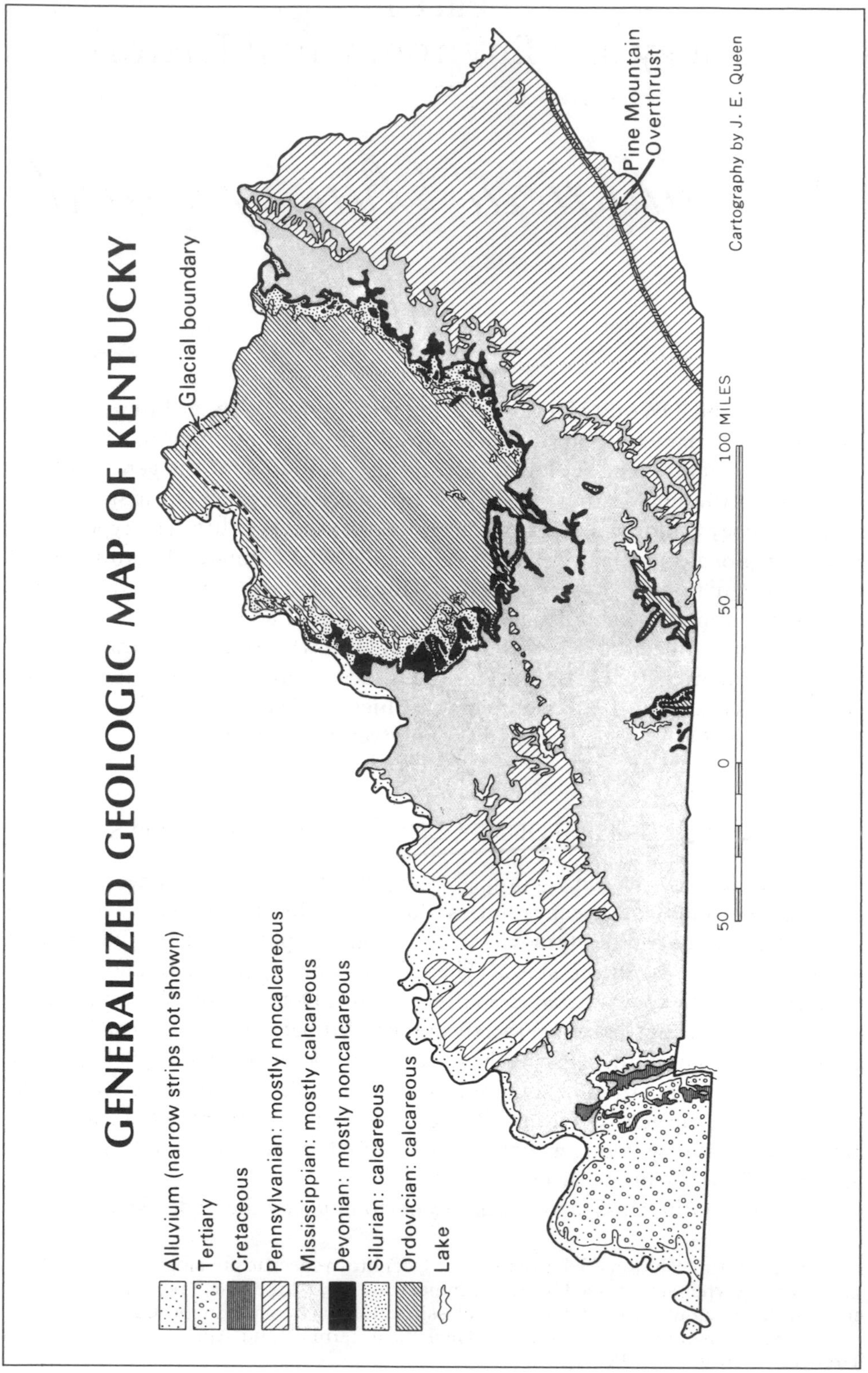
GENERALIZED GEOLOGIC MAP OF KENTUCKY
Alluvium (narrow strips not shown)
Tertiary
Cretaceous
Pennsylvanian: mostly noncalcareous
Mississippian: mostly calcareous
Devonian: mostly noncalcareous
Silurian: calcareous
Ordovician: calcareous
Lake
Glacial boundary
Pine Mountain Overthrust
50
0
50
100 MILES
Cartography by J. E. Queen

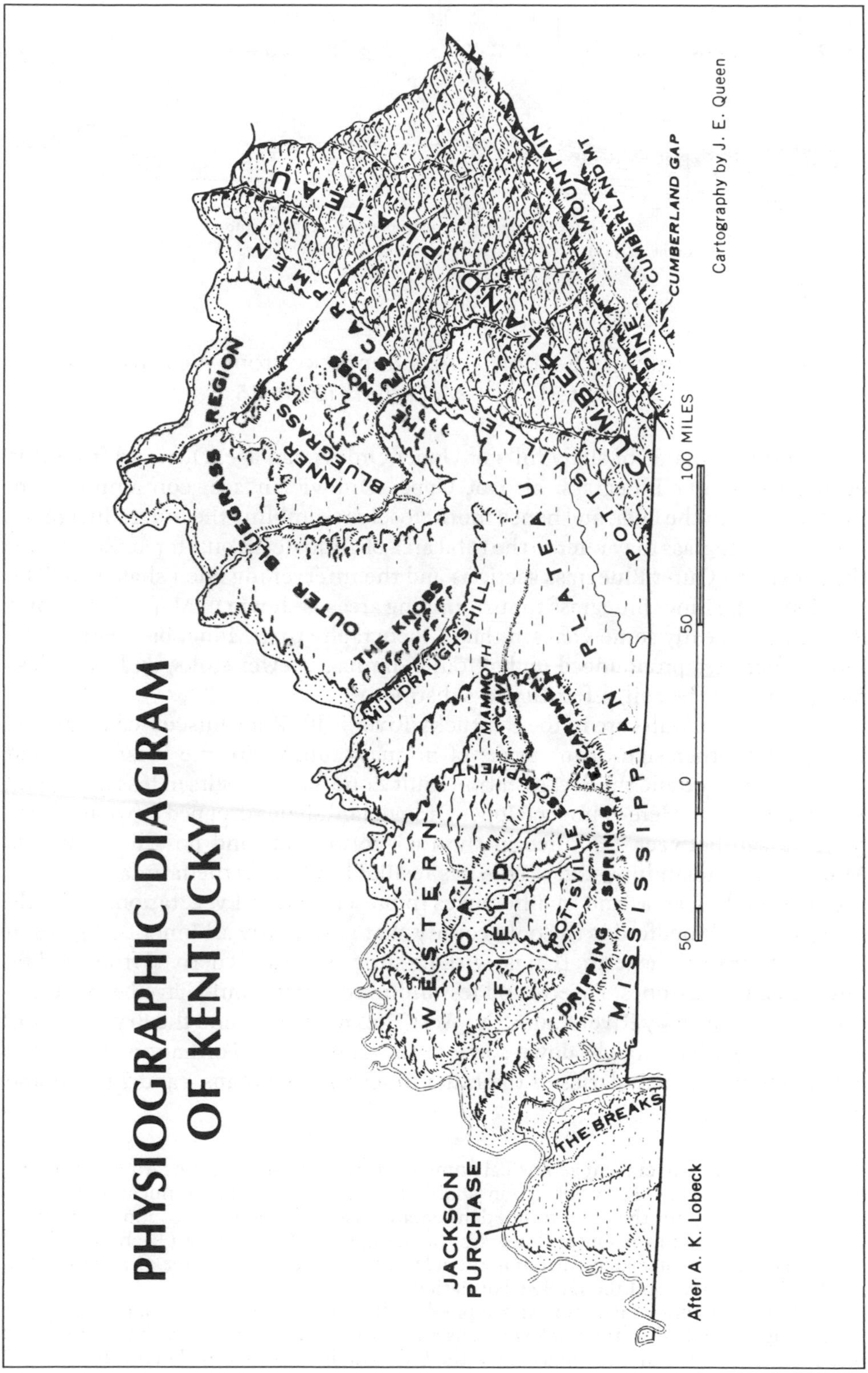

PHYSIOGRAPHIC DIAGRAM OF KENTUCKY

After A. K. Lobeck

Cartography by J. E. Queen

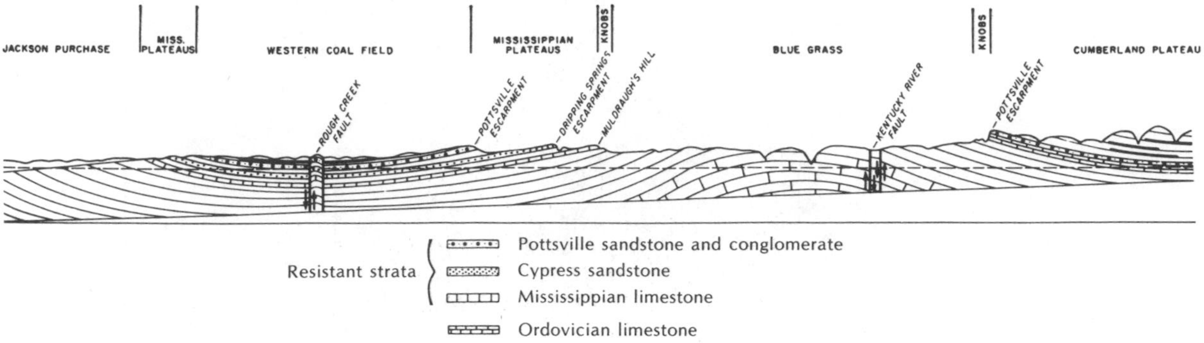

Figure 1. Structure Section across Kentucky from West to East. Adapted from McFarlan (1958), 15.

"Eden hills," an area of shaly hills of Upper Ordovician age. Outward from this occurs the Outer Bluegrass, also of Upper Ordovician age, containing more limestone than the Eden and hence more closely resembling the Inner Bluegrass.[3] The term Bluegrass may refer to the total area of Ordovician outcrop in Kentucky: the Inner and Outer Bluegrass sections and the intervening Eden shale belt. The relation of the Inner Bluegrass to surrounding areas is shown in Map 5. The Outer Bluegrass is locally somewhat similar in topography to the Inner but has slightly more relief, less pronounced underground drainage, fewer sinks, and, with less phosphorus in the soil, a fertility less distinctive.

The major faults are in the Kentucky River Fault Zone (discussed below, pp. 15-18). Two other significant zones of normal faulting are the West Hickman Creek Fault Zone and the Bryan Station Fault Zone, narrow belts in Jessamine and Fayette counties. Here younger (Upper Ordovician) shales dropped down millions of years ago between fractures in the rock formations and now lie alongside Middle Ordovician limestone. This has resulted in less fertile farmland than in the surrounding areas and in differences in present natural vegetation. It should be noted that Woodford is the only county that is virtually all Inner Bluegrass in the strict sense of the term: that is, with its surface and soils derived from Middle Ordovician limestones. Fayette and Jessamine counties would have been were it not for the Kentucky River faults, the West Hickman fault, and the Bryan Station fault, all of which brought down some of the Clay's Ferry Formation. To see the exact extent and boundaries of the Inner Bluegrass, see Maps 1 and 2 (front and back endsheets).

3. According to current geological nomenclature, the names of the formations in the Eden belt are the Clay's Ferry Formation (shale with interbedded tabular limestone) and the Garrard siltstone, but the older term Eden remains useful for general section designation (Weir and Greene). In the Outer Bluegrass the old names Maysville and Richmond limestones have been replaced in current nomenclature by the Calloway Creek limestone, the Ashlock Formation, and the Drakes Formation.

"Outer Bluegrass" is sometimes applied to all areas of Upper Ordovician outcrop but is more aptly applied in the narrower sense only to the limestone area that bears more resemblance to the Inner Bluegrass than the hilly and less calcareous Eden belt.

Map 5. The Inner Bluegrass in Relation to Surrounding Physiographic Areas and to the Cincinnati Arch. From Palmquist and Hall, 5.

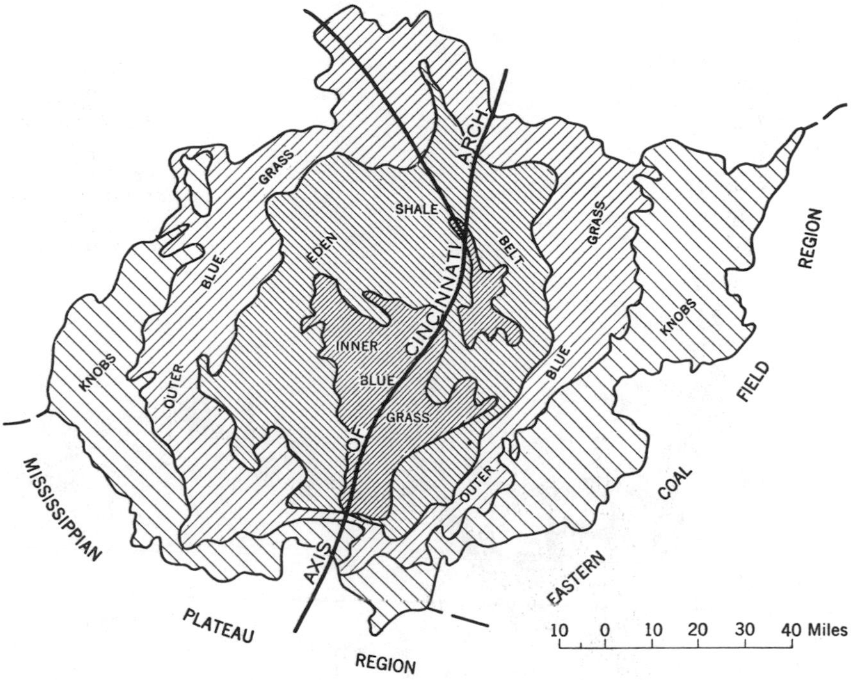

The oldest of the Middle Ordovician limestones are the Camp Nelson, Oregon, and Tyrone formations, composing the High Bridge group, all of which outcrop only in the vicinity of the Kentucky River and its immediate tributaries (Map 6). They are predominantly massive-bedded, cliff-forming, dolomitic limestones. The Camp Nelson, which is the oldest formation in the state, is a fine-grained, mottled limestone, 200-350 feet thick, containing some dolomitic beds; the Oregon, a calcareous dolomite, is 10-65 feet thick; and the Tyrone, the uppermost of the three, is a lithographic limestone 60-90 feet thick. In the early literature, the Tyrone was called the Birdseye limestone from the dark facets of calcite on the white surfaces of the weathered stone. The Oregon is less resistant than the other two, principally because of exfoliation in weathering; for this reason, creeks passing from the Tyrone to the Camp Nelson have waterfalls at the Oregon, and on the river bluffs there is usually a shelf at the top of the Camp Nelson.

The High Bridge group of formations are of Black River and lower Trenton age (McFarlan, 1943; Nosow and McFarlan). At the time of their deposition, Kentucky would have been a complex of warm carbonate tidal flats and intervening shallow marine lagoons, similar to the area around the Bahamas today, with the tidal flats shifting position from time to time. The deposition of fine lime sediment would have been at the rate of approximately 4 cm per 1,000 years; the

Map 6. Outcrop Area of the High Bridge Group.
From Cressman and Noger, 2.

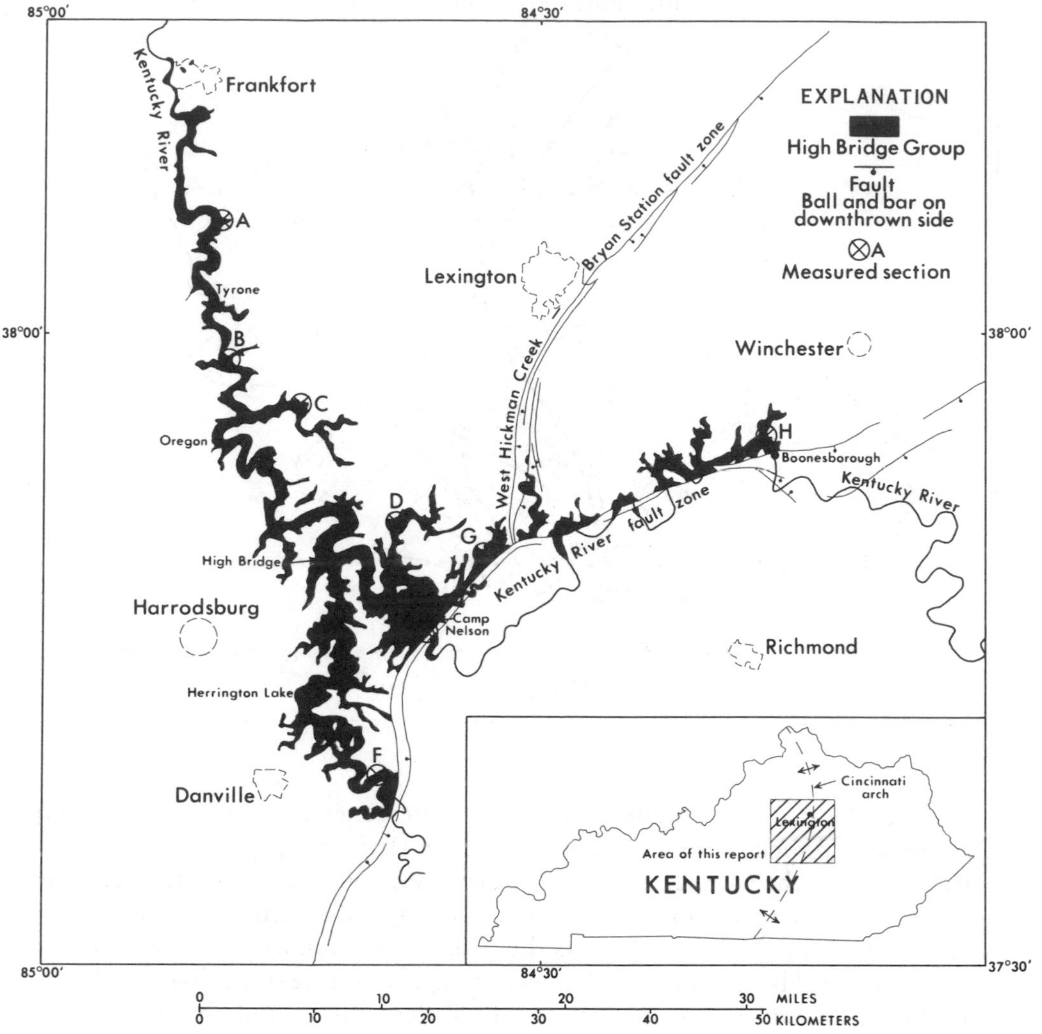

High Bridge group, therefore, would represent about 5 million years (Cressman and Nager).

The Tyrone formation contains several thin layers of bentonite (volcanic ash). The Pencil Cave layer, found 14-20 feet below the top, is present throughout and is composed of two or more ash falls; other layers occur locally. The volcanoes would have been located east of Kentucky in the Land of Appalachia.

The High Bridge group is overlain unconformably by the Lexington limestones deposited later in the Middle Ordovician. These bioclastic limestones, totalling about 300 feet in thickness, underlie most of the Inner Bluegrass. At the time of their deposition, the former mud flats were covered by a slightly deeper sea laying down coarsely crystalline limestone. The resulting formations contain more fossil shells and some thin layers of shale; all are thinner bedded than the

High Bridge group. The Lexington limestone is correlated in age with the Trenton (McFarlan, 1943; Nosow and McFarlan).

The Lexington limestone is composed of eight members: Curdsville, Logana, Grier, Brannon, Tanglewood, Devil's Hollow, Millersburg, and Nicholas. The Curdsville, Grier, and Tanglewood members, which are the highly phosphatic limestones, occur throughout the region. The others are local in extent; with the exception of the Nicholas limestone, these are argillaceous limestones or they contain some interbedded shale. Approximately two-thirds of the Lexington limestone is composed of the Grier and Tanglewood members. As now defined, the Lexington includes the former Cynthiana limestone (Black et al.). Its uppermost beds span the transition between the Middle and Upper Ordovician, and the Clay's Ferry formation sometimes intertongues with the upper member of the Lexington.

Map 1 shows the extent of the Lexington limestone in the counties involved and hence delineates the boundary of the Inner Bluegrass. Some authors and some maps in the past have differed as to whether to include the "Cynthiana limestone" in the Inner Bluegrass. McFarlan (1943) so includes it, however, and since the present interpretation is to treat the "Cynthiana" as the upper two members of the Lexington, it is indeed a part of the Inner Bluegrass.

The soils derived from these Middle Ordovician limestones are dark brown silt loams. In extensive interstream areas with minimum soil erosion, deep residual soils of great fertility have formed. On the Bluegrass Plain, which is the area of Lexington limestone, the prevailing soil is the Maury silt loam, deep and well drained, on slopes of 2-12%; on slopes of 12-30% the soil is the McAfee. Lowell soils, with less permeability than the Maury, occur especially near the periphery of the Inner Bluegrass. In the vicinity of the Kentucky River gorge the excessively steep slopes above the river and its tributaries have a shallow and rocky soil, the Fairmont, on 6-50% slopes with rock outcrops. The deep soil of the river floodplain is the Huntington (USDA 1968 A and B). The Inner Bluegrass soils are essentially residual; the most extensive transported soils are on the floodplains. The alluvium of the Kentucky River has had its source in sandstone and shale of the Cumberland Plateau as well as Ordovician limestone in the watershed. This should be noted when considering it as a botanical habitat, in terms of both geographical affinities and soil chemistry. The South Fork of the Licking River arises in the Inner Bluegrass and hence does not introduce extraneous material except a small amount from the Clay's Ferry Formation on its sides downstream.

It should be emphasized that "Inner Bluegrass" as here defined refers only to the area of Middle Ordovician limestone outcrop and soils derived largely from the weathering of these rocks. Contained within the boundary of the area are pockets of other materials. The largest of these are in the Hickman Creek and Bryan Station fault zones. Examples of smaller tracts are Trumbo Bottom and the lowland surrounding Devil's Backbone in Franklin County and Alton swamp in Anderson County, which are thick deposits of Pliocene alluvium, acid and poorly drained, in abandoned meanders or oxbow lakes of the ancient Kentucky River. From the standpoint of human geography, the people living in all of these areas can consider themselves living in the Inner Bluegrass since they are surrounded by Inner Bluegrass. But as Inner Bluegrass botanical habitats, these areas should be excluded, being islands of chemically and physically different materials producing growing conditions for plants different from those produced by the rock formations responsible for determining the Inner Bluegrass.

The fact that the soils are derived from limestone excludes acid-requiring plants, includes many lime-requiring plants as well as species having a wide pH range, and adapts most of the land to profitable agriculture. Filson (1784) reported that the land produced 100 bushels of corn per acre, and both Filson and Michaux (1802) reported that the land was too rich for wheat until it had been reduced by four or five years of corn cultivation. (We can add that the process also involved leaching from uncovered land through the winters.)

These formations in Kentucky are similar to others laid down in Middle Ordovician seas, but one significant difference is a much higher phosphate content, a feature that makes this area outstandingly adapted for livestock production. Late in the nineteenth century Dr. Robert Peter studied the influence of soil and underlying rock strata, and wrote that bluegrass grown in other regions does not yield the results it gives in this section. "The peculiar richness of our bluegrass pastures is not in the bluegrass per se but is dependent on the soil, which is abundantly supplied with the indispensable mineral elements of vegetable and animal nutrition" (Peter, 1882, 25). This statement was based on both observation and chemical analysis of the ash of several plant species grown here compared with the ash of the same species grown elsewhere. Animals are physically affected by the vegetation on which they feed, vegetation is modified by the chemical composition of the soil, and the soil is influenced by the chemistry of the geological formation from which it was derived. Very few soils in the world, Peter wrote, excel or even equal this area in richness of composition. The spring water containing dissolved minerals from the unique limestone formations found here also contributes to the mineral nutrition of animal life. The result of such soil and water is the tendency to form solid but light bones, strong tendons, and strong, firm, and elastic muscles, and to favor general stamina (Peter, 1882, 11-26). More recently, Louis Bromfield (314) said, "It is not without reason that the best race horses in the world are bred and raised in Ireland and in the bluegrass, limestone areas of Kentucky. It is so because both soils were limestone soils containing also high percentages of phosphorus. These two elements [calcium and phosphorus] in conjunction with the trace elements existing in limestone not only produce, but are essential to, the production of bone, stamina, vigor, and intelligence." Hence soil chemistry, derived from rock chemistry, has influenced plant and animal life and man's use of the land in the production of high-quality livestock in the Inner Bluegrass.

GEOLOGIC AND PHYSIOGRAPHIC HISTORY

Since the Ordovician Period, eastern United States has been uplifted, worn down to a peneplain, depressed below sea level, uplifted and worn down again—all repeated over and over. The last peneplain affecting the Kentucky Bluegrass region occurred in the Miocene Epoch of the mid-Tertiary and is designated as the Lexington peneplain. All of Kentucky except the Cumberland Plateau and the Cumberland Mountains had at that time been worn down to a nearly flat, poorly drained lowland with lazily meandering streams; at the same time other downstream areas in eastern United States had been similarly reduced. The Lexington peneplain is correlated with the Harrisburg peneplain in Pennsylvania. As uplift occurred in the Pliocene (800-900 feet in this area), streams were rejuvenated, downcutting within their old courses (Jillson 1945). The Kentucky River in its meandering course had massive-bedded, resistant rock to cut into as it passed through what we now call the Inner Bluegrass. Hence today it is characterized by entrenched meanders: a sinuous, old-age course that developed on a low plain, now incised and confined between rock walls. Such entrenched meanders are relatively rare throughout the world. The river has now cut to its base level and the valley is being widened. Tributary streams are still downcutting, and near the river their gradients are steep.

The uplift from the flat lowland or peneplain to the present elevation occurred in three stages, of which the second was the greatest, and the final one (possibly as late as the Pleistocene) was the least. The interval between the first and second uplifts was long enough for the river to cease downcutting, develop a floodplain, and cut off some meanders, leaving oxbows. Today several old high-level channels may be seen, each several miles long, on which lie fluvial sands and gravels, including quartz pebbles from conglomerates far upstream in eastern Kentucky. In the old, high-level oxbow near Little Hickman, northeast of Camp Nelson in Jessamine County, the sands and gravels are 60 feet thick. Another example is the old Warwick channel in Woodford County, 25 miles long and including the Clover Bottom meander, the Dark Hollow meander, and the Wildcat meander. These high-level fluvial deposits, 150-200 feet below the level of the Bluegrass Plain, lie on river hills that are intermediate between the uplifted peneplain surface and the present gorge. At an intermediate level, on several cliffsides where the river's course has not changed, a fluvial terrace with the same type of quartz pebbles may be seen. Further evidence for this long quiescent interval may be found on some tributaries (for example, Boone Creek) that cut off meanders or oxbows now left high and dry at an intermediate level (Jillson 1946, 1947), as shown in Map 7.

The remains of the old Lexington peneplain, a relic now uplifted, can be seen today in the accordant upland levels in the region. The present topography has developed since the Pliocene uplift (4 or 5 million years ago): the river cutting a gorge, tributaries downcutting to a lesser extent, and sinks and caves developing in the interstream uplands as rainwater dissolves some of the limestone. The new cycle of erosion has not progressed far because downcutting into the resistant, massive High Bridge limestone by the Kentucky River, the master stream, and its immediate tributaries has necessarily been slow.

Pleistocene glaciation, not reaching this area, had no effect on the physiography, but the climatic changes it brought would have influenced vegetation and animal life.

Map 7. A Portion of Ford Quadrangle, U.S.G.S. 7.5 Minute Series, Showing Abandoned Meanders of Boone Creek Cut Off in the Pliocene Epoch

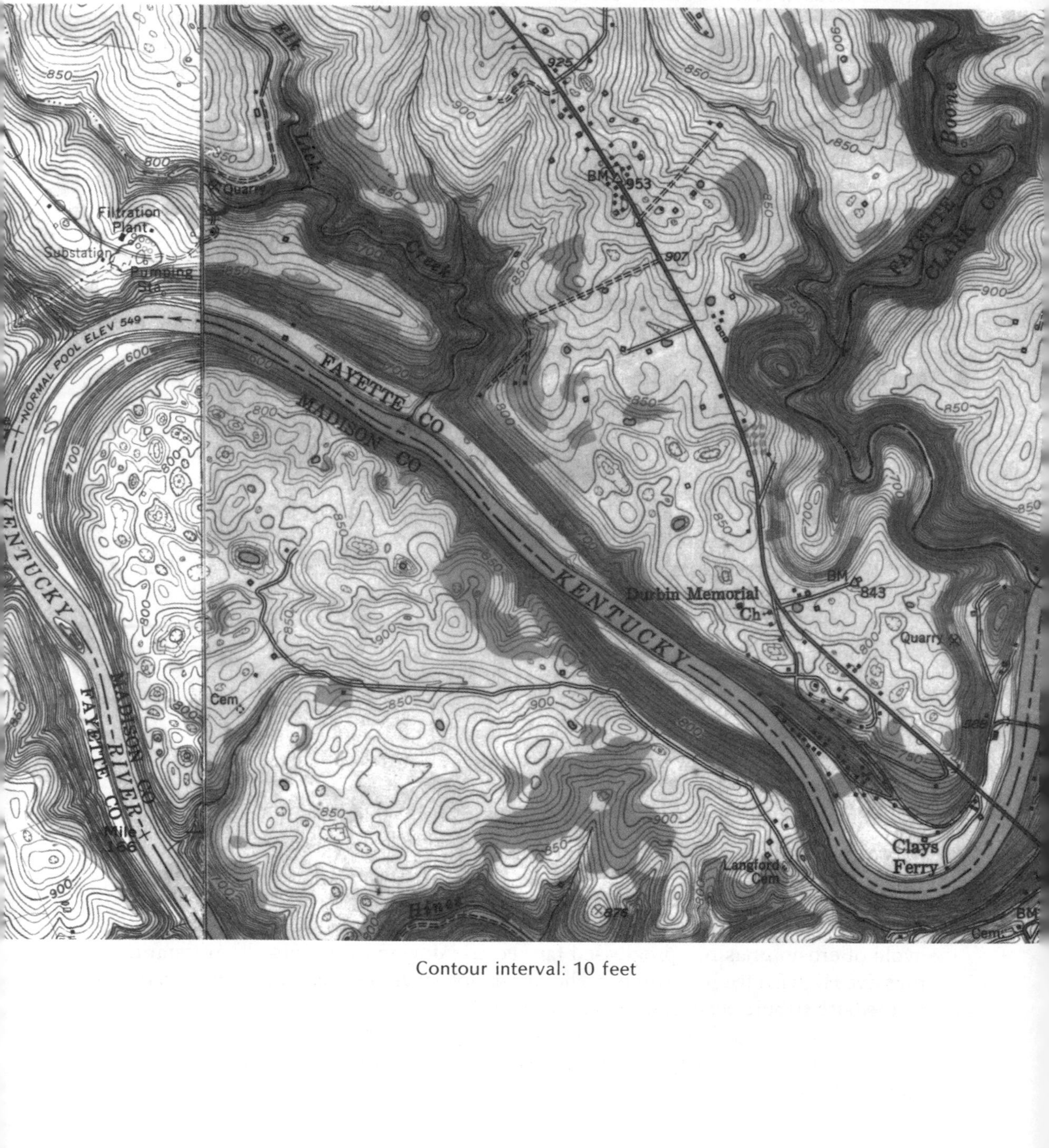

Contour interval: 10 feet

TOPOGRAPHY

Topographically the Inner Bluegrass has two extremes. By far the more extensive is the gently rolling, mildly karst plain or low plateau, pastoral in its modern aspect where it has not been destroyed by rapidly expanding urbanization. Basil Duke in his 1911 *Reminiscences* (pp. 20-21) described it: "The beauty of this country is much enhanced by its peculiar topography. It is neither hilly nor level, but undulates in all directions in a succession of wide 'swells,' rising to no great height, the depression of the intervening ground being so gradual that it rarely gives the impression of a valley." Into this plateau the Kentucky River has cut a deep and rugged gorge, and its tributaries in the vicinity of the river have cut deep, narrow, steep-sided valleys containing rapids and waterfalls. These two extremes have produced different vegetation types.

The highest elevation, 1,072 feet, is in northern Jessamine County near the Fayette County border; the lowest elevation, that of the Kentucky River below Frankfort, is 455 feet (McGrain and Currens). In the gorge of the river the water level is approximately 300-400 feet below the rim rock. On one side of the river the cliff drops somewhat precipitously to the water, while usually on the other there is a narrow floodplain at the foot of the cliff. These two situations alternate as the river follows its meandering course. This gorge through the Inner Bluegrass, often called the Kentucky River Palisades from Boonesborough to Frankfort, is about 100 miles long. The river is 250 miles in length from the confluence of its three forks to its mouth.

DRAINAGE

The Kentucky River is the master stream draining most of the Inner Bluegrass. Bourbon and Harrison counties, however, are in the watershed of the South Fork of Licking River. The largest tributaries of the Kentucky are the Dix River and Elkhorn Creek with its North and South forks; among other large creeks are Jessamine, Hickman, Boone, Raven, Clear, and Gilbert. Stoner, Townsend, and Hinkston creeks drain into the South Fork of Licking River.

The general direction of flow of the Kentucky River is northwestward from southeast Kentucky to the Ohio River, but when it reaches the Kentucky River Fault Zone it follows the trend of this zone, turning west and southwest before resuming a northward and northwestward course (Map 8). In its meanders it crosses the zone nine times (McFarlan, 1943), thus crossing a fault line eighteen times. Wherever the faulting brought down Lexington limestone to the level of the Camp Nelson, the precipitous rock cliffs are suddenly replaced by more gentle slopes.

The Kentucky River is believed to be an extraordinarily ancient river, over 100 million years old. Jillson's theory is that in the Mesozoic Era it flowed altogether northwestward from North Carolina into Indiana, long before the present Ohio River came into existence in the Pleistocene by a combination of old drainage systems at the glacial front. From the vicinity of Carrollton the Kentucky probably flowed northward into the ancient Teays system. The deflection

Map 8. Courses of the Kentucky River, Dix River, and Elkhorn Creek

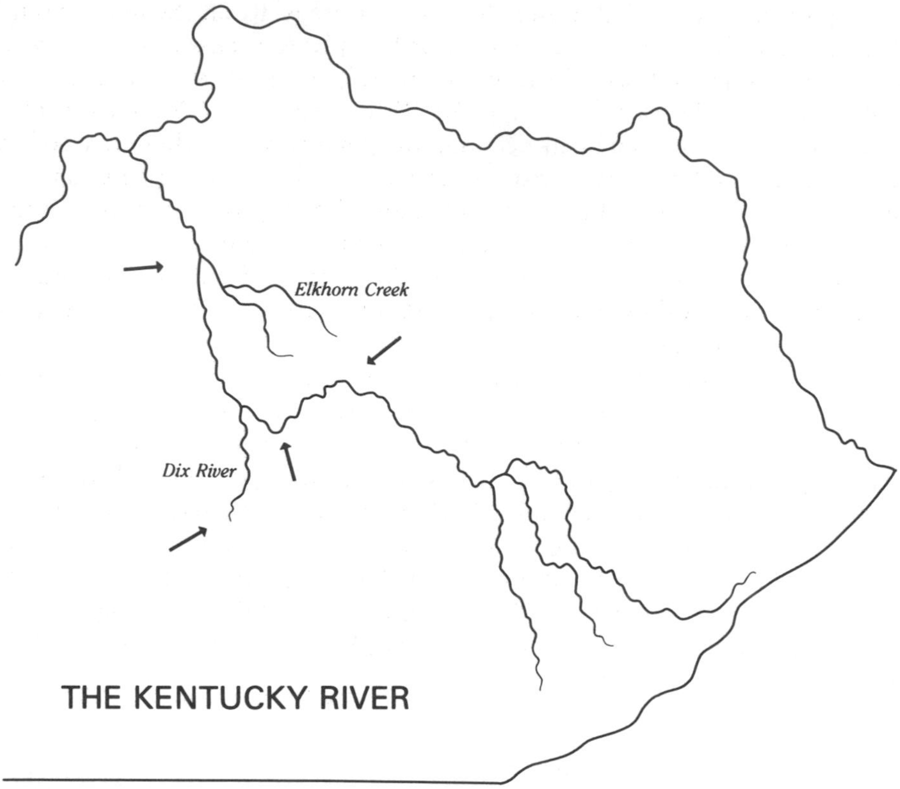

in the course resulted when the original faults, which had occurred at the close of the Paleozoic Era, were reactivated in the late Cretaceous or early Eocene. According to this theory, a portion of its Mesozoic course followed the present course of North Elkhorn Creek, and the Dix River joined it at the present mouth of the Elkhorn. After the deflection at the fault zone (as indicated by arrows on Map 8), the Kentucky adopted the northward course of the Dix, which therefore lost about two-thirds of its lower length (Jillson, 1963).

Most members of the Lexington limestone are soluble, especially the Grier and Tanglewood; hence sinks, underground drainage, and springs are prominent and important features. Jillson (1927) estimated that the Inner Bluegrass has over 3,000 sinks and 1,600 square miles of sinkhole topography plus an additional 75 square miles of truly karst topography with caves, sinking creeks, and subterranean streams, as well as sinks. These karst areas occur in several patches. Some sinkholes have nearly vertical sides that drop down as much as 40 feet to the water table, where solution has undermined the roof of a small cave, but many of the sinks have such gradually sloping, grass-covered sides (2-20% slope) that the average person may not immediately recognize them as such. These sinks are formed as surface water percolates downward into openings in the rocks, such as joints and bedding planes, dissolving the limestone. The dissolving of the underlying limestone results in depressions that gather rainwater and become larger as more solution is accomplished beneath. Most of the extensive high-level sand and gravel deposits that were a part of the Pliocene valley floor of the Kentucky River are pitted with sinkholes.

The solubility of the limestone, the sinking of rainwater underground, and the resulting underground drainage account for the attractive and desirable undulating topography. The peneplain surface has not been destroyed by surface stream erosion. By contrast the Eden hills, with their predominating shale with only some thin limestone interbedded, in the same length of time since rejuvenation have been eroded into a complex of hills and valleys, with little upland surface preserved because of the ease of erosion in a shale formation.

Leveling the undulations by man's machines—removing soil from the higher spots, leaving them with a too shallow cover above bedrock, and covering topsoil in the lower spots—interferes with the natural drainage and is a mistake.

Springs, both large and small, often emanating from caves, are numerous in the area; farm names such as "Cave Spring Farm" are frequent. The aquifers are shallow; the water in its downward movement is sometimes impeded by thin clay layers, impervious except at the joints, and moves along the top of these shaly beds to emerge as springs or seepage. The largest springs, such as the Royal Spring at Georgetown, Russell Cave Spring in Fayette County, and Spring Station Spring in Woodford County, are in the Grier member of the Lexington limestone (Mull; Van Couvering). Large springs influenced the location of many Bluegrass towns, including Georgetown, Cynthiana, Versailles, Harrodsburg, Nicholasville, and Lexington. Subsurface systems have a dendritic, or branching, pattern, as indicated by dye tracing studies, and a large spring has a major conduit.

The prevalence of subsurface drainage means that springs and wells can easily be polluted. Drainage from a septic tank, for instance, instead of filtering gradually through the soil, often quickly reaches a dissolved channel in the bedrock whence it moves without delay to wells, springs, or creeks that may provide water for someone else's household or livestock. With an expanding population, recognition of the fact that septic tanks in this area must be few and far between is essential for wise land use.

Although water sinking underground will eventually reemerge, an observant tourist, sensitive to land features, will note fewer surface streams in the Inner Bluegrass than in other areas with equal rainfall. As Basil Duke wrote in his *Reminiscences* (p. 21), "The only needful provision of nature which this region may be said to lack—more particularly that part of it lying between the Little Licking River on the north and the Kentucky on the south—is an adequate water supply. In periods of extreme drought this want is seriously felt, especially for livestock. . . . I did not thoroughly realize its deficiency in this respect until I traversed it with considerable bodies of cavalry during the Civil War. We found more difficulty in procuring water for our horses on the march than we had ever experienced in Tennessee and northern Alabama."

The Inner Bluegrass in general is well-drained, with its sinkhole topography and subsurface drainage. But some widely extending sinks covering several acres, such as Big Sink in Woodford County, may hold water for several days or even weeks in a rainy season and may temporarily resemble small lakes. Noteworthy are the sinking creeks, streams that drop into a sinkhole. One of these, named Sinking Creek, sinks four times, running underground from a quarter mile to a mile each time.

Swampy conditions in the region are rare and are found principally in seepage areas, broad sinks, and areas of sinking creeks. Among the largest swamps are Lee's Branch swamp in Woodford County and one along Sinking Creek in Jessamine County.

From the Lexington area creeks drain away in all directions, today carrying urban pollutants to neighboring districts. The location of pioneer Lexington was determined by a spring and by Town Branch, which flows into South Elkhorn Creek. Today, however, Lexington is one of the largest cities in eastern United States not situated on a major source of water.

CLIMATE

As with all of Kentucky and adjacent states, the climate is continental, with extremes and great changeability. Westerly winds bring low-pressure systems accompanied by southwest winds bearing warm moist air from the south; these are periodically displaced by high-pressure systems with cool dry northwest winds. The result is changeable weather in all seasons.

The average annual precipitation and temperature place the area in the warm temperate, humid category. The average annual precipitation of 44 inches is distributed throughout the year but with September and October usually having the least and March, May, June, and July usually the most. Droughts sometimes occur, the effects of which are intensified by the underdrainage of this limestone region. Either local flash floods or widespread flooding sometimes occurs, and flood damage is increasing due to more intensive use of the land: more runoff from the watershed and more activity to experience damage on the floodplains.

The minimum length of the growing season in the Inner Bluegrass, between the last killing freeze in the spring and the first killing freeze in autumn, is 181 days. Although the average annual temperature is 55 degrees F., midsummer highs may exceed 100 degrees and winter lows may reach below zero degrees F.; but such extremes usually last only a few days. The winters are usually somewhat mild, with an average of 15.9 inches of snow annually (Karan and Mather).

Gently undulating topography typical of the Bluegrass Plain. This develops with underground drainage in which rainwater soaks underground, dissolving some of the underlying limestone in the lower areas. [Upper photo: J.B. Varner; lower photo, Clyde Burke]

Sinking Creek, in Jessamine County, in one of the strongly karst areas of the Bluegrass Plain. Here the creek emerges from the ground, flows exposed to the sky for about 40 feet, then goes underground again. In the eighteenth century this source of water inspired the erection of a home, still occupied, and until recently supplied usable domestic water. Downstream, however, Sinking Creek has been ruined by unwise residential development with numerous septic fields. [Photos by R.W. Barbour]

Opposite page, above: Note the even skyline and the accordant upland levels of the Bluegrass Plain into which the Kentucky River has cut a gorge. In the gorge there is typically a precipitous cliff on the outside of a bend and a floodplain on the inside. [Photo by M.E. Wharton]

Opposite page, below: Elkhorn Creek, flowing on the Bluegrass Plain, contrasts with the creek canyons near the Kentucky River. [Photo by Clyde Burke]

Above: The gorge which the Kentucky River has cut in the Inner Bluegrass exposes massive-bedded limestone, the oldest rock in Kentucky. The resulting cliffs provide rugged and picturesque scenery. *Below*: Weathering of the Kentucky River cliffs produces narrow ledges, clefts, and crannies that provide a foothold for plants. (A foothold for botanists is sometimes questionable!) [Photos by J.B. Varner]

With weathering, the cliff face often suggests castle bastions, and further weathering occasionally results in some detached "chimney rocks" or "candlestick rocks." [Photos by R.W. Barbour]

Tributary creeks in the vicinity of the Kentucky River have cut picturesque canyons that contain a significant flora. (Top photo by M.E. Wharton; lower photo by J.B. Varner)

Elk Lick Falls. This so-called "petrified waterfall," a 61-foot drop, is one of the largest and most beautiful surface deposits of travertine in eastern United States. For its formation, groundwater containing carbon dioxide, having dissolved some calcium carbonate, emanates from springs above the falls. Agitation from the drop drives off some carbon dioxide necessary for holding calcium bicarbonate in solution; hence calcium carbonate is precipitated. Evaporation during a hot season also increases the precipitation of lime. [Photos by M.E. Wharton]

Left: The Kentucky River fault zone has numerous faults. This one is at Clay's Ferry. [Photo by R.W. Barbour]

Below: One of several faults that can be observed from U.S. Highway 27 in Garrard County near Camp Nelson. [Photo by J.B. Varner]

Above: Where the Kentucky River in the fault zone flows through an area in which "Eden shale" (the Clay's Ferry formation of Upper Ordovician age) was dropped down to the level of Middle Ordovician Camp Nelson limestone, there are fairly gentle, soil-covered slopes instead of steep or vertical cliffs of limestone. *Below*: The topography and soils in an extensive downfaulted block of "Eden shale" are typical of this formation and differ markedly from the true Inner Bluegrass. [Photos, in Jessamine County, by M.E. Wharton]

The Kentucky River gorge country, with its tributary creeks, should be preserved for aesthetic and scenic reasons as well as for its geological and biological significance. [Photos by J.B. Varner]

Planche 10
PÂTORIN DES PRÉS OU DU KENTUCKY
(Poa pratensis L.)

Left: It is certain that bluegrass (*Poa pratensis*) is a native of Europe that has been cultivated for centuries, but there is also evidence that it was growing wild in this area when the pioneers arrived.

Below: Although cane (*Arundinaria gigantea*) is found today only in small patches, usually on floodplains or creek banks, it densely covered large areas (measured in many miles) on Inner Bluegrass uplands as well as lowlands when the pioneers arrived.

[Photos by Patricia DeCamp]

Presettlement chinquapin oaks (*Quercus muehlenbergii*) in a remnant of an ancient savanna-woodland. (Harrison County) [Photo by M.E. Wharton]

An old Shumard oak (*Quercus shumardii*) that antedates settlement of the Bluegrass. (Bourbon County) [Photo by M.E. Wharton]

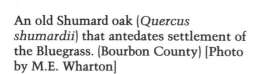

An ancient Biltmore white ash (*Fraxinus americana* var. *biltmoreana*). (Harrison County) [Photo by Bruce Poundstone]

Tall and stately blue ash trees (*Fraxinus quadrangulata*), remnants of a presettlement savanna-woodland. (Bourbon County) [Photo by M.E. Wharton]

The largest of the presettlement bur oaks (*Quercus macrocarpa*), over 400 years old. (Bourbon County) [Photos by R.W. Barbour]

Opposite page: Woodland pastures with bur oaks (*Quercus macrocarpa*). The "woodland pastures" of the Inner Bluegrass are the remnants of ancient savanna-woodlands, an irreplaceable treasure that should be protected. (Fayette County) [Photos by Clyde Burke]

Above: A woodland pasture dominated by blue ash (*Fraxinus quadrangulata*) over 200 years old. (Bourbon County)

Right: Ancient coffee trees (*Gymnocladus dioica*) in a woodland pasture. (Harrison County)

[Photos by M.E. Wharton]

2. *Presettlement Vegetation*

EARLY SURVEY RECORDS

During the period of white settlement, surveyors' "calls," or reference points, were usually trees. Reading several hundred eighteenth-century land surveys and early deeds for the Inner Bluegrass yields some information regarding prevailing species, although nothing concerning their density or community relations. To be useful, this information must be considered along with other sources. In the Bluegrass Plain the single species named most often in these early records was "sugar tree"; hackberry was also very frequent. Oak, "large oak," ash, and hickory were often named without indicating the species, although sometimes the calls specified bur oak, white oak, shellbark hickory, blue ash, and white ash. Other species mentioned many times were black walnut, white walnut, cherry, "lynn," locust, honey locust, "pea locust," elm, buckeye, mulberry, ironwood, box elder, and sycamore.

The lack of precision in common names and misidentification of species have to be reckoned with. "Black ash" was named several times but undoubtedly was not *Fraxinus nigra,* the black ash of northern bogs. The term may have referred to the green ash, which is present today but was not named in any survey. Michaux recognized that the Kentucky species was not the northern black ash. In his *North American Sylva* (3:60), he added the following note under the black ash of the North, which at that time was called *Fraxinus sambucifolia.* "Observation. Another lofty species of ash exists in Kentucky, which is also called Black Ash; but I am too imperfectly acquainted with it to attempt a description." It is unlikely that there existed an additional species of ash that is extinct today.

"Black oak" probably meant Shumard's red oak *(Quercus shumardii),* not *Q. velutina,* which we call black oak or quercitron oak. Michaux remarked in his *Travels* that when walking from Maysville to Lexington in 1802 he did not encounter the quercitron oak and did not believe it grew in the rich lands. "White oak," probably included *Quercus muehlenbergii,* which Short called "chestnut white oak," as well as *Q. alba;* both are in the "white oak group."

"Hoopwood," which was mentioned frequently, may have referred to hackberry, sometimes called hoop ash, according to Michaux in his *North American*

Sylva (1810-1813) and Peattie (1950), but may refer to any species of hickory. "Bettywood" in some surveys, especially in Bourbon County, possibly referred to something that made a bright light in burning. Bark from shagbark hickory was sometimes burned for light, "as a substitute for candles," according to Daniel Drake, writing in 1847 of life in Kentucky in the 1780s and 1790s, and this may have been what was called "bettywood" (possibly after Betty lamps).

An ecologically interesting corner in one survey was a reference to "an elm, hoopwood, and large ash in a cane brake." According to pioneers' journals, the extensive canebrakes had only a few scattered trees.

Trees mentioned in surveys near the Kentucky River cliffs and tributary gorges but not on the Bluegrass Plain were cedar, poplar, dogwood, and redbud; white oak was recorded more frequently and bur oak not at all; hackberry and both locusts were less frequent. Otherwise the species were essentially the same as in the rest of the Inner Bluegrass.

A significant deviation from the above list occurs in an area along the Kentucky River in Jessamine County, where the soil is derived from the Clay's Ferry Formation (Eden Shale) and hence is not true Inner Bluegrass. This deviation is caused by the Hickman Creek and Kentucky River faults. Here beech led in the surveys and was followed in frequency by buckeye, white ash, poplar, "sugar tree," white walnut, and hickory. Other species mentioned were white oak, red oak, elm, "lynn," black walnut, and hornbeam. This area is a part of what subsequently became known as "beech ridge" because it contained much more beech than did the adjacent true Inner Bluegrass.

REPORTS OF EARLY BOTANISTS

Early botanical records are few and sketchy. Françoix Michaux, who traveled through the Inner Bluegrass in 1802, included some scattered remarks concerning trees in his *Travels to the Westward of the Alleghany Mountains.* On the Dick's River, he said, Virginia cedar "affects elevated places where calcareous substance is nearest to the surface of the soil." Near Harrodsburg the woodlands surrounding the fields and orchards of General Adair's estate, where Michaux stopped, were "principally composed of those species of trees which are met with in the best districts, such as *Gleditsia 3-acanthos* [honey locust], *Guilandina dioica* [coffee tree], *Ulmus viscosa* [slippery elm], *Morus rubra, Corylus, Annona triloba* [pawpaw]" (171-73). He emphasized that especially the coffee tree, honey locust, and papaw denoted the richest lands. Other trees he listed for "first class land" (in which he placed the Bluegrass) were cherry, walnut, ash (white, blue, and "black"), hackberry, buckeye, bur oak, sugar maple, beech, poplar, and "plane tree." His itinerary included Dufour's vineyard on the Kentucky River in the "Big Bend," which, due to faulting, is not true Inner Bluegrass and was a part of the "beech ridge." On his departure from the vineyard for Hickman's Ferry, Michaux went four miles through the woods, where "beeches, walnuts, and oaks with large acorns form the principal mass of the forest. We, however, crossed parts of the level, adjoining the river, which are exclusively covered with superb plane-trees" (168).

In his *North Amerian Sylva* (1:121), Michaux, writing of a very large hickory near Lexington, said that "this extraordinary growth in several species of trees is rarely seen [east] of the Alleghany, and is attributable to the extreme fertility of the soil." Many of his comments concerning Kentucky probably pertain especially to the Bluegrass, where he apparently spent more time than in other sections, although the area is not pinpointed. A few excerpts from Michaux's accounts follow:

> BLACK WALNUT *(Juglans nigra)*. . . . In the states of Ohio and Kentucky, where the soil in general is very rich, it grows in the forests, with the Coffee-tree, Honey Locust, Red Mulberry, Locust, Shellbark Hickory, Black Sugar Maple, Hackberry, and Red Elm—all of which trees prove the goodness of the soil in which they are found. [1:104]
>
> COFFEE TREE *(Gymnocladus canadensis [G. dioica])*. . . . abundant . . . in Kentucky and Tennessee. . . . The presence of the coffee tree is an index of the richest lands, on which it habitually grows in company with the Black Walnut, the Red Elm, the Poplar, the Blue Ash, the Honey Locust, and the Hackberry. [1:182]
>
> LOCUST *(Robinia pseudo-acacia)*. . . . In these states Kentucky and Tennessee, it sometimes exceeds four feet in diameter and seventy or eighty feet in height. [2:93]
>
> SWEET LOCUST *(Gleditsia triacanthos)*. . . . It commonly grows with the Black Walnut, Shellbark Hickory, Red Elm, Blue Ash, Locust, Box Elder, and Coffee Tree, and forms a part of the forests that cover the most fertile soils. [2:109]
>
> WILD CHERRY TREE *(Cerasus virginiana [Prunus serotina])*. . . . It is nowhere more profusely multiplied, nor more fully developed, than beyond the mountains in the States of Ohio, Kentucky, and Tennessee. [2:148]
>
> BLUE ASH *(Fraxinus quadrangulata)*. The Blue Ash is unknown in the Atlantic parts of the United States, and is found only in Tennessee, Kentucky, and the southern parts of Ohio. The climate of these countries is mild, and the soil in some places so fertile that it is difficult, without having witnessed them, to form an idea of the luxuriance of vegetation and the productiveness of agriculture. [3:61]

Physician and botanist Charles Wilkins Short's "Florula Lexingtoniensis" (1828-1829) included all of Fayette County. Although its publication occurred fifty years after the pioneers' arrival, his observations would have antedated the 1820s, since he had grown up in this area. The work is incomplete, including only the spring-flowering species.

Short called the sugar maple one of the most common trees, and the black and white walnuts equally common. The hackberry was "very common throughout the best lands, attaining great height." The wild cherry was abundant on the richest soils and was one of the largest trees. The white oak, he said, was not often found in the rich land around Lexington but was abundant on the cliffs of the

Kentucky River. The "chestnut white oak" (probably *Quercus muehlenbergii*) grew in the richest soils. His "pin oak," most often found around Lexington and, like the bur oak, attaining great size, was undoubtedly *Quercus shumardii.* He described the bur oak as a noble tree towering above most others. *Quercus velutina,* the black oak, was rare here but abundant in the surrounding country (which we interpret as referring to the Eden Shale belt). White ash and blue ash were prominent, and he also mentioned the problematical "black ash," which the surveys included. The black locust occurred in "profuse abundance." The slippery elm had "almost disappeared from the forests around Lexington in consequence of its destruction by cattle" but remained on the cliffs of the Kentucky River and Elkhorn Creek. *Carya laciniosa,* the shellbark hickory, was one of the most abundant of the genus in this neighborhood. The common buckeye, *Aesculus glabra,* was abundant, but the yellow buckeye, *A. octandra,* a larger and straighter tree, he listed as confined to the alluvial bottoms of the Kentucky River.

Of the smaller trees, Short said, the dogwood was never found on first-rate land but "grows with redbud, white oak, and tulip poplar, and is confined to the thinner soils bordering the Kentucky River." There were once immense stands of papaw, but by 1828 cultivation and the ravages of cattle had greatly lessened them. The crab apple had formerly been more abundant, but at the time of Short's writing was found only occasionally in the more secluded woods of Fayette County. The hazelnut, *Corylus americana,* originally a native of Fayette County, was by 1828 no longer found growing wild there.

Among the declining herbaceous species, *Jeffersonia diphylla,* the twinleaf, once growing near Lexington, had by Short's time become restricted to secluded hillsides bordering the river and creeks. The blue cohosh *(Caulophyllum thalictroides),* which had once been abundant throughout the county, had almost disappeared from the more cultivated districts and was to be found only in unfrequented woodlands. The showy orchis *(Orchis spectabilis),* once frequent in moist rich woods, had almost disappeared as a result of the cultivation of the land and "the ravages of cattle."

Publications concerning the Kentucky flora by Constantine Rafinesque, the brilliant but erratic naturalist at Transylvania University between 1819 and 1826, are catalogs, essentially without annotations.

PIONEERS' DESCRIPTIONS OF THE AREA

A few of the Bluegrass pioneers and surveyors left journals that contain references to vegetation and animal life. In addition, in the 1840s and 1850s, John R. Shane and Lyman Draper interviewed elderly persons who had come to Kentucky in the early days, and these interviews, all incorporated in the Draper Manuscripts, present first-hand accounts of life in the pioneer period. Some of them contain meager and incidental reference to native vegetation and animals, although these are overpowered by accounts of Indian depredations.

Early records indicate that the Bluegrass was in general well timbered. More specifically, they show that the forests on most of the Bluegrass Plain were not dense, having an open canopy; that on the plain there were extensive canebrakes with a sparse tree cover; and that between the canebrakes there was open timber with grass and legumes forming natural meadows.

In 1773 Hancock Taylor surveyed for James and Robert McAfee in the vicinity of the present city of Frankfort. James recorded in his journal for July 16 that "We stopped and surveyed one tract of land . . . containing about 600 acres, about 100 of that meadowland." Later that month the party traveled to the area of the present city of Harrodsburg, and James's journal for July 31 stated that part of the journey was through canebrakes (Woods).

Thomas Hanson, one of a group of surveyors on North Elkhorn in 1774, recorded in his journal for July 8: "7 or 8 miles from the fork . . . the land is so good that I cannot give it due praise. Its undergrowth is clover, peavine, cane. Its timber is honey locust, black walnut, sugar tree, hickory, ironwood, hoopwood, mulberry, ash, elm, and some oak" (Draper MSS).

In 1775 James Nourse, traveling a buffalo road from the vicinity of Frankfort toward the present site of Lexington, wrote in his diary that on the plateau "it is light with timber, little oak—mostly sugar tree, walnut, ash, and buckeye. . . . The surface of the ground covered with grass . . . the ash very large and high, and large locusts of both sorts, some cherry. The growth of grass under amazing [sic]; blue grass, white clover, buffalo grass . . . and what would be called a fine swarth of grass in cultivated meadows; and such was its occurrence without end in little dells" (Nourse).

The pioneers coming to Boonesborough with Daniel Boone in 1775 were similarly amazed by the country before them, according to Felix Walker, one of the party. "As the cane ceased we began to discover the pleasing and rapturous appearance of the plains of Kentucky. A new sky and a strange earth seem to be presented to our view. So rich a soil we had never seen before; covered with clover in full bloom" (Ranck).

"Right before me . . . stands one of the finest elms that perhaps Nature ever produced in any region," wrote Colonel Richard Henderson at Boonesborough in his journal for 14 May 1775. "This tree is placed in a beautiful plain surrounded by a turf of fine white clover forming a green to its very stock, to which there is scarcely anything to be likened. The trunk is about four feet through to its first branches, which are about 9 feet high from the ground. . . . It so regularly extends its large branches on every side at such equal distances as to form the most beautiful tree that imagination can suggest. The diameter of its branches from the extreme ends is 100 feet—and every fair day it describes a semicircle on the heavenly green around it upwards of 400 feet, and anytime between 10 and 12[,] 100 persons may commodiously seat themselves under its branches. This divine tree . . . is to be our church, statehouse, council chamber, etc." (Ranck, 176-77). This great elm, which sheltered Kentucky's first legislature and first worshiping assembly, fell under the axe in 1828. Boonesborough also had immense sycamores.

Levi Todd, speaking of 1776, said, "The face of the country was, at the times I have been speaking [of], delightful beyond conception, nearly one half of it covered with cane, but between the brakes, spaces of open ground as if intended by nature for fields. The ground appeared fertile, and produced amazing quantities of weeds of various kinds, some wild grass, wild rye, and clover" (Draper MSS).

Josiah Collins, who came to Kentucky in 1778, related that he "joined 24 others all from Harrodsburg and went to Lexington that now is, and built a blockhouse. . . . Josiah Collins cutting the first tree, a burr oak about two feet across at the butt." (The blockhouse was erected at what is now the southwest corner of Main and Mill streets. The bur oak grew near a spring about 100 feet west of Mill Street and 50-60 feet south of Main Street.) Of a later episode, Collins wrote, "I and Ephraim January took off [pursued by Indians] through a canebrake and thus made our escape. We had run about one mile through the cane and crossed the road that led from Lexington to Bryant's Station" (Draper MSS).

John Bradford, the state's first publisher, in his newspaper, the *Kentucky Gazette,* published a series of "Notes on Kentucky." In one of these he told of a hunting party from Bryan's Station in 1780 setting out down the Elkhorn. After a while, "on looking back they discovered several Indians closely pursuing them; they therefore laid whip to their horses and for several miles when in open woods, could see the Indians in their rear" (Townsend 112-13).

Martin Wymore, describing another Indian attack near Lexington in 1781, in which his father was killed, observed that "the cane was so thick, my father and Donnolly could not be shot at, until they got into the open woods near the fort" (Draper MSS). In telling of an encounter with Indians in Bourbon County, William Clinkenbeard described the area as "a pretty open woods" (Draper MSS).

Vegetation is mentioned in the several records of the death of Daniel Boone's brother Edward in 1780. From the account given by one of Edward's grandsons we see that a grassy area, nut trees, and cane were in proximity: "Daniel and Edward Boone went hunting on Hinkston's [creek]. Found a good grassy spot and stopped to let the horses graze. Edward Boone picked up some nuts and commenced cracking them on a stone in his lap and watching the horses, while Daniel Boone said he would take a round and come back by the time the horses were through picking; and had scarcely gone when several guns cracked and he saw two or three Indians after him. He darted off into the cane. . . . Seven balls had been shot into Edward Boone and he must have been killed instantly" (Spraker, 71). The creek by which he died, then called Plum Lick, was subsequently named Boone's Creek, and a historical marker now indicates the spot.

Spencer Records, who migrated to Kentucky in 1783, related his experiences in a snowfall in December of that year: "We found ourselves in a large canebrake where we could get not wood to make a fire. . . . no broken wood was to be found. However, we found an old hickory stump about 15 feet high. We pushed it down . . . and put a fire to it" (Draper MSS).

James B. Finley, in his *Autobiography* (39), wrote that his father settled in 1790 on Cane Ridge in Bourbon County on "part of an unbroken canebrake extending for twenty miles." The site of Versailles in Woodford County was also a canebrake surrounding a spring at the headwaters of Glenns Creek. "Cane was all through here very thick, and courthouse was made in the midst of cane ten to twelve feet high. Very rank" (Jesse Graddy, Draper MSS). Georgetown and Harrodsburg also were situated at springs in canebrakes. The site of Winchester was a canebrake, with the first courthouse "in the middle of the cane" (McHargue 1941). And a canebrake extended all the way from Lexington to Walnut Hill Church, about 6 miles.

"The Elkhorn lands are much esteemed," wrote John Filson, Kentucky's first historian, in 1784. ". . . Here we find mostly first rate land, and near the Kentucke River second and third rate. This great tract is beautifully situated, covered with cane, wild rye, and clover; and many of the streams afford fine mill sites. . . . The country in general may be considered as well timbered, producing large trees of many kinds and to be exceeded by no country in variety." Filson mentioned the "sugar tree, which grows in all parts in great abundance and furnishes every family with plenty of excellent sugar. The honey-locust is curiously surrounded with large, thorny spikes, bearing broad and long pods in the form of peas, has a sweet taste, and makes excellent beer. The coffee-tree . . . grows large, and also bears a pod, in which is inclosed coffee. . . . Black mulberry trees are in abundance. The wild cherry tree is here frequent, of large size, and supplies the inhabitants with boards for all their buildings. . . . Here is a great plenty of fine cane on which the cattle feed and grow fat. . . . There are many canebrakes so thick and tall that it is difficult to pass through them. Where no cane grows there is abundance of wild rye, clover, and buffalo grass, covering vast tracts of country, and affording excellent food for cattle. The fields are covered with abundance of wild herbage not common to other countries" (Filson, 17-18, 22-25).

Thomas Hutchens, geographer and surveyor, in 1788 described "extensive meadows or savannas . . . 20-50 miles in circumference . . . [with] many beautiful groves of trees interspersed." Since he was speaking of land on both sides of the Ohio River (for example, Mason County in the Outer Bluegrass) rather than the Inner Bluegrass, we conclude that there were other tracts where soils and topography favored a savanna-like vegetational community but of smaller dimensions than were found on the Inner Bluegrass Plain.

In *The American Geography* (1789, 403-04), Jedidiah Morse wrote concerning "Elkhorn River" and the headwaters of Licking River and Hickman and Jessamine creeks: "The soil is deep and black, and the natural growth, large walnuts, honey and black locust, poplar, elm, oak, hickory, and sugar trees, etc."

"Where the soil is very rich there was a good deal of locust," said William Clinkenbeard. "Cane Ridge was also the greatest place for plumb [sic] bushes." He also noted that prickly ash *(Xanthoxylum)* grew very thick near Green Creek in Bourbon County (Draper MSS).

Asa Farrar, who had arrived in Lexington in 1788, told of clearing out the road "from Brennan's to Van Pelt's lane [now Rose Street] out to where the race ground was" after a hurricane had filled the passway. "There was one bur oak so large we couldn't get a saw long enough to run through. Had to cut on each side to let the saw in. Have no doubt the tree was four feet over. Forest of burr oaks and black walnuts" (Draper MSS).

Gilbert Imlay, a British traveler in Kentucky in the early 1790s, wrote of his journey to Bourbon Court House and Lexington that it was "as rich and as well-conditioned land as any in nature. . . . The country is immensely rich, and covered with cane, rye-grass, and the native clover. The cane is the reed that grows to the height frequently 15 or 16 feet, but more generally 10-12 feet, and is in thickness from the size of a goose-quill to that of two inches. . . . It is the most nourishing food for cattle on earth" (29).

Needham Parry, in his diary for 1794, wrote, "We came to a fine stream of water called Hinkston Creek . . . the land here being excellent and timbered with Walnut, Honey Locust, Buckeye, and Cherry trees. . . . The land I rode through today [fifteen miles after crossing Stoner Creek in Bourbon County] was of the first quality, being timbered like the rest with Walnut, Cherry, Blue Ash, Buckeye, Locust, and Hackberry" (1948).

John Bradbury, traveling here in 1809, wrote that "along the Elkhorn there were great beds of cane, and, at one pleasant spot, a prairie, grass-covered and treeless (except for a few wild plums)" (1809, 11).

General John B. Castleman, born in Fayette County in 1842, described the trees in the area in his boyhood: sugar maple, blue ash, oaks, hickory, and both black and white walnuts, he said, indicated good land and abounded here; beech and poplar did not. He also referred to "beech ridge," the divide between the drainage basins of the Kentucky and South Licking rivers on the Fayette-Bourbon boundary, and the areas of the Hickman and Bryan Station faults, all of which have more clay than most of the Inner Bluegrass and originally had more beech and tulip poplars.

In the foregoing accounts there is no question regarding the identity of the trees mentioned or concerning cane *(Arundinaria gigantea)*, a grass of the bamboo tribe. But there is a problem in interpreting the common names of some of the herbaceous species. Wild rye would undoubtedly be species of *Elymus*, especially *E. villosus* and *E. virginicus*, which are frequent today in open woods and woodland borders. "Buffalo grass" would have been a common grass on which the bison fed; it definitely is not the short grass *(Buchloe)* called buffalo grass on the Great Plains of the western states. Imlay (233) described it as coarse, 9-18 inches tall, with a broad leaf. This suggests several large species formerly in the genus *Panicum* (now *Dichanthelium commutatum*, *D. clandestinum*, and *D. boscii*), which today may be found in open woods and at the edge of woods.

Clover would have been a legume, undoubtedly of the genus *Trifolium*, of which we have only two native American species: *T. stoloniferum* and *T. reflexum*, both called buffalo clover. The peavine is probably *Amphicarpa bracteata*. Imlay described it as 1½–2 feet long, climbing on cane and shrubs by means of tendrils, and having slightly reddish flowers. *Amphicarpa*, however, twines, and its flowers can be pale purplish. *Vicia caroliniana* has tendrils, but the flowers are white.

A question that may never be answered is whether the bluegrass mentioned by the early pioneers was *Poa pratensis* and whether this was indigenous. For nearly a century and a half since giving its name to the region, this species has been called "Kentucky bluegrass." All species of the genus *Poa* are bluegrasses, of which there are seven other species in the Bluegrass region (but only four of them native), nine others in the state, and twenty-five in the northeast quarter of the United States. A few of this large number are weedy, several are introduced, and some are of forage value. *Poa pratensis* is by far the most important, however; it is the principal lawn and pasture grass in the northeast quarter of the nation. It requires lime and a rich soil; hence it flourishes here, but in many places where it is grown it must be nursed. The four species known to be native to this region grow in woods and nowhere form a ground cover dense enough to suggest significant forage.

Where did *Poa pratensis,* "Kentucky Bluegrass," come from? For centuries it has been grown in England and may not be native even there; it may have been introduced from farther east, on the Continent, in the Middle Ages. Though sometimes called "bluegrass" in England, it is more often called "meadow grass." In the American seaboard colonies where it was introduced, it was referred to as "English grass" about as often as "meadow grass" or "bluegrass." Was that grass also growing in the rich meadowlands and open forests west of the Appalachian Mountains when the pioneers arrived? The earliest record of bluegrass in a natural situation is that of Christopher Gist, written in 1751 of an area on the Miami River in Ohio, the description of which could fit the Bluegrass region of Kentucky: "fine rich level land, well timbered with large walnut, ash, sugartrees, cherry trees, etc., it is well-watered . . . and full of beautiful natural meadows; covered with wild rye, blue grass, and clover" (Johnston, 133).

One bit of evidence that "Kentucky bluegrass," "English grass," or "meadow grass" was growing wild here is found in a court case of 1805, at a time when there were many legal disputes over land titles and boundaries. The land in question was on Grassy Lick in Montgomery County near the Bourbon and Clark County lines. The case was *Higgins' heirs* versus *Darnall's devisees* (*Hardin's Kentucky Reports,* 1806, 57-58). Darnall's entry had noted "a piece of low ground remarkable for Bluegrass or English grass and extending on both sides of the creek, northward for quantity." Twelve witnesses testified that they had seen "English grass," "Bluegrass," or "English bluegrass" growing there in the 1770s. One testified that in 1775 "we discovered great quantities of English grass in this bottom . . . said to be the bottom land alluded to in Darnall's entry." Other witnesses saw it there in 1776, in 1778, and so on. The pioneers brought grain and vegetable seed with them, but there is no authentic record of any grass seed being brought or sown that early.

Further evidence of indigenous bluegrass is found in an account by Septimus Scholl, grandson of Daniel Boone, written for his children and placed at the disposal of Shane (Draper MSS). In 1780 Daniel Boone and his brother Edward, returning from Blue Licks, where they had gone for buffalo, stopped and unloaded their horses to let them graze on "indigenous bluegrass" where it "sprang up pretty fresh." Scholl knew that bluegrass had been brought in after 1780 and sown where it did not grow naturally, but in the 1840s he was convinced that some was indigenous.

About all we know with certainty is that the "Kentucky Bluegrass Seed" purchased from a seed store today was harvested from a strain of grass that years ago came from England, but this does not prove that some native populations were not growing here before the white settlers arrived.

In summary, to reconstruct the probable appearance in 1770 of the inter-stream plateau areas of the Inner Bluegrass which we call the Bluegrass Plain, we can visualize dense canebrakes with scattered trees, meadowlands, and open forests of oak, ash, walnut, cherry, hickory, sugar maple, and others, with an abundance of grasses (including cane), legumes, and other herbaceous plants flourishing beneath as ample light reached the ground. Dense, closed forests undoubtedly covered land near the rivers and creeks.

PRESETTLEMENT TREES REMAINING TODAY

The trees that greeted the pioneers are seen today in rapidly diminishing numbers. The chief causes of their loss are recent industrial and residential developments and highway construction, although natural mortality through lightning and wind damage to the tallest objects has also taken its toll. Most of the remaining patriarchs are on large stock farms; some are in parks and city cemeteries. The largest and oldest trees in the 200- to 450-year-old category are bur oaks *(Quercus macrocarpa)*; the most numerous trees over 200 years old are blue ash *(Fraxinus quadrangulata),* with chinquapin oak *(Quercus muehlenbergii)* running second numerically. Their contemporaries still living include Shumard oak *(Q. shumardii),* white ash *(F. americana),* shellbark hickory *(Carya laciniosa),* hackberry *(Celtis occidentalis),* and coffee tree *(Gymnocladus dioica).*

Davidson (1950) plotted the locations of old bur oaks that were visible from federal, state, and county roads throughout Fayette County, as well as those in public parks and cemeteries. In 1950, 370 of these venerable monarchs could be seen by the public, not including specimens far back on private estates and not visible from a road. In 1978 the present author (MEW), following Davidson's map, traversed every public road in Fayette County, as well as parks and cemeteries, and found only 199 remaining. Thus in twenty-eight years we lost 171 bur oaks, some from wind and lightning but most from human activity. If this rate continues, by the year 2000, there will be left in Fayette County, where the public can see them, only 30 bur oaks that antedate the settlement of the state, although the species is capable of living 500 years. (Several are known to have been lost since 1978, although no other complete count has been taken.)

Much more scarce than individual old trees are assemblages of trees over 200 years old, vestiges of the ancient open forests or savanna-woodlands. We call the presettlement open forests "savanna-woodlands," meaning open forests in which trees are dominant but with a well-developed grassy undergrowth. In a true savanna the tree density is so low that the actual dominants of the community are the grasses and other herbaceous vegetation. Nowhere in today's vestiges does the original ground vegetation remain, and there undoubtedly is much more space between the standing trees now than there was originally. Some species may have lacked the longevity of the remaining ones, and some species would have been removed for specific uses, such as black walnut and wild cherry cut for lumber and sugar maple killed by overtapping. Hence the ecologist's "importance value," if calculated for the various species in the remnant stands, would not represent that of the original communities. Nevertheless, these "woodland pastures," as they have been called, are the best that remain from the vegetation of the

Table 1. Diameters of Selected Large Trees in a Harrison County Woodland Pasture

white ash (Biltmore variety)	5′10¾″	DBH
blue ash	4′0″	DBH
chinquapin oak	4′7½″	DBH
Shumard oak	4′5½″	DBH
shellbark hickory	3′4¾″	DBH
pignut hickory	2′9¾″	DBH
coffee tree	3′4½″	DBH

primeval Bluegrass Plain, a heritage of inestimable value that should be zealously protected.

The most remarkable of these woodland pastures is a 90-acre tract in Harrison County near the Bourbon County border, a portion of a farm that has been in the same family for seven generations. Many of its trees would have been large when the first white men arrived. Stately blue ash and massive, widely spreading chinquapin oaks are the dominant trees, with shellbark hickory next in importance. Also present are numerous old white ash, Shumard oak, coffee tree, shagbark hickory, and others. The tract averages six ancient trees per acre. Although the ground has never been plowed (the sod not turned), fescue *(Festuca pratensis)* has been added; it is grazed by cattle and is mowed annually or biannually. Selected trees in this tract were measured in 1980, with the results shown in Table 1.

In a smaller tract on the same farm stand seven great old bur oaks, one of which is 5 feet 11½ inches in diameter at breast eight (DBH). A chinquapin oak here is 4 feet 11 inches (DBH), and a hackberry is 3 feet 11/2 inches (DBH).

Young trees 2-12 inches in diameter in both these tracts are confined to the edges of small streams and sinks where they have not been mowed. Of these, black walnut is the most numerous; other species are honey locust, black locust, American elm, shellbark hickory, hackberry, white ash, and hawthorn; there are only a few blue ash. In the smaller tract only two young bur oaks are among the many young trees along fencerows and small ravines. Hence the presettlement canopy is not being regenerated.

An example in Bourbon County is an eighteen-acre tract of pasture and lawn that contains 120 trees estimated to be over 200 years old. They include 87 blue ash, 5 bur oak, 5 sugar maple, 5 coffee tree, 4 hackberry, 3 chinquapin oak, 3 white ash, 3 bitternut hickory, 1 shellbark hickory, 1 American elm, 1 Ohio buckeye, 1 black locust, and 1 honey locust.

Bourbon County also has a seven-acre tract, including lawn and paddock, having the following trees estimated to be over 200 years old: 28 blue ash, 2 Shumard oaks (one approaching the national record for size in this species), and 2 bur oaks. One shellbark hickory and several blue ash are probably slightly under 200 years.

On another Bourbon County stock farm, in lawn and adjacent pasture (about 25 acres), there are 56 trees estimated to be from 175 to 350 years old: 26 chinquapin oaks, 20 blue ash, 9 bur oaks, and 1 coffee tree. This tract and another

Table 2. Diameters and Estimated Ages of Bur Oaks on a Former Farm in Fayette County

Circumference, DBH	Diameter, DBH	Estimated Age (years)
19′8″	6.26′	413
19′7″	6.23′	412
17′11″	5.70′	377
14′2″	4.51′	298
13′3.5″	4.23′	280
12′6″	3.98′	264
11′2″	3.56′	237

For estimating age, rings were counted in stumps of the same species, the average number of rings per inch was determined, and the diameter of living trees was measured.

pasture nearby also contain mature trees less than a century old of the following species: black walnut, black locust, white ash, blue ash, coffee tree, and a single bur oak.

On a Fayette County horse farm, two contiguous pastures totalling 40 acres contain the following trees estimated to be over 175 and up to 350 years old: 86 blue ash, 16 bur oaks, 1 chinquapin oak, and 2 coffee trees, as well as many blue ash approximately a century old. In the 50-year category are numerous black walnuts, several coffee trees, a few blue ash, 1 shagbark hickory, and 1 Ohio buckeye. In another pasture of 25 acres on the same farm are 24 blue ash, 15 bur oaks, and 1 shagbark hickory, all estimated to be between 175 and 300 years old, with numerous younger black walnuts in a fencerow. Unfortunately a tornado several years ago brought down many of the great old trees on this farm, and many of the remaining ones show lightning damage.

The most significant bur oak population the authors have seen in the Bluegrass region is a former farm southeast of Lexington, now a large residential subdivision. It was noteworthy not only because of the large concentration of old bur oaks but also because of the much better regeneration of young ones than at any other place. For this reason, it is included in our quantitative studies of current plant communities, where it is listed under "Relic Communities" (pages 59-60). The bur oak population here included 29 trees over 200 years old and 72 trees from 12 to 200 years old. Also present were 3 blue ash, 2 chinquapin oak, 1 white oak, and 1 shellbark hickory over 200 years old. One bur oak that had been cut recently showed growth of 10-12 years per inch and averaged 11 years per inch, thereby enabling us to estimate the age of those still standing. Some of the large bur oaks were measured in the late 1970s with the results shown in Table 2.

DISCUSSION AND INTERPRETATION

Trees in a dense forest grow tall but lack low branches and have upper branches not widely spreading. The survivors of the presettlement Bluegrass are notably widespreading trees with low branches (with the exception of the blue ash, which rarely develops such a silhouette), indicating that they were well spaced even in their youth and did not develop in a dense forest.

The mere presence of the bur oak is a significant indicator. In overall geographic distribution the species grows in central and northern United States; its stronghold is west and northwest of Kentucky, principally Illinois, Iowa, Wisconsin, Minnesota, and eastern Nebraska. It is a tree characteristic of the savannas, which are transitional between our eastern forests and our midcontinent prairies; it grows in the "oak openings" or "prairie groves" of the Midwest (Peattie 1950). At the northern and western limits of its range, however, it usually does not attain the gigantic size seen here. In Kentucky the species is most frequent in the Inner Bluegrass but occurs also in the Outer Bluegrass and Mississippian Plateau, also limestone. It is noteworthy that the species was first named and described by André Michaux in 1795 from a tree about twelve miles from the present city of Nashville, Tennessee, in the Nashville Basin, which is underlain by limestone of the same age as that in Kentucky's Inner Bluegrass. The bur oak is rarely found in a dense forest; its seedlings cannot tolerate shade and cannot become established in the subdued light of a closed canopy.

On a Woodford County farm that has 92 old trees (41 blue ash, 28 bur oaks, 13 black walnut, 6 chinquapin oak, 1 shellbark hickory, 1 bitternut hickory, 1 coffee tree, and 1 sugar maple), the owner about 1968 fenced off approximately one acre of open ground near seven large oaks (3 bur and 4 chinquapin) to observe what species would invade in the absence of grazing or mowing. Fifteen years later it was a dense thicket, predominantly of walnut and silver maple (the latter species having been planted in the farm's front lawn in the 1880s or 1890s), but also with a large number of wild cherry, box elder, and others. Six bur oaks were found underneath the hundreds of other trees, which are much faster growing species; three of these are sickly and will definitely not survive, and the survival of the other three is doubtful. Several sugar maples beneath a faster growing canopy looked healthy, but no blue ash were found here. The only young blue ash observed was next to a fallen tree at the side of an otherwise shady lawn—thereby escaping the mower and growing in the sunshine resulting from the opening.

The occurrence of bur oak, a savanna species, in Kentucky is anomalous, since all of the state has ample rainfall for the growth of dense forests, not the reduced rainfall of a savanna climate. Wherever we find bur oaks in the Bluegrass region, they tell us that in those places the original "forest" was open. Davidson noted that in Fayette County the old bur oaks were found north, south, east, and west of Lexington. This means that in a forest-producing climate having 44 inches of annual rainfall, there were in this section parklike groves carpeted with grass and legumes. In many places the presence of topsoil thicker and darker than is normal for soils formed under forests suggests partial grassland derivation (USDA 1968A). This applies to about 30-40 percent of Maury soils. All of this anomaly seeks an explanation.

At the time white settlers arrived, most of the vegetation here was apparently stabilized but held at a subclimax, not a climatic climax. Periodic burning by aborigines to encourage big game has been suggested as a contributing factor in holding it, since fires were known on the prairies. In the so-called "Barrens" of west-central Kentucky, grassland had been maintained and trees excluded largely by fire (McInteer 1946). In the Bluegrass area, however, there were trees. Although bur oak is considered fire-resistant, its associates are not known to be, and sugar maple, the species most often named in the early surveys and said by Short to be one of the most common trees, is definitely fire-sensitive. The early settlers left no statement to suggest that they thought Indians had burned any of this land. If fire had been a factor in determining the existing vegetation type, it would have been used by an earlier population, such as the Fort Ancient Culture (c. 1000-1700) or a still earlier culture. Burning would have to have been very infrequent for it not to eliminate the cane. When the settlers burned the cane once, it encouraged new shoots which the cattle ate, but with repeated burning it was entirely killed.

Probably the most potent factor in the continuance of a savanna-like situation was the activity of the large herbivores: great herds of bison trampling down tree seedlings as they grazed on cane and other grasses, and numerous elk and deer browsing on the tree seedlings. As Marsh pointed out (119), "The bison . . . could not convert the forest into a pasture, but he would do much to prevent the pasture from becoming a forest." This would only account for the perpetuation of a savanna or savanna woodland, however, not for its origin; nor would it account for the initial presence of the bur oak here.

To explain the origin of savanna in this area, we must go back several thousand years to a "xerothermic interval," beginning about 6,000 years ago and lasting approximately 3,000 years, when the climate was warmer and drier than the present. The extension of prairie into Ohio at that time has been studied by Transeau (1935) and Sears (1942). The climatic climax vegetation for our karst, limestone areas could well have been savanna at that time, for underdrainage makes a drought more pronounced than in areas without sinks. But a savanna ecosystem in the Bluegrass probably dates back to late Wisconsin time in the glacial epoch. Vertebrate remains dated as 13,000 years old in a Woodford County cave were of prairie, semi-prairie, and boreal woodland fauna, indicating that the vegetation at that time would likely have been semi-prairie or parkland.

Thus the fertile, parklike lands that charmed the early settlers were relic communities. Their origin was in the distant past, and their continuance in this mildly karst country after the climate became more moist was accomplished largely by beasts now long gone. A few bur oaks stand today as patriarchs, as narrators of prehistory. The remaining woodland pastures are antique treasures deserving the utmost protection, and their component species should be propagated lest we lose a natural flavor of the Bluegrass region.

3. Presettlement Animal Life

THE FIRST record of animals in the Bluegrass region is in the rocks that underlie the region. These animals were invertebrates inhabiting the warm shallow seas that covered this part of the country about 400 million years ago: cephalopods and other molluscs, brachiopods, crinoids, and bryozoa. Although later seas covered the area, their deposits, including later marine life, were eroded away when the land was several times uplifted out of the sea. No trace of the earliest terrestrial life has been left in the Bluegrass, although swamp life was preserved in the coal-bearing rocks of eastern and western Kentucky.

The next record here is at the time of Pleistocene glaciation, when great mastodons, mammoths, giant sloths, tremendous early bison, primitive horses, musk oxen, moose, and caribou left their remains in the Outer Bluegrass: at Big Bone Lick in Northern Kentucky and at Blue Licks in Nicholas County, only a few miles from the edge of the Inner Bluegrass. The bones of vertebrates no longer with us, buried in mire near the salt licks, cover a span of tens of thousands of years, from about 9,000 to over 100,000 years ago. From later periods, there are bones of extant species of bison, elk, deer, and bear. Other Pleistocene mammals have been found in Bluegrass caves: a polar bear in Fayette County from the time of glacial ice to the north, and tapirs in Fayette and Scott counties, indicating a warm interglacial climate.

In Welch Cave, between Nonesuch and Mundy's Landing in Woodford County, an impressive array of mammalian species was found in 1965 (Guilday et al.). Carbon dating placed the age of the specimens at 12,950 years ± 500 years. The habitat requirements of the species recovered (see Table 3) indicate prairie, semi-prairie, open parkland, boreal woodland, and open country in general.

In addition to four extinct species, the cave contained many species that are no longer known to occur in Kentucky. The latter include six northern species: the water shrew and snowshoe hare, which occur along the Appalachian crest south into Tennessee; the red squirrel, which extends south along the Appalachians into eastern Tennessee and westward into southern Indiana; the spruce vole, which now ranges no nearer Kentucky than the northern border of the

United States; the yellow-cheeked vole, whose present range lies in western Canada north of latitude 50 degrees but which apparently was common in the Appalachians in the late Pleistocene; and the porcupine, which occurs southward along the Appalachian crest into West Virginia. The grizzly bear, represented by an adult and a cub in Welch Cave, is now an exclusively western species.

Three of the species represented are characteristic of prairies or savannas. The nearest present range of the thirteen-lined ground squirrel is some 200 miles north of Kentucky; from the number of individuals recovered, one would infer that the environment around Welch Cave some 13,000 years ago was eminently suitable for the species. The species of the pocket gopher specimens could not be determined, but no member of the genus is now known in Kentucky; the Inner Bluegrass lies some 300 miles southeast of the range of the plains pocket gopher and roughly 400 miles north of the range of the southeastern pocket gopher. The badger is rarely observed in Kentucky today and here seems limited to a narrow band along the shore of the Ohio River south of Cincinnati; it is essentially a prairie creature whose eastern distribution in the United States roughly coincides with the distribution of the thirteen-lined ground squirrel.

Two species found in the cave still live in Kentucky, although not in the Bluegrass: the pigmy shrew, which now occurs sparingly across the state, and the red-backed vole, a northern species that now occurs only on the higher wooded mountains along the southeastern border of Kentucky. The least weasel has been extending its range and has recently been collected from the Inner Bluegrass.

Six of the Welch Cave species are common throughout Kentucky today: the short-tailed shrew; the eastern mole, which is common except in the higher southeastern mountains (one specimen found in the cave may be of relatively recent origin); the brown bat, which could be any of four species, two of which now occur at least occasionally in the Inner Bluegrass; the pipistrelle, probably *P. subflavus*, now common in the Bluegrass; the meadow vole, three species of which now occur in the Inner Bluegrass, all partial to grasslands; and the pine vole, the commonest vole at the cave and at present common in the Inner Bluegrass.

The conclusion is that central Kentucky 13,000 years ago was boreal semi-prairie or parkland.

The Adena people inhabited the Bluegrass and surrounding areas from approximately 500 B.C. to 600 A.D. Through their scraps and other leavings we have considerable information on the wildlife of the Inner Bluegrass during their tenure here. Their middens contain remains of deer, elk, rabbits, meadow vole, skunk, muskrat, gray squirrel, woodchuck, thirteen-lined ground squirrel, bear, raccoon, dog, otter, and beaver. Of birds, wild turkey, trumpeter swan, and great horned owl have been identified.

For the Indians the Inner Bluegrass was a favorite hunting ground. In the 1750s and 1760s adventurous white hunters and trappers from the eastern colonies wandered beyond the mountains and found an incredible land abounding in game, a hunter's paradise. Fur traders, such as John Finley in 1752, swapped goods for furs obtained by the Indians, but most did their own killing. They planned to

Table 3. Mammalian Species Found in Welch Cave

Species	No.	Present Status
Dire wolf (*Canis dirus*)	2	Species extinct
Mammoth (*Mammuthus* sp.)	1	Species extinct
Horse (*Equus* sp.)	1	Species extinct
Flat-headed peccary (*Platygonus compressus*)	31	Species extinct
Water shrew (*Sorex palustris*)	2	No longer in Kentucky
Snowshoe hare (*Lepus americanus*)	1	No longer in Kentucky
Red squirrel (*Tamiasciurus hudsonicus*)	1	No longer in Kentucky
Spruce vole (*Phenacomys* sp.)	1	No longer in Kentucky
Yellow-cheeked vole (*Microtus xanthognathus*)	2	No longer in Kentucky
Porcupine (*Erethizon dorsatum*)	2	No longer in Kentucky
Grizzly bear (*Ursus arctos horribilus*)	2	No longer in eastern North America
Thirteen-lined ground squirrel (*Spermophilus tridecemlineatus*)	43	No longer in Kentucky
Pocket gopher (*Geomys* sp.)	3	No longer in Kentucky
Badger (*Taxidea taxus*)	1	Rare in Kentucky
Pigmy shrew (*Microsorex hoyi*)	2	In Kentucky but no longer in Bluegrass
Red-backed vole (*Clethrionomys gapperi*)	1	No longer in Bluegrass
Least weasel (*Mustela nivalis*)	1	No longer in Inner Bluegrass
Short-tailed shrew (*Blarina brevicauda*)	2	Common throughout Kentucky
Eastern mole (*Scalopus aquaticus*)	1	Common throughout Kentucky except in higher southeastern mountains
Brown bat (*Myotis* sp.)	1	Two *Myotis* spp now occasional in Inner Bluegrass
Pipistrelle (*Pipistrellus* sp.) (probably *P. subflavus*)	1	*P. subflavus* common in Bluegrass
Meadow vole (*Microtus* sp.)	11	3 species now occur in Inner Bluegrass
Pine vole (*Microtus pinetorum*)	13	Common in Inner Bluegrass

take large loads back east for great profit, but sometimes Indians would steal them. The Long Hunters, a group of forty men from the Yadkin Valley of North Carolina—so named because they were long away from home—had the misfortune in 1770 to have 2,300 deer skins stolen. (This probably included elk hides also.) Another group lost 1,500 to Indians. Squire Boone brought back to North Carolina two packloads of skins and also pelts of otter and beaver, but had one load stolen.

The Bluegrass region was a special haven for large herbivores. The rich soil, high in calcium and phosphorus, provided nutritious food that made them strong and healthy, the topography was to their liking, and salt licks were nearby. The immense herds of bison amazed the pioneer settlers. Few kept any records of the wildlife they lived with, but some early accounts have survived:

Daniel Boone, for example, reported to Filson, "We found everywhere abundance of wild beasts of all sorts. . . . The buffaloes were more frequent than I have ever seen cattle in the settlements, browsing on leaves of cane, or cropping the herbage of those extensive plains, fearless because ignorant of the violence of man. Sometimes we saw hundreds in a drove" (Filson, 51). Felix Walker, who came to Boonesborough in 1775, wrote: "On entering the plain we were permitted to view a very interesting and romantic sight. A number of buffaloes of all sizes, supposed to be between two and three hundred, made off from the lick in every direction; some running, some walking, others loping slowly and carelessly, with young calves playing, skipping, and bounding through the plain. Such a sight some of us never saw before, nor perhaps may never again" (Ranck, 166).

Mrs. Joice Craig Falconer, who came to David's Fork in Fayette County in 1779, said in an interview (Draper MSS) that "there were pretty near perhaps a thousand [buffalo] in number, and the woods roared with their tramping, almost as bad as thunder." Martin Wymore (Draper MS) related that "Buffalo used to be passing by Lexington everyday and sometimes all day long."

Simon Kenton, a Virginia youth who had become entranced by hunters' tales of Kentucky and was eager to see the cane lands, came in 1771 at the age of sixteen. Two or three years later he and two companions set out to explore. At May's Lick they "fell in with the great buffalo trace, which in a few hours brought them to Lower Blue Lick. The flats on each side of the river were crowded with immense herds of buffalo . . . and a number of elk were seen upon the bare ridges which surround the springs. . . . After remaining a few days at the lick and killing an immense number of deer and buffalo, they crossed the Licking [River] and passing through the present counties of Scott, Fayette, Woodford, Clark, Montgomery, and Bath, where, falling in with another buffalo trace, it conducted them to the Upper Blue Lick where they again beheld elk and buffalo in immense numbers" (McClung 86)

John Filson provided the most detailed description of the buffalo in 1784:

> Among the native animals are the urus, bison, or zorax bison described by Caesar, which we call a buffalo, much resembling a large bull, of a great size, with a large head, thick, short, crooked horns, and broader in his forepart than behind. Upon his shoulder is a large lump of flesh, covered with a thick boss of long wool and curly hair, of a dark brown color. They do not rise from the ground as our cattle, but spring up at once upon their feet; are of a broad make, and clumsy appearance, with short legs, but run fast, and turn not aside for anything when chased, except a standing tree. They weigh from 500 to 1000 weight, are excellent meat, supplying the inhabitants in many parts with beef, and their hides make good leather. I have heard a hunter assert, he saw one thousand buffaloes at Blue Licks at once; so numerous were they before the first settlers had wantonly sported away their lives. There still remains a great number in the exterior parts of the settlement. They feed upon cane and grass, as other cattle, and are innocent, harmless creatures. . . . The amazing herds of buffaloes which resort thither [to salt licks] by their size and number, fill the traveler with

> amazement and terror, especially when he beholds the prodigious roads they have made from all quarters, as if leading to some populous city; the vast space of land around these springs desolated as if by a ravaging enemy. [pp. 27, 32]

At the Blue Licks there was a pond of salty water and sand that the buffalo had tread into a mire, which prevented its running into the river. The flats on both sides of the stream were nearly always crowded with buffalo that had come to lick the salty earth. Kenton reported counting 1,500 passing down a road at one time; he had to climb a tree to let the herd pass. The enormous herds on their way to a salt lick would pause to wallow in the shoals of streams, and no canoe could pass until the buffalo had shaken themselves free of water and mire and had moved on. These wallows, or "stamping grounds," resulted in bare spots covering several acres. There were three large stamping grounds in central Kentucky, although the name has been retained only for the one in Scott County.

The roads the bison made and traveled, especially from their feeding grounds of cane and meadow grass to the salt licks, were well laid out along the ridges and creeksides and always crossed a river or other stream at the most strategic and negotiable points. They were about forty feet broad, trampled hard, with bordering vegetation destroyed. These roads were adopted by the settlers, being especially useful in penetrating the canebrakes and crossing the rivers. They determined the lines of travel, transportation, and settlement. Between Maysville and Frankfort, for instance, settlements were first established along the buffalo road, and later the turnpike and railroad closely followed the route made by these animals.

The early settlers, besides eating buffalo meat—their principal food during the hard winter of 1779-1780—and using their hides, wove buffalo wool with a warp of nettle fibers to make cloth. But very little of any one buffalo killed was utilized. "Four of us went out and got 24, killed them, and got all the wool off," wrote William Clinkenbeard (Draper MSS). "They did destroy and waste them at a mighty rate. If one wasn't young and fat, it was left and they went on to kill another." Without salt, no fresh meat could be preserved.

One of the chief occupations of frontier life was hunting, not only for food and skins for the family, but for trade across the mountains, exchanging skins and pelts for manufactured articles. Most of the pioneers' accounts of animal life related to its abundance, how many they had killed, and how they had killed them.

Deer were abundant at the time of settlement and were wantonly killed for meat and for their skins, which were home-tanned for hunting pants and shirts, although linsey woolsey was also used. The stately elk, more properly called wapiti, was often mentioned in connection with buffalo. It provided leather that was stronger and more durable than deerskin and was therefore used for moccasins; elk meat had the flavor of venison but was tougher. Bearskins covered the pioneers' beds, and bear meat was relished on log-cabin tables. Bears and raccoons were unwelcome visitors in cornfields. Wolves and panthers were forest dwellers that occasionally made nocturnal raids on settlements. Clinkenbeard (Draper

MSS) recorded the presence of "a good many traps round the station [Strode's] to catch wolves. . . . the fort yard was a great place for wolf baiting. Caught a panther once."

Another common article on the menu was turkey, which was substituted for bread until a corn crop could be harvested and ground for meal. "It was the greatest country for turkey I ever saw," said Clinkenbeard. "I've seen a hundred turkeys roosting within sight of our station," said Joice Craig Falconer of Craig's Station in Fayette County (Draper MSS). An easy way to kill turkeys, according to Daniel Trabue (Young 1981, 71), was to shoot them while they roosted in the trees on a moonlit night. Since they would not fly away at night, one man could, and often would, kill the entire flock.

Daniel Boone and Richard Henderson perceived the fate that lay ahead for Kentucky's wildlife if profligate killing continued. Colonel Henderson, addressing delegates from the four settlements in "Kentucke" assembled at Boonesborough on 23 May 1775, mentioned "the wanton destruction of our game . . . this, together with the practice of many foreigners, who make a business of hunting in our country, killing, driving off, and lessening the number of wild cattle and other game, whilst the value of the skins and furs is appropriated to the benefit of persons not concerned or interested in our settlement." Boone thereupon introduced a bill for the preservation of game, and his brother Squire introduced one for the preservation of the range. These were among the nine laws enacted in the three-day session under "the great elm tree," and showed wisdom and foresight on the part of the delegates. But wasteful practices continued (Ranck, 204-7).

By 1775 there was already a noticeable reduction in big game. The phenomenally severe winter of 1779-1780 brought death through starvation and freezing to many thousands of mammals and birds—any species that depended on food from the ground, which for months lay covered with ice and snow. The settlers suffered also during that winter because they depended on a meat diet exclusively. Trabue complained that starving turkeys were "too poor to eat" (Young, 74).

In October 1780, Daniel Boone reported that there were no longer any buffalo in the vicinity of Cross Plains (at Boone's Station), and that they had to go all the way to Blue Lick for buffalo meat. Cross Plains (now Athens) was so named because two buffalo traces crossed there.

By the close of the 1780s buffalo bones covered all the ground along Stoner Creek in Bourbon County. Hunters would "kill them for sport and leave them lie," said John Hedge in an interview (Draper MSS). Jesse Graddy, in Woodford County, reported that "when we came to this country in 1787 the buffalo were gone." An account entitled "Some Particulars Relative to Kentucky," which appeared in the *National Gazette* in 1791, noted that "the Buffaloes have entirely quitted the cultivated parts of Kentuckey and the Deer have become scarce" (Schwaab, 60).

By 1800 all bison had been eliminated from the state, and the mighty herds that had fed on the rich herbage were but a memory. Elk too had become very rare in Kentucky, and after a few years would live on only in many place names in the state.

Daniel Boone left Kentucky in 1799 but returned for a visit in 1810, at the age of 76. He told John James Audubon that he "rambled about to see if a deer was still living in the land. But, ah! Sir, what a difference thirty years make in the country! . . . [Now] only a few signs of deer were to be seen, and as to the deer itself, I saw none" (Audubon, 115).

Most pioneer accounts ignore small creatures, although Filson (26-27) mentions a few: "Serpents are not numerous, and are such as are to be found in other parts of the continent, except the bull, the horned, and the moccasin snakes. Swamps are rare, and consequently frogs and other reptiles common to such places. There are no swarms of bees, except such have been introduced by the present inhabitants." Of birds, Filson also speaks of "the Parroquet, a bird every way resembling a parrot, but much smaller; [and] the ivory-billed wood-cock." The brilliantly colored Carolina parakeet, now extinct, was once common throughout Kentucky. "When we first came out," reported Clinkenbeard concerning Strode's Station in Bourbon County, "there were a great number of paroquets in the country. Lived on cuckleburrs [*sic*]. Flew in large gangs." The ivory-billed woodpecker, magnificent and majestic, has long been extinct in Kentucky and is probably extinct elsewhere. Clinkenbeard also commented on the ravens, which had been very plentiful, but "they went off as well as the buffalo" (Draper MSS).

No other bird in primeval America was as numerous as the passenger pigeon. Early Kentuckians described the darkening of the sky at noonday when a flock flew past. Its greatest nesting sites were north of Kentucky, and many of the birds wintered south of us, but the species both nested and wintered in Kentucky. It is not known whether the passenger pigeon had either a nesting or a roosting site in the Inner Bluegrass, but they flew overhead, and some documented breeding sites were in the Outer Bluegrass, including one near Shelbyville that was 40 miles long and several miles wide. The ornithologist Alexander Wilson described the flight of millions of birds over Frankfort in 1808 or 1809. He conservatively estimated the breadth of the column as at least one mile, and it took four hours in passing. If the pigeons were flying at a rate of one mile in one minute, the column would have been 240 miles long. Calculating three birds per square yard, Wilson reached a figure of 2,230,272,000 birds in the flock (2:201-03).

The passenger pigeon was so abundant that it was held in contempt, and in its nesting and roosting places in early Kentucky it was slaughtered prodigiously. Hogs would be driven to the site to feed on dead birds, while relatively few were taken for human consumption. At Duncan Tavern in Paris, a "bill of fare" in the early 1800s listed several meats, the cheapest of which was pigeon. The slaughter mounted on a commercial basis in the northern states in the second half of the nineteenth century, and the species has been extinct since 1914. The last passenger pigeon killed in Kentucky was shot near Winchester in 1899.

Thus wrought the hand of man on native creatures.

4. Early Modification of the Presettlement Ecosystems

THE PREHISTORIC human residents of Kentucky lived with the land and its other inhabitants, harvesting only what they needed, rather than attempting to modify them to their own designs. But with the astounding rate of migration from the eastern states and the rapidity of settlement in the Inner Bluegrass, immediate inroads were made into the natural ecosystems. According to Aubudon, writing in the early nineteenth century, "Cultivation and introduction of cattle and horses, and other circumstances connected with the progress of civilization, have greatly altered the face of the country" (Peattie 1940, 55).

The pioneer was impressed by the richness of the land, as evidenced by its bountiful natural production, but—not interested in that bounty per se—sought to adapt the richness to producing what he had previously known. What was abundant in nature, be it plant or animal, was treated carelessly or even with contempt.

FROM PUBLIC DOMAIN TO PRIVATE OWNERSHIP

Both France and England claimed the Ohio valley until France relinquished it at the end of the French and Indian War in 1763. Although both French and English had set foot on Kentucky soil in the seventeenth century, they did not reach that heart that we call the Inner Bluegrass. By the mid-eighteenth century, scouts, hunters, and fur traders from the frontier settlements of Virginia and North Carolina were penetrating Kentucky in increasing numbers, but few reached the Inner Bluegrass until after 1750. Dr. Thomas Walker, scouting for a land company, entered Kentucky at Cumberland Gap, erected a cabin, and raised a crop of corn in 1750 near the present site of Barbourville. He explored as far north as Levisa Fork but missed the Bluegrass. Christopher Gist entered Kentucky from Ohio in 1751 and went as far south as Pine Mountain, skirting the Inner Bluegrass. John Finley, who hunted and fur-traded in Kentucky in 1752, especially in Clark County but also in Woodford County, returned in 1767 and came again in 1769 with Daniel Boone. Boone, hunting and land prospecting on a two-year trip in 1769-1771 and on a second trip in 1773, was more thorough in exploring the Inner Bluegrass than anyone previously.

Boone said he esteemed this area "a second paradise" (Filson, 56). His reports and those of other explorers and hunters spread rapidly and stimulated interest to the extent that it was generally believed to be a "Promised Land" or "another Eden." To quote Moore, "Kentucky came to be idealized as an earthly paradise within the grasp of anyone willing to move west, an American Eden just beyond the Cumberland Gap." Emigrants to Kentucky were not deterred by Indian attacks; to get here they would brave any hardship or danger. Felix Walker, arriving at Boonesborough in 1775, wrote, "We felt ourselves as passengers through a wilderness, just arrived at the fields of Elysium, or at a garden where there was no forbidden fruit" (Ranck). George Rogers Clark, in a letter to his brother on 6 July 1775, wrote, "A richer and more beautiful country than this I believe has never been seen in America yet" (James 9-10).

Following the adventurous hunters and roving scouts came surveyors, then land squatters, and finally land claimants. By 1775 about 300 persons were already residing in the Bluegrass region, most of them at the four stations: Boonesborough, Fort Harrod, St. Asaph's, and Boiling Springs. The scramble for Kentucky land was under way. By 1784 the population of Kentucky was estimated at 30,000. The census of 1790 listed 73,677; all Kentucky towns at this time were either within or on the margin of the Greater Bluegrass. In 1800 the state census was 220,955; in 25 years Kentucky's population had grown to be nearly as great as Connecticut's, two-thirds that of Maryland, more than half that of Massachusetts, more than one-third that of Pennsylvania, and one-fourth that of Virginia. Imlay (173) said in 1795 that emigration to Kentucky in the previous year was 14,000.

Every person, of whatever class, who set out for this "second Eden" came to better his lot. Many were middle-class farmers who were not prospering on land worn out by continuous tobacco culture, some were recent arrivals from across the ocean, and some were patricians of the landed gentry—younger sons of aristocratic families who in a system of primogeniture would inherit little of the family estate in the Old Dominion. Sometimes slaves and overseers were sent in advance to make preparations and erect temporary housing before the family set out. Imlay wrote in 1795, "This extraordinary fertility enables the farmer who has but a small capital, to increase his wealth in a most rapid manner" (167). Toulmin reported in 1793, "The produce of an acre [in Kentucky] is double that of the Shenandoah valley, and you can send it to market for less money." Moreover, land prices in the Shenandoah valley were two or three times as high as those in Kentucky; those near Hagerstown, Maryland, were nine times as high; and those in Lancaster County, Pennsylvania, eighteen times as high (Tinling and Davies). Another advantage was that land ownership could be obtained on easy terms, and much land was given away. After a few years many Bluegrass Kentuckians had established elegant estates.

The earliest surveys in the archives of the Kentucky Land Office in Frankfort are those for land granted by Virginia for service in the French and Indian War. The first surveying party in Kentucky was headed by Captain Thomas Bullitt in 1773. Other surveys were made later in 1773 and in 1774, 1775, and 1776 by Hancock Taylor, John Floyd, James Douglas, and Isaac Hite, deputy surveyors under Colonel William Preston, surveyor of Fincastle County, Virginia, of which Kentucky was a part (Taylor 1975). Surveying was discontinued during the American Revolution but was resumed in 1780. Most of these French and Indian War land grants were in the Inner Bluegrass and near the Ohio River from the Falls upstream. They were for a specified number of acres, usually 1,000, but sometimes 500, 2,000, or 3,000, and occasionally as few as 50. They were to be located, surveyed, and then entered in the land office for the receipt of title. Location was by watercourse and adjoining surveys.

The earliest settlers, however, were squatters without survey or title. Virginia enacted legislation in 1776 granting 400 acres to any person living in Kentucky prior to June of that year. In 1779 a new land law stated that every settler who had raised a crop of corn prior to January 1, 1778, was entitled to a 400-acre settlement grant at $2.25 per 100 acres and was allowed the right to preempt an additional 1,000 acres at $40.00 per hundred. This law excluded the lands between the Green and Cumberland rivers, which Virginia was reserving for grants to officers in the American Revolution. This law further stipulated that future purchases be by treasury warrants: that is, the purchaser would pay for the acreage desired and secure a warrant, then he would select a tract and blaze the trees on the boundary, enter a description of his claim in the land office, have it surveyed, and finally receive a patent for the land. The descriptions of claims written by individuals and filed in the land office were called entries. They were vague, and tracts were odd-shaped, bounded by trees, rocks, and creeks. The individuals did not know what lands had already been claimed; hence there were many overlapping entries, which resulted in mammoth confusion. An entry was valid only if there was no prior claim—the date of entry establishing a prior claim—but often descriptions were too vague for this to be determined. A military grant always had precedence.

Before Kentucky became a state in 1792, Virginia had issued 9,564 land grants in all categories listed above. Almost all of the Inner Bluegrass land had been claimed and settled before 1792, with grants in all categories. It should be noted that the military grants here were for service in the French and Indian War rather than the Revolutionary War. Of the 9,034 "Old Kentucky Grants" made by Kentucky after statehood in 1792, very few are in the Inner Bluegrass, and of these most were surveyed earlier but not recorded (Jillson 1925). No more than approximately a half-dozen seem to have been surveyed after 1800. This chronology is significant in understanding how early the natural aspect of the Inner Bluegrass was altered.

It appears that most of the French and Indian War grants were not settled by the one to whom the award was made, and usually the 1,000, 2,000, or 3,000 acres did not long remain intact. In Fayette County, for example, Samuel Meredith, Jr., came west in 1790 to claim and settle the grant made to his father, Colonel

Map 9. Examples of Boundaries of French and Indian War Military Land Grants Determining Early Roads, Now Secondary Roads

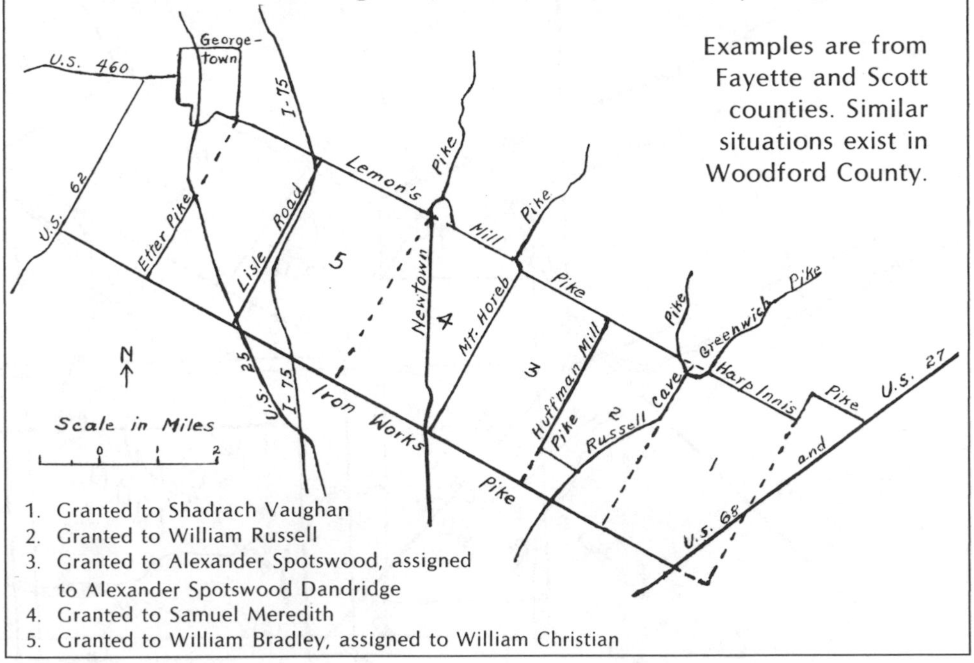

Samuel Meredith. Within a few years he sold all but 600 acres. A grant was made to William Russell in recognition of the service of his brother Henry, who had been killed in Lord Dunsmore's War. In 1773, his son Henry, en route to Kentucky with Daniel Boone, was killed by Indians, and not until 1783 did two other sons attempt to come to Kentucky, William, Jr., taking 800 acres (including "Russell's Cave" and the big spring), and Robert, taking 1,200 acres. Joseph Rogers bought Colonel Preston's military grant of "2000 acres," which turned out to be 3,000 acres. The Bryan Station settlers did not know that their station was on land that had been surveyed as Colonel Preston's military grant, and hence, when Rogers came to take possession, they had to abandon the station. Shadrack Vaughan and Joseph Beckley were other examples of the many who sold their Bluegrass land without settling on it themselves. Also many sold their 1,400-acre settlement and preemption grants, and many sold ("assigned") their warrants to others who in turn had the land surveyed and either settled or sold it.

The military grants on the Bluegrass Plain were for some of the choicest land, and it is interesting to note that in some instances boundaries remained stable long enough for an early road pattern to develop around them. In parts of Fayette, Woodford, and Scott counties these roads continue as county or state roads today, as shown in Map 9. In the total picture of Virginia's land policies in Kentucky, however, confusion and entanglement were rampant, and overlapping claims were the order of the day. The reasons were several. During the American Revolution, Virginia was too busy fighting a war to devise a satisfactory system of

Map 10. Overlapping Claims in the Bluegrass. Original in Jonathan Truman Dorris Museum, Eastern Kentucky University

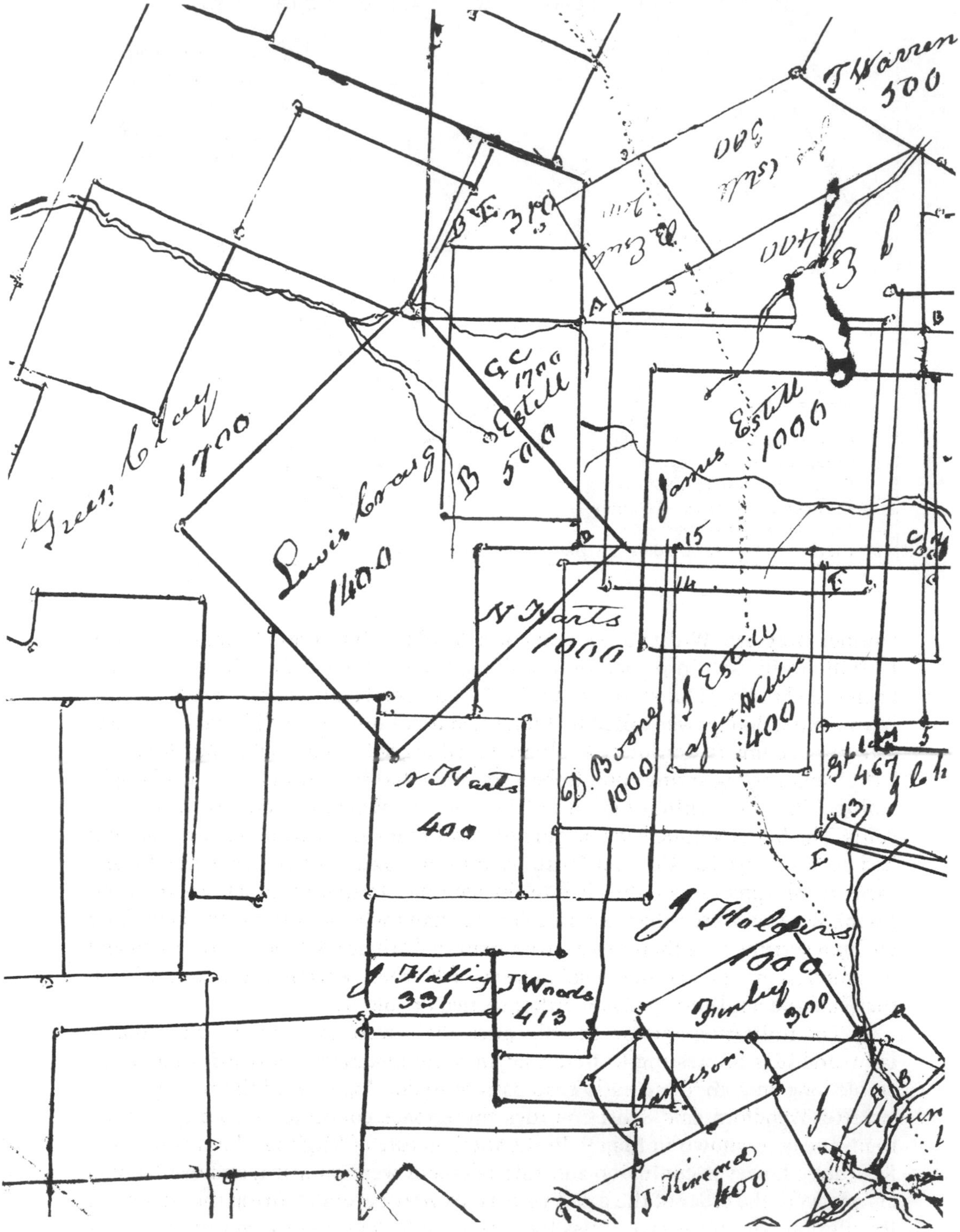

surveys for Kentucky before settlers moved in. The result was chaos. In addition to a crude technique of surveying by chains and links, the surveyors were beset with fear of Indian attack, and some were indeed killed by Indians (for instance, Hancock Taylor and John Floyd). Sometimes mathematical skills were questionable. All of this resulted in a frequent lack of accuracy, with the surveyed and claimed area usually being of greater acreage than the warrant designated. In addition, records in the land office were not precise, with surveyors' calls being such vague points as "a large oak tree" or "a stone in the creek." Military grants overlapped settlement and preemption rights, and land presumably unclaimed and purchased by treasury warrants overlapped both. It was often impossible for a later surveyor to determine the original calls because after a few decades the notched and blazed trees had healed. The only part of Kentucky surveyed according to the section and township plan established by the Federal Land Ordinance of 1785 was the Jackson Purchase of 1819, surveyed prior to its opening to settlers.

So much litigation concerning disputed ownership had been initiated in the 1790s that enterprising young attorneys, such as John Breckinridge and Henry Clay, saw great opportunity for a lucrative law practice in Kentucky. Land litigation in the Bluegrass reached its peak in the early 1800s.

This situation was also an opportunity for entrepreneurs with a bit of ready cash for investment in Kentucky land in the 1780s. One representative example is Eli Cleveland, a Revolutionary War officer who came to the Bluegrass from the Virginia Piedmont about 1782. He was at different times engaged in various projects, including one of the first water mills in Kentucky, a rope walk, a warehouse on the Kentucky River for collecting and inspecting goods to be shipped, and a ferry across the river in partnership with Green Clay of Madison County—"Clay's Ferry," with the Fayette side known as "Cleveland's Landing."

The old land entries show that between 1782 and 1792, Eli Cleveland entered over 17,000 acres, though a few thousand were noted as "withdrawn," evidently meaning there were prior claims, and several thousand were apparently outside the Inner Bluegrass. Over 6,000 were in Fayette County along the Kentucky River, Boone Creek, Elk Lick Creek, and Raven Run. In the same area in 1786, he added by purchase the 1,400-acre settlement and preemption rights of John Holder and also purchased 206 acres from another man. In 1787 Cleveland began selling his Fayette County land. Between that time and 1816 he sold 5,233 acres in 22 parcels, ranging in size from 12 to 622 acres. Then, in 1816, he conveyed to Levi Hart all remaining land he had not previously sold between Elk Lick and Raven Run, believed to be about 1,000 acres, by quit claim deed so that he would not be responsible in the event of any prior claims. Before 1819 he sold an additional 1,066 acres in two tracts.

Such a division of land into smaller tracts was common. Another example among many is approximately 900 acres near the Kentucky River in Jessamine County which the owner sold in the early 1800s as nine parcels varying from 28 to 312 acres each. Selling was easy because demand was great, with the strong and persistent migration into Kentucky. In regard to land history and the impact on nature, small tracts received much more intensive use in succeeding decades than did land remaining in large estates.

FROM CANEBRAKES AND SAVANNA-WOODLANDS TO FIELDS AND PASTURES

For a short time after settlement, life was on a subsistence basis: clearing and building houses, barns, and stockades. The chief project the first year was to clear sufficient ground for a corn crop and to plant a few garden vegetables (pumpkins and beans in the corn field; also sweet potatoes, Irish potatoes, and turnips). Corn provided bread, hominy, and mush for the table and food for all domestic livestock. For several years it continued to be the major crop. According to Filson, the land was too rich for wheat until it had grown corn four or five summers and had been subjected to leaching for as many winters.

The settlers liked to choose cane lands, but they eliminated the cane despite the knowledge that the young cane shoots were highly nutritious for stock. John Hedge in Bourbon County mentioned "the abundance of cane and the ease of raising cattle" (Draper MSS). The Englishman Imlay (1797) characterized cane as "the most nourishing food for cattle on earth. No other milk or butter has such flavor and richness as that which is produced from cows which have fed upon the cane." In clearing a small portion of a canebrake a man would cut the stems with a large knife or cutlass, place them in heaps, and burn them when dry. Extensive canebrakes would be burned off if the ground was not too damp. William Clinkenbeard "thought they never would get it [cane] out of the country when I came, but now it is scarce and a curiosity" (Draper MSS)

The sugar maple tree was the only source of sugar until steamboats were available to bring cane sugar up the Mississippi River from southern plantations. Since the sugar maple was one of the most common trees, the settlers evidently thought they need not be careful in tapping it. Imlay described their method of obtaining sap by chopping a large gap in the trunk. Audubon, in noting that the trees did not last many years, said, "I have no doubt, however, that with proper care the same quantity of sap might be obtained with less injury to the trees; and it is now fully time that the farmers and land-owners should begin to look to the preservation of their sugar maples" (317).

Within a few years after settlement began, wheat, barley, oats, tobacco, and hemp were being grown, and by the early and mid-1780s production was in excess of home consumption. The year 1787 marked the first shipment to New Orleans via the Kentucky, Ohio, and Mississippi rivers, a commerce that prospered until 1860. This first cargo contained hams, bacon, flour, salt, hogsheads of tobacco, and other products. Until there were steamboats to come up the river, the crude flatboats were dismantled and left in the South while the crews walked home. The first steamboat on the Kentucky River was built in 1816, and by 1820 there were several. But little navigation was possible in slack water until after the construction of locks and dams was started in 1836. By 1842 five locks (of the eventual fourteen) were opened to navigation.

On the Bluegrass Plain away from the river, tobacco culture, though initiated, was discontinued for many decades because it depended on river transportation to market. Prior to the growing of Burley tobacco after the Civil War, it was packed in hogsheads, each weighing 1,000 to 1,300 pounds, which were too difficult to transport overland. Much tobacco was grown in the Eden shale belt, in the Outer Bluegrass, and in other places that had easy access to a river. In the Inner Bluegrass tobacco was confined to areas near the Kentucky River or the Licking River. (See Axton.)

Hemp soon became the chief cash crop in the Inner Bluegrass. William Clinkenbeard related in an interview that he planted hemp at Strode Station in Clark County as early as 1780 (Draper MSS). The *Kentucky Gazette* in 1788 carried an advertisement of hemp seed produced by a local farmer. By the time Inner Bluegrass farms were well established, they were producing chiefly livestock, hemp, and grain. Hempen products were being shipped downstream to New Orleans as early as 1790 to supply sails and rigging for the navy, the hemp grown in the eastern states being insufficient. The invention of the cotton gin in 1793, stimulating cotton-raising in the South, also gave impetus to hemp-raising in Kentucky to supply the needs of the cotton plantations, and this area soon became foremost in hemp production. For decades Kentucky led the nation in hemp, all of it grown in the Bluegrass region, principally in the Inner Bluegrass (especially Fayette, Bourbon, Scott, Woodford, Jessamine, and Clark counties), but also in Mason and Shelby counties of the Outer Bluegrass. In 1849 over half of the nation's hemp came from these counties. A deep, rich soil was necessary, and the Kentucky climate was favorable. To produce the rank growth necessary for long fibers without too much wood, a highly fertile soil was essential. Hemp as a crop did not exhaust the soil as tobacco, corn, and cotton do; it covered the ground solidly, not in rows, and many successive crops could be grown without fertilization. After cutting and in preparation for breaking, it was spread for "dew rotting" on the ground that produced it; soluble minerals were thus leached back into the soil, and humus was added by the leaves. (See Hopkins.)

In the Inner Bluegrass hemp brought the highest monetary return of any crop. Hemp manufacturing was important from 1790 through 1860. John Melish of Scotland visited Lexington and the Bluegrass in 1811 and reported, "The principal manufactures of Lexington are hemp . . . of which the country yields amazing crops. . . . There are thirteen extensive rope-walks, five bagging manufactories, and one of duck [cloth]" (Melish, 2:184-86). Of Kentucky exports in 1830, hempen fabrics were second only to livestock. The demand was increasing with the expansion of cotton culture in the South, since hemp was used to make the bags for cotton picking and the cordage and canvas for cotton bales.

Although hemp fields differed drastically from canebrakes, there was one utilization of Bluegrass land that allowed some of its original character to be retained: the savanna-woodlands were converted to woodland pastures by altering the ground vegetation and retaining the canopy trees. There are numerous early descriptions.

An account entitled "Some Particulars Relative to Kentucky" in the *National Gazette* of 1791 included the following description of this section: "The stories told of the abundance of grass in the woods are in many instances true. . . . The woods . . . afford abundance of food for cattle, and in consequence of this abundance the people pay very little attention to making and improving pasture lands" (quoted by Schwaab, 55-56). By 1790, however, the landowners were beginning to replace the native grasses of the savanna-woodlands with sown timothy and bluegrass, although, according to Imlay, wild rye was "a very good and valuable grass." Also the clover was being replaced by the European white clover.

The tree-studded pastures were aptly called "grazing parks" by Samuel R. Brown writing in 1817 for the *Western Gazetteer.* James Hall, writing in the *Western Monthly Magazine* in 1834 and 1835, included this description: "The surface is not broken by hills, nor is it level—but of that beautifully rolling or undulating character, which is, above all others, the most pleasing to the eye, and the best adapted to the purpose of husbandry. . . . The soil is of the richest kind, and the improvements superior to any that I have seen in any part of the United States. . . . The dwellings are all commodious and comfortable, and the most of them very far superior to those usually inhabited by farmers. . . . The woodland pastures, which are peculiar to this section of the country, are remarkably beautiful, giving to its extensive farms an unusual degree of elegance, and to the whole character of the scenery an originality. . . . This pleasing effect is produced by a simple procedure . . . the underwood and useless trees are removed, and the valuable timber trees are left, standing sufficiently wide apart to admit the rays of the sun and the free circulation of air between them. The ground is then sown with grass, and extensive tracts . . . are thus converted into spacious lawns studded with noble trees. These are so numerous and of such extent as to form a prominent feature in the scenery. . . . The fine country of which I am speaking extends something like twenty miles in every direction from Lexington, and no district of the United States, of equal extent, perhaps none in the world, exhibits a more fertile body of land, or a tract more firmly embellished by good improvements and judicious cultivation."

Samuel Allen wrote in the *American Agriculturist* in 1843 concerning a farm in Woodford County, ". . . adjoining this [residence and yard] is a noble park. . . . These are usually termed woodland pastures in Kentucky; yet in most instances, they better deserve the name of park, than many of those on noblemen's estates in Europe" (quoted in Schwaab, 292).

These parklike woodland pastures continued to be a substantial part of the rural landscape throughout the nineteenth century. James Lane Allen wrote in *The Blue-Grass Region of Kentucky* (11), "Characteristically beautiful spots on the Blue-Grass landscape are the woodland pastures—a loveliness unique and local." Knight and Greene, in *Country Estates of the Bluegrass,* included several photographs of woodland pastures.

Today, unfortunately, the few old, unplowed woodland pastures with presettlement trees are rare indeed. Although they are not the original ecosystem, lacking bison and elk and having a different and less diverse ground cover, they do retain some of the original dominants of those anomalous savanna-woodlands and are the best remnants of primeval vegetation extant on the Bluegrass Plain. The old trees in these situations are not reproducing themselves because seedlings are mowed down.

The rugged, densely forested land near the Kentucky River and its tributaries had a different settlement history. The creeks provided excellent sites for grist mills, and building stone was quarried here. Most of the land was divided into tracts smaller than the farms of the Bluegrass Plain and was intensively farmed, with the exception of cliffland. Creek cliffs provided building materials, fuel, and maple sap for home use; timber from the river cliffs was commercially clearcut and floated downstream to sawmills.

FROM BISON AND ELK TO CATTLE AND HORSES

The early settlers keenly grasped the phenomenal suitability of this region for domestic stock—this area where bison, elk, and deer had flourished on luxuriant herbage. One of the nine laws adopted in 1775 by the Boonesborough assembly, the first legislative body west of the Appalachian Mountains, concerned the improvement of the breeds of horses. On this rolling, well-drained terrain with rich soil, the livestock industry grew with unprecedented rapidity; it was a natural development.

The *Kentucky Gazette* from 1788 on carried advertisements of stud horses, both good saddle horses and racing stock. Throughout the 1790s excellent race horses from Virginia were being brought to this section of Kentucky, and in 1795 the first imported English Thoroughbred to come beyond the mountains was brought to Scott County. "For some time past," noted François Michaux, the French botanist who visited Kentucky in 1802, "the inhabitants of Kentucky have engaged in breeding horses . . . the number of horses, which is already considerable, augments daily. Almost all the inhabitants employ great care in breeding and improving the breeds. . . . The southern states, and particularly South Carolina, are the principal markets for the fine horses of Kentucky. They are taken there in troops of 15, 20, or 30 together." Michaux also noted that "If a traveler arrives, his horse is valued as soon as they see him" (1805, 231-32, 234, 239-40).

Thomas Smith, Jr., of Lincolnshire, England, traveled in the Bluegrass in 1819. His journal for October 11 recorded: "Walked thirteen miles to Mr. Steele's plantation [in Woodford County]. . . . The plantations here are very fine and well cleared, the land excellent. . . . The kentuckians pay great attention to the breeding of cattle. Their horses are the best in the United States" (Appleton).

A Virginia correspondent to the *American Farmer* (10, no. 50:398) wrote in 1829 that Kentucky will be "second if not first in their stock ere long," and by 1840 Kentucky had superseded all other states in producing superior horses (Hervey). This early prominence in horse breeding was due to the physical attributes of the land together with the propensities of the people. Many of the persons who came were already interested in horse quality and breeding and were attracted here by the land. In addition to the significance of Thoroughbreds, the early Kentucky saddler was the forerunner of the American Saddlebred horse, a breed that developed largely in the Inner and Outer Bluegrass.

The cattle industry had begun before 1790 and developed rapidly. Soon herds of cattle and hogs were driven to Philadelphia, Baltimore, and other eastern cities. Beginning in 1787 they were shipped by river down to New Orleans. The first importation to Kentucky of high quality English cattle for breeding was in 1817. In the 1830s especially, there was extensive importation of Durham Shorthorns of illustrious quality from lines already renowned in Britain. Large-scale cattle raising in the United States, with careful upbreeding, began in the Kentucky Bluegrass and spread to other parts of the Ohio valley, thence to the Midwest, and finally, after 1860, to the West (Henlein).

Kentucky stockmen imported high quality jacks and jennets from France, Spain, and Malta. The jack Montezuma was advertised in the *Kentucky Gazette* in 1810. The breeding of superior jack stock in the Bluegrass was aimed at improving the size and strength of mules, most of which were sent to the cotton plantations of the South.

The Bourbon County Agricultural Society was formed in 1821 to promote the breeding of superior strains of cattle, sheep, and horses. In 1826 the Kentucky Association for the Improvement of Breeds of Stock was organized in Lexington. This was especially a racing association, the founders of which perceived the race course as a testing ground for the quality of horses.

Thus the rich land that had produced phenomenal populations of large indigenous animals soon gained renown for domestic livestock.

Above left: The steep wooded slopes above creeks tributary to the Kentucky River afford excellent habitats for wildflowers. Here we have wild blue phlox (*Phlox divaricata*).

Above right: The twinleaf (*Jeffersonia diphylla*) grows on rich wooded slopes in limestone regions. Hence it is more frequent in the Inner Bluegrass than elsewhere in Kentucky.

Left: Early saxifrage (*Saxifraga virginiensis*) is frequent at the edge of mossy ledges on cliffs in the Inner Bluegrass. Its basal rosettes of leaves are green all winter, and flowers appear early.

All photos in this section are by R.W. Barbour.

Above: The white trout-lily (*Erythronium albidum*) is one of the earliest spring flowers on wooded south-facing limestone slopes, often covering them with a floral blanket in the Inner Bluegrass. *Below left*: The yellow-wood (*Cladrastis kentukea*), a handsome tree with graceful, pendulous panicles of white flowers in late spring, grows on Kentucky River cliffs in the Inner Bluegrass and is only rarely found in the wild elsewhere in Kentucky. *Below right*: The shooting-star (*Dodecatheon meadia*) grows in moist areas on wooded cliffs, especially where there is a small amount of dripping water.

Above left: The aromatic aster (*Aster oblongifolius*), rooted in crevices of limestone cliffs, is abundant and showy on the Kentucky River cliffs in October.

Above right: Short's aster (*Aster shortii*) is the most frequent aster in the woods of the Bluegrass.

Right: The so-called "wild baby's-breath" (*Arenaria patula*), a delicate and graceful little annual inhabiting a harsh environment, requires a mere film of soil on limestone ledges and boulders.

The beautiful and showy wild pink (*Silene caroliniana* var. *wherryi*) is very restricted in its distribution in the state. In the Inner Bluegrass it often creates a mass of bright pink on cliffs, where it is locally profuse.

The pink stonecrop or widow's-cross (*Sedum pulchellum*) grows in thin soil on limestone, either moist or dry. In full sunlight the flower color is deeper than in the shade.

Blue-eyed Mary (*Collinsia verna*) is locally profuse in the Inner Bluegrass and in such areas creates a spectacular display.

Left: The valerian (*Valeriana pauciflora*) grows in moist humus in rich woods on lower slopes and is more frequent in the Inner Bluegrass than elsewhere in the state.

Below left: Although generally somewhat rare in its range in eastern United States, synandra (*Synandra hispidula*) is frequent in the Inner Bluegrass, where it grows in deep humus of rich moist woods. It is a lovely species of late spring.

Below right: The false rue-anemone (*Isopyrum biternatum*) is a characteristic species of Bluegrass woods in early spring. In Kentucky it is apparently confined to calcareous regions.

Squirrel-corn (*Dicentra canadensis*) and its close relative, Dutchman's-breeches, grow in deep humus in rich mesophytic woods on well drained slopes.

Wild hyacinth (*Camassia scilloides*) is found in fairly sunny situations in calcareous soil and is frequent both on the Bluegrass Plain and in the vicinity of the Kentucky River gorge.

Columbine (*Aquilegia canadensis*) grows especially on limestone ledges, frequently south-facing.

Purple phacelia (*Phacelia bipinnatifida*), although widespread in rich woods throughout the state, is most frequent in the Inner Bluegrass, where it grows in leafmold on rocky slopes and ledges.

Miami mist (*Phacelia purshii*), typically a species found in alluvial woods, is common throughout the Bluegrass, where it may be seen even along the sides of long-established roads.

Above photos: Bulblet fern (*Cystopteris bulbifera*) is often profuse hanging from shaded, moist (often dripping) limestone ledges a few feet above a creek.

Left: Purple cliffbrake (*Pellaea atropurpurea*) is found on limestone ledges and cliffs.

The rosefin shiner (*Notropis ardens*) is moderately abundant and spawns in riffles.

The longear sunfish (*Leponis megalotis*) occurs in all major drainages of Kentucky.

The rainbow darter (*Etheostoma caeruleum*) breeding males are among the most colorful of the darters.

The midland mud salamander (*Pseudotriton montanus diastictus*) is a short, stout-tailed, brown-eyed red salamander.

The red-spotted newt (*Notophthalmus viridescens viridescens*) is seen at left in its terrestrial phase, and below in its aquatic phase.

Above: The bullfrog (*Rana catesbeiana*) is the largest frog in Kentucky. *Below*: Adults of the American toad (*Bufo americanus americanus*) congregate in March or April to mate and lay their eggs.

The red-eared slider (*Trachemys scripta elegans*) has a broad, usually red, patch behind each eye, unique among Kentucky turtles, but the red is sometimes replaced by yellow.

The northern fence lizard (*Sceloporus undulatus*) is found in dry, open, sunny woodlands.

The eastern rough green snake (*Opheodrys aestivus*) feeds almost exclusively on insects, as well as a few spiders, snails, and an occasional tree toad.

A number of yellow-crowned night herons (*Nycticorax violaceus*) have for several years nested in a wooded section on the campus of the University of Kentucky.

The lovely northern cardinal (*Cardinalis cardinalis*) is a common permanent resident.

The song sparrow (*Melospiza melodia*) is a common resident of a number of brushy habitats.

The tremulous call of the eastern screech owl (*Otus asio*) is a pleasant sound at night.

White-footed mice (*Peromyscus leucopus*) are nocturnal and are active throughout the year.

This young eastern cottontail (*Sylvilagus floridanus mearnsi*) is about 10 days old.

The southern flying squirrel (*Glaucomys volans volans*) generally forages for food in trees at night.

The fox squirrel (*Sciurus niger rufiventer*) is strictly diurnal and forages on the ground.

The red bat (*Lasiurus borealis borealis*) is a tree dweller.

Above: The raccoon (*Procyon lotor lotor*) is omnivorous, and its food habits depend in large part upon what is most readily available. *Below*: The gray fox (*Urocyon cinereoargenteus cinereoargenteus*), although chiefly nocturnal, is occasionally encountered in daylight.

Part II
Habitats and Natural Community Organization

5. Plant Communities

THE INNER Bluegrass section is in the Western Mesophytic Forest Region as defined by Braun (1950), as is all of the state west of the Cumberland Plateau. This region is transitional between the Mixed Mesophytic Forest Region of the western Appalachians and the Oak-Hickory Forest Region centering in the Ozarks. The Western Mesophytic Region contains a wide variety of vegetation types and, influenced by underlying rock and physiography, forms a mosaic of forest types, including mixed mesophytic, mixed hardwoods, oak-hickory, cedar glades, and swamp forests.

In a region such as the Inner Bluegrass, where soils are of prime value for crops and pastures and where space for construction is now in great demand at a high price, wooded areas are virtually restricted to steep slopes and narrow stream valleys. It is estimated that natural plant communities here have now been reduced to about 4 percent of the area. No truly virgin tracts remain. A traveler notices the sudden change from pastoral beauty on the Bluegrass Plain to rugged picturesqueness in the deep gorge and steep wooded cliffs of the Kentucky River and its tributaries. With such great physiographic differences, an account of Inner Bluegrass vegetation must be in two divisions.

THE KENTUCKY RIVER GORGE AND VICINITY

River Banks. The bank of the Kentucky River is dominated by water maples (*Acer saccharinum*) with numerous box elder *(A. negundo)* and a few elm *(Ulmus americana)* and sycamore *(Platanus occidentalis)*; elderberry *(Sambucus canadensis)* is sometimes present as a shrub layer. This marginal strip, which is inundated several times a year, is devoid of herbaceous vegetation, although innumerable water maple seedlings may be present.

Floodplains. The river floodplains have all been cleared at some time, and most of them now are either cultivated or used for resort camps. Some have returned to woodland consisting principally of sycamore *(Platanus occidentalis)*, water maple

(Acer saccharinum), box elder *(A. negundo),* American elm *(Ulmus americana),* black walnut *(Juglans nigra),* and great shellbark hickory *(Carya laciniosa),* with an occasional beech *(Fagus grandifolia)* or white basswood *(Tilia heterophylla).* Cane *(Arundinaria gigantea),* papaw *(Asimina triloba),* spice bush *(Lindera benzoin),* and elderberry *(Sambucus canadensis)* frequently comprise a shrub layer. Characteristic herbaceous ground plants include *Aster pilosus, Eupatorium coelestinum, Helianthus tuberosus, Impatiens capensis, I. pallida, Lobelia siphilitica, Phacelia purshii, Rudbeckia laciniata, Sorghum halepense, Viola striata, V. papilionacea,* and *Verbesina alternifolia.*

Cliff Bases. Talus slopes at the base of cliffs and above the river's floodplain offer a favorable habitat. One such slope was found to have the following composition: hackberry *(Celtis occidentalis),* 33 percent; Kentucky coffee-tree *(Gymnocladus dioica),* 21 percent; black sugar maple *(Acer nigrum),* 15 percent; black walnut *(Juglans nigra),* 9 percent; sugar maple *(Acer saccharum),* 5 percent; Ohio buckeye *(Aesculus glabra),* 5 percent; butternut *(Juglans cinerea),* 4 percent; red mulberry *(Morus rubra),* 4 percent; great shellbark hickory *(Carya laciniosa),* 3 percent; and wild black cherry *(Prunus serotina),* 1 percent.

Other species of trees frequently found in such situations but absent from the preceding are sycamore *(Platanus occidentalis),* black locust *(Robinia pseudoacacia,* and chinquapin oak *(Quercus muehlenbergii).*

Cliffsides. The cliffsides are essentially forested, although a portion of each contains some sheer rock. The steep wooded slopes frequently have slight shelves on top of the most resistant beds. The cliffs are now and then notched with small coves where more humus accumulates and provides for a richer flora than on the vertical cliff faces. Root anchorage is difficult on these steep slopes, and windthrow is frequent.

The forests of the river cliffs were almost entirely cleared in the nineteenth century, when logs were easily floated downstream to the many flourishing sawmills along the river. Photographs of the Kentucky River gorge in *Art Work of the Bluegrass* by J. Soule Smith, published in 1898, show smaller and much less plentiful timber on the cliffs than is present today. Only one sizable uncut area (approximately 35 acres) on cliffs with large original trees is known to us. The species include sugar maple, black sugar maple, blue ash, white ash, basswood, hackberry, black walnut, Shumard oak, chinquapin oak, and coffee tree.

Most of the cliffside forests are maple-oak-ash or oak-ash-maple or oak-hickory-cedar, depending on the exposure and the depth of soil. A mesic situation exists even on some of the lower south-facing slopes, in addition to that on north- and northeast-facing slopes, due to underground water draining toward the river. In total floristic composition, these mesophytic forests are intermediate between the Mixed Mesophytic Association of eastern Kentucky and the plant communities of the remainder of the Inner Bluegrass. Their closer affinity to the former could be due partly to the fact that the Kentucky River has its source in Mixed Mesophytic domain, making the valley a possible route for plant migration. The

Kentucky River gorge thus constitutes a westward extension of some elements of the Mixed Mesophytic Association, such as yellow buckeye.

Trees most frequently associated with sugar maple *(Acer saccharum)* on the mesic cliffs are red oak *(Quercus rubra),* chinquapin oak *(Q. muehlenbergii),* Shumard oak *(Q. shumardii),* white oak *(Q. alba),* white ash *(Fraxinus americana),* blue ash *(F. quadrangulata),* black walnut *(Juglans nigra),* shellbark hickory *(Carya laciniosa),* bitternut hickory *(C. cordiformis),* coffee tree *(Gymnocladus dioica),* American elm *(Ulmus americana),* slippery elm *(U. rubra),* basswood (*Tilia* spp.), tulip poplar *(Liriodendron tulipifera),* and Ohio buckeye *(Aesculus glabra).* The yellow buckeye *(A. octandra)* is rare, and beech *(Fagus grandifolia)* is infrequent.

Understory trees and shrubs that are either characteristic or frequent in these mesic communities are dogwood *(Cornus florida),* black haw *(Viburnum prunifolium* and *V. rufidulum),* hornbeam *(Carpinus caroliniana),* yellowwood *(Cladrastis kentukea),* bladdernut *(Staphylea trifolia),* and spicebush *(Lindera benzoin).*

Toward the upper portions of a cliff, where the water table is deeper, and on many dry, south-facing exposures, the percentages of red cedar *(Juniperus virginiana),* oaks (especially *Quercus alba* and *Q. muehlenbergii*), hickories (*Carya ovata, C. ovalis,* and *C. cordiformis),* blue ash *(Fraxinus quadrangulata),* and redbud *(Cercis canadensis)* increase, while sugar maple and other mesic species are few or lacking. Such communities would be designated as oak, oak-ash, oak-hickory, or oak-cedar.

Among ground plants commonly found on the cliffs (both mesic and moderately dry) are the following: *Aster shortii, Campanula americana, Cardamine douglassii, Collinsonia canadensis, Cystopteris protrusa, Delphinium tricorne, Dentaria laciniata, Diarrhena americana, Erythronium albidum, E. americanum, Euonymus obovatus, Hydrophyllum macrophyllum, Jeffersonia diphylla, Phacelia bipinnatifida, Phlox divaricata, Polymnia canadensis, Senecio obovatus, Silene virginica, Solidago flexicaulis, S. ulmifolia, Stylophorum diphyllum, Thalictrum thalictroides, Thaspium barbinode, Tradescantia subaspera, Trillium sessile, Vicia caroliniana, Viola pensylvanica, V. sororia, Woodsia obtusa,* and *Zizia aptera.*

Tables 4-6 compare the canopy composition of several types of cliff forest. Transect counts were made and percentages figured for each species.

Cliff Summits. The cliff summits may be slightly or strongly xeric, depending on the exposure and steepness of the bluff. Soils are thin and the water table deep; the driest crests have red cedar communities. Although red cedar *(Juniperus virginiana)* is a common pioneer tree in secondary succession, here, where the xeric conditions prevent many species from becoming established, it is primary, stable, and essentially perpetual. It has been thus since presettlement. James McAfee in his 1773 journal said, "We crossed the [Kentucky] river at high hills and cedar banks" (Woods). McMurtrie in 1819 described the Kentucky River cliffs, "some of which are from four to five hundred feet in height, crowned with groves of red cedars" (207-30). On the less xeric summits, oaks, hickories, and ashes are associated with cedar. These include chinquapin oak *(Quercus muehlenbergii),* white oak *(Q. alba),* pignut hickory *(Carya glabra),* shagbark hickory *(C. ovata),*

Table 4. Composition of Canopy, Maple-Ash-Oak Forests, on Mesic Cliffs of the Kentucky River

Species	North facing, transect 100 ft. wide, down very steep cliff, trees large, never logged (Madison County)		North facing, transect 100 ft. wide, down cliff (Mercer County)		East facing, transect 100 ft. wide, down cliff along small ravine (Garrard County)	
Maple						
Acer saccharum	23%					
A. nigrum	11%	36%		39%		42%
A. negundo	2%					
Ash						
Fraxinus americana	2%	13%	7%	28%	5%	16%
F. quadrangulata	11%		21%		11%	
Oak						
Quercus muehlenbergii	4%				8%	
Q. shumardii	5%	10%		7%		26%
Q. rubra	1%				18%	
Basswood						
Tilia sp.		10%		5%		5%
Walnut						
Juglans nigra	7%	8%		8%		2%
J. cinerea	1%					
Hickory						
Carya cordiformis	4%		5%	7%		
C. glabra	1%	7%	2%		4%	
C. ovalis	2%					
Hackberry						
Celtis occidentalis		7%		2%		3%
Elm						
Ulmus americana		2%		3%		
Coffee Tree						
Gymnocladus dioica		2%				
Yellowwood						
Cladrastis kentukea						2%
Beech						
Fagus grandifolia		1%		1%		
Cherry						
Prunus serotina		1%				
Buckeye						
Aesculus glabra	1%	2%				
Ae. octandra	1%					
Hop hornbeams						
Ostrya virginiana		1%				

bitternut hickory *(C. cordiformis)*, blue ash *(Fraxinus quadrangulata)*, white ash *(F. americana)*, hop hornbeam *(Ostrya virginiana)*, and rock elm *(Ulmus thomasi)*. Characteristic shrubs and understory trees are redbud *(Cercis canadensis)*, bittersweet *(Celastrus scandens)*, New Jersey tea *(Ceanothus americanus)*, and aromatic sumac *(Rhus aromatica)*. *Agave virginica* and *Swertia caroliniensis* are often among the herbaceous plants here.

Table 5. Composition of Forest Canopy, Kentucky River Cliffs, from Xeric to Slightly Mesic

Species	*Oak-Ash* East facing, upper ⅓ of cliff. Transect 75 ft. wide paralleling river (Garrard County)		*Oak-Maple-Ash* West facing, transect 100 ft. wide, down the cliff (Garrard County)		*Oak-Cedar-Ash* Southwest facing, transect 100 ft. wide, down steep cliff; rocky soil (Garrard County)		*Oak-Maple-Hickory* South facing, transect 75 ft. wide, mid-cliff, paralleling river (Fayette County)	
Oak		42%		47%		40%		47%
Quercus muehlenbergii	39%		13%		21%		14%	
Q. shumardii	1%				10%		17%	
Q. rubra	2%		30%		7%		11%	
Q. alba			4%		2%		5%	
Ash		42%				16%		11%
Fraxinus americana	5%				10%		6%	
F. quadrangulata	37%		11%		6%		5%	
Maple								21%
Acer saccharum		5%		31%		6%	19%	
A. nigrum							2%	
Hickory				3%				12%
Carya ovata			1%			1%	5%	
C. ovalis							4%	
C. glabra		2%	2%				3%	
Cedar								
Juniperus virginiana		4%		5%		37%		2%
Coffee tree								
Gymnocladus dioica								1%
Walnut								
Juglans nigra								2%
Cherry								
Prunus serotina								2%
Honey locust								
Gleditsia triacanthos								1%
Hackberry								
Celtis occidentalis								1%
Elm								
Ulmus thomasi		4%						
Yellowwood								
Cladrastis kentukea		1%						
Hop hornbeam								
Ostrya virginiana				3%				

Microclimates. In the gorge area—river cliffs and tributaries—microclimates are numerous and significant. Rock ledges and boulders support *Arenaria patula, Aquilegia canadensis, Aster oblongifolius, Asplenium rhizophyllum, Heuchera villosa, Nothoscordum bivalve, Sedum pulchellum, S. ternatum, Silene caroliniana* var. *wherryi, Saxifraga virginiensis,* and *Solidago sphacelata.* (Some of the preced-

Table 6. Comparison between Canopy Species on Opposite Cliffs of Creek
Transect counts, each 75 feet wide in mid-slope, Elk Lick Creek, Fayette County

Species	North Facing Slope		South Facing Slope	
	Species	Total	Species	Total
Maple				
Acer saccharum		31%	11%	12%
A. nigrum			1%	
Oak				
Quercus muehlenbergii	10%	32%	30%	61%
Q. shumardii	17%		26%	
Q. rubra	5%		4%	
Q. alba			1%	
Ash				
Fraxinus americana	4%	5%	1%	9%
F. quadrangulata	1%		8%	
Hickory				
Carya cordiformis	3%	6%	3%	6%
C. ovalis	2%			
C. ovata			3%	
C. laciniosa	1%			
Basswood				
Tilia sp.		9%		
Hackberry				
Celtis occidentalis		2%		1%
Poplar				
Liriodendron tulipifera		3%		
Cedar				
Juniperus virginiana				7%
Walnut				
Juglans nigra	5%	6%		2%
J. cinerea	1%			
Cherry				
Prunus serotina		5%		
Buckeye				
Aesculus glabra				2%
Elm				
Ulmus americana		1%		

ing are in shade only, some in sun only, and some in either.) Sheer rock faces often have *Pellaea atropurpurea* and *Asplenium ruta-muraria* in crevices. Springs and seepage areas on a cliff will provide for *Cardamine bulbosa, Cystopteris bulbifera, Dodecatheon meadia, Iodanthus pinnatifidus, Mertensia virginica,* and *Valerianella umbilicata.*

Tributary Valleys. Throughout the nineteenth century and into the twentieth, commercial lumbering was limited along steep slopes on the tributaries, with their narrow valleys, rapids, and waterfalls, because of the difficulty of getting logs to the sawmills along the river. Such activity was restricted to times of heavy flooding. But there was considerable timber cutting by individual landowners for farm use both as fuel and as building material. Also farmers who owned wooded ravines tapped their sugar maples, often overtapping to the point of eventual death. Except near the top, the steep slopes of the tributary gorges were not clearcut, as the river cliffs were, and that is indicated by a difference in herbaceous cover. Today the creek slopes have a greater proportion of those species requiring a deep, rich humus buildup, such as *Adiantum pedatum, Allium tricoccum, Arisaema atrorubens, Asarum canadense, Botrychium virginianum, Dentaria diphylla, Dicentra canadensis, D. cucullaria, Dryopteris marginalis, Isopyrum biternatum, Hepatica acutiloba, Polemonium reptans, Synandra hispidula, Trillium flexipes,* and *Valeriana pauciflora.*

Although the sides of tributary gorges tend to have a richer herbaceous flora than that on the river cliffs, there is little difference in canopy trees: sugar maple dominating on mesic slopes, red cedar dominating in the most xeric situations, and varying percentages of oaks in the gradations between.

Old Fields and Succession to Woodland. Old fields abandoned from agriculture and allowed to return to woodland are relatively scarce in an area as fertile as the Inner Bluegrass. There are some, however, and since most of them are in the vicinity of the Kentucky River, they will be described here.

The upland topography near the Kentucky River is more hilly and dissected than that in most of the Inner Bluegrass, and the soils are thinner. Consequently, in the initial settling, the landed aristocracy tended to choose the gently undulating lands with deep, rich soil, which often continued to be well maintained as large estates. Filson (18) spoke of the Elkhorn lands as being first-rate and the Kentucky River lands as second- and third-rate. In the latter the holdings were frequently 1,400 acres each at first, and a typical landowner grazed and cultivated the hilly and relatively level lands, operated a water mill, and quarried building stone. As decades passed most of these lands were divided and sold as smaller and smaller tracts. By the turn of the present century the lands less productive and with a lesser carrying capacity were largely in small farms, more intensively worked to support a family than were the larger estates on more productive lands. Therefore, some overgrazed, overcropped, and eroded lands do exist in this area and are returning to woodland. There are exceptions, however. A notable one is a farm of approximately 1,300 acres in a river bend in Madison County; this was not divided and remained in the same family for six generations before being sold and subdivided in the 1970s. As a result, the aspect and condition of its land were until recently different from many farms in the river vicinity.

In old-field succession, following annual and perennial weed stages, there is an invasion of woody plants. The shrubs include blackberries (*Rubus* spp.), buckberry *(Symphoricarpos orbiculatus),* sumac *(Rhus glabra),* and trumpet vine *(Campsis radicans).* The chief invading tree species are hackberry *(Celtis occidentalis* and *C. tenuifolia),* redbud *(Cercis canadensis),* hawthorn (*Crataegus* spp.), persimmon *(Diospyros virginiana),* white ash *(Fraxinus americana),* honey locust *(Gleditsia triacanthos),* black walnut *(Juglans nigra),* red cedar *(Juniperus virginiana),* Osage orange *(Maclura pomifera),* red mulberry *(Morus rubra),* wild plum *(Prunus americana),* wild cherry *(P. serotina),* black locust *(Robinia pseudoacacia),* sassafras *(Sassafras albidum),* and American elm *(Ulmus americana).* Not all species occur in any one field, of course; sometimes red cedars constitute over 50 percent of the invading trees.

THE BLUEGRASS PLAIN

The fertile, undulating Bluegrass Plain is characterized by farms, cities, and towns; hence natural, intact, organized plant communities are scarce, and fragmentary at best. Yet it is here that the greater vegetational anomaly lies. Where creeks run through farms that use other water for livestock, there exist some limited botanical areas.

Pastures and Creek Bank Communities. A 20-acre pasture in Scott County has trees representing three age groups. Trees over 175 years old—mostly 200-300 years old—are: 24 blue ash *(Fraxinus quadrangulata),* 2 chinquapin oak *(Quercus muehlenbergii),* 8 bur oak *(Q. macrocarpa),* 1 white ash *(Fraxinus americana),* 1 coffee tree *(Gymnocladus dioica),* and 1 shellbark hickory *(Carya laciniosa).* Trees 75 to 175 years old—mostly 100-150 years old—are: 33 blue ash *(F. quadrangulata),* 2 chinquapin oak *(Q. muehlenbergii),* 1 white ash *(F. americana),* and 1 sugar maple *(Acer saccharum).* Trees less than 75 years, most of which are less than 50 years, are restricted to fencerows and a sinkhole: 30 hackberry *(Celtis occidentalis),* 17 black walnut *(Juglans nigra),* 10 coffee tree *(Gymnocladus dioica),* 6 wild cherry *(Prunus serotina),* 3 black locust *(Robinia pseudoacacia),* 2 bitternut hickory *(Carya cordiformis),* 1 box elder *(Acer negundo),* 1 bur oak *(Quercus macrocarpa),* and 1 blue ash *(Fraxinus quadrangulata).*

Where North Elkhorn Creek runs through this farm, there occurs the following tree canopy: box elder *(Acer negundo),* Ohio buckeye *(Aesculus glabra),* white ash *(Fraxinus americana),* blue ash *(F. quadrangulata),* black walnut *(Juglans nigra),* Osage orange *(Maclura pomifera),* sycamore *(Platanus occidentalis),* wild cherry *(Prunus serotina),* chinquapin oak *(Quercus muehlenbergii),* and American elm *(Ulmus americana).* One sycamore tree is 19 feet 8 inches in circumference and 6 feet 3 inches in diameter DBH, and another is 10 feet 2 inches in circumference, 3 feet 3 inches in diameter DBH. The shrub layer here is composed of lance-leaf buckthorn *(Rhamnus lanceolata),* buckberry *(Symphoricarpos orbiculatus),* wahoo *(Euonymus atropurpureus),* and Japanese honeysuckle *(Lonicera japonica).* Herbaceous plants, being a combination of "wildflowers" and "weeds," indicating some disturbance, are: *Alliaria petiolata, Allium vineale, Barbarea vulgaris, Claytonia virginica, Conium maculatum, Corydalis flavula, Galium aparine, Glechoma hederacea, Hydrophyllum macrophyllum, Lamium purpureum, Mertensia virginica, Phacelia purshii, Polygonatum biflorum, Saxifraga virginiensis, Smilacina racemosa, Stellaria media, Viola papilionacea,* and *V. striata.*

A plant community at another locality along North Elkhorn Creek in Scott County has the following composition: The canopy and understory trees are sugar maple *(Acer saccharum),* box elder *(A. negundo),* hornbeam *(Carpinus caroliniana),* shellbark hickory *(Carya laciniosa),* hackberry *(Celtis occidentalis),* redbud *(Cercis canadensis),* hawthorn (*Crataegus* sp.), hop hornbeam *(Ostrya virginiana),* sycamore *(Platanus occidentalis),* wild cherry *(Prunus serotina),* chinquapin oak

(Quercus muehlenbergii), Shumard oak *(Q. shumardii)*, and black willow *(Salix nigra)*. The shrub layer is composed of wahoo *(Euonymus atropurpureus)*, winter-creeper *(E. kiautechovicus)*, *Lonicera maackii*, and gooseberry *(Ribes cynosbati)*.

Herbaceous species found in this community are: *Alliaria petiolata, Aster shortii, Campanula americana, Corydalis flavula, Delphinium tricorne, Dentaria laciniata, Lamium purpureum, Mertensia virginica, Phacelia purshii, Polygonatum biflorum, Ranunculus abortivus, R. micranthus, Saxifraga virginiensis, Thalictrum dioicum, T. thalictroides, Tradescantia subaspera,* and *Viola papilionacea*.

A Bur Oak Relic Community. The pasture described above is typical of the region in that it has few bur oaks and blue ashes under 75 years of age. The current practice of mowing where they grow discourages or prevents their natural regeneration. The only bur oak community with a significant regeneration known to the authors was one southeast of Lexington, now developed as a residential subdivision. Hence planned planting of these species, as well as conservation of existing individuals, should be encouraged to foster a perpetuation of this aspect of Bluegrass character.

This significant relic savanna-woodland with bur oak as a dominant was analyzed before any residential development was under way. It contained 29 bur oaks over 200 years old and 72 between 12 and 200 years. (Sizes and ages are given in Table 2, p. 30.) On this same farm were some small open areas near bur oaks where, for the period from approximately 75 years ago to 12-15 years ago, there was grazing but little mowing. Only one seedling was found because all open areas have been mowed recently. In a strip 40 feet wide and 214 feet long, 52 trees were counted, ranging in size from 2 inches to 1 foot DBH. There were 19 shagbark hickory, 15 bur oak, 8 hackberry, 6 black walnut, 2 wild cherry, 1 honey locust, and 1 hawthorn.

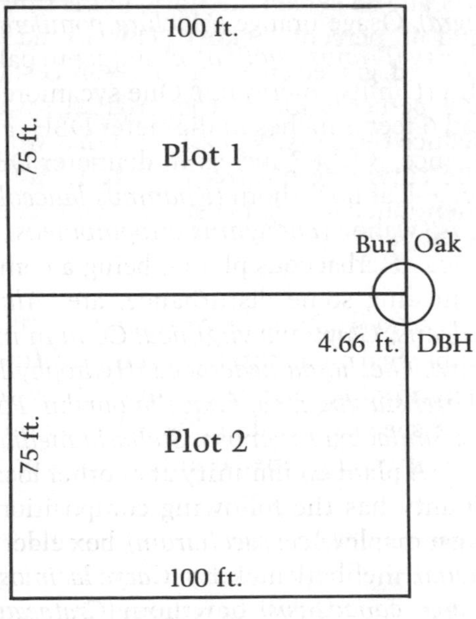

Two contiguous plots, each 75 by 100 feet, with a large bur oak between them, contained the following trees: Plot 1 had 72 trees from 2 inches to 17½ inches DBH: 29 shagbark hickory, 26 shellbark hickory, 7 white ash, 5 bur oak, 4 black locust, and 1 wild cherry. Of these, 10 (including 2 bur oaks) were 11-17½ inches DBH and 62 were 2-10 inches DBH. In Plot 2, 105 trees were counted, ranging from 1½ to 8½ inches DBH: 37 bur oak, 27 shagbark hickory, 21 black locust, 7 wild cherry, 3 white ash, 3 black walnut, 3 box elder, 2 shellbark hickory, 1 hackberry, and 1 American elm.

Elsewhere in this relic savanna-woodland, 3 large bur oaks and 1 large blue ash, the branches of which meet overhead in a closed canopy, formed a circle

Table 7. Importance Value (Sum of Relative Density and Relative Dominance) of Tree Species in Four Relic Savanna-Woodlands

	Stand A (Scott County) I.V.	*Stand B* (Woodford County) I.V.	*Stand C* (Harrison County) I.V.	*Stand D* (Bourbon County) I.V.	I.V. Average
Fraxinus quadrangulata	129.96	80.81	58.38	165.71	107.97
Quercus macrocarpa	19.70	46.21		11.57	19.37
Quercus muehlenbergii	9.21	10.82	50.38		17.60
Quercus shumardii	30.65	3.30			8.49
Carya laciniosa		11.16	20.79		7.99
Juglans nigra	1.86	9.03	12.94		5.96
Ulmus americana	9.50	3.26		10.57	5.83
Carya ovata			20.79		5.20
Fraxinus americana		2.96	16.79		4.94
Celtis occidentalis		5.83	7.92	5.57	4.83
Gymnocladus dioica		2.55	6.94	6.57	4.02
Platanus occidentalis		13.01			3.25
Acer saccharum		8.97	1.98		2.74
Robinia pseudoacacia	2.10		1.98		1.02
Liriodendron tulipifera		2.09			0.52
Morus rubra			1.10		0.28

100 feet in diameter. Within the circle and in the shade under the four large trees were the following species over 2 inches DBH; 174 shagbark hickory, 23 blue ash, 23 hackberry, 18 American elm, 12 bur oak, 8 wild cherry, 6 black walnut, and 2 shellbark hickory. Thus under the closed canopy the trees were 4.5 percent bur oak and 66 percent hickory; in the three open plots they were 25 percent bur oaks and 45 percent hickory. This would indicate that bur oaks require open, unmowed, grazed areas for successful establishment. But there were other factors in the perpetuation of the original savanna. Trampling by bison would greatly reduce the density of all trees that would survive and would not be selective. Of the surviving old trees, there is not a high percentage of hickory, and trees mentioned in original surveys and deeds do not indicate a great preponderance of hickory.

Other Relic Savanna-Woodlands. In 1980, Bryant, Wharton, Martin, and Varner published a quantitative study of fifteen remnant stands in the Inner Bluegrass, determining relative density, relative dominance, and importance value of the tree species found. Table 7 lists the importance value—"IV" (sum of relative density and relative dominance)—for tree species in the four principal stands.

Swamps. Swamps are rare in the characteristically well drained Inner Bluegrass, occurring only in such situations as sinking creeks, widely extending sinks, and areas of groundwater seepage. They produce a flora somewhat distinct from the remainder of the region, and therefore many years ago interested the author

(MEW), who studied them and made collections from them. More recently Meijer (1976) published a paper concerning the flora of the Sinking Creek system.

Swamp white oak *(Quercus bicolor)* may dominate in one locality, white ash *(Fraxinus americana)* in another, and green ash *(F. pennsylvanica* var. *subintegerrima)* in yet another. Associated species are red maple *(Acer rubrum),* box elder *(A. negundo),* water maple *(A. saccharinum),* shellbark hickory *(Carya laciniosa),* hackberry *(Celtis occidentalis),* sycamore *(Platanus occidentalis),* basswood *(Tilia americana),* and American elm *(Ulmus americana).*

Sedges are more prominent here than in any other Bluegrass habitat, although some of them may be found on pond margins. These sedge meadows include *Cyperus strigosus, Eleocharis obtusa, E. palustris, Scirpus atrovirens, S. lineatus, S. validus,* and many species of *Carex,* including *C. amphibola, C. blanda, C. cephalophora, C. conjuncta, C. frankii, C. jamesii, C. leavenworthii, C. lurida, C. lupulina, C. normalis, C. shortiana, C. stipata,* and *C. vulpinoidea.*

Other herbaceous plants found in swampy situations, some of which are also found on stream banks, are: *Asclepias incarnata, Astranthium integrifolium, Bidens cernua, B. frondosa, Chelone glabra, Cicuta maculata, Epilobium coloratum, Eupatorium perfoliatum, Glyceria striata, Helenium autumnale, Impatiens capensis, I. pallida, Juncus tenuis, Lycopus americanus, L. virginicus, Lysimachia ciliata, Ludwigia palustris, Leersia oryzoides, Lobelia cardinalis, L. siphilitica, Laportea canadensis, Lindernia dubia, Penthorum sedoides, Rumex altissimus, Saururus cernuus, Silphium perfoliatum, Spiranthes cernua, Scutellaria lateriflora,* and *Valerianella* ssp.

In summary, natural plant communities, already scarce and fragmentary on the Bluegrass Plain, are diminishing still further, and even those in the area of the Kentucky River are threatened with development. In Part I we described the vegetation of the past. In a few years will Part II also be relegated to what *was* and no longer *is*?

6. Vertebrate Animal Habitats

A WIDE variety of habitats is available for animals in the Inner Bluegrass, and they readily fall into five major groups. We have subdivided these, present some information on each of the subdivisions, and name some animals that may be commonly encountered in each.

OPEN FIELD HABITATS

Pastures. Paddocks and small pastures offer poor habitats for most vertebrates other than horses, although one commonly sees starlings, English sparrows, and sometimes crows in such places. Pine voles and meadow voles may make their runs in the taller grasses under the fences and between the paddocks. Larger pastures, not so intensively used, support a variety of mammals and birds and even an occasional reptile or amphibian. Fox squirrels, woodchucks, rabbits, meadow mice, pine mice, prairie deer mice, and eastern moles are commonly encountered. Woodpeckers favor old trees, and various hawks, especially in winter, perch high in trees and scan the landscape for food. Short-eared owls sometimes appear in flocks in winter and feed largely on meadow mice. Often in the warmer seasons, especially if the pasture is rocky, milk snakes, rat snakes, and occasionally black racers or common garter snakes seek shelter under the stones. Sometimes an American or Fowler's toad is encountered in such a site.

Cultivated Fields. Fields being intensively cultivated provide poor habitats, save for squirrels, woodchucks, and raccoons feeding on corn. Later, however, when the crops have been harvested, a variety of animals feed on the leavings and/or on the animals feeding thereon.

White-footed mice, deermice, and the ubiquitous house mice and Norway rats feed on the scattered leavings by night, and an owl frequently feeds on the rodents. Also by night, the white-tailed deer, which is not commonly encountered unless one knows where to look, feeds on the scattered grain, sometimes within hailing distance of a thickly populated subdivision. During the day feral pigeons and native crows, doves, and a variety of sparrows feed on the leavings, and occasionally a hawk takes one of the lesser scavengers. In early fall a milk snake, a rat snake, or a black racer may be encountered in such a habitat, where they are no doubt seeking a meal of mouse or bird.

Hayfields. If not mowed overly often, grassy hayfields provide an excellent habitat for a variety of animals. Least and short-tailed shrews are present, with the tiny least shrew considerably outnumbering its larger counterpart. Two species of meadow voles, as well as pine voles and lemming mice, are abundant. Cottontail rabbits are common, and red and gray foxes hunt and sometimes den in such areas. Woodchucks often den in hayfields, although here they seem more prone to den in fencerows, woodland edges, or rock piles.

Several of our rarest nesting birds in the Bluegrass select such areas: bobolinks, dickcissels, and Henslow's and savannah sparrows all favor tall, thick grass.

Weed Fields. Weed fields furnish the required habitat for at least two species of mammals in the Bluegrass area. The tiny harvest mouse, *Reithrodontomys humulis,* seems essentially retricted to such areas. It sometimes inhabits fallow fields that exhibit a rank growth of weeds, but seems to favor upland fields that remain weedy over long periods of time. The meadow jumping mouse favors rank weedy growth of weeds and grasses reaching heights of five or six feet or even higher. Since such rank growth usually occurs in the river bottoms, it is there that this species often reaches its greatest abundance, but it does occur in uplands where suitable cover is available. This species has extremely large hind legs and a surprisingly long tail. It is a great jumper, sometimes leaping three feet high and four or five feet forward. It seems strange that such a leaper would elect to live in vegetation so dense that it could rarely find a spot in which to jump more than a foot or so. Actually, the jumping mouse usually creeps about on the ground and jumps only when disturbed.

A large number of species of birds find food and shelter in old weedy fields in the fall and winter. Included are a number of sparrows, bluebirds, wrens, titmice, chickadees, and assorted others.

WOODLAND HABITATS

Mature Forests. These forests are mostly in the gorges cut by the rivers and their major tributaries as they traverse the Bluegrass area, but some are randomly scattered throughout this region. Many species of vertebrates seem more abundant and more diversified in the forests along the streamside bluffs than elsewhere in the Bluegrass. There may well be several reasons. The bluff forests, though sometimes narrow, are often quite elongate and offer a wide variety of habitats. Additionally, the waterways serve as avenues of invasion into the Bluegrass for individuals from the high populations of woodland forms in the mountains to the east.

There is at least one relatively clear-cut example of this latter phenomenon. The white-footed mice of the bluff forests in Fayette and Jessamine counties are much more closely related in size and body proportions to their upstream congeners than to those in the brushy fields and woods of the adjacent uplands. Since they interbreed freely, it appears not only that white-footed mice came from the mountain form but that continual recruitment from the huge upstream population is essential to the continuing survival of this race along the bluffs. The phenomenon may well extend on down the Kentucky River, but the necessary information is not yet available.

Other mammals of these woodlands include opossums, shrews, gray and flying squirrels, woodchucks, raccoons, both red and gray foxes, and assorted other species.

Great horned and screech owls are relatively common, as are nesting hawks. An occasional grouse is encountered, but this species, although common in the woodlands to the east, is quite rare in the Bluegrass. Various thrushes occur in season, with wood thrushes nesting there. Vireos, tanagers, and warblers frequent the woods, along with chickadees, titmice, nuthatches, and others.

Under stones, logs, and leaf litter in the forest one may find a variety of snakes, the most common of which are worm and ringnecks. An occasional box turtle, fence lizard, or blue-tailed skink (broad-head or five-lined) appears, but most abundant vertebrates in such places are the salamanders, especially the slimy, the zig-zag, and the ravine.

Brushlands. Scattered throughout the Bluegrass are areas of thick brush and small trees that provide outstanding food and shelter for various animals. Such areas are most abundant along the streamside bluffs. Most are dry, rocky areas, but some occur in spring-fed ravines or draws where the ground is soggy except in the driest seasons. In most cases these brushlands are of mixed deciduous species and red cedar, but the proportions vary widely. Some are almost wholly comprised of red cedar, others are mostly of deciduous species. These thickets provide food and shelter for a considerable assemblage of animals, but a few species use them far more than most, and a few seem almost limited to them in this region.

The more deciduous brushlands supply both food and daytime cover for white-tailed deer, which often seek shelter in the cedar thickets in inclement weather.

The beautiful golden mouse formerly inhabited these brushlands, favoring those supporting a rank growth of greenbriers. Members of this species construct nests under logs or stones for inclement weather, and softball-sized leaf nests up in the trees among the vines, where they live when the weather is dry and mild. The species appears to be gone from the area, their habitat destroyed.

Field sparrows, towhees, indigo buntings, yellow-breasted chats, prairie warblers, white-eyed vireos, and assorted other birds occupy at least the periphery of such thickets, either in summer or in winter, or both. Robins by the hundreds often winter in the cedar thickets.

Rat snakes, racers, milk snakes, and kingsnakes often feed in such areas. In the more soggy thickets one may sometimes flush a woodcock in season, or encounter dusky, small-mouthed, and two-lined salamanders, as well as an occasional newt or frog.

Woodland Edges. Many species, especially of mammals and birds, can be found along woodland edges. The high population density is due at least in part to the juxtaposition of two or more habitat types. Woodchucks, chipmunks, skunks, and foxes often dig their burrows here. Some species, such as the rufous-sided towhee and the wood peewee, seemingly prefer woodland edges, both as nesting and as feeding areas. Box turtles, green snakes, black racers, rat snakes, milk snakes, and copperheads all favor such areas, and American and Fowler's toads and tree frogs may often be encountered here.

River Cliffs. The rocky cliffs lining much of the gorge of the Kentucky River and the lower portions of its major tributaries provide shelter and nesting sites for several species of birds and home sites for some mammals. In most places, there are sufficient narrow flats on the cliffs to give foothold to a number of species of woody and herbaceous plants, and enough cracks, crevices, and small to large caves to supply homesites for various mammals and a few amphibians and reptiles.

The cliff rat is an immaculately clean, curious, and handsome animal, far removed from its distant relative, the obnoxious introduced Norway rat. Wood rats inhabit the deeper cracks and crevices and caves of the bluffs, and their homesites can be readily recognized by the piles of leaves, sticks, scraps of paper, bits of shiny metal, and other debris that comes their way. They are not evenly distributed, of course, because the sites suitable to them are not uniformly distributed. The handsome little white-footed mouse also lives along the bluffs and inhabits cracks and crevices but makes no such decorative piles of trash.

Both black and turkey vultures nest in shallow sheltered cavities in the cliff faces, and phoebes frequently build their nests under overhanging rocks. The peregrines and ravens of by gone times no longer cruise the river or nest on the cliffs, but they are not yet extinct and perhaps may some day again grace the river bluffs.

AQUATIC HABITATS

Rivers and Major Tributaries. The larger bodies of flowing water provide food and shelter for a wide variety of aquatic and semi-aquatic animals ranging through the five major classes of vertebrates.

The graceful otter is now apparently absent, but raccoons, mink, beaver, and muskrats still feed along the shores or in the shallow waters. Bats often feed over the water and at dusk frequently drink from the rivers by flying barely above the surface and scooping up a mouthful of water with their lower jaws. They sometimes misjudge and tumble into the water but readily take flight from the surface. Perhaps such accidents explain the occasional presence of a bat in the stomach of a bass or a bullfrog.

Great blue and little green herons often feed along the shores, and an occasional osprey takes a fish. Kingfishers are abundant, and their raucous rattle can often be heard as they fly swiftly up and down the streams. Several species of ducks frequent the streams in season; probably the most abundant is the colorful wood duck. These beautiful birds nest in tree cavities along the stream banks and around woodland ponds. The newly hatched babies scramble out of the nest cavity and jump to the ground, sometimes as far as forty or so feet below them.

Snapping, stinkpot, map, red-ear, and spiny softshell turtles bask along the shores and may sometimes be seen, but the painted turtles are much less abundant in the larger streams. The northern water snake is probably the most abundant snake along the larger streams, and the queen water snake a distant second.

Two species of permanently aquatic salamanders inhabit the larger streams. The smaller, the mudpuppy, has bushy external gills and is sometimes caught by fishermen. The hellbender is a huge salamander (up to 2.5 feet long), flattened, dark, and wrinkled, sporting a broad flat head with tiny eyes. It has a fleshy fold of skin between the fore and hind limbs on either side and a similar fold along the top and bottom of the laterally flattened tail. Sometimes a fisherman catches one, and on occasion an article appears in one of the local newspapers about some "prehistoric monster," complete with a photograph of a poor hellbender caught in one of the larger streams.

Several species of frogs and toads inhabit the river banks, including bull, bronze, pickerel, and an occasional leopard frog. Both American and Fowler's toads may sometimes be heard along the banks, and in early spring the choruses of spring peepers and later in the season an occasional chorus of gray tree frogs around quiet pools and backwaters adds to the delightful din.

Fishes, of course, are the major vertebrate inhabitants of the larger streams; 120 species have been recorded in the waters of the Inner Bluegrass. Several species formerly common to abundant are now either exterminated in this region or exceedingly rare. Such magnificent fishes as the lake sturgeon, the shovel-nosed sturgeon, and the American burbot are almost surely gone. The peculiar paddlefish is only rarely encountered in the Kentucky River. The native muskellunge is in real trouble in Kentucky as a whole, especially in the Bluegrass, but is still occasionally encountered in the streams of the Knobs.

Small Streams. Reptiles and fishes account for most of the species living in the small streams. Snakes of two species are common, especially in streams with rocky bottoms flowing through open pasturelands. The most common is the queen water snake, which attains a length of about three feet. It feeds almost exclusively on crayfish but occasionally takes small fish, salamanders, frogs, tadpoles, or snails. These snakes seem reluctant to bite, even when picked up, and rarely can be induced to bite, even when handled roughly. Northern water snakes inhabit the same streams and take shelter under the same stones but feed mostly on fishes. These latter snakes are as vicious as their coinhabitants are docile. They bite savagely, frequently, and deeply when carelessly handled. Sixteen snakes of these two species were once gathered up with one grasp of two bare hands from under an overturned stone in a Bluegrass stream. All seven of the northern water snakes bit, repeatedly, but not one of the nine queen snakes bit once. The hands were those now penning these lines.

Small, usually wooded streams supporting few or no fish and only an occasional water snake are frequently used as breeding sites by two-lined salamanders, but the major vertebrate in such streams is the essentially terrestrial small-mouthed salamander, *Ambystoma barbouri.* Many of these lunged, air breathing, dark brown to almost black salamanders forsake their shelters in the woods and migrate to the streams on rainy nights in late fall or early winter; a second contingent leaves the woods on rainy nights in January or February to enter the streams. They must surely crawl into cracks and crevices in the rocky stream banks with the advent of freezing weather, for such streams sometimes freeze solid in many places. By late December they begin to mate and lay their eggs. The eggs are laid on the underside of the submerged flat rock, one at a time, about an inch or so apart in a row of four or five eggs. The female then turns in another direction and repeats the process, over and over, until a flat, roughly hand-sized, one-egg-deep sheet of eggs is deposited. If there is sufficient space under the rock, sometimes several females will lay their eggs together; the resulting sheets of eggs may be as large as eighteen inches across. The female turns upside down to deposit the eggs, and may brace herself in place with her stout tail. This activity continues off and on, sometimes into March, and then the adults leave the streams to go into the woods, where they may be encountered on the surface but more likely beneath a rock or log. That they sometimes go deep in the ground is indicated by the discovery of an individual, previously marked with a radioactive tag, some twenty inches underground on a dry, hot summer day. The recently transformed larvae must surely go underground soon after they leave the stream, for a great deal of searching has revealed only one juvenile, and that one was buried in the humus beneath a pile of rotten logs and brush. They apparently remain so hidden until they reach sexual maturity.

It is remarkable that these creatures survive so well. During the breeding season their body temperature must be at or near the water temperature, which is often barely above freezing or even slightly below freezing due to the currents. The rocks sheltering the eggs are often frozen into the surface ice, and if a rain raises the level of the stream, the ice may go out, sometimes dragging the rocks along the bottom and destroying the eggs or tilting the rocks so the eggs are left above the normal water level, where they cannot hatch. In spite of all these misadventures, by late spring or early summer the stream supports thousands of larvae of assorted sizes. But their troubles are still not over. Every time enough rain falls to raise the level of the stream and increase the water flow, numerous larvae are washed varying distances downstream, where hungry fishes wait to devour them. In one spot near Lexington, fishes come upstream until they reach a pool at the base of a low waterfall they cannot traverse. After every hard rain, the pool contains a number of larvae washed down from upstream, but within two or three days all have disappeared. Fishes are known to feed voraciously on the larvae, and it must be an exceptionally lucky larva that metamorphoses from a pool supporting fish.

Even so, many larvae do metamorphose, and some become adults; over the last 32 years the population has remained relatively constant, with but minor fluctuations. They survive in a cold and cruel world.

The small-mouthed salamanders (*Ambystoma texanum*) of Kentucky and adjacent Indiana are unique. Throughout the rest of the range of the species, the breeding behaviour is in sharp contrast. Elsewhere the females generally lay their eggs in small clumps attached to the upper, exposed surface of leaves, sticks, or other organic matter, or in the quiet water of mud-bottomed ponds and sloughs.

Springs and Seeps. These generally small areas provide sanctuary for several species of vertebrates. Meadow voles and Bluegrass bog lemming mice often inhabit the rank grasses usually found in such areas. Sometimes woodcock are found here, and Wilson's snipe are often present along muddy spots in spring and fall. An occasional box turtle may reside here in the heat of summer, and such places often provide hibernaculae for garter snakes, which overwinter underground in such wet spots. Cave salamanders sometimes occupy springs and seeps, as do the midland mud and an occasional red salamander. Leopard frogs inhabit such areas; even an occasional bronze frog or bullfrog is encountered if the spring provides sufficient water.

Normally there are no fishes in such sites, save perhaps an occasional sculpin in a small spring, probably having arrived there through some tortuous connection with an underground stream. If the spring is large and empties into a relatively nearby stream supporting fishes, one might well find a variety of fishes in the spring.

Swamps and Marshes. Such natural areas are rather rare in the Bluegrass, but the coming of the farm pond and larger reservoirs has provided a number of obviously semi-permanent marshes and swamps, especially at the upper end of the catchment basin.

At least one marshy site in the Inner Bluegrass supports a colony of meadow jumping mice. Meadow mice, *Microtus pennsylvanicus,* often abound in the tall dense grasses around the margins of such areas. Along their well worn runways neat piles of short lengths of tall grass stems mark the spots where they felled a stalk bit by bit until the tender leaves and seed heads descended within reach of their busy jaws. The prairie vole, *Microtus ochrogaster,* sometimes inhabits such areas but seems to prefer more upland situations.

In some swamps and marshes where there is more or less permanent water, spotted and Jefferson's salamanders congregate to lay their eggs, and newts are common. In an occasional woodland pool, a chorus of spring peepers may be heard, sometimes as early as the first week in March. Red-spotted newts seem to be drawn to the breeding sites of the other salamanders. They readily eat the jelly coats surrounding the eggs, often consuming much of the future *Ambystoma* larvae food in the process, the eggs themselves, and the surviving larvae. In ponds particularly densely populated with newts, they can consume most of a given year's spawns of the other salamanders.

Several swampy or marshy areas in the Bluegrass support a breeding colony of spring peepers, but they are considerably less common than they were some thirty years ago. Various other frogs and toads occur in the swamps and marshes, and an occasional turtle or water snake is observed.

Raccoons, mink, muskrats, and assorted other mammals inhabit such areas, and a variety of birds occur. Such areas provide excellent habitats for red-winged blackbirds, and frequently little green herons nest in the sheltering trees. A wide variety of birds utilize these habitats, especially in migration, and a birdwatcher should be particularly observant in such areas.

Reservoirs and Ponds. Man-made reservoirs, usually for municipal water supplies, provide living space for many species of fish, several kinds of frogs and toads, turtles and various snakes, and many species of birds, especially the aquatic and shore birds. Muskrats often dig their bank dens or construct their domed houses of cattails and other vegetation in shallow water. Raccoons, skunks, opossums, and an occasional mink prowl the shores for food. It is around the larger reservoirs that one most often encounters gulls and terns, perhaps because many other large bodies of water in this region lie at the bottom of a deep gorge. Gulls and terns generally favor larger expanses of open area and usually avoid tight spots.

During the past several years many hundreds of farm ponds have been constructed across Kentucky, and they are particularly abundant in the Bluegrass region. These ponds apparently have had a profound effect on the population of pond turtles and bullfrogs; their numbers have increased dramatically, almost surely due to the tremendously expanded availability of admirably suited habitat. Surprisingly, the ponds seem not to have had such a striking effect on the populations of water snakes, which seem to prefer the streams or else do not wander far enough from the streams to encounter many ponds.

Ponds are sometimes invaded by muskrats, and the propensity of these animals for digging holes frequently results in the draining of a pond, or at least a drop in the water level. Although beaver have been seen in farm ponds, they apparently do not establish residence there.

Little green herons, bitterns (both American and least), redwinged blackbirds, grackles, and assorted other birds, including some shorebirds, frequent farm ponds. They constitute a favorite haunt of several species of ducks, but probably the most common ones are wood ducks and blue-winged teal in season. Almost any species will alight on a farm pond on occasion, however; even an oldsquaw, rare in Kentucky, was seen resting on one in Madison County.

Various turtles, almost always including snapping turtles, soon take up residence in a new farm pond and are well established within a year or so. Sometimes a milk, rat, black, or garter snake appears around a pond, but this seems purely incidental. Northern water snakes sometimes take up residence, especially if the pond is near a permanent stream.

Bullfrogs are quite characteristic of farm ponds, but several other varieties of anurans may appear. Bronze, leopard, or pickerel frogs may occur, and American and Fowler's toads sometimes breed in the ponds. About 30 years ago spring peepers were reasonably common in farm ponds of the Inner Bluegrass; today they are almost nonexistent there except in the river valleys. They are much more common in the Outer Bluegrasses and especially in the Knobs.

Farm ponds are generally stocked with fish; largemouth bass and bluegill are probably the most commonly stocked species. Crappies, channel catfish, and even bullheads are frequently stocked, and one might well encounter almost any species of freshwater fish in a farm pond. Some ponds are stocked with bait minnows of various species, with fathead minnows a common choice.

CAVES

Apparently no accurate count of the caves of the Inner Bluegrass exists, but the number must be tremendous. It is probably well in excess of 500, counting only those caves with over a thousand feet of passageways through which a person can travel.

Although an occasional opossum, raccoon, skunk, mink, gray fox, or white-footed mouse may venture deep enough into a cave to be beyond the lighted zone, and all may occasionally feed on bats, the major mammal inhabitants of our caves are bats, with the woodrat a poor second.

Woodrats do not generally wander far into the unlighted recesses of a cave. The finding of woodrat sign far back in a cave does not necessarily indicate that the animal came along the same trail you did. We tend to forget that they can travel passageways that we might not even notice and that we, after traveling thousands of feet underground, may be no more than a few yards, either horizontally or vertically, from a sunny forest.

These delightful creatures often assemble bushel-sized or larger accumulations of leaves (often green), sticks, bones, and assorted debris cast aside by human visitors. Generally such accumulations are stashed away in a sheltered spot, such as beneath a huge fallen slab of ceiling that forms a triangular, elongate cavity along a cave wall. Woodrats dig rounded cavities two or three inches into the surface of the pile, which they curl into and sleep. They fit exactly and are surprisingly difficult to see until they are frightened and move. Occasionally as many as three or four adult-sized animals may be frightened at one time from as many cavities in a single mound.

Bats are clearly the most populous vertebrates inhabitating the caves of this area, although only 9 of the 15 species recorded in Kentucky have been recorded in the Inner Bluegrass. Four of these sometimes enter caves, but not regularly, and apparently only singly. The other 5 species regularly inhabit caves in winter, and one of these inhabits caves throughout the year. This latter is the gray bat, an endangered species. A colony currently inhabits a Bluegrass cave, and apparently another colony occupied a cave in the Outer Bluegrass until about 30 years ago.

The most frequently encountered bat in the caves of this region is the tiny pipistrelle, which winters in caves and in summer presumably roosts in the tops of tall trees. They begin to enter the caves in fall and become more abundant as the winter progresses; probably the colder weather drives them from less suitable sites into the caves. They occupy many, if not most of the caves in the area. They usually hang singly, but sometimes two or three are found in close proximity. An individual pipistrelle will usually hang in one spot for a fortnight or so and then move to another site, sometimes in an entirely different section of the cave. It usually has only a few spots where it hangs, however, and seems to shift about with considerable regularity. There is some evidence that an individual may use the same sites from one season to another. In any event, after a summer's absence, a banded pipistrelle was found in the fall hanging from the exact same pea-sized projection from a wall deep in a cave where it had hung intermittently the year before. Clearly, the bat found that tiny projection in absolute darkness, after traversing several hundred yards of tortuous, pitch-black passageways. Is it possible that that tiny creature remembered that particular pattern of echoes out of the untold thousands it had responded to since it last heard that pattern? Did it, perhaps, recognize its own lingering odor after a lapse of nearly six months? Such phenomena boggle one's mind.

The Indiana bat, another endangered species, may be encountered in fall and winter in some of the caves of this region, but they are much more abundant both to the east and to the west. They spend the summer north of the Bluegrass.

Big brown bats are frequently encountered in caves in winter, usually fairly near the entrance, tucked back in a horizontal crevice, sometimes in the ceiling, sometimes in the wall.

In summer, gray bats are the only resident bats in the caves of the Inner Bluegrass. They prefer deep wet caves and are particularly averse to disturbance. If overly disturbed, they will simply desert the site. Since suitable caves are rather scarce, it is no wonder the species is endangered. Any summer colony of bats in a cave in Kentucky should be left strictly alone.

We have no cave-frequenting birds in Kentucky, but a pair of phoebes may build their nest and rear their young on a sheltered ledge at or near the mouth of a cave, or even a bit inside.

Rat snakes sometimes enter caves and have been known to feed on bats, but they surely must do so near the entrance. Worm, ringneck, milk, garter, and other snakes may be encountered at cave entrances, but such locations are generally not particularly good snake habitat. Box turtles, fence lizards, and five-lined skinks sometimes are encountered around the entrances to caves.

Sometimes a two-lined, slimy, Richmond's, zig-zag, or dusky salamander is found in a cave entrance or near the mouth, but the cave salamander is the most common species encountered. During the day they are generally hidden in the caves, but they come out at dusk to feed on insects and worms in and about the cave entrance by night. A toad may be encountered at a cave entrance, but other than the pickerel frog, which often winters deep in a cave, frogs are conspicuous by their absence.

Fishes are scarce in Bluegrass caves. Occasionally one encounters a surprisingly pale sculpin, usually in winter, deep in a cave. Where permanent streams enter and/or depart a cave, one frequently finds minnows and sometimes other fishes. Apparently there are no true cave fishes in the caves of the Inner Bluegrass.

SPECIAL HABITATS

Cemeteries, Golf Courses, Airports, etc. Places such as these are among the easiest to reach and often support an amazing number of birds. They are especially good spots to observe birds in spring and fall, when the migrants are going through. One can see almost every species that appears in an area save some of the water and shore birds. The open-field birds appear at the airports and golf courses, and the tree- and brush-loving types stop over in many of the cemeteries. If there are ponds, some of the water and shore birds will almost certainly appear.

Buildings. Farm buildings may, on occasion, be occupied by a variety of mammals other than the farmer's livestock. Raccoons, Norway rats, house mice, white-footed mice, and bats, or signs of their presence, are often encountered. Tall barns with sufficient hiding places just beneath the roof frequently provide living space for a maternity colony of big brown bats or their smaller relatives, the little brown bats.

Churches, warehouses, garages and other buildings providing adequate shelter may be utilized by maternity colonies of bats, and in many cases the people using the building are quite unaware of their associates in the attic.

The graceful barn swallows often build their mud nests on the ceiling joists of barns, garages, and other buildings. A pair may bring off two or sometimes three broods of four or five youngsters each in a single season. English sparrows may nest among the rafters, and domestic pigeons may also find locations for their nests. A pair of barn owls may find a suitable site for a nest, sometimes in a haymow, and bring off a brood of graduated young. The female begins to incubate when the first egg is laid, and the first hatched of the brood is a week or more old when the last chick emerges.

Rat snakes and milk snakes often frequent little-used barns, where they feed on small mammals and birds. Not infrequently a blue-tailed skink may be seen on the barn siding, and sometimes a fence lizard is encountered here also.

Residences are sometimes blessed (or plagued, depending on your attitude) with assorted vertebrates that accidentally or deliberately enter. About the only wild mammals to come into a residence regularly are the handsome little white-footed mice, house mice, gray squirrels, flying squirrels (rarely), and assorted bats.

White-footed mice frequently take up residence in a country home especially in winter. They do little damage except when one dies in an inaccessible spot and creates a bad odor for a few days. The delightful pitter-patter of their feet as they scamper across the top of the ceiling affords sufficient recompense for a few days of minor discomfort.

Any species of bat moving through or residing in this area may accidentally enter a home. If one does, it probably wants out as much as the owner wants it out. The solution is to open the door and shoo it out. It will not get in hair, nor will it deliberately bite unless picked up carelessly or managed in some other manner to interpose human epidermis between its teeth. The bat will not be the aggressor.

Many of the large old homes, especially the brick ones, in the Bluegrass area harbor a maternity colony of big brown bats in their attics and sometimes in the walls. Little brown bats occur in such places also but are not nearly so common. They do no particular damage unless the colony is a particularly large one; in this latter case the droppings accumulating on the attic floor sometimes becomes a problem. The manure is extremely high in nitrogen content and is an outstanding fertilizer for a flower garden. But it should be used sparingly, lest it damage the plants. Sometimes in extremely hot weather a colony in the attic will move down into the walls in search of cooler quarters. It is at such times that the colony is most likely to come to the attention of the residents. If left alone, they will go back up into the attic when the hot spell ameliorates.

A maternity colony of bats in a neighborhood will devour untold thousands of flying insects and make a sizable dent in the nearby insect populations.

Three species of snakes account for probably 95 percent of the uproar that generally ensues when one is found in a residence or even nearby. In early spring the garter snakes emerge from their underground hibernaculae, and since the vegetative growth is minimal at that time, they are highly visible. These animals are completely harmless and do no damage to anything except the animals they eat. Garter snakes are surely much more afraid of people than people are of them, and seem to make every effort to avoid humans. They are intriguing creatures and deserve to be left to their own devices.

In fall, young black rat snakes about 18 inches long and hatched the previous summer intuitively crawl about seeking a spot below frost line to spend the coming winter. Residences supply an abundance of such sites, and young snakes that encounter such a place in their wanderings sometimes may find a hole and crawl in. Most wind up in crawl spaces, but the unlucky ones wind up on a basement floor at best, and on the ground floor, at worst. If left alone they soon disappear into some crevice. If the animal must be gotten out of the house, it should be picked up and carried out. It will likely bite, but the bite of such a baby is no more than a pin prick, and they are not at all venomous. The squeamish should wear a pair of gloves and grasp the animal just behind the head.

Sometimes an adult rat snake or a milk snake gets into a residence while seeking a meal of mouse or bird. Under such a circumstance, one should open the door, take up a broom, and shoo the creature out. It may coil and lash out, but it can usually be driven or swept out unhurt with a minimum of effort. A big rat snake (they attain a length of over six feet) is not to be taken so lightly. They are largely bluff, however, and by no means a match for a determined householder.

7. Present Status of Vertebrates

FISHES

ABOUT 120 species of fishes are currently known in the streams and rivers of the Inner Bluegrass, out of 229 known in the state. Several of these are relatively recent introductions, and some of them are doing well. On the other hand, we have essentially lost several species of magnificent fishes that were abundant when the white man first came to the Bluegrass—lake sturgeon, shovelnose sturgeon, muskellunge, paddlefish, and American burbot.

A surprising number of fish species occur commonly in the headwaters of the Licking and Kentucky rivers that do not occur in equivalent-sized tributaries of these rivers as they traverse the Inner Bluegrass region. The reason seems quite clear: the headwater streams have sand and/or gravel bottoms to which the species are adapted. Tributary streams in the Inner Bluegrass have bottoms of bare limestone, limestone rubble, or mud, or some combination of these, and do not provide the requisite hiding, feeding, or resting sites for many upstream species. Additionally, the chemistry of sandstone waters and that of limestone waters are quite different and surely have different effects on the fishes.

AMPHIBIANS

Twenty-six of the 49 species of Kentucky amphibians occur in the Inner Bluegrass, and the status of two more is still unclear. Sixteen of the 26 species are salamanders, ten are frogs or toads.

There are essentially no data on the amphibian fauna of Kentucky in pioneer days; almost every particle of our present store of information about them has been accumulated in the past 160 or so years, and probably 95 percent of that in the last 50 years.

One of the most intriguing parts of our knowledge of the amphibian fauna is not so much what is here as what is not here. Several species having widespread distribution in the eastern United States do not seem to occur at all in the Bluegrass and are found only sparingy in the Knobs. Some of the more striking of these are the four-toed salamanders, wood frogs, upland chorus frogs, and mountain chorus frogs. All four of these species occur to the edge of the Knobs in at least three of the four cardinal directions. We do not know why they skip the Bluegrass region, but likely it is related to habitat; perhaps this limestone country is insufficiently acid for their requirements.

Thirty years ago, the ubiquitous spring peeper could be heard commonly in the Inner Bluegrass. Today, most are gone and the little ponds are silent.

REPTILES

Of the 54 species of reptiles known in Kentucky, only 27 occur in the Inner Bluegrass; they are comprised of 8 turtles, 4 lizards, and 15 snakes.

Our snakes are in real trouble. Urban sprawl annually renders many acres of the Inner Bluegrass unsuitable for wildlife habitat and, more importantly for the snakes, brings more people in contact with them. In such encounters, the snake almost always loses. A surprising number of otherwise reasonable people have an overwhelming fear of snakes and make every effort to destroy every one they encounter. Actually, snakes are of considerable value to the farmer, are attractive (if one would only look), inoffensive, more afraid of humans than humans are of them, and on the whole completely harmless. Some snakes are venomous and their bite is serious, but they are reluctant to bite, much preferring to slip away unnoticed, and have become extremely rare.

In the past 33 years one of us (RWB) has spent hundreds of hours looking for snakes in the Inner Bluegrass and has seen thousands of them. Only twice has he encountered a venomous snake (a copperhead, in both cases), and both were on the river bluffs, one in Jessamine County several years ago, and another in Fayette County in 1980. He has seen one other copperhead found by a student on the river bluffs in Frankfort. In hundreds of hours of botanizing, MEW has encountered only two copperheads, both on the river bluffs in Fayette County, and neither of them recently.

There are 4 unrecorded species of snakes that should occur in the Inner Bluegrass, judging from their habitats and distribution. Three of the four missing snakes, the eastern ribbon snake *(Thamnophis sauritus)*, the earth snake *(Virginia valeriae)*, and the red-bellied snake *(Storeria occipitomaculata)* are nowhere common in the state and may have been overlooked. If they occur in the Inner Bluegrass at all, however, they are extremely local in distribution or quite rare. The other missing snake is the timber rattlesnake, *Crotalus horridus*. It was surely here in pioneer times, and a flood-transported individual might be found along the river bluffs at any time. It seems almost certain that there is no breeding population of timber rattlesnakes anywhere in the Inner Bluegrass.

BIRDS

Of the 322 species of birds recorded in Kentucky, 257 have been observed in the Inner Bluegrass. We have divided the local birds into several groups on the basis of their residence, as follows:

Permanent Residents (46 species). These species are present in all seasons, but not necessarily the same individual birds or in the same numbers in different seasons. Some of our permanent residents are quite migratory, but the Inner Bluegrass is so situated geographically as to be in the southern portion of their nesting area and in the northern portion of the wintering grounds of some. Consequently, we have the species but not necessarily the same individuals all year round, with a noticeable increase in spring and fall, when the migrants are passing through.

Summer Residents (63 species). These birds spend the summer here, nesting and rearing their young. They arrive from the south in spring and depart in the fall. These birds are most numerous in spring and fall, when the resident population is augmented by those individuals just passing through.

Winter Residents (22 species). These birds arrive from the north in fall, spend the winter here, and depart for their northern nesting ground in spring.

Migrants (96 species). These are the migratory birds that nest to the north of us, and winter to the south. We normally see them only in spring and fall as they pass through. In mild winters a few individuals may overwinter, and sometimes a slightly incapacitated individual will summer here.

Vagrants and Accidentals (30 species). Some species of birds, particularly the youngsters when they have attained their full growth in late summer or early fall, are prone to wander over the countryside, showing up at places far out of their normal range. These vagrants are sometimes fairly regular but sometimes quite erratic in their movements. Individual birds may become lost and wander or be blown far off course into regions where they do not normally occur. These are often termed "accidentals."

Obviously, there is no season in which fewer than two of these groups are present, and parts of every group may well be represented. In early fall, for example, our permanent residents are here, our summer residents are beginning to leave, the vanguard of our winter residents is arriving, and the migrants are passing through in numbers. Some of the vagrants are most likely to appear in early fall, and accidentals may appear at any time.

It appears that the total numbers of individuals of most species of local birds is declining precipitously. Whether the trend will continue remains to be seen. Probable factors are urban sprawl, habitat destruction, and the increasing use of pesticides and herbicides. A vicious cycle seems to be operating—the greater the use of pesticides, temporarily the fewer the insects; the fewer the insects, the fewer the birds; the fewer the birds, the more the insects, the greater the use of pesticides—*ad nauseam.*

Our agricultural practices result in increased yields, and less time- and energy-consuming methods of harvesting generally result in more grain left in the fields. Herein lies one of the contributions to the increasing numbers of such gramnivorous birds as grackles, starlings, crows, pigeons, and doves. These practices also contribute to the survival of our wintering sparrows, but to a lesser extent. Most of our native sparrows prefer to feed where there is some substantial ground cover, as along the overgrown edges of cultivated land, while the preceding birds prefer more open areas.

The saddest part of all is what we have lost. Golden and bald eagles no longer cruise the Kentucky River, and the magnificent peregrine falcon no longer nests on the river bluffs. No more do we hear the croak of a raven, the drumming of a grouse, or the gobble of a wild turkey from the sparse woodlands of the Inner Bluegrass. The passenger pigeons are extinct; we cannot even conceive of the enormous flocks that once occurred here. The magnificent ivory-billed woodpecker is gone, but we still have his counterpart, the pileated woodpecker, in our woodlands and along the bluffs.

We have gained some foreign avian species by introductions in recent years. The starling is one of our commonest birds, and the house sparrow is not far behind. The house finch is perhaps our most recent acquisition; it arrived here a few years ago and is becoming more numerous. It is now a breeding species in Lexington. Rock doves (the ubiquitous "pigeon") are abundant pests in towns and around farm buildings. Monk parakeets have been reported. Personally we would be delighted to trade all the individuals of these introduced species in the Bluegrass for one nesting pair of any of the species we have lost.

MAMMALS

Of the 63 species of mammals recorded in Kentucky, 44 are known to occur in the Inner Bluegrass: 1 marsupial, 5 insectivores, 9 bats, 1 lagomorph, 5 squirrels, 13 rodents, 9 carnivores, and 1 ungulate. Our mammalian fauna is an interesting mixture of northern and southern elements, with another mixture of eastern woodland and western prairie species interposed. This mixing of fauna is probably due in part to man's actions in clearing the forests but must surely have its basic roots back in Pleistocene times.

At least 3 species of mammals surely could, but apparently do not, occur in the Inner Bluegrass. The southeastern shrew, *Sorex longirostris,* the eastern big-eared bat, *Plecotus rafinesquii,* and the golden mouse, *Ocrotomys nuttalli,* occur around the Inner Bluegrass in three of the four cardinal directions, in some cases ranging into the Knobs and the outer fringes of the Outer Bluegrass. If they occur in the Inner Bluegrass, they must be extremely local or exceedingly rare or both.

Some notable changes in our mammalian fauna can be laid squarely at the door of the white man. Since he appeared here a little over two hundred years ago, we have lost nearly all our largest mammals, and some of the smaller ones are now in serious jeopardy. The beaver, gray wolf, black bear, otter, cougar, bobcat, white-tailed deer, and bison have been eliminated from the mammalian fauna of the Inner Bluegrass. Within the last 25 years, however, we have managed, by transplanting wildcaught animals, to have beaver and white-tailed deer once again living wild in the Inner Bluegrass.

Part III
Annotated Lists

Vascular Plants

THIS LIST is compiled from collection records, but only collections that are unmistakably from those portions of the counties in which the soil is derived from Middle Ordivician limestone—Inner Bluegrass in the strictest sense. No sight records are included unless they are so specified, as, for example, a rare species found in only one place in numbers too few to collect. In the case of very common species, it may be stated that according to the author's observation they occur in every county, although, as with Kentucky bluegrass, they may in fact have been collected in only some counties. On the distribution maps the lack of a symbol in a county does not necessarily mean that the species does not grow there, only that the records used did not include collections from that county.

Nomenclature, for the most part, follows Fernald in *Gray's Manual of Botany,* Eighth Edition (1950). Where the name used is a revision, the one in *Gray's Manual* is listed as a synonym. In the list of plant species, names of orders are not included; families are listed under class or subclass in the sequence in which they would occur in the orders involved.

Terms used to denote abundance are as follows, in descending order: abundant, common, frequent, infrequent, and rare. "Abundant" and "common" indicate that the species occurs in considerable quantity where found, in addition to being found frequently. The rating applies only to the habitat in which the species grows. A species occurring plentifully in a scarce habitat would not be termed "frequent," as it is not frequently seen throughout the region but only in a given situation. For some species, it is stated without restriction that they are common or frequent, implying that they are found in different situations and the frequency rating applies throughout.

The records on which the list is based are as follows:

(1) Collections by Mary E. Wharton, most of which are in the University of Kentucky Herbarium; designated (MEW) in the text and W on maps.

(2) Collections by Johnnie B. Varner, which are in the Varner private herbarium; designated (JBV) in the text and V on maps.

(3) Collections from the study of the Kentucky River Palisades by the Kentucky Chapter of The Nature Conservancy and deposited in the herbarium at Eastern Kentucky University; designated (Pal) in the text and P on maps.

(4) Miscellaneous collections in the University of Kentucky Herbarium and

the College of Agriculture Herbarium; both designated (UK) in the text and H on maps.

(5) Unpublished county floras; designated C on maps, and in the text as follows: Bourbon County: Edi Guharja (EG); Clark County: Mary Ruth Becket (MRB); Jessamine County: James McFarland (McF); Woodford County: Elwood Carr (EC). The first three references are theses at the University of Kentucky. The Bourbon and Clark County specimens are in the University of Kentucky Herbarium; James McFarland's Jessamine County specimens were destroyed by fire at the University of Kentucky in 1948. Carr's specimens are in the Carr Herbarium, now at Pine Mountain Settlement School.

(6) Studies of special groups; designated X on maps, and in the text as follows: ferns: Thomas McCoy (McC); Ray Cranfill (RC). Grasses and sedges: W.A. Anderson (WA); composites: Willem Meijer (Mei).

(7) Records of the Nature Preserves Commission; designated (NP) in the text and N on maps.

(8) A few of Braun's records (*An Annotated Catalog of Spermatophytes of Kentucky*). Only a few can be used because Braun designated distribution only by counties; we need to know which part of a county. Those records used are designated (ELB) in the text and B on maps.

(9) Collections of Julian Campbell and Max Medley, designated C&M in the text and M on the maps.

Miscellaneous collections for Franklin County: Hal Bryan (HB); Steve Rice (SR); William Blackburn (WB).

A few collections in Anderson County by W.S. Bryant (Bry).

(10) Other records, for which the name of the collector is given.

Identification by collectors other than the author is taken at face value.

On the distribution maps the outer boundaries of the peripheral counties are left open to emphasize the fact that only a portion of each is included. Thirteen counties are included. A fourteenth, Nicholas, has a very small amount of Inner Bluegrass (Middle Ordovician) land northeast of part of the Bourbon County line, principally valley slopes of Hinkston Creek and its tributaries. The only records known to the author from this area are 132 species collected by Varner. Most of these are of general distribution in the state; the twelve that are either characteristic of the Inner Bluegrass or more frequent here than elsewhere in Kentucky are indicated on the maps by a V beyond Bourbon County.

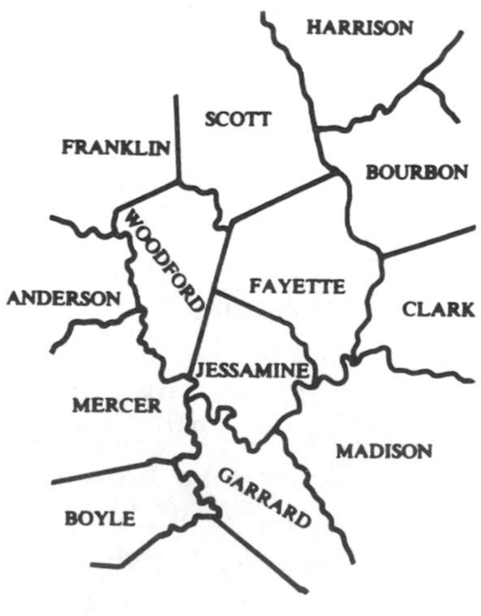

No floristic account of a region is ever complete because every square meter of ground cannot be covered at all seasons. This one would have been more complete if ill health had not prevented the author from continuing field work and visiting other herbaria. It is hoped that other botanists will be stimulated to study this unique area.

Class *Lycopodineae* CLUBMOSSES

Lycopodiaceae: Clubmoss Family

Lycopodium digitatum A. Braun
[= *L. complanatum* L. var. *flabelliforme* Fernald]
RUNNING PINE, GROUND-CEDAR
Associated with red cedar on uplands above the Kentucky River. Rare. Fayette (MEW); Jessamine (RC).

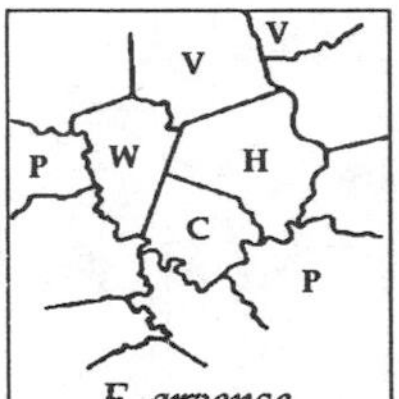

E. arvense

Class *Equisetineae* HORSETAILS

Equisetaceae: Horsetail Family

Equisetum arvense L. FIELD HORSETAIL
Along margins of rivers and creeks and on floodplains. Infrequent, but locally forming large colonies.

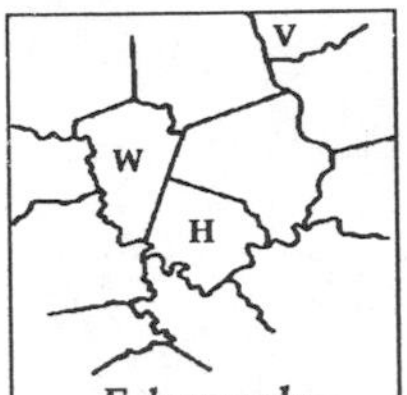

E. hyemale

Equisetum hyemale L. var. *affine* (Engelm.) A. Eaton
SCOURING RUSH
Along watercourses, especially on alluvial flats. Infrequent, but locally extensive.

B. dissectum

Class *Filicineae* FERNS

Ophioglossaceae: Adder's-tongue Family

Botrychium dissectum Spreng. var. *obliquum* (Muhl.) Small COMMON GRAPE-FERN
Fairly frequent in open woods, woodland borders, and thickets; occasional in old pastures.

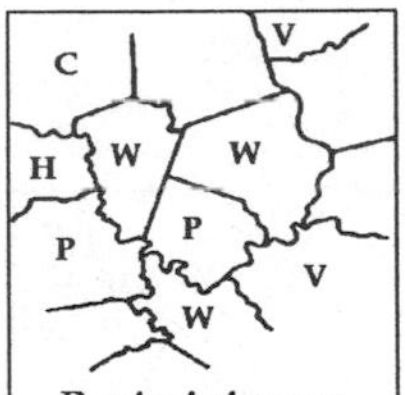

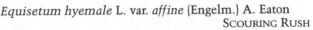

B. virginianum

Botrychium virginianum (L.) Sw.
VIRGINIA GRAPE-FERN, RATTLESNAKE FERN
Frequent in moist, rich woods; less frequent in dry woods.

Ophioglossum engelmanii Prantl
ADDER'S-TONGUE FERN
In cedar woods on dry hillsides. A single record; Clark (UK).

O. pycnostichum

Ophioglossum pycnostichum (Fernald) Love & Love
[= *O. vulgatum* L. var. *pycnostichum* Fernald]
ADDER'S-TONGUE FERN
In grassy woods and red cedar thickets. Rare.

A. pedatum

Pteridaceae: Bracken Fern Family

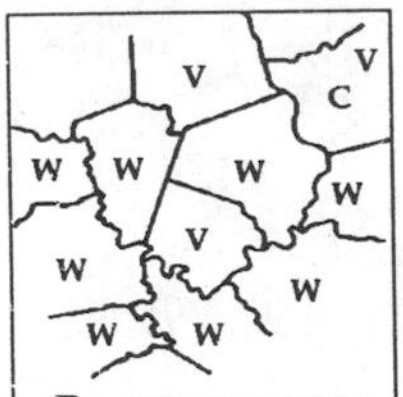

P. atropurpurea

Adiantum pedatum L. MAIDENHAIR FERN
Frequent in rich mesic woods on slopes.

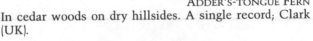

Pellaea atropurpurea (L.) Link PURPLE CLIFFBRAKE
Frequent on limestone cliffs and ledges; most frequent in the vicinity of the Kentucky River and its immediate tributaries.

Pellaea glabella Mett. ex Kuhn SMOOTH CLIFFBRAKE
On limestone cliffs and ledges in the vicinity of the Kentucky River. Infrequent. Franklin, Jessamine, Mercer (all UK).

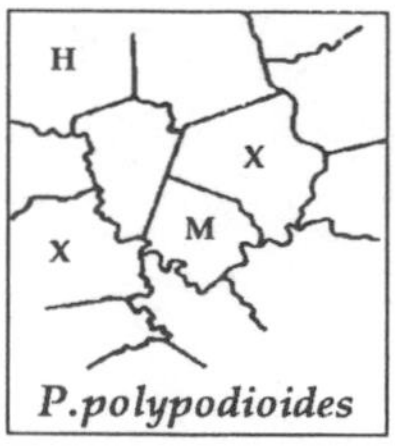

P.polypodioides

Polypodiaceae: Polypody Family

Polypodium polypodioides (L.) Watt
RESURRECTION FERN
An epiphyte growing on tree trunks. Rare.

Polypodium virginianum L. POLYPODY
Very rare in the Bluegrass. With Appalachian affinities in Kentucky, it apparently has migrated from the southeast along the Kentucky River gorge, where it grows on shaded cliffs. Jessamine (McC); Mercer (McC).

A.ebenoides

Aspleniaceae: Spleenwort Family

Asplenium X *ebenoides* R.R. Scott (Hybrid between *A. platyneuron* and *A. rhizophyllum*)
On mossy limestone ledges and boulders. Infrequent.

A.platyneuron

Asplenium platyneuron (L.) Oakes EBONY SPLEENWORT
One of the most common ferns. Found especially in dry or rocky second-growth woods, often associated with red cedar, but also in mesophytic habitats. Var. *incisum* (Howe) Robinson is less common than the typical. Clark (MRB); Fayette (JBV); Mercer (MEW); Woodford (MEW).

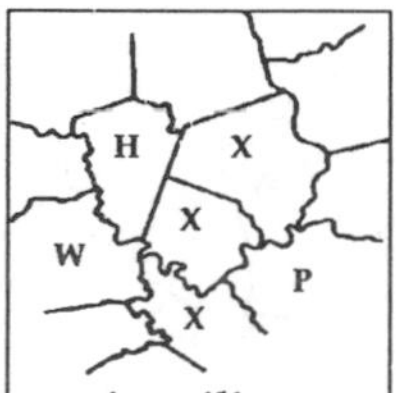

A.resiliens

Asplenium resiliens Kunze BLACKSTEMMED SPLEENWORT
In shaded moist crevices of limestone cliffs in the vicinity of the Kentucky River and its immediate tributaries. Infrequent.

A.rhizophyllum

Asplenium rhizophyllum L.
[= *Camptosorus rhizophyllus* (L.) Link] WALKING FERN
Frequent on moss and humus on shaded ledges, cliffs, and boulders, especially near Kentucky River and its tributaries.

A.ruta-muraria

Asplenium ruta-muraria L. WALL-RUE
Fairly frequent in crevices of limestone cliffs.

Asplenium trichomanes L. MAIDENHAIR SPLEENWORT
On moist, shaded cliffs. Rare. Fayette (UK).

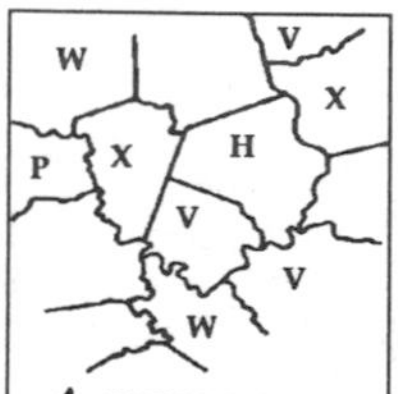

A.pycnocarpon

Aspidiaceae: Shield Fern Family

Athyrium pycnocarpon (Spreng.) Tidestr. GLADE FERN
Fairly frequent in rich mesophytic woods.

C.bulbifera

Cystopteris bulbifera (L.) Bernh. BULBLET FERN
Common on shaded, moist (often dripping) moss-covered limestone ledges, usually close above a creek and especially in the vicinity of the Kentucky River.

C.protrusa

Cystopteris fragilis (L.) Bernh.
(var. not distinguished) FRAGILE FERN
Anderson (Pal); Woodford (McC).

Cystopteris protrusa (Weatherby) Blasd.
[= *C. fragilis* var. *protrusa* Weatherby] FRAGILE FERN
Frequent on rocky wooded slopes and in moist pockets on wooded cliffs.

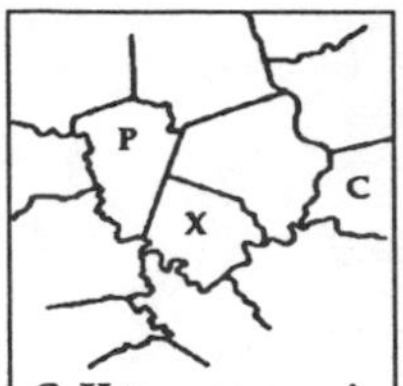

C. X tennesseensis

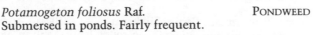

Cystopteris X *tennesseensis* Shaver (Hybrid between *C. fragilis* and *C. bulbifera*)
Open wooded slopes and bluffs. Infrequent.

D. marginalis

Dryopteris marginalis (L.) Gray MARGINAL SHIELD-FERN
Frequent on rich wooded slopes.

Onoclea sensibilis L. SENSITIVE FERN
A common fern of wet ground, rare in the Bluegrass; usually found in situations more acid than those in this region. A single record, "Clays Ferry," Fayette or Madison (UK).

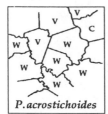

P. acrostichoides

Polystichum acrostichoides (Michx.) Schott CHRISTMAS FERN
Common on rich wooded slopes.

W. obtusa

Woodsia obtusa (Spreng.) Torr. BLUNT-LOBED WOODSIA
Frequent on rocky wooded slopes and cliffs.

Class *Gymnospermae* GYMNOSPERMS

Cupressaceae: Cypress Family

J. virginiana

Juniperus virginiana L. RED CEDAR
In thin soil on ridges and south-facing cliffs; also an invader of old fields and overgrazed, eroded slopes. Abundant.

Class *Angiospermae* FLOWERING PLANTS
Subclass *Monocotyledoneae* MONOCOTYLEDONS

Typhaceae: Cattail Family

T. latifolia

Typha latifolia L. CATTAIL
Common on pond margins and in other marshy ground.

Potamogetonaceae: Pondweed Family

Potamogeton diversifolius Raf. PONDWEED
Predominantly submersed, partly floating, in ponds. A single record, Harrison (JBV).

P. foliosus

Potamogeton foliosus Raf. PONDWEED
Submersed in ponds. Fairly frequent.

Potamogeton nodosus Poir. FLOATING PONDWEED
In ponds, infrequent. Fayette (UK); Harrison (JBV).

Najadaceae: Naiad Family

Najas flexilis (Willd.) Rostk. & Schmidt WATER NYMPH
Submersed in ponds. A single record, Fayette (MEW).

Alismataceae: Water Plantain Family

Alisma subcordatum Raf. WATER PLANTAIN
In pond margins, sloughs, and ditches that are permanently wet. Infrequent. Franklin (UK); Jessamine (UK).

Sagittaria australis (J.G. Sm.) Small ARROWHEAD
In mud or shallow water at edges of ponds. A single record, Clark (MRB).

Sagittaria calycina Englm.
[=*Lophotocarpus calycinus* (Englm.) J.G. Smith]
ARROWHEAD
Same habitat as the species above. Infrequent. Franklin (SR); Harrison (JBV); Woodford (JBV).

S. latifolia

Sagittaria latifolia Willd. [including var. *obtusa* (Muhl.) Wieg. and forma *gracilis* (Pursh) Robins, in addition to the typical] ARROWHEAD, DUCK-POTATO
Same habitat as the species above. Fairly frequent.

Sagittaria longirostra (Michx.) J.G. Smith ARROWHEAD
Same habitat as the species above. Infrequent. Fayette (UK); Franklin (UK).

Poaceae: Grass Family

Aegilops cylindrica Host. GOAT GRASS
On roadsides and in waste places. A single record, Harrison (JBV). Introduced.

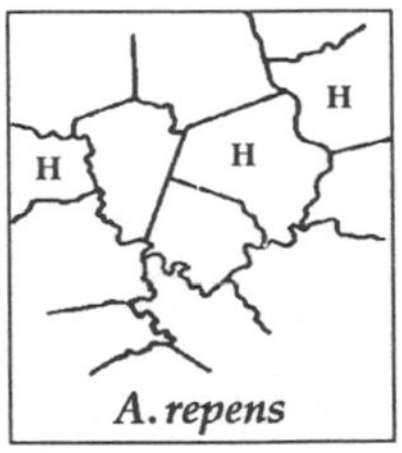

A. repens

Agropyron repens (L.) Beauv. QUACK GRASS
A weed, in fields and on roadsides. Infrequent. Introduced.

Agropyron smithii Rydb. WESTERN WHEAT GRASS
In fields and on roadsides. Infrequent. Fayette (WA); Madison (MEW). Introduced.

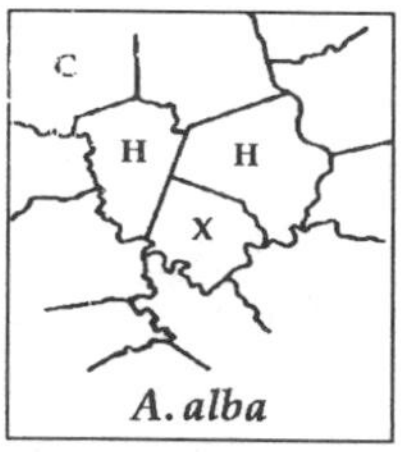

A. alba

Agrostis alba L. REDTOP
Escaped from cultivation in meadows. Fairly frequent. Introduced.

A. alba var. *palustris* (Huds.) Pers.
Along streams. Infrequent. Fayette (UK); Mercer (UK).

Agrostis elliottiana Schultes BENT GRASS
In dry fields. A single record, Jessamine (McF).

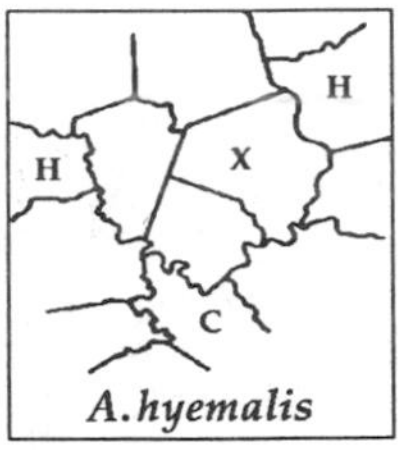

A. hyemalis

Agrostis hyemalis (Walt.) BSP BENT GRASS
In old fields and on roadsides. Fairly frequent.

A. perennans

Agrostis perennans (Walt.) Tuckerm. BENT GRASS
In open woods and thickets, on rocky banks, and in old fields. Frequent.

Alopecurus myosuroides Huds. FOXTAIL
In waste places. Recorded only from Fayette (WA, UK). Introduced.

Alopecurus pratensis L. MEADOW FOXTAIL
In fields and waste places. Recorded only from Fayette (WA, UK). Introduced.

Andropogon elliottii Chapm.
On a dry ridge. Rare. Jessamine (C&M).

Andropogon gerardii Vitman BIG BLUESTEM
A single collection, Fayette (UK).

A. virginicus

Andropogon saccharoides Swartz SILVER BEARDGRASS
On roadsides. Infrequent. Fayette (UK); Harrison (JBV).

Andropogon virginicus L. BROOM SEDGE
Common in old fields and overgrazed pastures.

Anthoxanthum odoratum L. SWEET VERNAL GRASS
In meadows and on roadsides. Recorded only from Fayette (WA, UK). Introduced.

Aristida oligantha Michx. TRIPLE-AWN GRASS
In dry eroded field. A single record, Harrison (JBV).

Arrhenatherum elatius (L.) Presl. TALL OATGRASS
Open situations. Recorded only from Fayette (UK). Introduced.

A. gigantea

Arundinaria gigantea (Walt.) Chapm. CANE
Once abundant, now only fairly frequent and nowhere extensive. On wooded floodplains, in open woods, and in fencerows.

B. erectum

Brachyelytrium erectum (Schreb.) Beauv. HUSK GRASS
In woods. Infrequent.

Bromus arvensis L.
A single record, Fayette (WA). Introduced.

Bromus catharticus Vahl RESCUE GRASS
An escape in open, grassy woods. A single record, Harrison (JBV). Introduced.

Bromus ciliatus L. FRINGED BROME
In open woods and on rocky slopes. A single record, Woodford (Pal).

B. commutatus

Bromus commutatus Schrad. HAIRY CHEAT
A weed in cultivated ground and waste places. Fairly common. Introduced.

B. japonicus

Bromus inermis Teyss HUNGARIAN BROME
In fencerows and waste places. Fayette (UK); Madison (Pal). Introduced.

Bromus japonicus Thunb. JAPANESE BROME
A common weed along roadsides and in waste places. Introduced.

B. purgans

Bromus purgans L. (typical, or var. not distinguished) CANADA BROME
Frequent in woods on dry or mesic slopes.

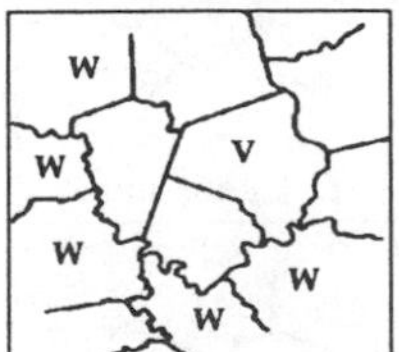

B. purgans f. laevivaginatus

B. purgans forma *laevivaginatus* Wieg.
Same habitat and frequency as the typical.

B. secalinus

Bromus secalinus L. CHEAT
In fields, waste places, and occasionally open woods. Fairly common. Introduced.

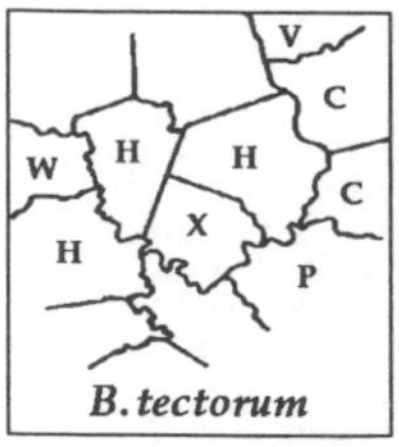

B. tectorum

Bromus tectorum L. Downy Cheat
In fields, in waste places, and on roadsides. Common and weedy. Introduced.

C. latifolium

Chasmanthium latifolium (Michx.) Yates
[=*Uniola latifolia* Michx.]
Frequent on wooded stream banks, on floodplains, and in other moist situations.

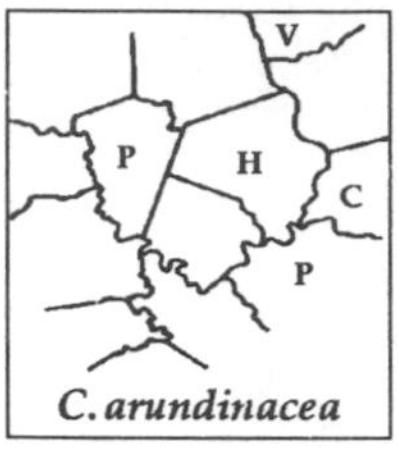

C. arundinacea

Cinna arundinacea L. Wood Reed
Fairly frequent in open, moist grassy woods, especially on floodplains and banks.

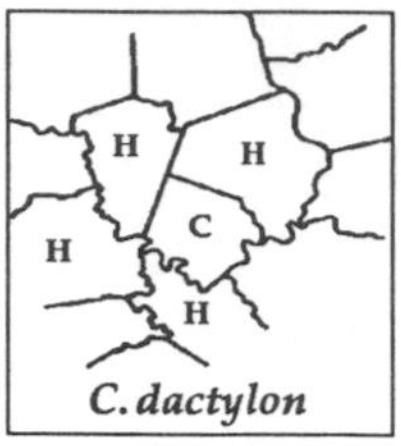

C. dactylon

Cynodon dactylon (L.) Pers. Bermuda Grass
In fields and waste places. Frequent. Introduced.

D. glomerata

Dactylis glomerata L. Orchard Grass
Common on roadsides and in pastures, fields, and open woods. Introduced.

Danthonia sericea Nutt. Downy Oatgrass
In dry open woods. A single record, Fayette (Pal).

D. spicata

Danthonia spicata (L.) Beauv. Poverty Grass
Fairly frequent in dry open woods on thin soil.

Deschampsia caespitosa (L.) Beauv. var. *glauca* (Hartm.) Lindm.
Tufted Hairgrass
On rocky river banks. Jessamine (C&M).

D. americana

Deschampsia flexuosa L. Crinkled Hairgrass
Fayette (UK).

Diarrhena americana Beauv.
Common in rich woods on slopes.

D. boscii

Dichanthelium boscii Poir.
[=*Panicum boscii* Poir.]
Frequent on rich wooded slopes, creek banks, and woodland borders.

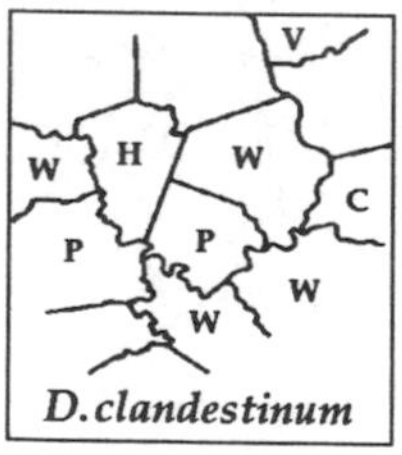

D. clandestinum

Dichanthelium clandestinum L.
[=*Panicum clandestinum* L.]
Frequent in open woods, thickets, and fencerows, especially on low ground.

D. ischaemum

Dichanthelium commutatum Schult.
[=*Panicum commutatum* Schult.]
In open woods and thickets. Infrequent. Harrison (JBV); Jessamine (Pal).

D. sanguinalis

Digitaria ischaemum (Schreb.) Muhl. Small Crabgrass
A weed in cultivated and waste ground. Introduced.

Digitaria sanguinalis (L.) Scop. Crabgrass
A common weed in cultivated ground and lawns. Introduced.

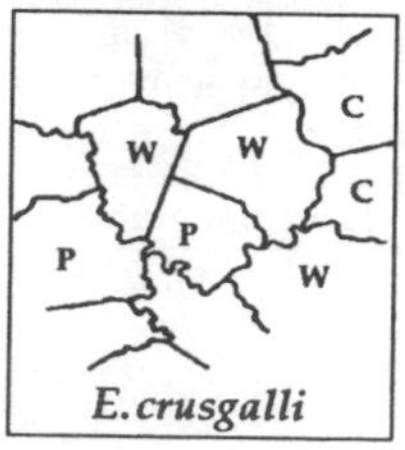

E. crusgalli

Echinochloa crusgalli (L.) Beauv. Barnyard Grass
Frequent in wet ground, including sinks and pond margins.

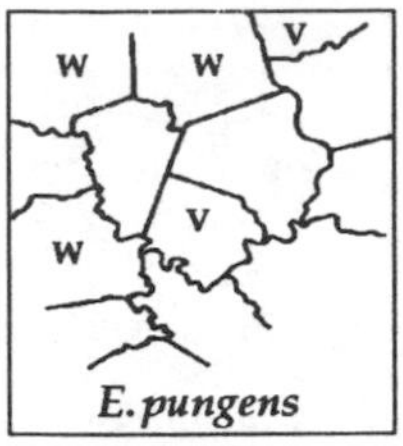

E. pungens

Echinochloa pungens (Poir.) Rybd.
[= *E. muriata* (Michx.) Fernald] BARNYARD GRASS
Frequent in pond margins and other wet areas.

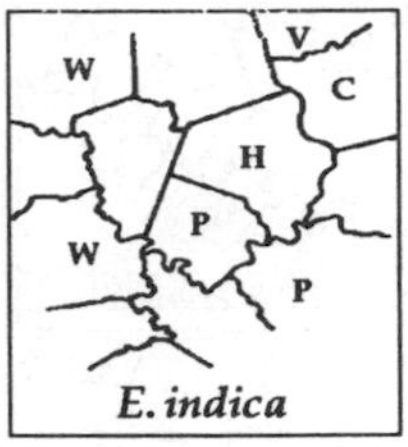

E. indica

Eleusine indica (L.) Gaertn. GOOSE GRASS
A common weed in gardens, lawns, pastures, and farm roadways. Introduced.

Elymus canadensis L. CANADA WILD RYE
A single record, Woodford (EC).

Elymus glaucus Buckl. WILD RYE
A single record, Anderson (Pal).

Elymus riparius Weig. WILD RYE
On creek banks and wooded slopes above streams. Infrequent. Clark (MEW); Fayette (UK); Jessamine (C&M).

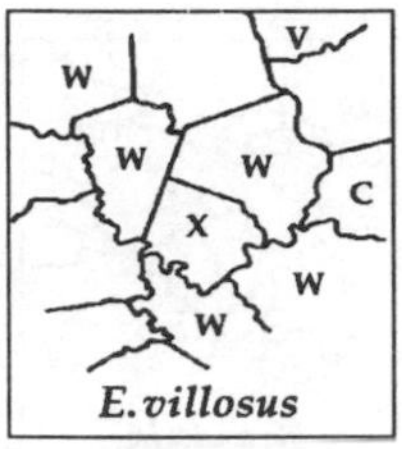

E. villosus

Elymus svensonii Church
Rare. Franklin (C&M).

Elymus villosus Muhl. WILD RYE
Frequent in open woods, dry or moist.

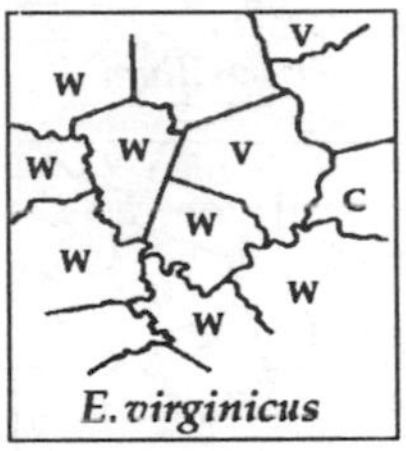

E. virginicus

Elymus virginicus L. [including var. *intermedius* (Vasey) Bush, var. *glabriflorus* (Vasey) Bush, and var. *jejunus* (Ramaley) Bush, as well as the typical] WILD RYE
Common in open woods, thickets, and old fields.

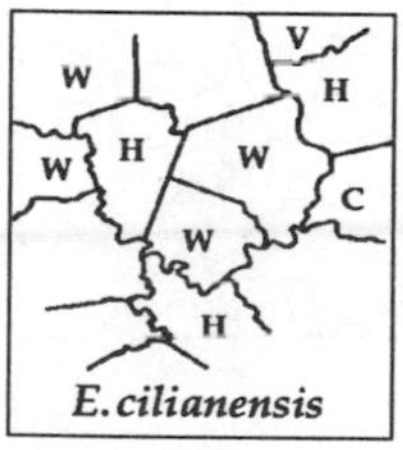

E. cilianensis

Eragrostis capillaris (L.) Nees CAPILLARY LOVE GRASS
Open woods and fields. A single record, Fayette (WA).

Eragrostis cilianensis (All.) Lutati STINK GRASS
[= *E. megastachya* (Koel.) Link]
A frequent weed in cultivated ground and overgrazed pastures. Introduced.

Eragrostis frankii C. A. Meyer LOVE GRASS
Moist, sunny situations. Infrequent. Fayette (UK); Woodford (MEW).

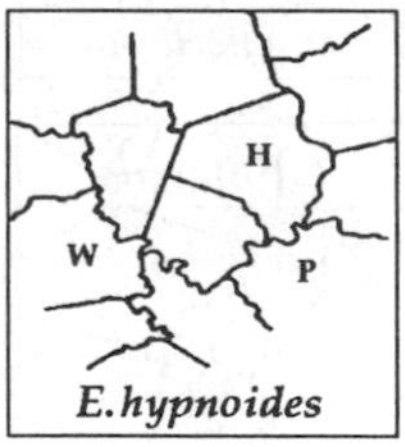

E. hypnoides

Eragrostis hypnoides (Lam.) BSP LOVE GRASS
Fairly frequent on floodplains and muddy banks.

Eragrostis pectinacea (Michx.) Nees LOVE GRASS
A weed in cultivated fields and other open areas. Infrequent. Fayette (UK); Franklin (SR); Jessamine (WA).

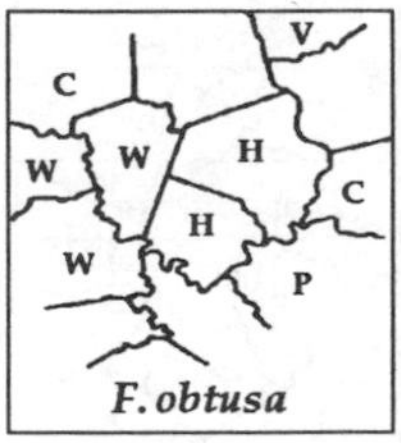

F. obtusa

Eragrostis pilosa (L.) Beauv. INDIA LOVE GRASS
A weed in moist open ground. A single record, Madison (Pal). Introduced.

Festuca obtusa Biehler NODDING FESCUE
Frequent on mesic wooded slopes and wooded floodplains.

Festuca ovina L. SHEEP'S FESCUE
A single record, Scott (UK). Introduced.

Festuca paradoxa Desv.
A single record, Fayette (WA).

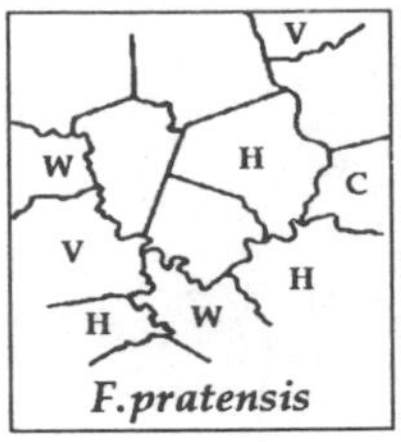

F. pratensis

Festuca pratensis Huds.
[=*F. elatior* L.] MEADOW FESCUE, TALL FESCUE
Abundant and widely planted along roadsides and in pastures and meadows. Introduced.

Festuca rubra L. RED FESCUE
A single record. Franklin (NP).

Glyceria melicaria (Michx.) Hubbard MANNA GRASS
On border of lowland field; a single record, Woodford (MEW).

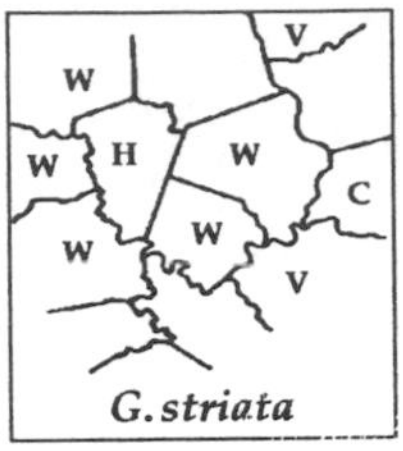

G. striata

Glyceria striata (Lam.) Hitch. MANNA GRASS
Common in wet situations; on creek banks either woody or sunny, under dripping cliffs, and in marshy ground.

H. pusillum

Holcus lanatus L. VELVET GRASS
In fields and waste places. Recorded only from Jessamine (UK). Introduced.

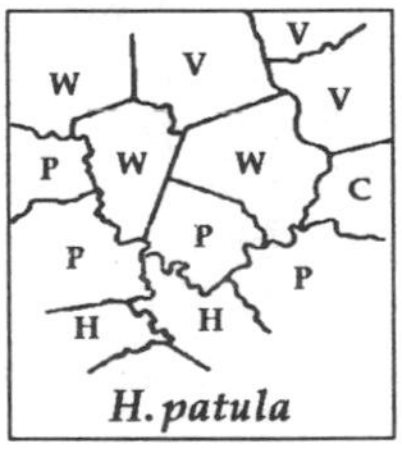

H. patula

Hordeum pusillum Nutt. LITTLE BARLEY
In old fields and other open areas. Infrequent.

Hystrix patula Moench BOTTLEBRUSH GRASS
Very frequent in woods.

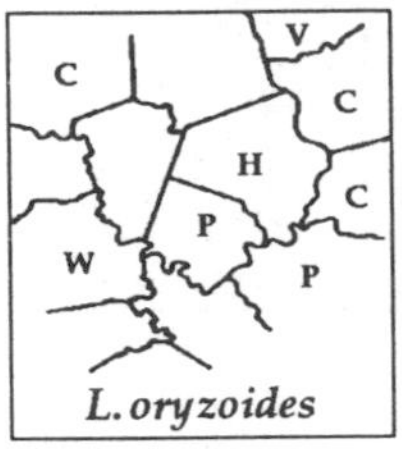

L. oryzoides

Leersia oryzoides Willd. RICE CUTGRASS
Frequent in wet meadows, pond margins, and other marshy situations.

L. virginica

Leersia virginica Willd. CUTGRASS
Fairly frequent in moist woods and thickets.

L. filiformis

Leptochloa filiformis (Lam.) Beauv. RED SPANGLETOP
A weed in fields and gardens. Infrequent.

Leptoloma cognatum (Schultes) Case
FALL WITCH GRASS
A single record, Fayette (WA).

Lolium multiflorum Lam. ITALIAN RYE GRASS
An escape from cultivation. Fayette (UK). Introduced.

Lolium perenne L. ENGLISH RYE GRASS
An escape from cultivation. Fayette (UK). Introduced.

M. mutica

Melica mutica Walt. MELIC GRASS
Fairly frequent in open woods and thickets.

Melica nitens Nutt. MELIC GRASS
In woods. Rare. Jessamine (UK); also an old collection by C.W. Short from "cliffs of the Kentucky River" (UK).

M. viminium

Miscrostegium viminium (Trinius) A. Camus
[=*Eulalia viminius* (Trin.) Kuntze] EULALIA
In moist ground, especially on floodplains. Locally extensive, although not frequent. Introduced.

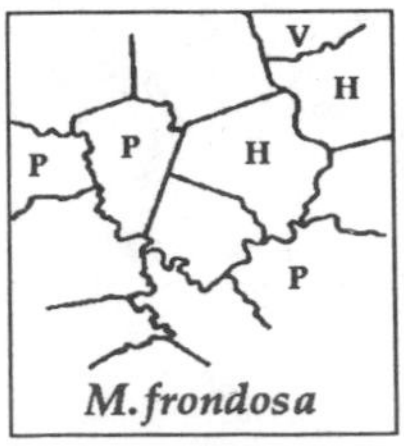

M. frondosa

Muhlenbergia frondosa (Poir.) Fernald MUHLY
In thickets, fencerows, and creek banks. Frequent.

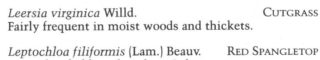

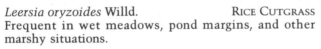

M. schreberi

M. sobolifera

Muhlenbergia schreberi J.F. Gmel. NIMBLEWILL
A common weed in lawns and gardens.

Muhlenbergia sobolifera (Muhl.) Trinius MUHLY
Fairly frequent in woods.

Muhlenbergia tenuifolia (Willd.) BSP SLENDER MUHLY
In woods. A single record, Fayette (WA).

O. racemosa

Oryzopsis racemosa (Sm.) Ricker RICE GRASS
In woods. Infrequent.

Panicum anceps Michx.
In moist ground. A single record, Madison (Pal).

P. capillare

Panicum capillare L. WITCH GRASS
A common weed in cultivated fields and other open areas.

P. dichotomiflorum

Panicum dichotomiflorum Michx. FALL PANIC GRASS
In fields, roadsides, and other open places, especially in low ground. Frequent.

P. dichotomum

Panicum dichotomum L. PANIC GRASS
In fields and open woods. Infrequent.

P. flexile

Panicum flexile (Gattinger) Scribn. PANIC GRASS
Frequent in open woods.

P. gattingeri

Panicum gattingeri Nash PANIC GRASS
In sunny areas. Infrequent.

P. lanuginosum var. fasciculatum

Panicum lanuginosum Ell. var. *fasciculatum* (Torr.) Fernald PANIC GRASS
Frequent in open woods and old fields.

P. lanuginosum var. *implicatum* (Scribn.) Fernald
A single record, Fayette (UK).

P. lanuginosum var. lindheimeri

P. lanuginosum var. *lindheimeri* (Nash) Fernald
In open woods and old fields. Infrequent.

Panicum latifolium L. PANIC GRASS
In woods. Infrequent. Fayette (JBV); Jessamine (McF).

Panicum laxiflorum Lam.
[=*P. xalapense* HBK] PANIC GRASS
In open woods. Infrequent. Anderson (Pal); Jessamine (McF).

Panicum linearifolium Schribn. PANIC GRASS
Rare. Fayette (UK, coll. C.W. Short).

Panicum microcarpon Muhl. PANIC GRASS
A single record, Boyle (UK).

Panicum miliaceum L. BROOM-CORN MILLET
A single record, Woodford (WA). Introduced.

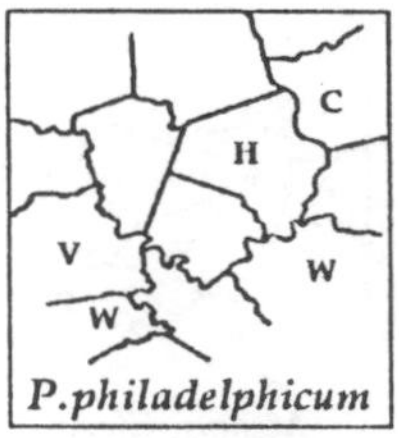

P.philadelphicum

Panicum philadelphicum Bernh. PANIC GRASS
Frequent in fields, open woods, and woodland borders.

Panicum rigidulum Bosc ex Nees
[= *P. agrostoides* Spreng.] MUNRO GRASS
Rare. Clark (MRB); Fayette (UK, coll. C.W. Short).

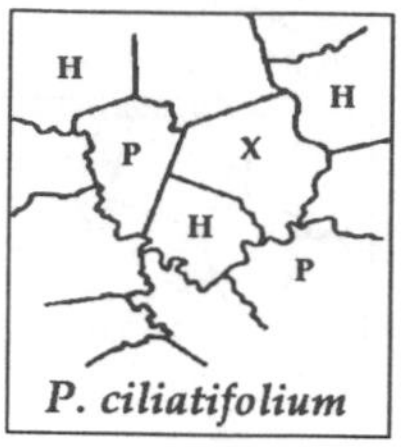

P. ciliatifolium

Panicum virgatum L. SWITCH GRASS
Infrequent. Fayette (UK); Scott (UK).

Paspalum ciliatifolium Michx. BEADGRASS
In fields and on roadsides. Infrequent.

P.pubiflorum

Paspalum laeve Michx. BEADGRASS
In fields and on roadsides. Harrison (JBV); Scott (MEW).

Paspalum pubiflorum Rupr. var. *glabrum* Vasey
BEADGRASS
Frequent in low fields, in roadside ditches, and on creek banks.

P.pratense

Phalaris canariensis L. CANARY GRASS
In waste places. Fayette (UK); Franklin (SR). Introduced.

Phleum pratense L. TIMOTHY
Frequent in fields, in clearings, and on roadsides. Introduced.

Phragmites australis (Cav.) Trin. ex Steud.
[= *P. communis* Trin.] GIANT REED
Along Kentucky River. A single record, Woodford (EC).

P. annua

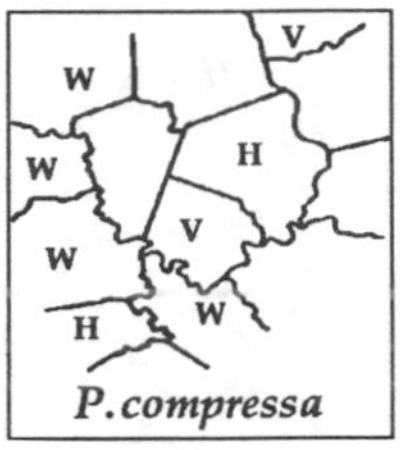

P.compressa

Poa alsodes A. Gray WOODLAND BLUEGRASS
In woods. A single record, Fayette (WA).

Poa annua L. ANNUAL BLUEGRASS
Frequent in moist ground in the open, often near springs. Introduced.

Poa autumnalis Muhl. WOODLAND BLUEGRASS
On wooded slopes. Infrequent. Fayette (Pal); Garrard (MEW).

P.cuspidata

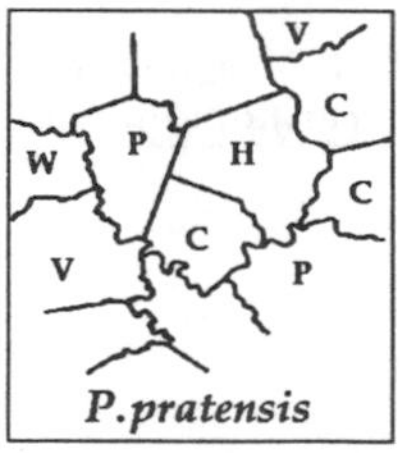

P.pratensis

Poa compressa L. CANADA BLUEGRASS
Frequent in rocky ground. Introduced.

Poa cuspidata Nutt. WOODLAND BLUEGRASS
Fairly frequent on wooded slopes.

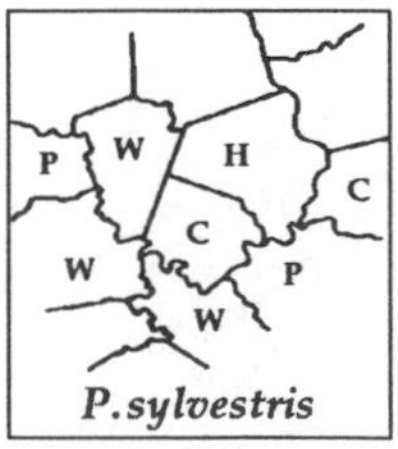

P.sylvestris

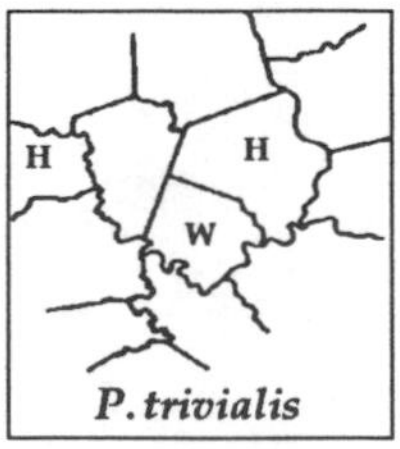

P.trivialis

Poa pratensis L. KENTUCKY BLUEGRASS
Cultivated in pastures and lawns; often an escape. Abundant, occurring in every Bluegrass county.

Poa sylvestris Gray WOODLAND BLUEGRASS
Frequent in woods.

Poa trivialis L. ROUGH BLUEGRASS
In wet ground. Infrequent. Introduced.

S. scoparium

Schizachne purpurascens (Torr.) Swallen
On rocky points. Rare. Jessamine (C&M).

Schizachyrium scoparium (Michx.) Nash
[=*Andropogon scoparius* Michx.] LITTLE BLUESTEM
In dry woods and woodland borders. Infrequent.

Setaria faberi Herrm. FOXTAIL
A weed in cultivated ground and on roadsides. Fayette (UK); Woodford (UK). Introduced.

S. glauca

Setaria geniculata (Lam.) Beauv. FOXTAIL
Franklin (SR); Woodford (EC).

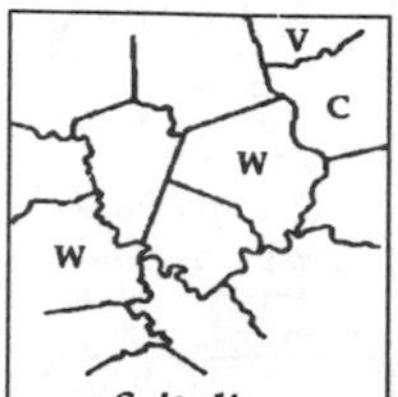

S. italica

Setaria glauca (L.) Beauv.
[=*S. lutescens* (Weigel) Hubb.] FOXTAIL
A common weed in cultivated ground, on roadsides, and in waste places. Introduced.

Setaria italica (L.) Beauv. FOXTAIL MILLET
An escape from cultivation. Introduced.

Setaria verticillata (L.) Beauv. FOXTAIL
A weed in cultivated ground. Fayette (UK); Woodford (UK). Introduced.

S. viridis

Setaria viridis (L.) Beauv. FOXTAIL
A common weed in cultivated ground, on roadsides, and in other open places. Introduced.

S. obtusata

Sphenopholis nitida (Biehler) Schribn. WEDGE GRASS
On wooded slopes. Infrequent. Fayette (UK); Franklin (SR); Jessamine (McF).

Sphenopholis obtusata (Michx.) Scribn. var. *major* (Torr.) Erdman
[=*S. intermedia* (Rydb.) Rydb.] WEDGE GRASS
Fairly frequent in open woods in moist ground.

Sphenopholis pallens (Biehl.) Scribn. WEDGE GRASS
Infrequent. Fayette (UK); Jessamine (UK).

S. bicolor

Sorghastrum nutans (L.) Nash INDIAN GRASS
In open woods. A single record, Fayette (WA).

S. halepense

Sorghum bicolor (L.) Moench
[=*S. vulgare* Pers.] BROOM CORN, MILO
An escape from cultivation. Introduced.

Sorghum halepense (L.) Pers. JOHNSON GRASS
A common weed in moist ground. Introduced.

Sporobolus asper (Michx.) Kunth DROPSEED
A single record, Mercer (UK).

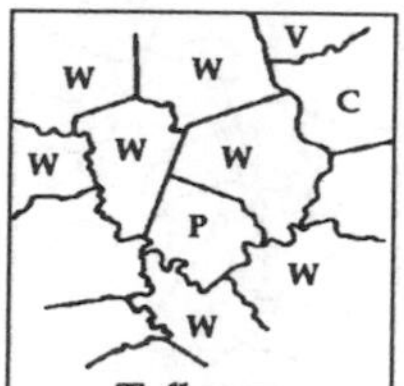

T. flavus

Tridens flavus (L.) Hitchc.
[=*Triodia flava* (L.) Smith] PURPLE TOP, GREASE GRASS
Common in old fields, woodland borders, open woods, pastures, and roadsides.

V. octoflora

Vulpia octoflora (Walt.) Rydb.
[= *Festuca octoflora* (Walt.) Rydb.] SIX-WEEKS FESCUE
In open areas. Fairly frequent.

C. albursina

Cyperaceae: Sedge Family

Carex albursina Sheldon
Frequent in rich mesophytic woods.

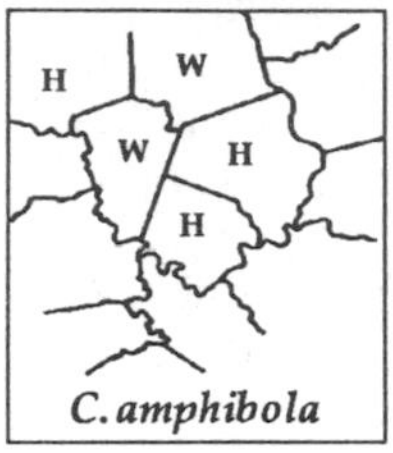

C. amphibola

Carex amphibola Steud. (typical)
Frequent in wet situations: creek banks, creek beds, and floodplains.

C. amphibola var. *rigida* (Bailey) Fernald
Same habitat as the typical. Woodford (Pal).

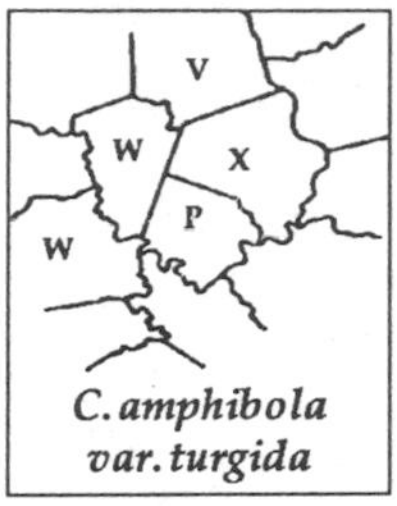

C. amphibola var. turgida

C. amphibola var. *turgida* Fernald
Same habitat as the typical.

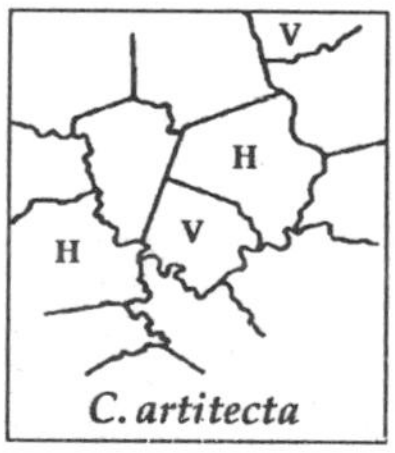

C. artitecta

Carex annectans (Bickn.) Bickn.
A single record, Fayette (UK).

C. blanda

Carex artitecta Mack.
Fairly frequent in woods.

Carex blanda Dewey
Frequent in woods: wet, dry, or mesic.

Carex bromoides Schkuhr
Recorded only from Fayette (UK).

C. cephalophora

Carex careyana Torr.
In rich woods. Infrequent. Fayette (UK); Jessamine (C&M); Woodford (UK).

Carex cephalophora Muhl.
Frequent in woods.

Carex communis Bailey
A single record, Jessamine (UK).

C. conjuncta

Carex complanata Torr. & Hook.
In open areas. Infrequent. Fayette (UK); Jessamine (C&M); Madison (UK).

Carex conjuncta Boot
In woods. Infrequent.

Carex cristatella Britt.
In wet ground. A single record, Jessamine (McF).

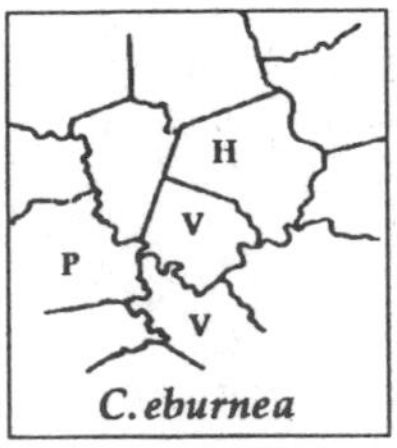

C. eburnea

C. festucacea

Carex davisii Schriv. & Torr.
In woods. Infrequent. Fayette (UK), Harrison (JBV).

Carex eburnea Boot.
Frequent on ledges and in crevices of limestone cliffs.

Carex festucacea Schkuhr
Fairly frequent in open woods and woodland borders, usually in moist soil.

Carex flaccosperma Dewey
Woodford (UK).

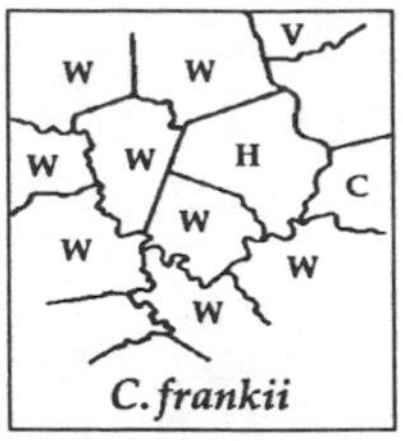

C. frankii

Carex frankii Kunth.
Common in wet situations: creek margins, floodplains, and swamps.

Carex gracilescens Steud.
In woods. Recorded only from Jessamine (WA, McF).

C. granularis

Carex granularis Muhl.
Near springs, in marshy ground, and in moist woods. Infrequent.

Carex gravida Bailey
Infrequent. Fayette (WA); Woodford (UK).

Carex grayii Carey
Recorded only from Fayette (WA, UK).

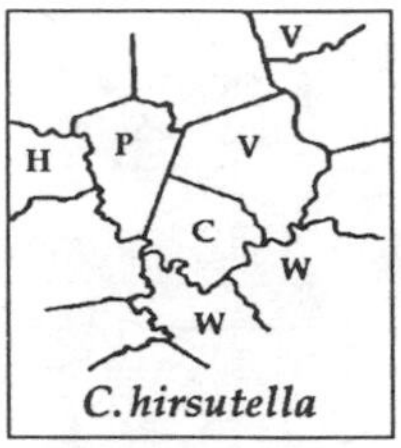

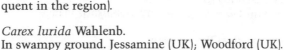

C. hirsutella

Carex hirsutella Mack.
Frequent on dry or mesic wooded hillsides, on creek banks, and in dry clearings.

C. hitchcockiana

Carex hitchcockiana Dewey
Fairly frequent in rich woods.

Carex hyalinolepis Steud.
In swamps and marshes. Rare. Franklin (UK); Woodford (UK).

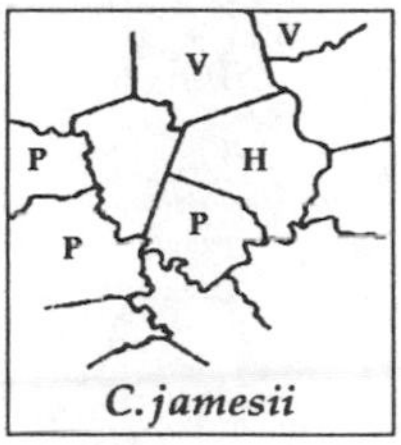

C. jamesii

Carex jamesii Schwein.
Frequent in rich woods and moist open areas.

Carex laevivaginata (Kukenth.) Mack.
Along streams. Rare. Jessamine (UK); Woodford (UK).

Carex laxiculmis Schwein.
In woods. A single record, Anderson (Pal).

Carex laxiflora Lam.
In woods. Infrequent. Fayette (UK); Jessamine (UK).

C. leavenworthii

Carex leavenworthii Dewey
In woods. Infrequent.

C. lupulina

Carex lupulina Muhl.
Frequent in marshy or swampy ground (which is infrequent in the region).

Carex lurida Wahlenb.
In swampy ground. Jessamine (UK); Woodford (UK).

Carex mesochorea Mack.
In dry open woods. Jessamine (JBV); Woodford (UK).

C. muhlenbergii

Carex muhlenbergii Schkuhr (typical)
In open woods, pastures, and roadsides. Infrequent.

C. muhlenbergii var. *enervis* Boott.
A single record, Harrison (JBV).

C. oligocarpa

Carex normalis Mackenz.
In woods. Jessamine (UK); Woodford (UK).

Carex oligocarpa Schkuhr
Frequent on rich wooded hillsides.

C. pensylvanica

Carex pensylvanica Lam.
Frequent in dry open woods.

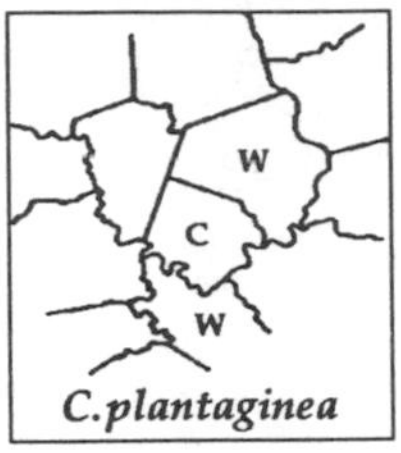

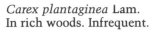

C. plantaginea

Carex picta Steud.
In woods. A single record, Jessamine (UK).

Carex plantaginea Lam.
In rich woods. Infrequent.

C. platyphylla

Carex platyphylla Carey
Frequent in rich mesophytic woods.

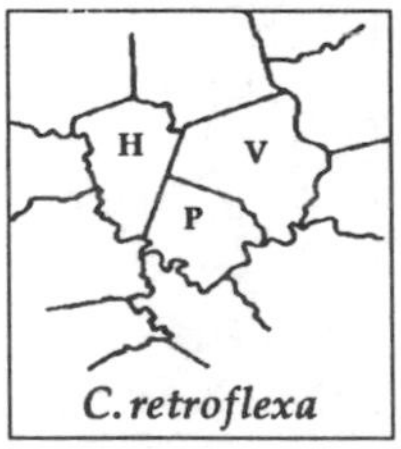

C. retroflexa

Carex prasina Wahlenb.
In wet woods. Recorded only from Jessamine (UK).

Carex retroflexa Muhl.
In edges of woods. Infrequent.

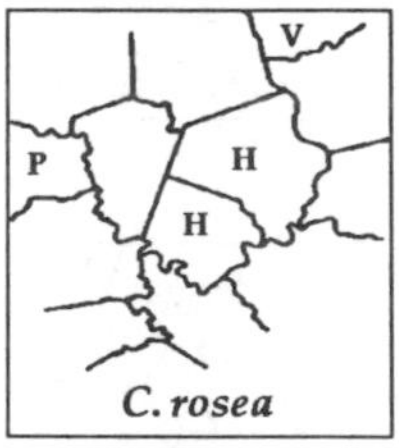

C. rosea

Carex rosea Schkuhr
Frequent in woods and thickets.

C. shortiana

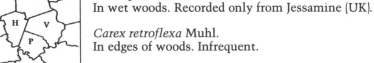

Carex rostrata Stokes
On margin of small stream. A single record, Fayette (UK).

Carex shortiana Dewey
Fairly frequent on stream margins and in moist woodlands.

C. sparganioides

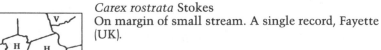

Carex sparganioides Muhl.
Fairly frequent in rich woods and woodland openings.

C. spicata

Carex spicata Huds.
In fields and on roadsides. Infrequent. Introduced.

Carex squarrosa L.
In wet ground in pastures. Franklin (SR); Jessamine (UK).

Carex stipata Muhl.
On stream banks. Fayette (UK); Woodford (UK).

Carex texensis (Torr.) Bailey
In dry open woods. Recorded only from Fayette (UK).

Carex tribuloides Wahl.
On creek banks and river floodplains. Infrequent. Franklin (UK); Madison (JBV).

C. vulpinoidea

Carex umbellata Schkuhr
In open areas. Anderson (Pal); Jessamine (C&M).

Carex vulpinoidea Michx.
Common in wet ground.

Carex willdenowii Schkuhr
A single record, Fayette (UK).

Carex woodii Dewey
In open woods. Infrequent. Anderson (Pal); Jessamine (UK).

Cyperus aristatus Rottb.
In mud along creeks and in cedar glades near the Kentucky River. Infrequent. Fayette (UK); Mercer (UK).

Cyperus densicaespitosus Mattf. and Kukenth.
[=*C. tenuifolius* (Steud.) Dandy]
In swampy ground. Infrequent. Fayette (WA); Franklin (HB); Woodford (UK).

Cyperus diandrus Torr.
In wet ground. A single record, Fayette (WA).

C. flavescens

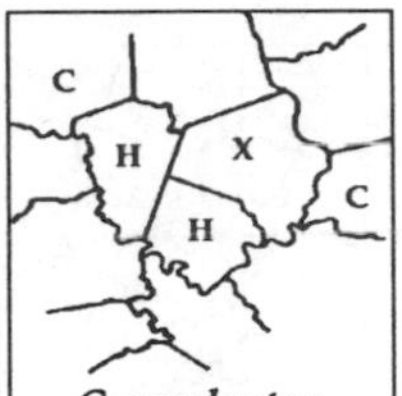

C. esculentus

Cyperus esculentus L. YELLOW NUTGRASS
Wet ground. Infrequent.

Cyperus flavescens L. var. *poaeformis* (Pursh) Fernald
Fairly frequent in wet, sunny situations.

Cyperus lancastriensis Porter
A single record, from a stream bank; Bourbon (EG).

Cyperus refractus Engelm.
Infrequent. Madison (Pal); Woodford (EC).

C. strigosus

Cyperus rivularis Kunth
Fayette (UK).

Cyperus strigosus L. UMBRELLA SEDGE
Common in wet situations: pond margins, stream beds, floodplains, and sinks.

Eleocharis engelmanni Steud. SPIKE-RUSH
On margins of ponds. Infrequent. Clark (MRB); Fayette (UK).

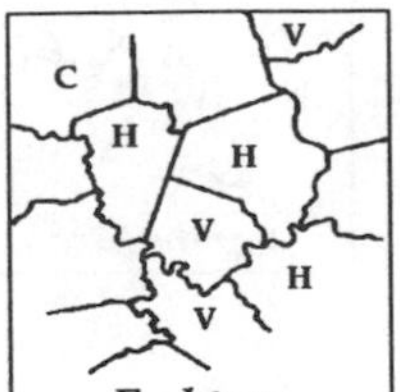

E. obtusa

Eleocharis erythropoda Steudel
[=*E. calva* Torr.] CREEPING SPIKE-RUSH
In marshy ground. A single record, Woodford (UK).

Eleocharis obtusa (Willd.) Schult. SPIKE-RUSH
Common in marshy ground and on muddy margins of ponds.

Fimbristylis autumnalis (L.) R. & S.
A single record, Jessamine (UK).

Hemicarpha micrantha (Vahl) Britt.
In wet ground. Infrequent. Fayette (UK); Scott (UK).

Rhynchospora capitellata (Michx.) Vahl BEAK-RUSH
A single record, from bottom of sink; Harrison (JBV).

S. atrovirens

Scirpus americanus Pers. THREE-SQUARE
In swamps. A single record, Woodford (UK).

Scirpus atrovirens Willd. BULRUSH
Frequent in marshy areas such as the bottoms of sinks and in creek beds.

Scirpus georgianus Harper
[= *S. atrovirens* var. *georgianus* (Harper) Fernald]
BULRUSH
Same habitat as the above species but less frequent. Franklin (MEW); Jessamine (McF).

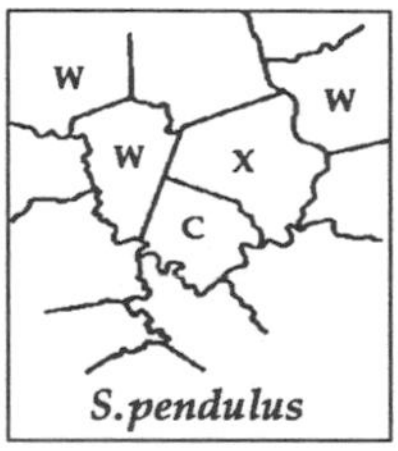

S. pendulus

Scirpus pendulus Muhl.
[= *S. lineatus* of authors, not Michaux.]
Frequent in wet ground along small, sluggish streams.

S. validus

Scirpus rubricosus Fernald WOOL-GRASS
A single record, Fayette (WA).

Scirpus validus Vahl var. *creber* Fernald
GREAT BULRUSH
In shallow water of pond margins. Infrequent.

A. atrorubens

Araceae: Arum Family

Arisaema atrorubens (Ait.) Blume
[typical and forma *viride* (Engelm.) Fernald]
JACK-IN-THE-PULPIT
Frequent in rich mesophytic woods.

A. dracontium

Arisaema dracontium (L.) Schott GREEN DRAGON
Fairly frequent in moist woods and seepage areas.

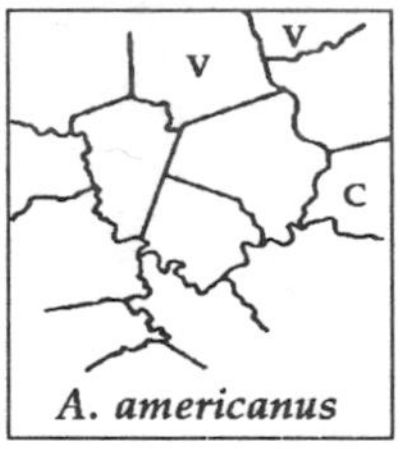

A. americanus

Acorus americanus Raf. SWEET FLAG
[= *A. calamus* L.]
In swales and shallow water. Infrequent.

L. minor

Lemnaceae: Duckweed Family

Lemna minor L. DUCKWEED
Fairly frequent on surface of ponds.

S. polyrhiza

Spirodela polyrhiza (L.) Schleid. DUCKWEED
Frequent on surface of ponds.

W. punctata

Wolffia punctata Griesb. WATER-MEAL
On surface of ponds. Infrequent.

Xyridaceae: Yellow-eyed Grass Family

Xyris caroliniana Walter YELLOW-EYED GRASS
In wet ground. A single record, Woodford (EC).

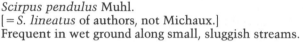

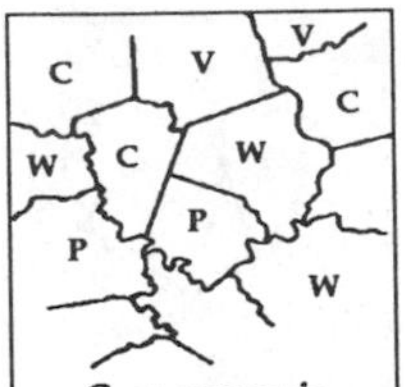

C. communis

Commelinaceae: Spiderwort Family

Commelina communis L. COMMON DAYFLOWER
Common in dooryards, roadside ditches, and other places near human habitation, especially in moist ground. Introduced.

Commelina diffusa Burm. f. DAYFLOWER
In wet ground. Infrequent. Harrison (JBV); Woodford (EC).

T. subaspera

Commelina virginica L. DAYFLOWER
In moist ground near the mouth of a creek. Rare. Mercer (JBV).

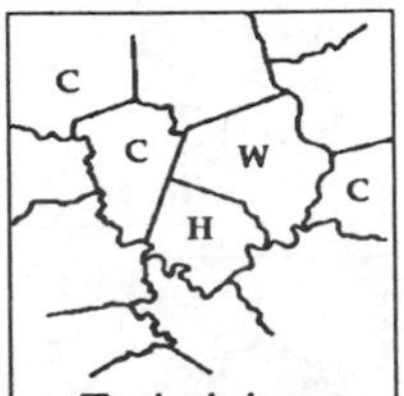

T. virginiana

Tradescantia subaspera Ker. SPIDERWORT
Common in open woods and woodland borders.

Tradescantia virginiana L. SPIDERWORT
In open woods. Infrequent.

Pontederiaceae: Pickerelweed Family

Heteranthera limosa (Sw.) Willd.
A single record: a collection by C.W. Short in 1838 from Woodford County (UK).

Heteranthera dubia (Jacq.) MacM. WATER STARGRASS
A single record: a collection by C.W. Short from "Kentucky River" (UK).

Juncaceae: Rush Family

J. tenuis

Juncus effusus L. RUSH
A common species but rare in the region. In wet ground along creeks. A single record, Harrison (JBV).

Juncus tenuis Willd. PATH RUSH
Common in paths and farm roadways.

J. tenuis forma anthelatus (Wieg.) Hermann
Jessamine (MEW).

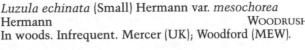

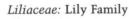

J. tenuis var. *uniflorus* (Farw.) Farw.
[=*J. dudleyi* Wieg.]
In wet ground. Infrequent. Franklin (UK); Woodford (UK).

Luzula echinata (Small) Hermann var. *mesochorea* Hermann WOODRUSH
In woods. Infrequent. Mercer (UK); Woodford (MEW).

A. canadense

Liliaceae: Lily Family

A. cernuum

Allium canadense L. WILD GARLIC
Fairly frequent in open woods, woodland paths, and roadsides, usually in moist situations.

Allium cernuum Roth NODDING WILD ONION
Frequent on dry open-wooded slopes and rocky banks.

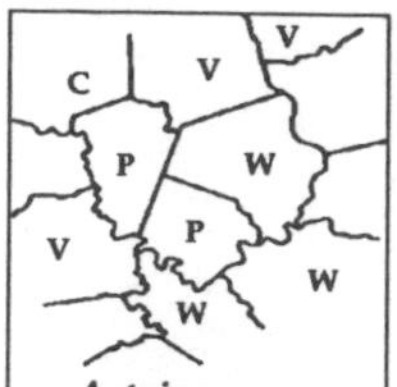

A. tricoccum

Allium tricoccum Ait. WILD LEEK
Frequent in rich mesophytic woods.

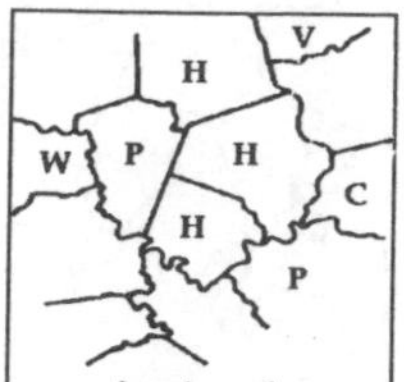

A. vineale

Allium vineale L. FIELD GARLIC
A common weed on roadsides and in fields, pastures, and lawns. Introduced.

A. officinalis

Asparagus officinalis L. ASPARAGUS
An escape from gardens, frequently growing in weedy fencerows, in waste places, and along roadsides. Introduced.

C. scilloides

Camassia scilloides (Raf.) Cory WILD HYACINTH
Frequent on open-wooded, rocky banks, moist or somewhat dry.

E. albidum

Erythronium albidum Nutt. WHITE TROUT-LILY; WHITE FAWN-LILY
Locally extensive on south-facing, steep wooded slopes and cliffs.

E. americanum

Erythronium americanum Ker. YELLOW TROUT-LILY; YELLOW FAWN-LILY
Frequent on wooded slopes, especially north-facing, and in wooded ravines.

H. fulva

Hemerocallis fulva L. DAY-LILY
A common escape on roadsides. Introduced.

Lilium canadense L. CANADA LILY
In dry open woods and old meadows. Rare. Fayette (MEW); Woodford (EC).

Muscari botryoides (L.) Mill. GRAPE-HYACINTH
An escape from cultivation. Fayette (MEW); Woodford (EC). Introduced.

Muscari racemosum (L.) Mill. GRAPE-HYACINTH
An escape from cultivation. Fayette (UK). Introduced.

N. bivalve

O. umbellatum

Nothoscordum bivalve (L.) Britt. FALSE GARLIC
Frequent in dry, sunny areas on limestone outcrops or in thin soil, often growing with red cedar.

Ornithogalum umbellatum L. STAR-OF-BETHLEHEM
Frequent on old homesites, in lawns, and along roadsides. Originally an escape from cultivation. Introduced.

P. biflorum

P. commutatum

Polygonatum biflorum (Walt.) Ell. SOLOMON'S-SEAL
Frequent in woods.

Polygonatum commutatum (Schultes f.) Dietr.
[=*P. canaliculatum* (Muhl.) Pursh]
GREAT SOLOMON'S-SEAL
Frequent in rich, moist woods, especially in wooded ravines.

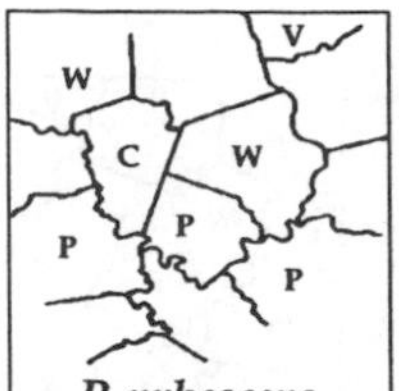

P. pubescens

Polygonatum pubescens (Willd.) Pursh SOLOMON'S-SEAL
Frequent in woods.

S. racemosa

Smilacina racemosa (L.) Desf. FALSE SOLOMON'S-SEAL
Frequent in woods.

Smilax bona-nox L. BRISTLY GREENBRIER
Very frequent in thickets and open, disturbed woodlands.

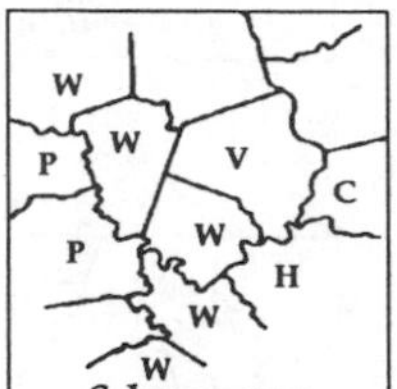

S. bona-nox

Smilax ecirrhata (Engelm.) S. Wats. ERECT CARRION-FLOWER
Rich woods. Rare. Jessamine (JBV); Woodford (UK).

S. glauca

Smilax glauca Walt. SAWBRIER, CATBRIER
Fairly frequent in old fields, thickets, and clearings.

Smilax herbacea L. CARRION-FLOWER
Fairly frequent on wooded slopes.

S. herbacea

Smilax hispida Muhl.
Common in second-growth woods and thickets.

S. hispida

Smilax lasioneuron Hook. CARRION-FLOWER
In woods. Rare. Fayette (UK); Jessamine (UK).

Smilax pulverulenta Michx. CARRION-FLOWER
On wooded ravine slopes. Infrequent.

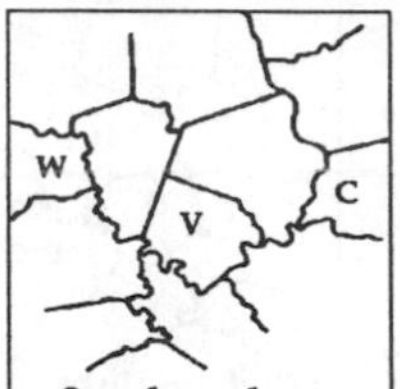

S. pulverulenta

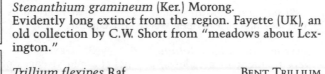

Smilax rotundifolia L. GREENBRIER
Frequent in thickets, woodland borders, and clearings.

S. rotundifolia

Stenanthium gramineum (Ker.) Morong.
Evidently long extinct from the region. Fayette (UK), an old collection by C.W. Short from "meadows about Lexington."

T. flexipes

Trillium flexipes Raf. BENT TRILLIUM
Frequent in woods on rich, mesic slopes.

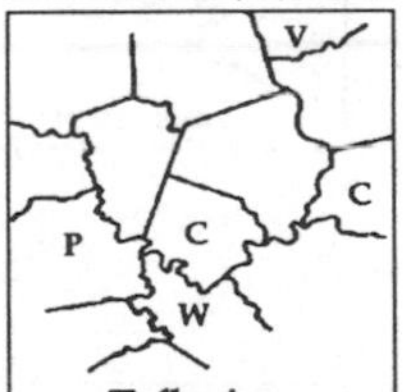

T. flexipes f. walpolei

T. flexipes forma walpolei (Farw.) Fernald
Same habitat as the typical but less frequent.

Trillium grandiflorum (Michx.) Salisb. LARGE WHITE TRILLIUM
A single record, Fayette (UK).

Trillium nivale Riddell SNOW TRILLIUM
On wooded slopes and ledges. Very rare. Jessamine (MEW); Mercer (UK).

T. sessile

Trillium sessile L. WAKE-ROBIN
Very frequent in woods, especially on slopes and cliffs.

U. grandiflora

Uvularia grandiflora Sm. BELLWORT
Frequent on wooded slopes and cliffs.

Uvularia perfoliata L. BELLWORT
In woods. Rare in the region. Fayette (UK); Franklin (WB); Jessamine (JBV).

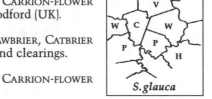

Dioscoreaceae: Yam Family

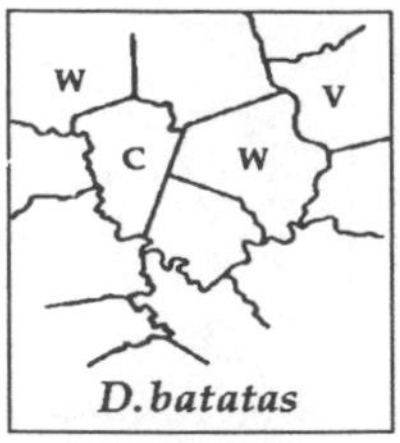

D. batatas

Dioscorea batatas Dcne. CINNAMON VINE
An escape from former cultivation. Introduced.

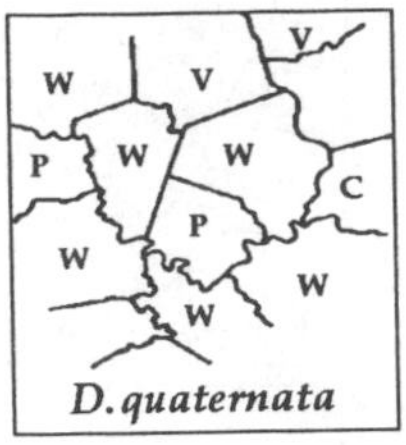

D. quaternata

Dioscorea quaternata (Walt.) Gmel. WILD YAM
Frequent in woods, thickets, and woodland borders.

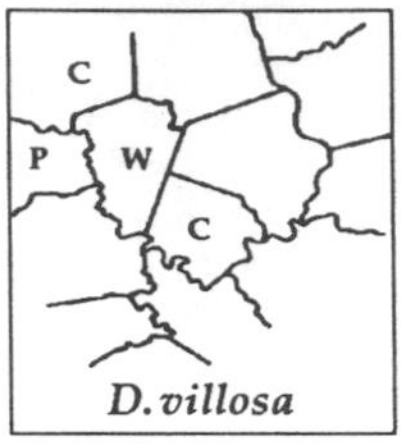

D. villosa

Dioscorea villosa L. WILD YAM
In woods, thickets, and woodland borders. Infrequent.

Veratrum woodii Robbins
In rich woods near the Kentucky River. Very rare in the region but locally plentiful. Franklin (NP).

Amaryllidaceae: Amaryllis Family

A. virginica

Agave virginica L. FALSE ALOE
Fairly frequent on dry ledges of south-facing cliffs.

Hypoxis hirsuta (L.) Coville YELLOW STARGRASS
On top of a Kentucky River cliff. Recorded only from Jessamine (UK).

Iridaceae: Iris Family

B. chinensis

Belamcanda chinensis (L.) DC. BLACKBERRY-LILY
Naturalized in open woods and at edges of woods. Fairly frequent. Introduced.

I. cristata

Iris cristata Ait. CRESTED DWARF IRIS
In Kentucky River gorge. Rare.

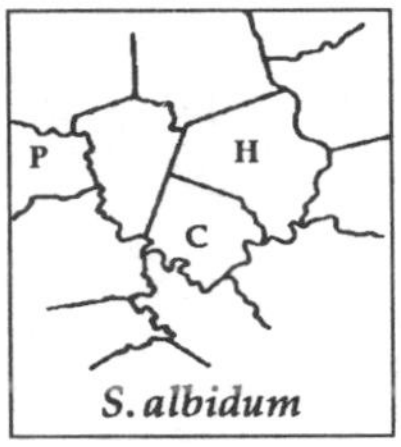

S. albidum

Sisyrinchium albidum Raf. BLUE-EYED GRASS
In grassy places and open woods. Infrequent.

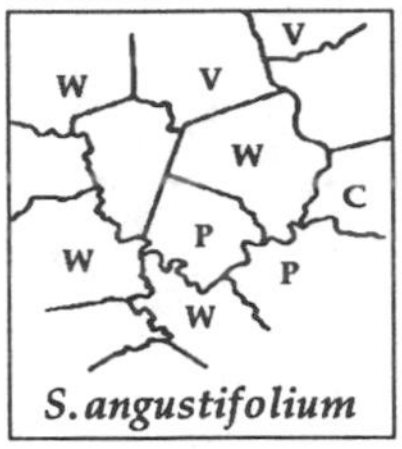

S. angustifolium

Sisyrinchium angustifolium Mill. BLUE-EYED GRASS
Very frequent in meadows, in thickets, and at edges of woods.

Orchidaceae: Orchid Family

Aplectrum hyemale (Muhl.) Torr. PUTTY-ROOT
In rich woods. A single record, Madison (Pal).

Corallorhiza odontorhiza (Willd.) Nutt. CORAL-ROOT
In woods. Rare. Anderson (Pal); Fayette (JBV).

C. wisteriana

Corallorhiza wisteriana Conrad CORAL-ROOT
Fairly frequent on rocky wooded slopes.

Galearis spectabilis (L.) Raf. SHOWY ORCHIS
[= *Orchis spectabilis* L.]
The last record for this region was collected in 1879, Fayette (UK).

Goodyera pubescens (Willd.) R. Br. RATTLESNAKE-PLANTAIN
In woods. Rare. Fayette (MEW); Harrison (JBV).

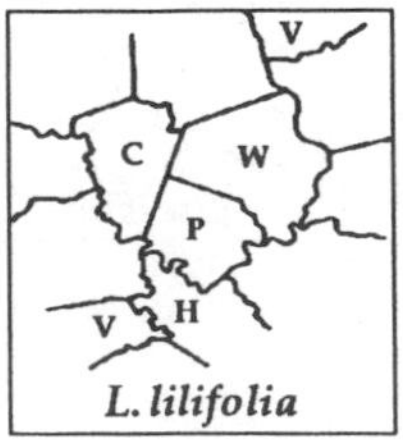

L. lilifolia

Liparis lilifolia (L.) Richard. TWAYBLADE
On wooded uplands, slopes, and banks. Infrequent.

Spiranthes cernua (L.) Richard.
NODDING LADIES'-TRESSES
In damp ground. Rare. Jessamine (Pal); Madison (Pal).

Spiranthes gracilis (Bigel.) Beck.
SLENDER LADIES'-TRESSES
In open woods and grassy thickets. Rare. Boyle (JBV); Harrison (JBV).

Spiranthes ovalis Lindl. LESSER LADIES'-TRESSES
In open grassy areas. Rare. Jessamine (Pal; C&M).

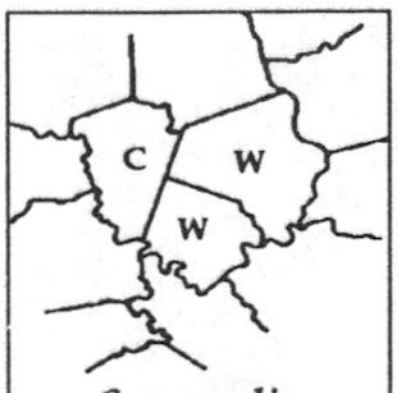

S. vernalis

Spiranthes tuberosa Raf. SMALL LADIES'-TRESSES
In open oak woods. A single record, Harrison (JBV).

Spiranthes vernalis Englm. & Gray
NARROW-LEAVED LADIES'-TRESSES
In woodland borders and grassy thickets. Infrequent.

T. discolor

Tipularia discolor (Pursh) Nutt. CRANEFLY ORCHID
On dry wooded slopes. Infrequent.

Subclass *Dicotyledoneae* DICOTYLEDONS

Saururaceae: Lizard's-tail Family

S. cernuus

Saururus cernuus L. LIZARD'S-TAIL
Fairly frequent in standing water in swamps and at the edges of ponds and quiet streams.

Salicaceae: Willow Family

P. alba

Populus alba L. WHITE POPLAR
Fairly frequent on old homesites and along roadsides. Introduced.

P. deltoides

Populus deltoides Marsh. COTTONWOOD
On stream banks. Infrequent.

Salix alba L. WHITE WILLOW
In low ground along roadsides and along small streams near roads. An infrequent escape from cultivation. Harrison (JBV). Introduced.

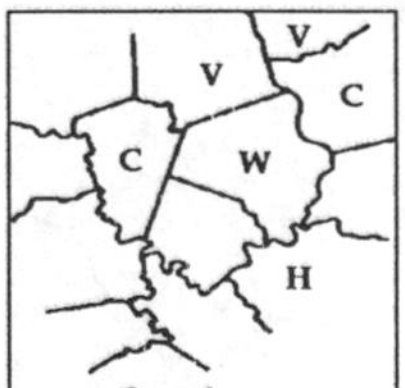

S. exigua

Salix caroliniana Michx.
On creek margins. Rare. Jessamine (C&M); Woodford (MEW).

Salix exigua Nutt.
[= *S. interior* Rowlee] SANDBAR WILLOW
Fairly frequent in pond margins and on bars in streams.

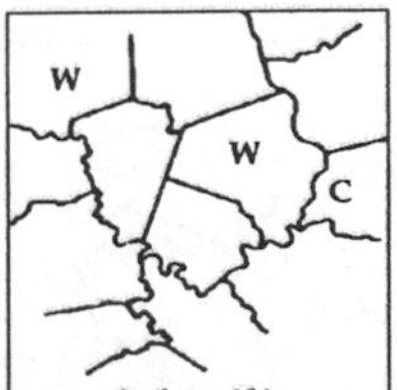

S. fragilis

Salix fragilis L. CRACK WILLOW
An escape from cultivation. Infrequent. Introduced.

Salix humilis March. PRAIRIE WILLOW
A single record, Fayette (UK)

Salix missouriensis Bebb.
A single record, Franklin (UK).

S. nigra

Salix nigra Marsh. BLACK WILLOW
Common on margins of rivers, creeks, and ponds.

Salix purpurea L. BASKET WILLOW, PURPLE OSIER
An escape from former cultivation. Jessamine (McF). Introduced.

Salix rigida Muhl. HEART-LEAF WILLOW
A single record, Jessamine (McF).

C. cordiformis

Salix sericea Marsh. SILKY WILLOW
On creek margins. Infrequent. Fayette (UK); Franklin (UK).

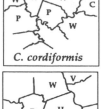

Juglandaceae: Walnut Family

Carya cordiformis (Wang.) K. Koch BITTERNUT HICKORY
Common in mesic woods, in pastures, and along roadsides.

C. glabra

C. laciniosa

Carya glabra (Mill.) PIGNUT HICKORY
Frequent on wooded cliffs; fairly frequent in dry, open upland woods.

Carya laciniosa (Michx.) Loud. KINGNUT, SHELLBARK HICKORY
Frequent in rich woods on slopes and bottomlands and in woodland borders.

C. ovalis

C. ovata

Carya ovalis (Wang.) Sarg.
[Including, in addition to the typical, var. *odorata* (Marsh.) Sarg.] SWEET PIGNUT
On river bluffs, in pastures, and in borders of woods. Infrequent.

Carya ovata (Mill.) K. Koch SHAGBARK HICKORY
With oaks on south-facing slopes and cliffs and in upland woods. Frequent.

C. tomentosa

J. cinerea

Carya tomentosa Nutt. MOCKERNUT HICKORY
On open-wooded river bluffs and dry, south-facing slopes. Infrequent.

Juglans cinerea L. BUTTERNUT, WHITE WALNUT
In rich woods. Infrequent.

J. nigra

Juglans nigra L. BLACK WALNUT
Common in fencerows, dooryards, and pastures and along roadsides. Frequent in mesic woods.

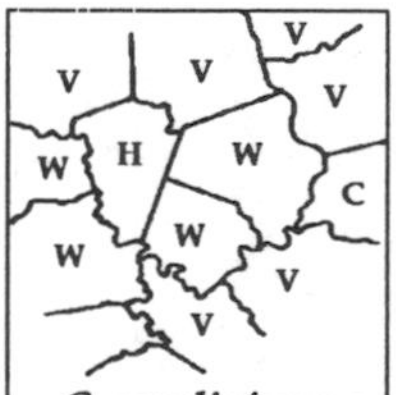

C. caroliniana

Betulaceae: Birch Family

Alnus serrulata (Ait.) Willd. ALDER
On floodplain of Kentucky River. A single record, Madison (JBV).

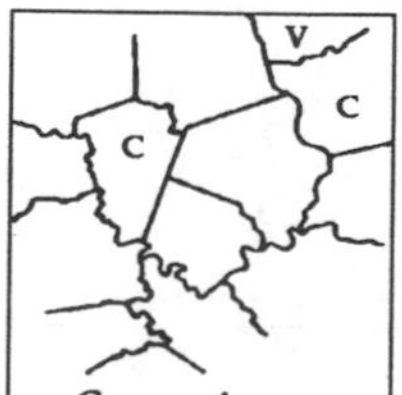

C. americana

Carpinus caroliniana Walt. var. *virginiana* (Marsh.) Fernald. HORNBEAN, BLUE BEECH
Common in wooded ravines and on creek banks.

O. virginiana

Corylus americana Walt. HAZELNUT
In fencerows in bottomlands. Rare.

Ostrya virginiana (Mill.) K. Koch IRONWOOD, HOP-HORNBEAM
Frequent on wooded cliffs, dry hillsides, and ridge tops.

Fagaceae: Beech Family

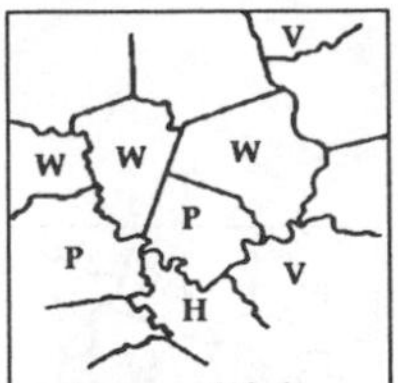

F. grandifolia

Fagus grandifolia Ehrh. BEECH
Infrequent but widely distributed in mesophytic woods.

F. grandifolia var. caroliniana

F. grandifolia var. *caroliniana* (Loud.) Fern. & Rehd.
Same habitat as the typical.

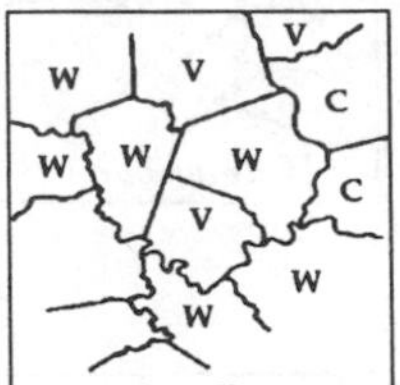

Q. alba

Quercus alba L. WHITE OAK
Fairly frequent on wooded cliffs and south-facing slopes.

Q. bicolor

Quercus bicolor Willd. SWAMP WHITE OAK
In swamps, on floodplains, and on creek margins. Infrequent but widely distributed.

Q. imbricaria

Quercus imbricaria Michx. SHINGLE OAK
In open woods and borders of woods. Infrequent.

Quercus lyrata Walt. OVERCUP OAK
In wet ground in a sink. A single locality, Jessamine (UK).

Q. macrocarpa

Quercus macrocarpa Michx. BUR OAK
Frequent in pastures and other open, grassy places in the plateau area of the Inner Bluegrass.

Q. muehlenbergii

Quercus muehlenbergii Engelm. CHINQUAPIN OAK
Common throughout the region. In pastures, along old roads, and on wooded bluffs, ravine slopes, and uplands.

Q. rubra

Quercus rubra L.
[= *Q. borealis* Michx. f. var. *maxima* Ashe] RED OAK
Common in mesophytic woods, especially on riverbank cliffs and ravine slopes.

Q. shumardii

Quercus shumardii Buckl. SHUMARD RED OAK
In rich, moist, well-drained soil on mesophytic wooded slopes, in pastures, and along old roads. A characteristic and fairly common tree of the region.

Q. stellata

Quercus stellata Wang. POST OAK
In dry open woods on rocky, often eroded, ground. Infrequent.

Q. velutina

Quercus velutina Lam. BLACK OAK, QUERCITRON OAK
In pastures and woodland borders on uplands. Very infrequent.

Ulmaceae: Elm Family

C. laevigata

Celtis laevigata Willd. SUGARBERRY
On lowlands. Very infrequent.

C. occidentalis

Celtis occidentalis L. HACKBERRY
A highly variable, polymorphic species. In open woods, pastures, old fields, fencerows, and roadsides in dry, mesic, or moist situations. Common.

C. tenuifolia

Celtis tenuifolia Nutt. (typical) DWARF HACKBERRY
In old fields and other open situations in dry ground. Frequent.

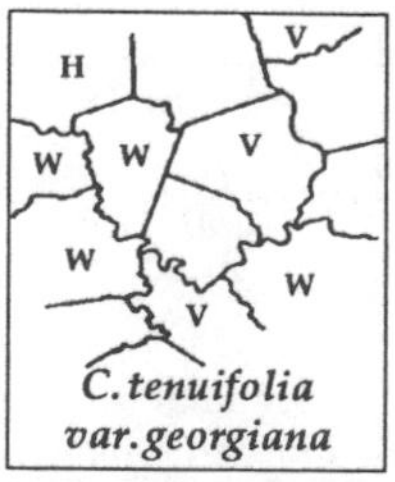

C. tenuifolia var. georgiana

C. tenuifolia var. *georgiana* (Small) Fern. & Schub.
Same habitat as the typical.

Ulmus alata Michx. WINGED ELM
On dry ridges, bluffs, and slopes. Rare. Jessamine (McF).

U. americana

Ulmus americana L. AMERICAN ELM
On river and creek banks, floodplains, and roadsides, and in wooded coves, pastures, and old fields. Large trees are becoming less common because of disease.

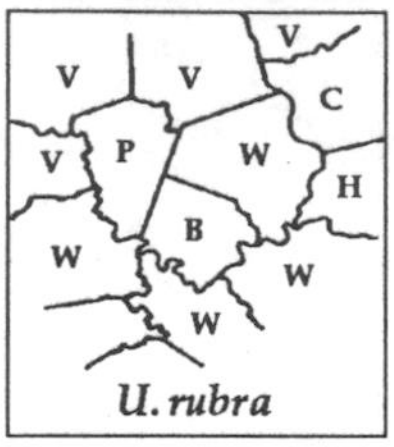

U. rubra

Ulmus rubra Muhl. SLIPPERY ELM
In open woods, woodland borders, and old fields, in both dry and moist situations. Frequent.

Ulmus serotina Sarg. SEPTEMBER ELM
On river floodplains. Rare. Fayette (JBV); Harrison (JBV).

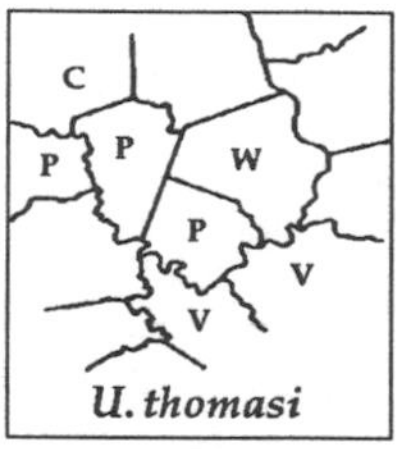

U. thomasi

Ulmus thomasi Sarg. ROCK ELM, CORK ELM
Fairly frequent on dry limestone bluffs and slopes, especially in rock at cliff edges.

Moraceae: Mulberry Family

B. papyrifera

Broussonetia papyrifera (L.) Vent. PAPER MULBERRY
An escape in waste places and along farm roads. Infrequent. Introduced.

M. pomifera

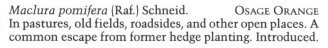

Maclura pomifera (Raf.) Schneid. OSAGE ORANGE
In pastures, old fields, roadsides, and other open places. A common escape from former hedge planting. Introduced.

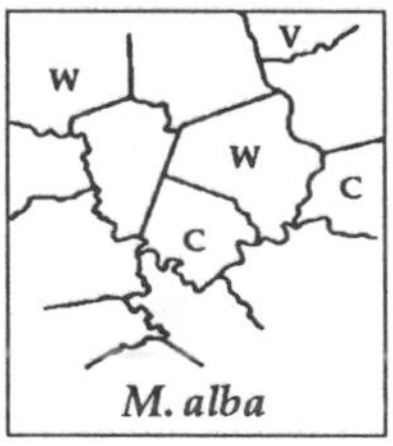

M. alba

Morus alba L. WHITE MULBERRY
In fencerows, along roadsides, and in other open places to which it has escaped. Infrequent. Introduced.

M. rubra

Morus rubra L. RED MULBERRY
In thickets, fencerows, open woods and edges of woods. Common.

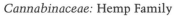

Cannabinaceae: Hemp Family

C. sativa

Cannabis sativa L. HEMP
A frequent escape from former cultivation. Introduced.

Humulus japonicus Sieb. & Zucc. JAPANESE HOPS
In waste places. Recorded only from Fayette (MEW). Introduced.

Urticaceae: Nettle Family

B. cylindrica

Boehmeria cylindrica (L.) Sw. FALSE NETTLE
Fairly common on banks and floodplains of rivers and slow creeks, usually wooded.

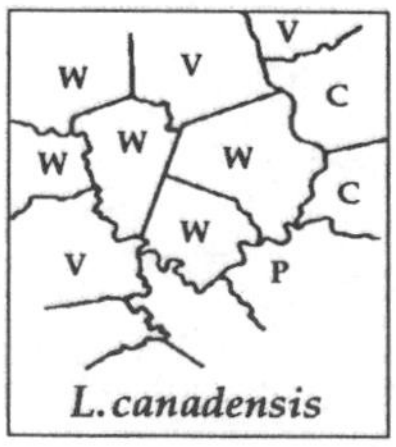

L. canadensis

Laportea canadensis (L.) Wedd. WOOD-NETTLE
Frequent on wooded creek banks, in swamps, and in mesophytic woods.

P. pensylvanica

Parietaria pensylvanica Muhl. PELLITORY
On open wooded slopes. Infrequent.

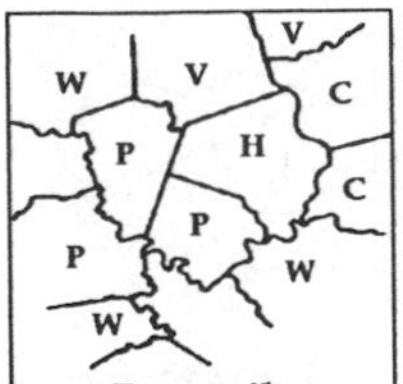

P. pumila

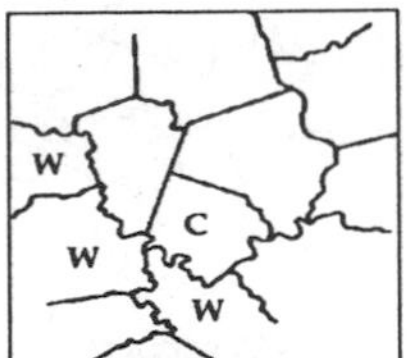

P. pumila var. deamii

Pilea pumila (L.) Gray (typical) CLEARWEED
Frequent on shady creek banks and in areas of springs.

P. pumila var. *deamii* (Lunell) Fernald
Same habitat as the typical but less frequent.

U. chamaedrioides

Urtica chamaedryoides Pursh NETTLE
Fairly frequent in moist woods and thickets.

Urtica dioica L. NETTLE
Infrequent. Scott (JBV); Woodford (EC). Introduced.

Urtica procera Muhl. NETTLE
A single record, Jessamine (McF).

Santalaceae: Sandalwood Family

Comandra umbellata (L.) Nutt. BASTARD TOADFLAX
On the top of a bluff above a creek. A single record, Franklin (MEW).

P. flavescens

Pyrularia pubera Michx. BUFFALO-NUT
A single record, Jessamine (McF).

Loranthaceae: Mistletoe Family

Phoradendron flavescens (Pursh) Nutt. MISTLETOE
Parasitic on several species of trees, most frequently on black walnut but occasionally on elm, hackberry, and others.

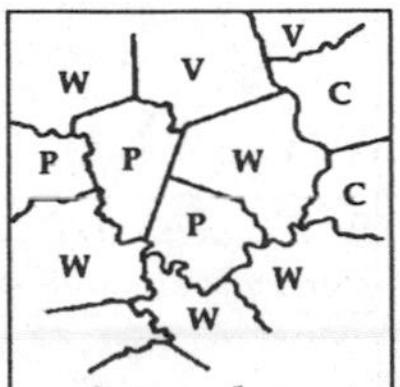

A. canadense

A. canadense var. acuminata

Aristolochiaceae: Birthwort Family

Aristolochia serpentaria L. VIRGINIA SNAKEROOT
A single record, Woodford (EC).

Asarum canadense L. (typical) WILD GINGER
Frequent in rich woods, especially on ravine slopes.

A. canadense var. *acuminata* Ashe
Same habitat as the typical variety.

P. aviculare

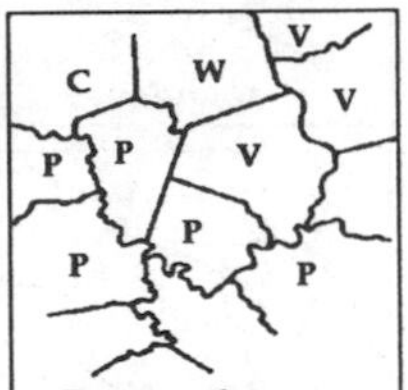

P. caespitosum

Polygonaceae: Buckwheat Family

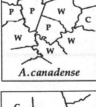

Polygonum aviculare L. KNOTWEED
A weed fairly frequent near dwellings, especially along paths and roadways. Introduced.

Polygonum caespitosum Blume var. *longisetum* (DeBruyn) Stewart
Fairly frequent in wet ground, such as creek banks and roadside ditches. Introduced.

P. convolvulus

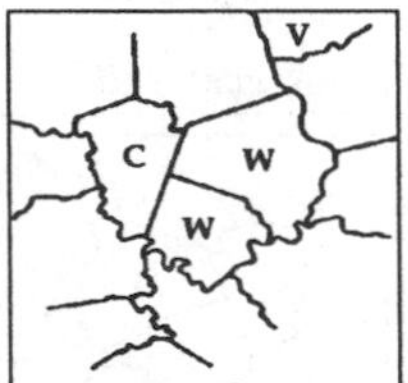

P. cuspidatum

Polygonum convolvulus L. BLACK BINDWEED
Fairly frequent on roadsides and in waste places. Introduced.

Polygonum cuspidatum Sieb. & Zucc. JAPANESE KNOTWEED
In waste places. An escape from cultivation. Introduced.

Polygonum dubium Stein SMARTWEED
On pond margins. Infrequent. Madison (MEW); Mercer (MEW). Introduced.

P. erectum

P. hydropiper

Polygonum erectum L. Knotweed
In waste places and other disturbed areas. Infrequent.

Polygonum hydropiper L. Water-pepper
Wet ground. Infrequent. Introduced.

Polygonum hydropiperoides Michx. Water-pepper
In wet ground. Infrequent.

P. hydropiperoides

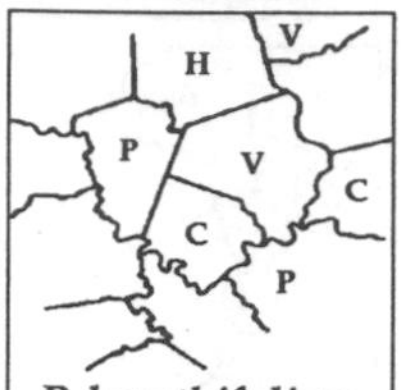

P. lapathifolium

Polygonum lapathifolium L. Smartweed
Fairly frequent in wet or moist situations, especially in disturbed areas.

Polygonum orientale L. Prince's Feather
An escape from cultivation. Fayette (UK); Jessamine (McF). Introduced.

P. pensylvanicum

P. persicaria

Polygonum pensylvanicum L. Smartweed
Common in moist, sunny situations, such as depressions in fields.

Polygonum persicaria L. Smartweed
A common weed in low ground. Introduced.

Polygonum punctatum Ell. (typical) Water-smartweed
On margins of ponds and slow streams and in swamps. Common.

P. punctatum

P. punctatum var. leptostachyum

P. punctatum var. *leptostachyum* (Meisn.) Small
Same habitat as the typical. Common.

Polygonum sagittatum L.
In wet situations. Infrequent. Fayette (UK); Jessamine (UK).

P. scandens

P. scandens var. cristatum

Polygonum scandens L. (typical)
Climbing False Buckwheat
Common in thickets, on edges of fields and woods, and on roadsides.

P. scandens var. *cristatum* (Engelm. & Gray) Gleason
In thickets and on edges of woods. Less common than the typical variety.

R. acetosella

R. altissimus

Rumex acetosella L. Field Sorrel, Sheep Sorrel
A common weed in fields and overgrazed pastures. Introduced.

Rumex altissimus Wood Water Dock
In standing water of swamps and on margins of quiet streams. Infrequent.

R. crispus

R. obtusifolius

Rumex crispus L. Curly Dock, Sour Dock
A common farm weed. Introduced.

Rumex mexicanus Meisn. Mexican Dock
On moist banks. Fayette (UK).

Rumex obtusifolius L. Bitter Dock
Fairly common in fields and barnyards. Introduced.

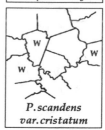

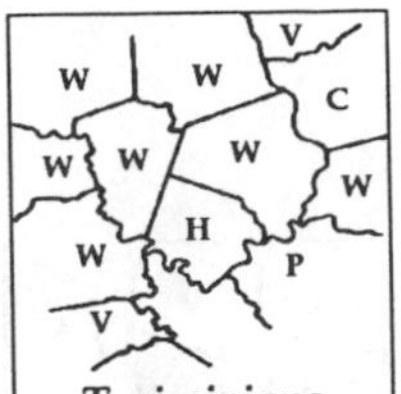

T. virginiana

Tovara virginiana (L.) Raf. JUMPSEED, VIRGINIA KNOTWEED

Common in moist thickets, on wooded mesic slopes, and on stream banks.

C. album

Chenopodiaceae: Goosefoot Family

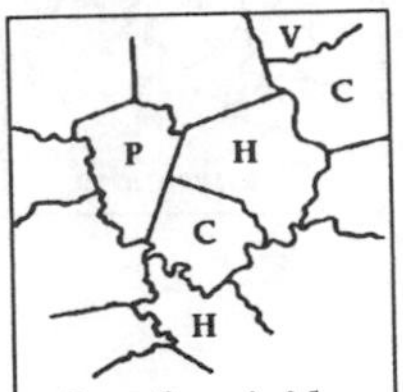

C. ambrosioides

Chenopodium album L. LAMB'S-QUARTERS

A very common weed in cultivated ground and barnyards. Introduced.

Chenopodium ambrosioides L. MEXICAN TEA

A weed in moist ground, especially near streams. Frequent. Introduced.

Chenopodium gigantospermum Aellen
[= *C. hybridum* L. var. *gigantospermum* (Aellen) Rouleau] MAPLE-LEAVED GOOSEFOOT

On rich wooded north slope above the Kentucky River. A single record, Mercer (MEW).

Chenopodium missouriensis Aellen
[= *C. paganum* Reichenb.] PIGWEED

Bourbon (EG); Fayette (UK).

Chenopodium murale L. WALL GOOSEFOOT

A single record, Woodford (EC). Introduced.

Chenopodium standleyanum Aellen
[= *C. hybridum* L. var. *standleyanum* (Aellen) Fernald]

A single record, Franklin (UK).

Amaranthaceae: Amaranth Family

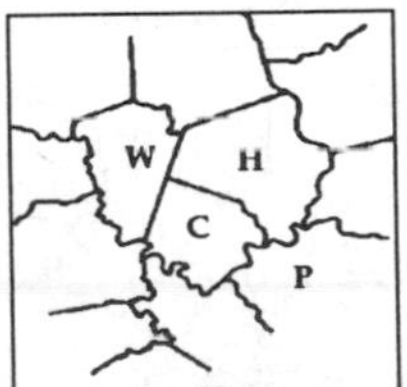

A. albus

Amaranthus albus L. TUMBLEWEED

A roadside weed. Infrequent.

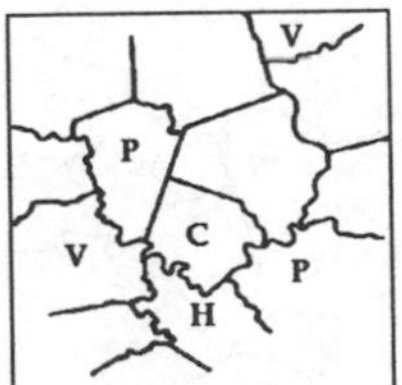

A. hybridus

Amaranthus cruentus L. PURPLE AMARANTH

Fayette (UK). Introduced.

Amaranthus graecizans L. TUMBLEWEED

Fayette (UK).

Amaranthus hybridus L. PIGWEED

A common weed in cultivated fields. Introduced.

Amaranthus retroflexus L. PIGWEED

A weed in cultivated fields. Fayette (UK); Jessamine (McF). Introduced.

A. spinosus

Amaranthus spinosus L. THORNY AMARANTH

A common weed on roadsides, in fields, and in gravelly creek beds. Introduced.

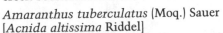

I. rhizomatosa

Amaranthus tuberculatus (Moq.) Sauer
[*Acnida altissima* Riddel] WATER HEMP

A single record, Franklin (HB).

Iresine rhizomatosa Standl. BLOODLEAF

In rich, moist woods, on north-facing cliffs and in alluvium at base of cliffs. Fairly frequent.

M. nictaginea

Nyctaginaceae: Four-o'clock Family

Mirabilis nictaginea (Michx.) Sweet UMBRELLA-WORT
In waste places and other open areas. Infrequent. Introduced.

P. americana

Phytolaccaceae: Pokeweed Family

Phytolacca americana L. POKEWEED
In borders of fields and woods, fencerows, disturbed areas within woodlands, waste ground, and roadsides. Abundant.

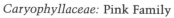

M. verticillata

Aizoaceae: Carpet-weed Family

Mollugo verticillata L. CARPET-WEED
A common weed in moist ground in gardens and cultivated fields. Introduced.

Portulacaceae: Purslane Family

Claytonia caroliniana Michx.
BROAD-LEAVED SPRING-BEAUTY
On rich wooded slopes. Rare. Clark (MRB); Fayette (UK).

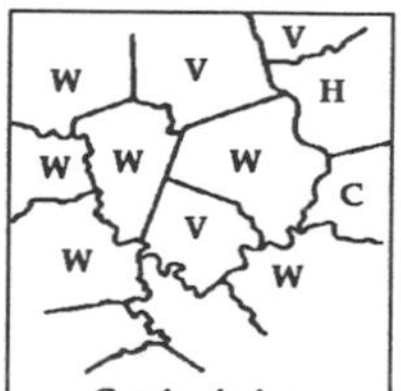

C. virginica

Claytonia virginica L. SPRING-BEAUTY
Frequent in forests and open woodlands. Locally abundant in parklands.

P. oleracea

Portulaca oleracea L. COMMON PURSLANE
A weed in gardens and cultivated fields. Frequent. Introduced.

Caryophyllaceae: Pink Family

A. githago

Agrostemma githago L. CORN COCKLE
In fields, on roadsides, and in waste places. Infrequent. Introduced.

A. fontinalis

Arenaria fontinalis (Short & Peter) Shinners
[= *Stellaria fontinalis* (Short & Peter) Robinson]
On dripping ledges above creeks. Rare. Clark (UK); Fayette (UK); Jessamine (C&M).

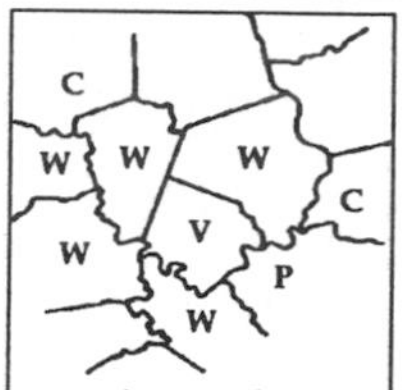

A. patula

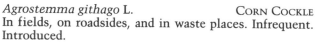

Arenaria patula Michx. (typical) SANDWORT, WILD BABY'S-BREATH
Frequent in thin soil on limestone cliffs and ledges.

A. serpyllifolia

A. patula var. *robusta* (Stey.) Maguire
Garrard (MEW).

Arenaria serpyllifolia L. THYME-LEAVED SANDWORT
Fairly frequent in dry rocky ground in open woods or gravelly stream banks and in other open situations. Introduced.

Cerastium arvense L. FIELD CHICKWEED
In grassy areas. Infrequent. Anderson (Bry.); Fayette (UK); Jessamine (UK).

C. glomeratum

Cerastium glomeratum Thuill.
[= *C. viscosum* of American authors, not L.]
MOUSE-EAR CHICKWEED
Frequent in grassy fields and on roadsides.

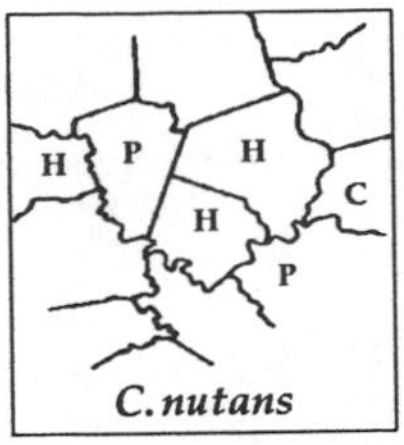

C. nutans

Cerastium nutans Raf. NODDING CHICKWEED
Frequent in moist soil in pastures, fields, and open, disturbed woods.

Cerastium viscosum L. MOUSE-EAR CHICKWEED
Waste places, fields, and roadsides. Fairly frequent. Fayette (UK); Woodford (EC). Introduced.

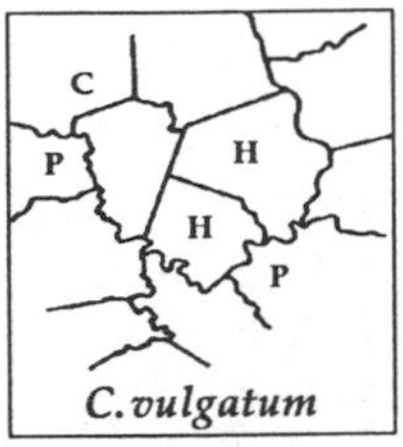

C. vulgatum

Cerastium vulgatum L. COMMON CHICKWEED
In pastures, cultivated fields, lawns, and roadsides. Very frequent. Introduced.

D. armeria

Dianthus armeria L. DEPTFORD PINK
In fencerows, old fields, thickets, edges of woods, and roadsides. Frequent. Introduced.

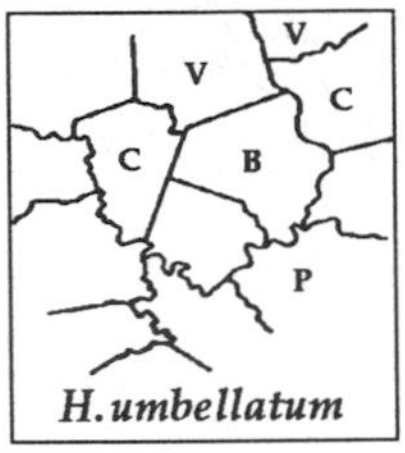

H. umbellatum

Holosteum umbellatum L. JAGGED CHICKWEED
In pastures, fields, and roadsides. Fairly frequent. Introduced.

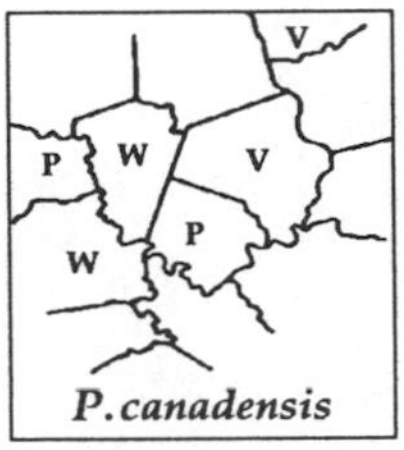

P. canadensis

Lychnis dioica L. RED CAMPION
A single record, Franklin (SR). Introduced.

Paronychia canadensis (L.) Wood. FORKED CHICKWEED
Fairly frequent in dry open woods, especially with red cedar on rocky slopes.

S. officinalis

Sagina decumbens (Ell.) T. & G. PEARLWORT
On paths and in openings in woods. Infrequent. Clark (MEW); Woodford (UK).

S. alba

Saponaria officinalis L. BOUNCING BET, SOAPWORT
Abundant along roadsides and railroad embankments; common on grassy banks and in other open areas. Introduced.

Silene alba (Mill.) Krause
[=*Lychnis alba* Mill.] WHITE CAMPION
A weed, especially common on roadsides. Introduced.

S. antirrhina

Silene antirrhina L. SLEEPY CATCHFLY
In open situations. Infrequent.

S. caroliniana

Silene caroliniana Walt. var. *wherryi* (Small) Fernald. WILD PINK
Frequent on cliffs in the gorges of the Kentucky River and tributary streams; locally profuse.

S. noctiflora

Silene cucubalus Wibel BLADDER CAMPION
Woodford (EC). Introduced.

S. rotundifolia

Silene noctiflora L. NIGHT-FLOWERING CATCHFLY
Along roadsides. Fairly frequent. Introduced.

Silene rotundifolia Nutt. ROUND-LEAVED FIRE-PINK
Under overhanging cliffs. Infrequent.

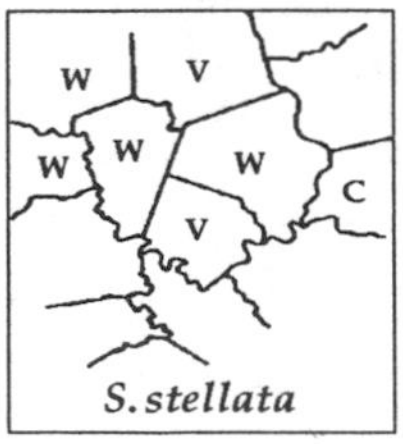

S. stellata

Silene stellata (L.) Ait. f. STARRY CAMPION
Frequent in open woods.

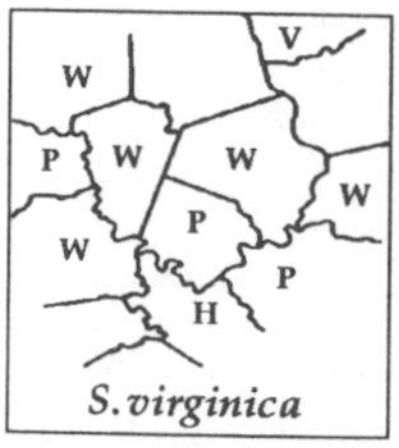

S. virginica

Silene virginica L. FIRE-PINK
Frequent on mesic and rocky wooded slopes and in open woods.

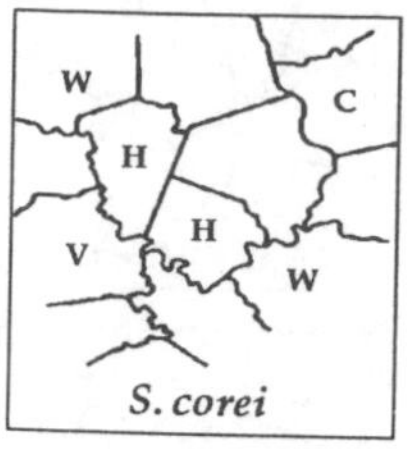

S. corei

Spergula arvensis L. SPURREY
A weed in cultivated ground. Fayette (UK). Introduced.

Stellaria corei Shinner
[*S. pubera* var. *silvatica* (Beguinet) Weath.]
GREAT CHICKWEED
Frequent on mesophytic wooded slopes.

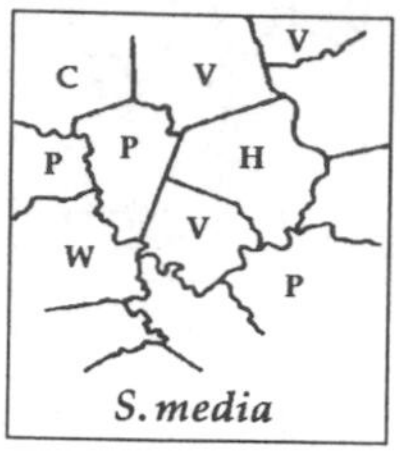

S. media

Stellaria media (L.) Cyrill. CHICKWEED
A weed abundant in lawns and gardens. Introduced.

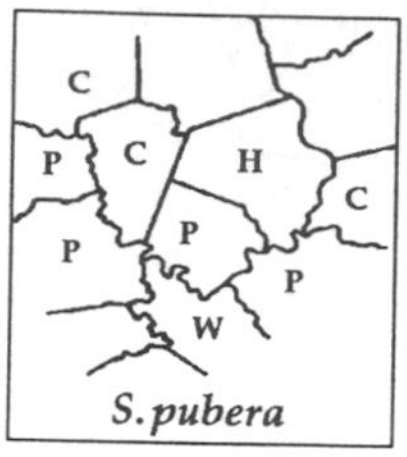

S. pubera

Stellaria pubera Michx. GREAT CHICKWEED
Frequent on mesophytic wooded slopes.

Nymphaeaceae: Water-lily Family

Nymphaea odorata Ait. WATER-LILY
In ponds. A single record, Jessamine (McF).

Nelumbonaceae: Lotus Family

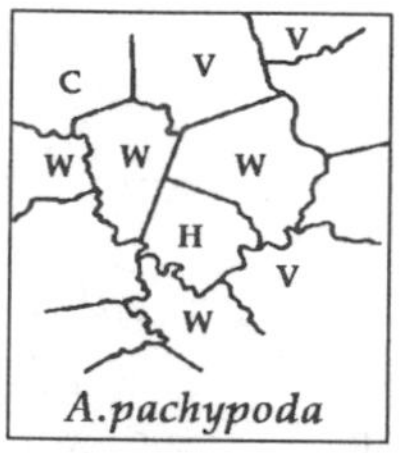

A. pachypoda

Nelumbo lutea (Willd.) Pers. AMERICAN LOTUS
In ponds. A single record, Jessamine (McF).

Ranunculaceae: Buttercup Family

A. virginiana

Actaea pachypoda Ell. WHITE BANEBERRY
Fairly frequent on rich, mesophytic wooded slopes.

Anemone virginiana L. TALL ANEMONE, THIMBLEWEED
Frequent at the edges of woods, in thickets, and in open woods.

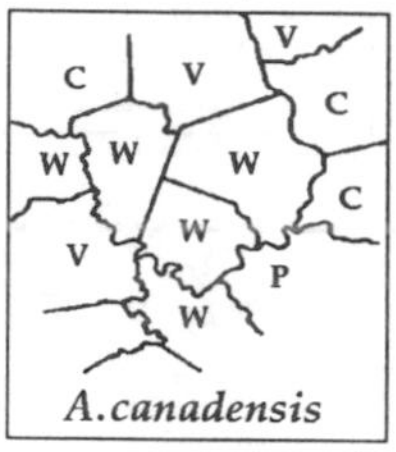

A. canadensis

Aquilegia canadensis L. COLUMBINE
Frequent on ledges and in crevices of cliffs and in rocky valleys.

Cimicifuga racemosa (L.) Nutt. BLACK COHOSH, BUGBANE
In rich moist woodlands. Rare. Fayette (UK).

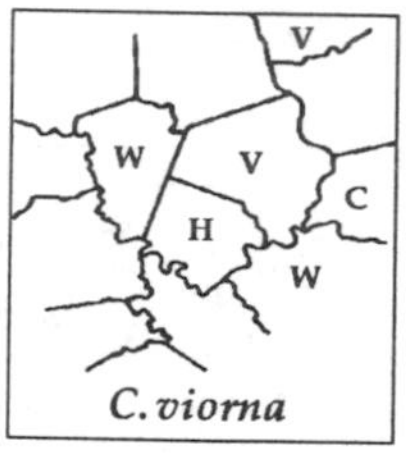

C. viorna

Clematis dioscoreifolia Levl. & Van.
On creek banks, an escape from cultivation. Bourbon (EG); Franklin (SR). Introduced.

C. virginiana

Clematis viorna L. LEATHER FLOWER
Fairly frequent in rich thickets and woodland borders.

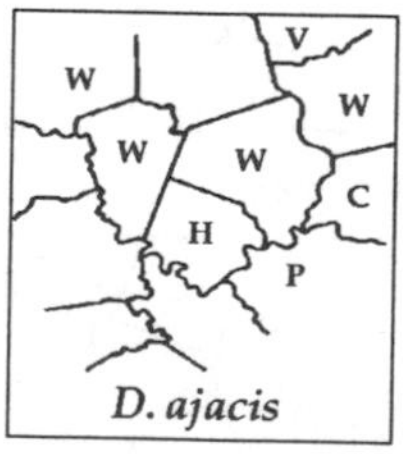

D. ajacis

Clematis virginiana L. VIRGIN'S-BOWER
Frequent in moist thickets and grassy edges of woods.

Delphinium ajacis L. LARKSPUR
A frequent escape from cultivation, found in sunny, rocky fields, on roadsides, and in other open situations. Introduced.

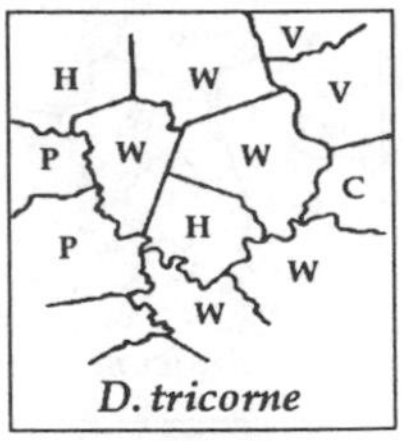

D. tricorne

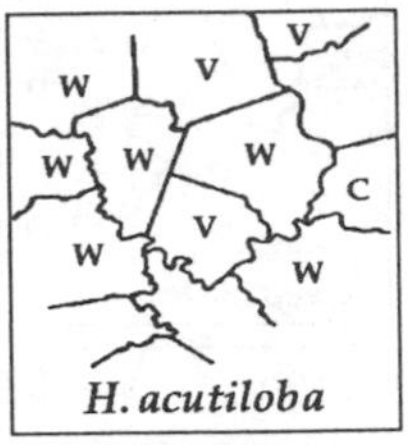

H. acutiloba

Dephinium tricorne Michx. DWARF LARKSPUR
Frequent in woods: on both dry rocky and rich mesic slopes. Locally profuse.

Hepatica acutiloba DC. HEPATICA
Frequent on rich mesophytic wooded slopes and north-facing cliffs.

Hydrastis canadensis L. GOLDENSEAL
On mesophytic wooded slopes. Now rare. Garrard (JBV); Harrison (JBV); Jessamine (JBV).

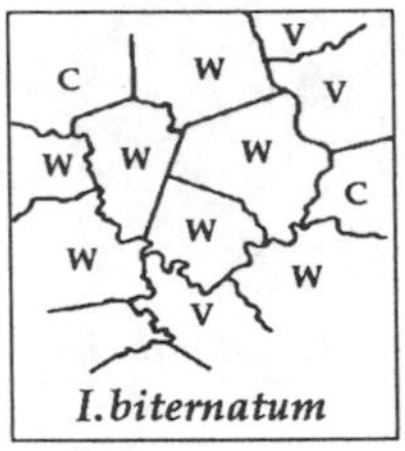

I. biternatum

Isopyrum biternatum (Raf.) T. & G. FALSE RUE ANEMONE
Frequent in rich mesophytic woods; locally profuse.

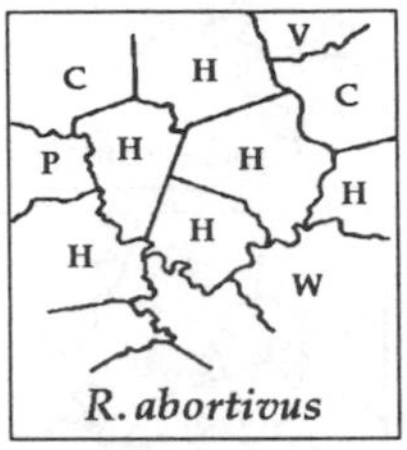

R. abortivus

Ranunculus abortivus L. SMALL-FLOWERED CROWFOOT
Frequent in woodlands and woodland borders. Introduced.

Ranunculus acris L. TALL BUTTERCUP
In low ground. Rare. Fayette (MEW); Franklin (WB). Introduced.

Ranunculus aquatilis L.
[=*R. trichophyllus* Chaix] WHITE WATER-CROWFOOT
Submersed in water. A single record, Fayette (UK).

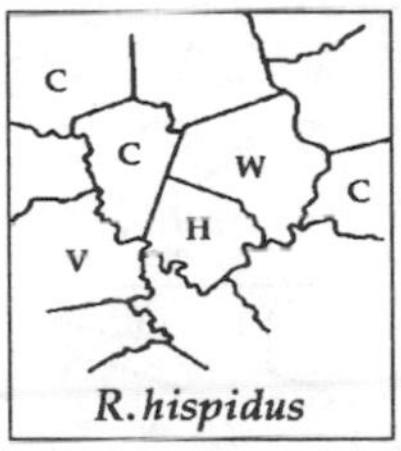

R. hispidus

Ranunculus fascicularis Muhl. EARLY BUTTERCUP
In open woods on dry slopes. Rare. Anderson (MEW); Jessamine (UK).

Ranunculus hispidus Michx. (typical) BUTTERCUP
On mesophytic slopes and margins of small streams. Infrequent.

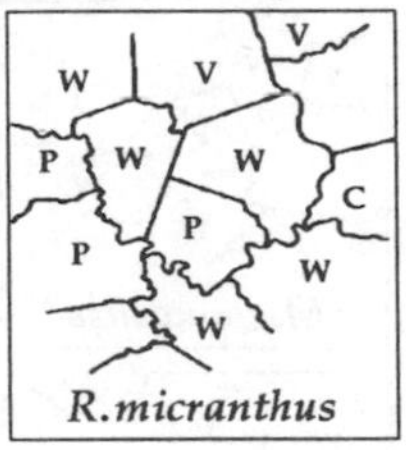

R. micranthus

Ranunculus longirostris Gordon WHITE WATER-CROWFOOT
In running water. A single record, Jessamine (UK).

Ranunculus micranthus Nutt. SMALL-FLOWERED CROWFOOT
Common in open woods, edges of woods, thickets, and meadows.

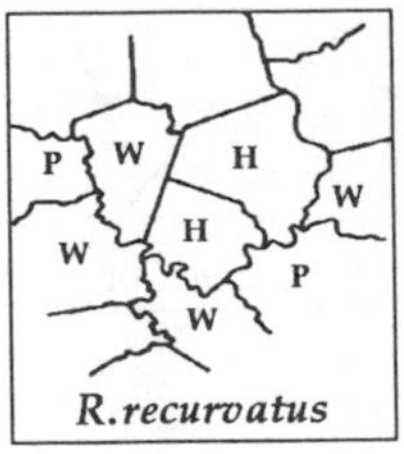

R. recurvatus

Ranunculus parviflorus L.

An introduced weed. A single record, Fayette (Benson).

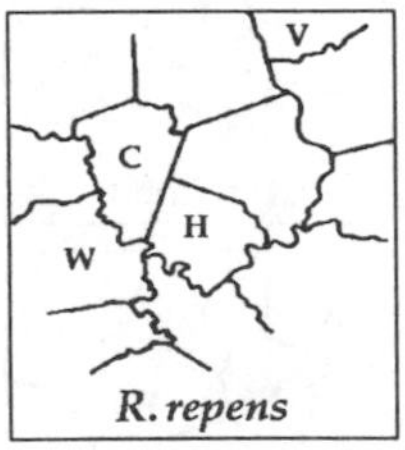

R. repens

Ranunculus recurvatus Poir. HOOKED CROWFOOT
Frequent on moist wooded slopes and in valleys.

Ranunculus repens L. CREEPING BUTTERCUP
An escape, occasionally naturalized in open, moist sites. Introduced.

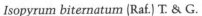

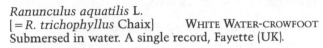

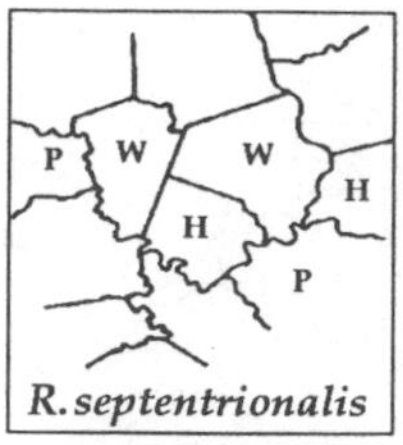

R. septentrionalis

Ranunculus septentrionalis Poir. SWAMP BUTTERCUP
On creek margins and floodplains. Infrequent.

T. dioicum

Thalictrum dioicum L. EARLY MEADOW RUE
Frequent on mesophytic wooded slopes.

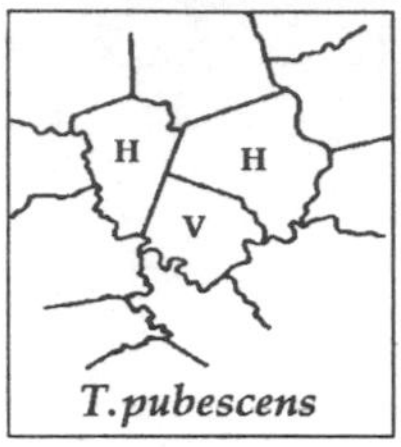

T. pubescens

Thalictrum pubescens Pursh.
[= *T. polygamum* Muhl.] MEADOW RUE
In alluvial woodlands and on grassy floodplains of Kentucky River. Rare.

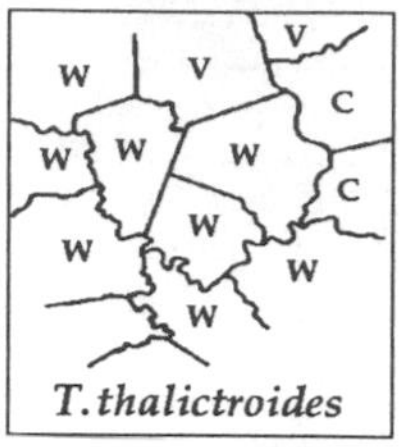

T. thalictroides

Thalictrum thalictroides (L.) Boivin
[= *Anemonella thalictroides* (L.) Spach.] RUE ANEMONE
In woods. Frequent.

Berberidaceae: Barberry Family

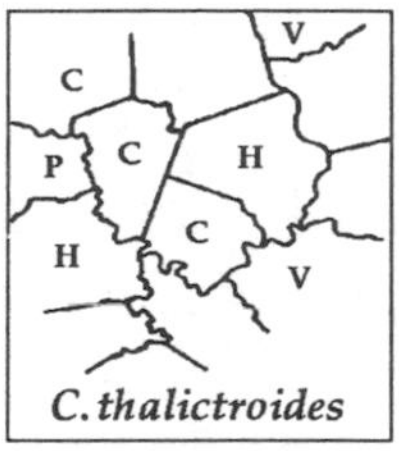

C. thalictroides

Caulophyllum thalictroides (L.) Michx. BLUE COHOSH
In rich mesophytic woods. Infrequent.

J. diphylla

Jeffersonia diphylla (L.) Pers. TWINLEAF
Frequent on rich wooded slopes, usually steep; locally profuse.

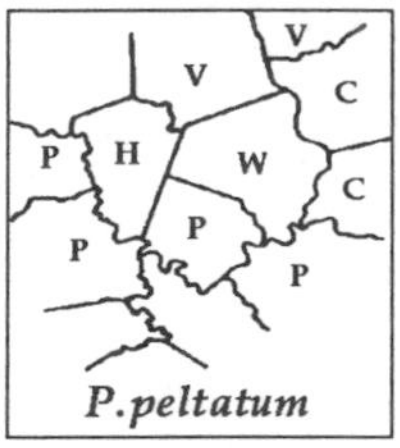

P. peltatum

Podophyllum peltatum L. MAY-APPLE
Fairly common in open woods.

Menispermaceae: Moonseed Family

C. carolinus

Cocculus carolinus (L.) DC. CAROLINA SNAILSEED
Fairly frequent in thickets and woodland borders; locally profuse.

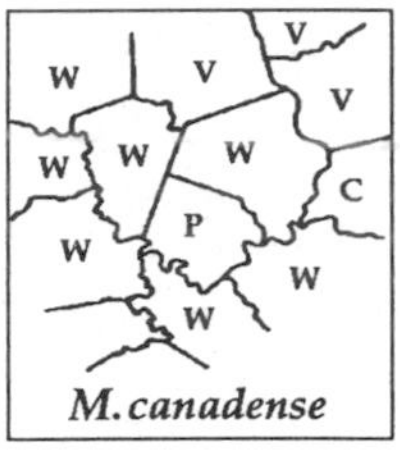

M. canadense

Menispermum canadense L. MOONSEED
Very frequent in thickets, open woods, and woodland borders.

Magnoliaceae: Magnolia Family

L. tulipifera

Liriodendron tulipifera L. TULIP POPLAR
Fairly frequent on rich mesic slopes and occasionally on the floodplain of the Kentucky River.

Annonaceae: Custard-apple Family

A. triloba

Asimina triloba (L.) Dunal. PAPAW
In thickets, woods, and open situations; on floodplains, creek banks, and hillsides. Common.

Lauraceae: Laurel Family

L. benzoin

Lindera benzoin (L.) Blume SPICEBUSH
On mesophytic wooded slopes and in valleys. Frequent.

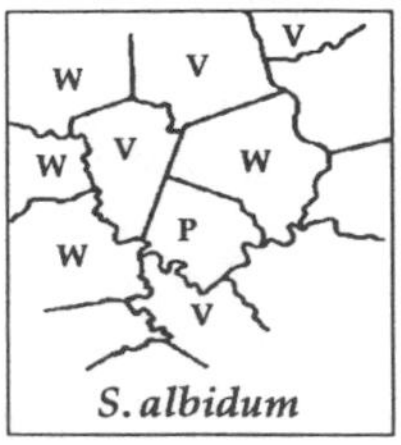

S. albidum

Sassafras albidum (Nutt.) Nees SASSAFRAS
Frequent in thickets and on open-wooded hillsides and bluffs.

Papaveraceae: Poppy Family

Argemone alba Lestib. WHITE PRICKLY POPPY
An escape from cultivation. Fayette (UK). Introduced.

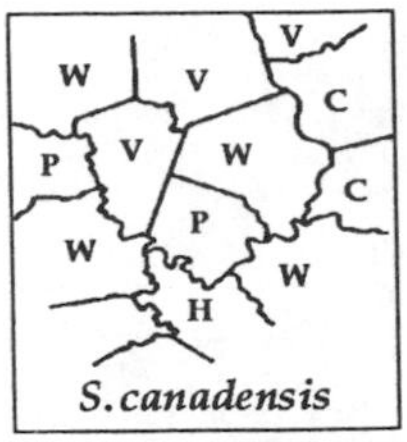

S. canadensis

Chelidonium majus L. CELANDINE
An escape in rich ground by road. Fayette (UK); Scott (MEW). Introduced.

Sanguinaria canadensis L. BLOODROOT
Frequent on wooded, mesic slopes and cliffs.

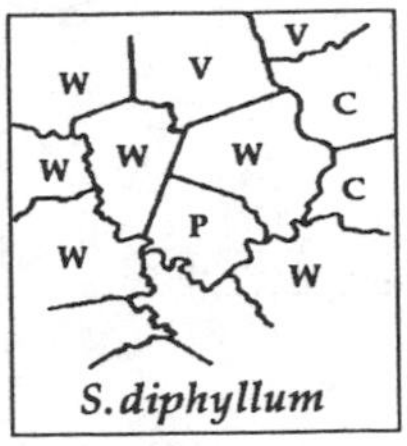

S. diphyllum

Stylophorum diphyllum (Michx.) Nutt. CELANDINE POPPY
Frequent in deep leaf-mold on rich, moist wooded slopes.

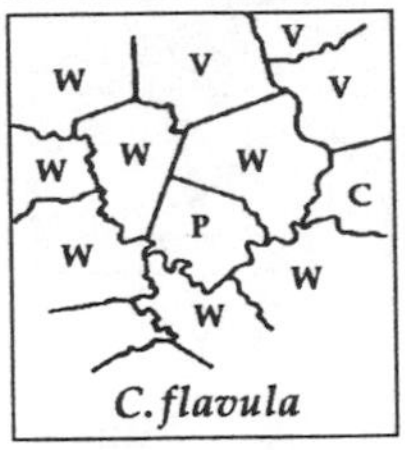

C. flavula

Fumariaceae: Fumitory Family

Corydalis flavula (Raf.) DC. YELLOW CORYDALIS
Common in rich soil in thickets, open woods, and edges of woods.

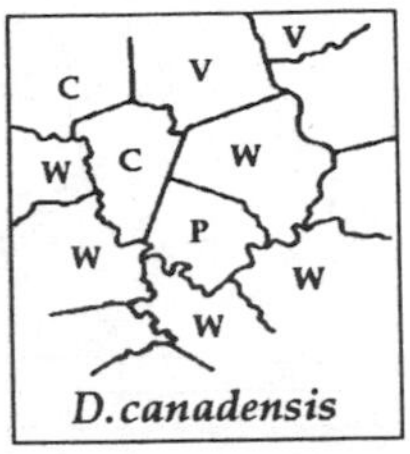

D. canadensis

Dicentra canadensis (Goldie) Walp. SQUIRREL-CORN
In deep humus on rich, wooded, mesic slopes. Less frequent than the following species.

D. cucullaria

Dicentra cucullaria (L.) Bernh. DUTCHMAN'S-BREECHES
Frequent on rich, wooded, mesic slopes.

Brassicaceae: Mustard Family

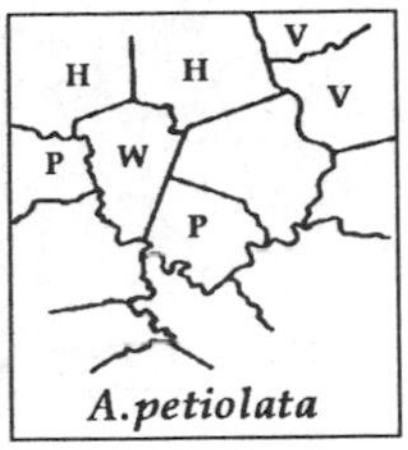

A. petiolata

Alliaria petiolata (Bieb.) Cavara
[= *A. officinalis* Andrz.] GARLIC MUSTARD
Along roadsides. Infrequent. Introduced.

Alyssum alyssoides L.
On roadside. A single record, Jessamine (McF). Introduced.

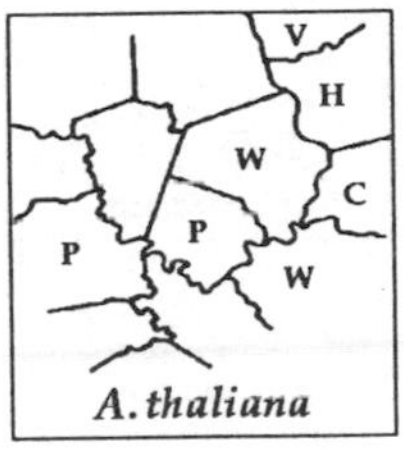

A. thaliana

Arabidopsis thaliana (L.) Heyn. MOUSE-EAR CRESS
Frequent in fields, in pastures, and on roadsides. Introduced.

Arabis canadensis L. SICKLEPOD
Dry rocky woods. Infrequent. Fayette (JBV); Woodford (JBV).

Arabis hirsuta (L.) Scop. var. *pycnocarpa* (Hopkins) Rollins
Rare. Franklin (NP).

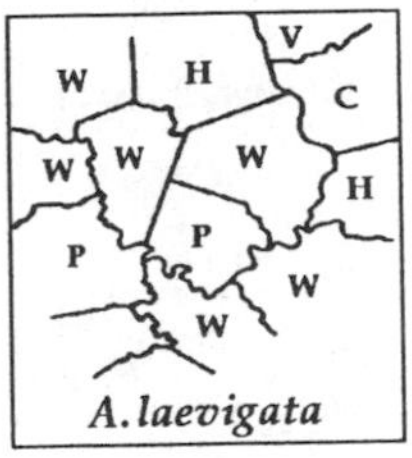

A. laevigata

Arabis laevigata (Muhl.) Poir. SMOOTH ROCKCRESS
Frequent in dry open woods.

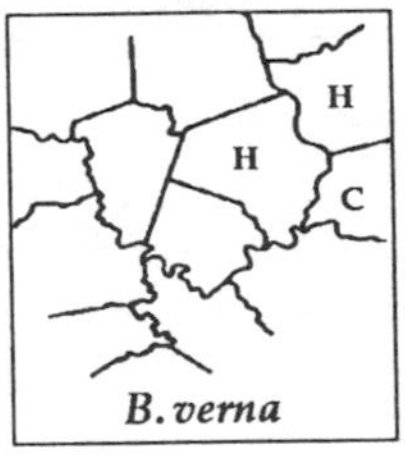

B. verna

Arabis perstellata Braun
In humus on steep rocky slopes in woods. Rare. Franklin (ELB). Var. *shortii* Fern., Franklin (SR).

Barbarea verna (Mill.) Aschers EARLY WINTERCRESS
On creek banks and in other moist situations. Introduced. Infrequent.

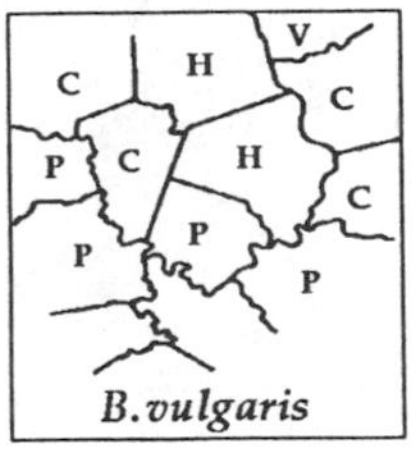

B. vulgaris

Barbarea vulgaris R. Br. YELLOW ROCKET
Abundant in sunny fields. Introduced.

B. nigra

Brassica napus L. TURNIP
In waste ground. A single record, Franklin (WB). Introduced.

Brassica nigra (L.) Koch BLACK MUSTARD
A fairly common weed on roadsides, in waste places, and in other open sites. Introduced.

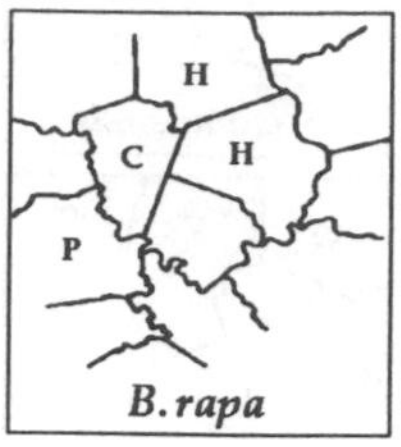

B. rapa

Brassica rapa L. BIRD'S RAPE
A weed in cultivated fields. Not common. Introduced.

C. bursa-pastoris

Camelina microcarpa Andrz. FALSE FLAX
A weed in fields. Infrequent. Jessamine (UK), Mercer (UK). Introduced.

Capsella bursa-pastoris (L.) Medic. SHEPHERD'S PURSE
A common weed in lawns, pastures, and other grassy places. Introduced.

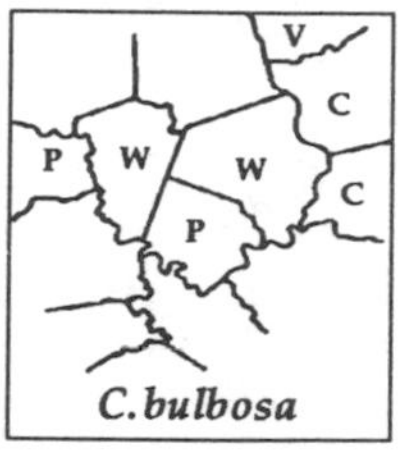

C. bulbosa

Cardamine bulbosa (Schreb.) BSP. SPRING CRESS
Frequent around springs and seepage areas, along creeks, and in other wet ground.

C. douglassii

Cardamine douglassii (Torr.) Britt. PURPLE CRESS
Fairly common in rich woods.

C. hirsuta

Cardamine flexuosa With.
On moist, moss-covered ledges. Rare. Fayette (MEW).

Cardamine hirsuta L.
Fairly frequent in old fields and disturbed areas in woods, especially in moist ground. Introduced.

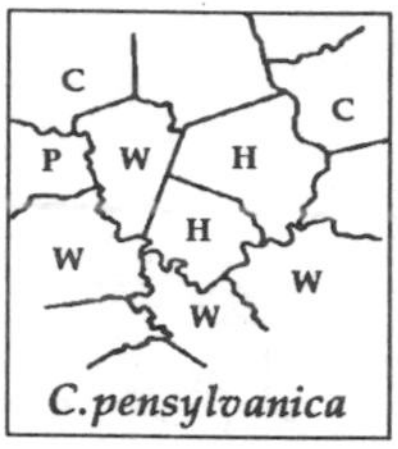

C. pensylvanica

Cardamine parviflora L.
Infrequent. Fayette (UK); Woodford (EC).

Cardamine pensylvanica Muhl. BITTERCRESS
Fairly frqurent in moist situations such as creek margins, cracks in limestone creek beds, and springs.

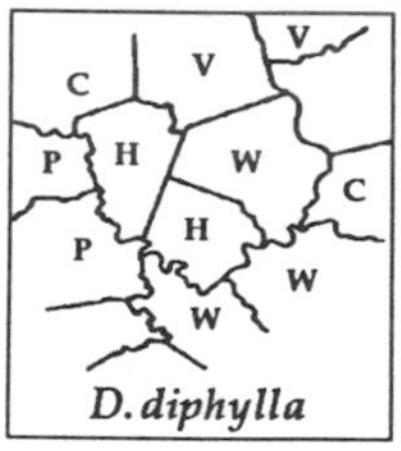

D. diphylla

Conringia orientalis (L.) Dumort HARE'S-EAR MUSTARD
A weed in yards. Fayette (UK). Introduced.

D. laciniata

Dentaria diphylla Michx. CRINKLE-ROOT, TWO-LEAVED TOOTHWORT
Fairly frequent in moist ravines in mesophytic woods.

Dentaria laciniata Muhl. CUT-LEAF TOOTHWORT
Common in woods, both mesic and somewhat dry.

Descurainia pinnata (Walt.) Britt. var. *brachycarpa* (Richards) Fernald TANSY-MUSTARD
In rocky ground. Rare. Fayette (Detling).

Descurainia sophia (L.) Webb TANSY-MUSTARD
Weedy areas. Rare. Franklin (SR); Harrison (JBV).

Diplotaxis muralis (L.) DC. WALL-ROCKET
A single record, Woodford (EC).

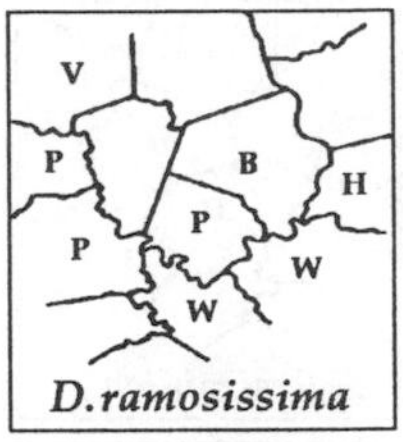

D. ramosissima

Diplotaxis tenuifolia (L.) DC. WALL-ROCKET
In waste ground. Bourbon (UK). Introduced.

Draba ramosissima Desv.
On moss-covered limestone ledges. Infrequent.

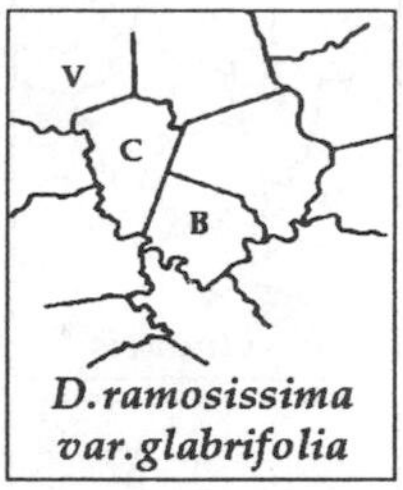

D. ramosissima var. glabrifolia

D. ramosissima var. *glabrifolia* Braun
Same habitat as the typical variety. Rare.

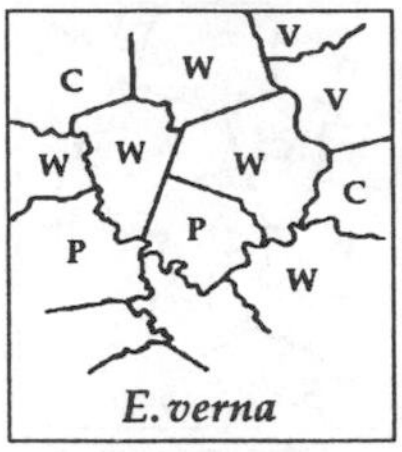

E. verna

Erophila verna (L.) Chev.
[=*Draba verna* L.] WHITLOW-GRASS
Common (though inconspicuous) in pastures, farm roadways, and other open places. Introduced.

Erysimum aspera (Nutt.) DC. WESTERN WALLFLOWER
A single record, Woodford (EC).

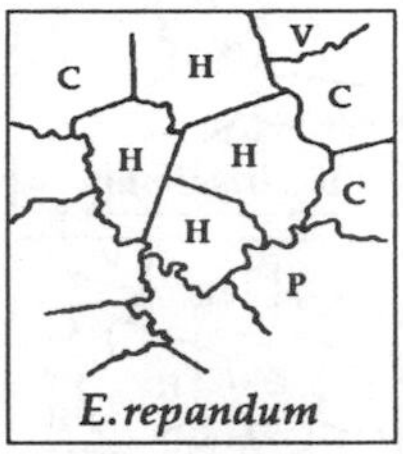

E. repandum

Erysimum repandum L. TREACLE MUSTARD
Frequent on roadsides and in weedy fields. Introduced.

H. matronalis

Hesperis matronalis L. DAME'S ROCKET, SWEET ROCKET
An escape from gardens, found occasionally on roadsides in rich, moist ground. Introduced.

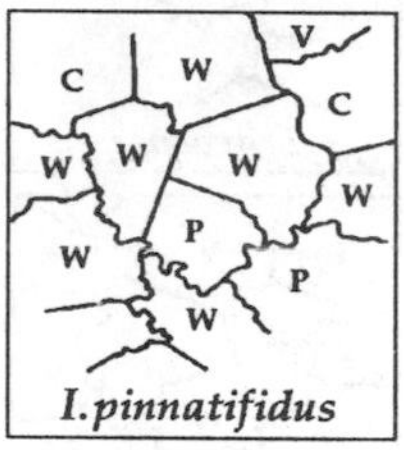

I. pinnatifidus

Iodanthus pinnatifidus (Michx.) Steud. PURPLE ROCKET
Frequent in shady, moist situations, such as wooded creek banks, spring and seepage areas, and wooded floodplains.

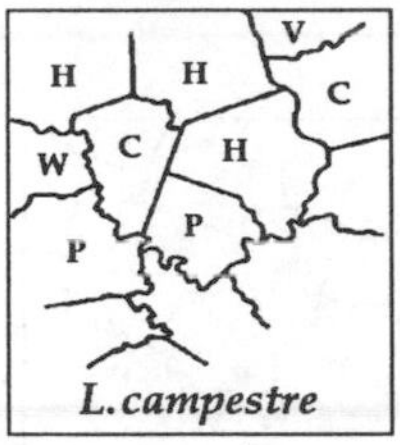

L. campestre

Lepidium campestre (L.) R. Br. FIELD PEPPERGRASS
A fairly common roadside weed. Introduced.

Lepidium densiflorum Schrad. PEPPERGRASS
A weed in fields. Woodford (UK). Introduced.

Lepidium ramosissimum Nels.
A single record, Franklin (SR). Introduced.

L. virginicum

Lepidium virginicum L. PEPPERGRASS
Common in dry open areas: fields, gardens, farm roadways, and roadsides.

L. giobosa

Lesquerella globosa (Desv.) Wats. BLADDER-POD
On limestone ledges. Infrequent.

N. officinale

Nasturtium officinale R. Br. WATERCRESS
Common in shallow water of brooks and springs. Introduced.

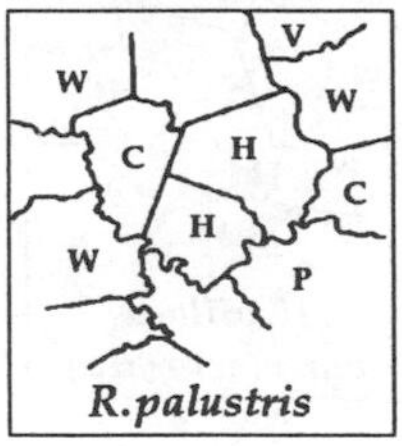

R. palustris

Rorippa palustris (L.) Bess. ssp. *fernaldiana* Butters & Abbe.
[=*R. islandica* (Oeder) Borbas var. *fernaldiana* Butters & Abbe] MARSH CRESS, YELLOW CRESS
Frequent on floodplains, on pond margins, and in other moist, sunny situations.

Rorippa sessilifolia (Nutt.) Hitchc. YELLOW CRESS
In wet depressions in fields and other moist places. Infrequent. Boyle (MEW); Franklin (SR); Jessamine (McF).

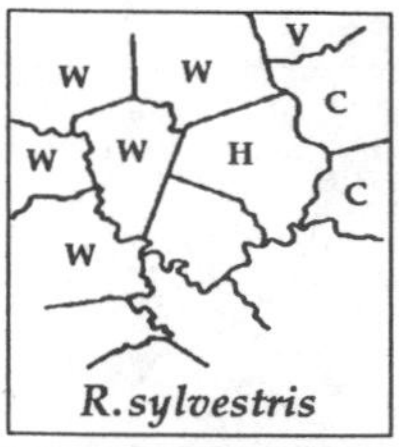

R. sylvestris

Rorippa sylvestris (L.) Bess. CREEPING YELLOW CRESS
Frequent and weedy in sunny, wet ground. Introduced.

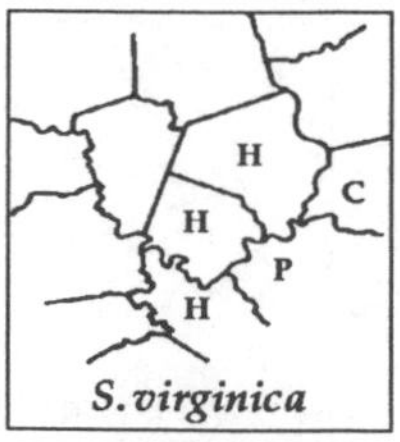

S. virginica

Sibara virginica (L.) Rollins
In fields and on roadsides. Infrequent.

Sisymbrium altissimum L. TUMBLE-MUSTARD
A roadside weed. Infrequent. Introduced.

S. altissimum

Sisymbrium officinale (L.) Scop. HEDGE MUSTARD
Common in fields, on roadsides, and in other open areas. Introduced.

S. officinale

Thlaspi arvense L. FIELD PENNY-CRESS
A fairly frequent weed in fields and on roadsides. Introduced.

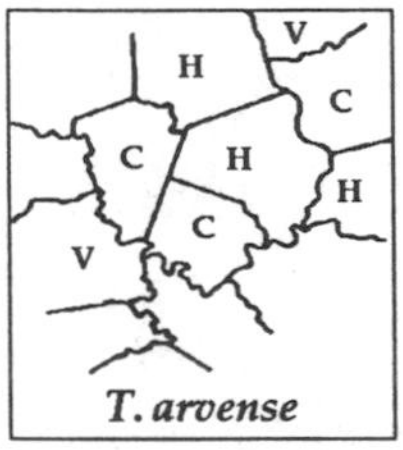

T. arvense

Thlaspi perfoliatum L. PENNY-CRESS
Frequent in fields, in overgrazed pastures, and on roadsides. Introduced.

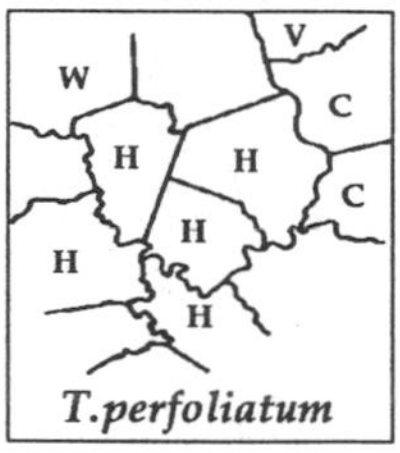

T. perfoliatum

Crassulaceae: Orpine Family

Sedum pulchellum Michx. PINK STONECROP, WIDOW'S-CROSS
Common on limestone ledges or in thin soil over bedrock, either wet or dry, usually sunny.

S. pulchellum

Sedum sarmentosum Bunge
An escape from cultivation. Bourbon (EG); Franklin (NP); Fayette (NP). Introduced.

Sedum ternatum Michx. STONECROP
Frequent on mossy ledges, boulders, and banks in mesophytic woods.

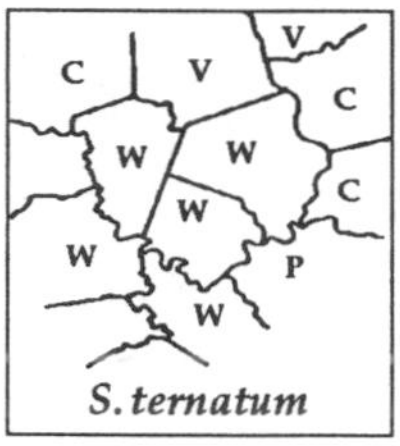

S. ternatum

Saxifragaceae: Saxifrage Family

H. americana

Astilbe biternata (Vent.) Britt. FALSE GOAT'S-BEARD
On wooded cliffs of Kentucky River. Rare. Fayette (UK); Woodford (UK).

Heuchera americana L. var. *brevipetala* R., B. & L. ALUM-ROOT
Frequent on wooded cliffs and slopes.

Heuchera longiflora Rydb. (typical) ALUM-ROOT
Rare. A single record, Fayette (Rosendahl, Butters, & Lakela).

Heuchera parviflora Bartl. ALUM-ROOT
A single record, Mercer (Pal).

Heuchera villosa Michx. var. *macrorhiza* (Small) R., B. & L. ALUM-ROOT
Frequent on moist wooded cliffs and ravine slopes.

H. villosa var. macrorhiza

H. villosa var. *intermedia* R., B. & L.
Jessamine (MEW).

H. villosa, variety not distinguished.
Anderson (Pal), Madison (Pal), Mercer (Pal).

H. arborescens

M. diphylla

Hydrangea arborescens L. HYDRANGEA
Frequent on moist wooded cliffs and ravine slopes.

Mitella diphylla L. BISHOP'S-CAP, MITERWORT
Rich mesophytic wooded slopes. Infrequent.

Penthorum sedoides L. DITCH STONECROP
Frequent on pond and stream margins and floodplains.

P. sedoides

Philadelphus inodorus L. MOCK-ORANGE
Spread from cultivation. A single record, Franklin (SR). Introduced.

R. cynosbati

Ribes cynosbati L. DOGBERRY
Frequent on ledges above creeks, overhanging cliffs, and sides of ravines.

R. missouriense

Ribes missouriense Nutt. GOOSEBERRY
Open woods and steep, rocky banks above creeks. Infrequent.

S. virginiensis

Saxifraga virginiensis Michx. EARLY SAXIFRAGE
Very frequent on mossy ledges and in crevices of shaded cliffs.

Tiarella cordifolia L. FOAMFLOWER
In rich woods. A single record, Woodford (EC).

Hamamelidaceae: Witch-hazel Family

H. virginiana

Hamamelis virginiana L. WITCH-HAZEL
Frequent on wooded ravine slopes, stream banks, and edges of woods.

Platanaceae: Plane Tree Family

P. occidentalis

Platanus occidentalis L. SYCAMORE
Abundant along streams both large and small.

Rosaceae: Rose Family

Agrimonia parviflora Ait. AGRIMONY
In moist ground. Infrequent. Jessamine (C&M).

A. pubescens

Agrimonia pubescens Wallr. AGRIMONY
Frequent in open woods and at edges of woods.

A. rostellata

Agrimonia rostellata Wallr. AGRIMONY
Fairly frequent in woods.

A. arborea

Amelanchier arborea (Michx. f.) Fernald SERVICEBERRY
Kentucky River cliffs, dry. Rare in the region.

Aruncus dioicus (Walt.) Fernald GOAT'S-BEARD
A single record, from a steep mesophytic wooded slope. Anderson (Pal).

Crataegus calpodendron (Ehrh.) Medic. HAWTHORN
On creek banks. Fayette (UK).

C. crus-galli

Crataegus crus-galli L. COCKSPUR THORN
On dry hillsides. Infrequent.

Crataegus intricata Lange HAWTHORN
In old fields. Infrequent. Harrison (JBV), Woodford (JBV).

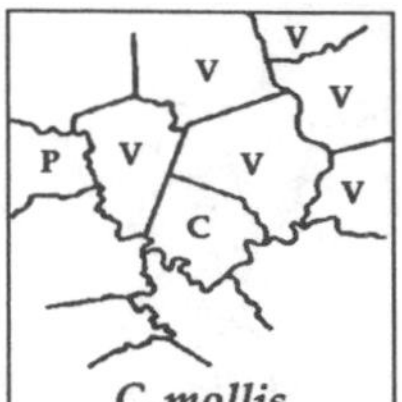

C. mollis

Crataegus margaretta Ashe HAWTHORN
A single record, from a fencerow. Harrison (JBV).

Crataegus mollis T. & G. HAWTHORN
Common in pastures, fencerows, and open woods near creeks.

Crataegus phaenopyrum (L. f.) Medic HAWTHORN
A single record, from a creek bank. Woodford (JBV).

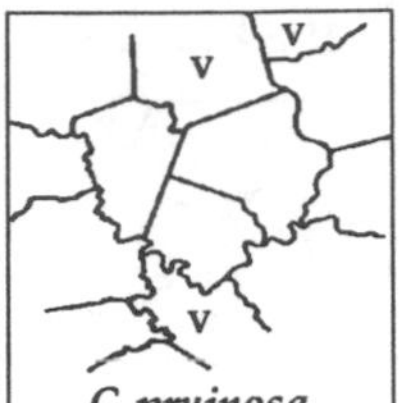

C. pruinosa

Crataegus pruinosa (Wendl.) K. Koch HAWTHORN
In thickets, old fields, and open woods on steep slopes. Infrequent.

Crataegus punctata Jacq. var. *microphylla* Sarg.
HAWTHORN
In open woods on dry south-facing slope. A single record, Garrard (JBV).

Crataegus rubella Beadle HAWTHORN
In rocky woods on cliffs above Kentucky River. A single record, Woodford (JBV).

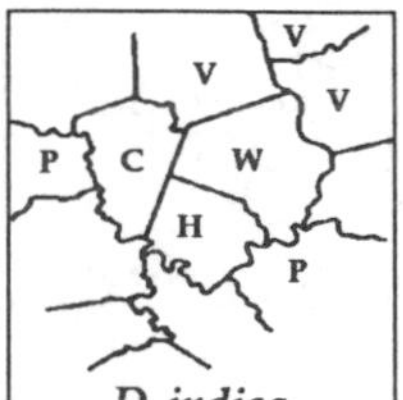

D. indica

Crataegus uniflora Muench HAWTHORN
On a sunny cliff. A single record, Garrard (JBV).

Duchesnea indica (Andr.) Focke MOCK STRAWBERRY,
INDIAN STRAWBERRY
A common weed in gardens, lawns, and other grassy areas. Introduced.

F. virginiana

Fragaria virginiana Duchn. [including the typical variety and var. *illinoensis* (Prince) Gray]
WILD STRAWBERRY
Common in old fields and clearings and on borders of thickets, railroad embankments, and other sunny banks.

G. canadense

Geum canadense Jacq. WHITE AVENS
Common in open woods, edges of woods, and thickets.

G. vernum

Geum vernum (Raf.) T. & G. SPRING AVENS
Frequent in sunny areas, grassy or weedy.

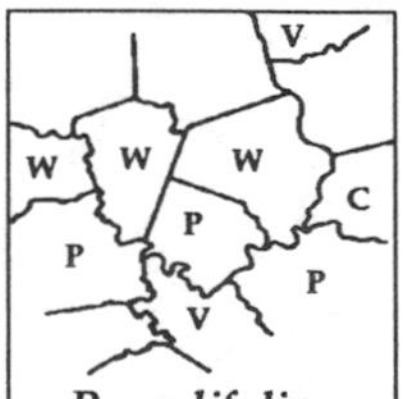

P. opulifolius

Physocarpus opulifolius (L.) Maxim. NINEBARK
Frequent on cliffs and ledges and in cracks of limestone in creek beds.

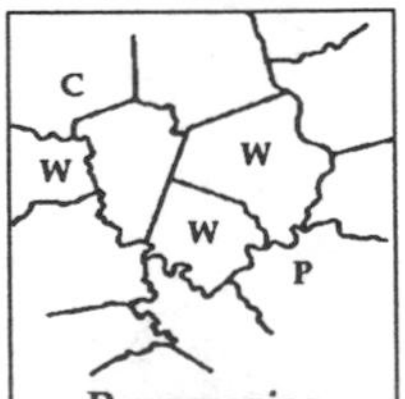

P. norvegica

Potentilla intermedia L.
A single record, Woodford (EC). Introduced.

P. recta

Potentilla norvegica L. ROUGH CINQUEFOIL
In fields and gardens and on roadsides. Fairly frequent.

Potentilla recta L. SULPHUR CINQUEFOIL
In fields and fencerows and on roadsides. Common. Introduced.

P. simplex

Potentilla simplex Michx. CINQUEFOIL
Fairly frequent in old fields, clearings, and edges of woods.

P. americana

Prunus americana Marsh. WILD PLUM
In fencerows, edges of woods, and old fields. Common.

Prunus angustifolia Marsh. CHICKASAW PLUM
Usually forming thickets. Infrequent. Fayette (UK); Jessamine (UK).

Prunus avium L. CHERRY
An escape from cultivation. Franklin (SR).

P. mahaleb

Prunus hortulana Bailey HORTULAN PLUM
Infrequent. Fayette (UK); Jessamine (UK).

P. munsoniana

Prunus mahaleb L. PERFUMED CHERRY
A fairly frequent escape from cultivation as grafting stock.

Prunus munsoniana Wight & Hedrick WILD-GOOSE PLUM
Forming thickets. Fairly frequent.

P. persica

Prunus nigra Ait.
[= *P. americana* var. *lanata* Sudw.] WOOLY-LEAF PLUM
Infrequent. Garrard (MEW), Harrison (JBV).

P. serotina

Prunus persica (L.) Batsch. PEACH
An escape, on roadsides and in dumps. Introduced.

P. virginiana

Prunus serotina Ehrh. BLACK CHERRY
A common tree in fencerows, on roadsides, and in other open areas; no longer a prominent constituent of a forest community.

P. communis

Prunus virginiana L. CHOKE CHERRY
On wooded rocky banks of creeks. Infrequent.

P. malus

Pyrus communis L. PEAR
An escape. Introduced.

Pyrus malus L. APPLE
An escape, on roadsides and in dumps. Introduced.

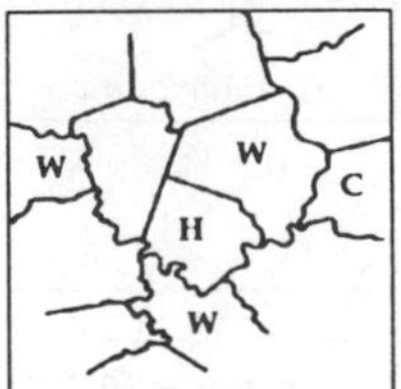

R. canina

Rosa canina L. DOG ROSE
In old pastures and old fields. Infrequent. Introduced.

R. carolina

Rosa carolina L. WILD ROSE
In dry open woods, edges of woods, old fields, and old pastures. Frequent.

Rosa eglanteria L. SWEETBRIER
An infrequent escape. Jessamine (UK); Madison (UK). Introduced.

R. multiflora

Rosa multiflora Thunb. MULTIFLORA ROSE
An escape from farm-hedge planting. Becoming frequent in open woods, edges of woods, and thickets. Introduced.

R. palustris

Rosa palustris Marsh. SWAMP ROSE
In wet ground. Rare.

R. setigera

Rosa setigera Michx. PRAIRIE ROSE
In old fields and woodland borders and on sunny creek banks. Frequent.

RUBUS, Subgenus *EUBATUS* BLACKBERRIES and DEWBERRIES
In old fields, dry or moist. Subgenus common.

Rubus allegheniensis Porter
Jessamine (McF).

Rubus argutus Link
Jessamine (McF).

Rubus flagellaris Willd.

Rubus louisianus Berger
Clark (MRB)

Rubus congruus Bailey
Clark (MRB)

Rubus pensylvanicus Poir.
Harrison (JBV), Mercer (JBV).

Rubus praepes Bailey
Clark (MRB)

RUBUS, Subgenus *IDAEOBATUS* RASPBERRIES

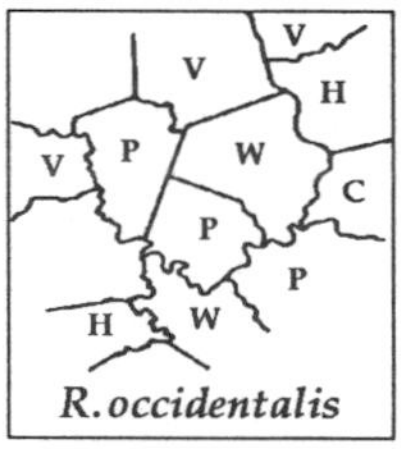

R. occidentalis

Rubus occidentalis L. BLACK RASPBERRY
In moist soil in partial shade. Common.

Waldsteinia fragarioides (Michx.) Trott.
On mesophytic wooded slopes. Rare. Anderson (Bry.), Fayette (MEW); Jessamine (UK).

A. bracteata

Fabaceae: Legume Family

Amphicarpa bracteata (L.) Fernald PEAVINE, HOG-PEANUT
Frequent in rich, moist open woods.

A. americana

Apios americana Medic. GROUNDNUT
In open woods in bottomlands. Fairly frequent.

Cassia fasciculata Michx. PARTRIDGE-PEA
In old fields in low ground; rare in the region. Variety not distinguished: Boyle (UK); Jessamine (McF). Var. *robusta* (Pollard) Macbr.: Woodford (MEW).

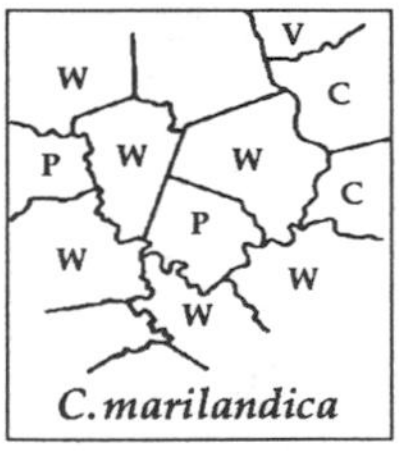

C. marilandica

Cassia marilandica L. WILD SENNA
Common in old fields, thickets, and woodland borders.

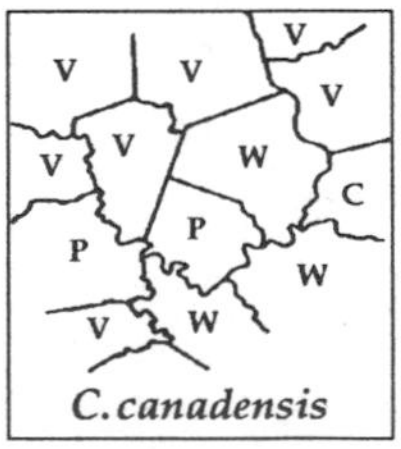

C. canadensis

Cercis canadensis L. REDBUD
In open woods and woodland borders. Common.

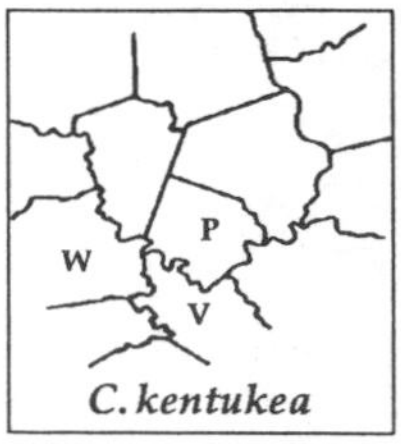

C. kentukea

Cladrastis kentukea (Dum.-Cours.) Rudd
[= *C. lutea* (Michx. f.) K. Koch]
On mesophytic wooded north-facing slopes and steep rocky cliffs. Locally restricted near the Kentucky River.

Coronilla varia L. CROWN VETCH
Commonly planted on roadside banks, from which it escapes. Bourbon (UK); Woodford (EC). Introduced.

Desmanthus illinoensis (Michx.) MacM.
ILLINOIS MIMOSA
In sunny, rocky ground. Rare. Anderson (MEW); Woodford (UK).

Desmodium cuspidatum (Muhl.) Loud.
At edge of woods. A single record, Anderson (MEW).

D.glutinosum

Desmodium glabellum (Michx.) DC.
A single record. Anderson (Pal).

Desmodium glutinosum (Muhl.) Wood TICK-TREFOIL
On north-facing slopes and cliffs above the Kentucky River and on sides of wooded ravines. Frequent.

Desmodium laevigatum (Nutt.) DC.
A single record, Jessamine (McF).

Desmodium nudiflorum (L.) DC.
On wooded slopes above creeks. Rare in the region. Anderson (Pal); Clark (MRB)

Desmodium obtusum (Muhl. ex Willd.) DC.
[=*D. rigidum* (L.) DC.]
A single record, Anderson (Pal).

D.paniculatum

Desmodium paniculatum (L.) DC. TICK-TREFOIL
In old fields and borders of woods. Frequent.

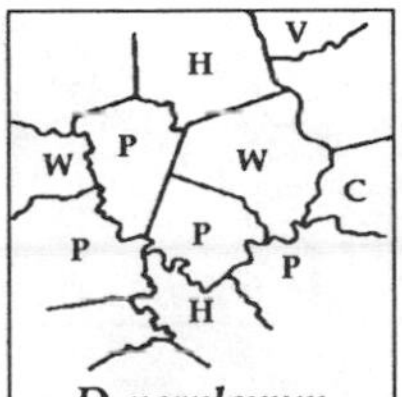

D.perplexum

Desmodium pauciflorum (Nutt.) DC.
On wooded slopes above creeks. Infrequent. Anderson (MEW); Woodford (JBV).

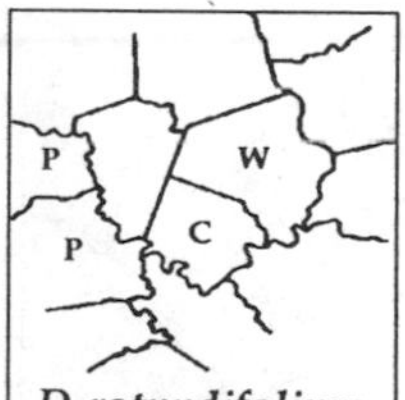

D.rotundifolium

Desmodium perplexum Schub.
Common in old fields, in woodland borders, and on roadsides.

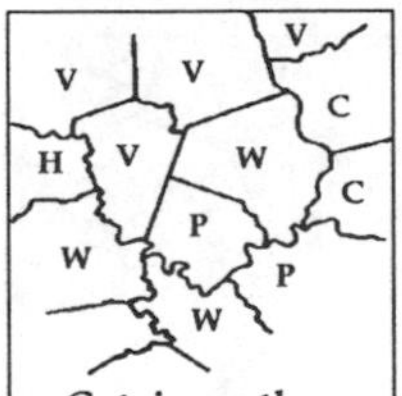

G.triacanthos

Desmodium rotundifolium DC. TRAILING TICK-TREFOIL
Dry woods. Infrequent.

Gleditsia triacanthos L. HONEY LOCUST
A common invader of old fields; also in fencerows and woodland borders.

G.dioica

Gymnocladus dioica (L.) K. Koch
KENTUCKY COFFEE-TREE
A common and characteristic tree of the area: on floodplains, on wooded slopes, and in pastures.

K.stipulacea

Kummerowia striata (Thunb.) Schindl.
[=*Lespedeza striata* (Thunb.) H. & A.]
JAPANESE CLOVER
In fields and on roadsides. Infrequent. Fayette (UK); Jessamine (McF). Introduced.

Kummerowia stipulacea (Maxim.) Makino
[=*Lespedeza stipulacea* Maxim.] KOREAN CLOVER
Frequent in fields and on roadsides. Introduced.

Lathyrus latifolius L. PERENNIAL PEA
An escape from cultivation. Bourbon (EG); Fayette (UK); Jessamine (McF). Introduced.

L. cuneata

Lathyrus sylvestris L. PERENNIAL PEA
A single record, Fayette (UK). Introduced.

Lespedeza cuneata (Dum.-Cours.) G. Don.
SILKY LESPEDEZA
In thickets and edges of fields and woods in dry ground. Infrequent.

Lespedeza intermedia (S. Wats.) Britt.
In dry open woods. A single record. Jessamine (C&M).

Lespedeza procumbens Michx.
TRAILING BUSH-CLOVER
In thin soil in dry, open cedar-oak woods. Infrequent. Fayette (MEW); Harrison (JBV).

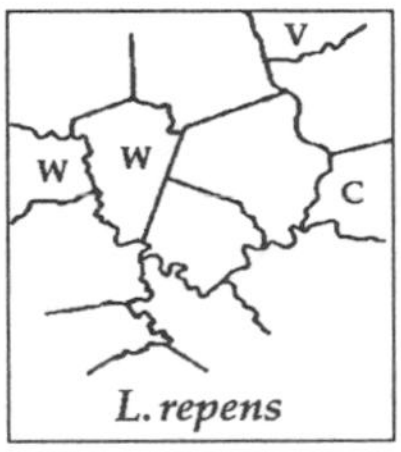

L. repens

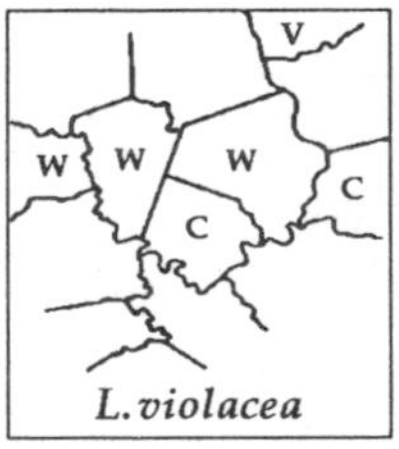

L. violacea

Lespedeza repens (L.) Bart. CREEPING BUSH-CLOVER
In thin soil on dry, open-wooded slopes and ridges. Infrequent.

Lespedeza violacea (L.) Pers. BUSH-CLOVER
Fairly frequent in dry open woods and edges of woods.

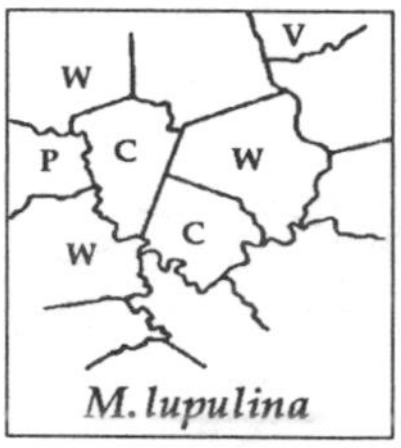

M. lupulina

Lotus corniculatus L. BIRD'S-FOOT TREFOIL
A single record, Woodford (EC). Introduced.

Medicago lupulina L. BLACK MEDIC
Common in lawns, fields, and pastures, and on roadsides. Introduced.

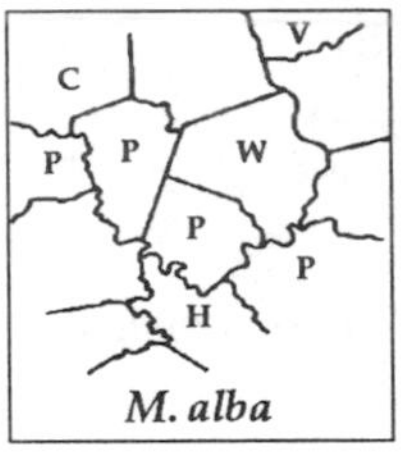

M. alba

Medicago sativa L. ALFALFA
A forage plant occasionally escaping to roadsides. Harrison (JBV); Jessamine (JBV). Introduced.

M. officinalis

Melilotus alba Desr. WHITE SWEET CLOVER
Common in fields and on roadsides. Introduced.

Melilotus officinalis (L.) Lam. YELLOW SWEET CLOVER
Abundant along roadsides and in waste places.

R. pseudoacacia

Phaseolus polystachios (L.) BSP. WILD BEAN
In open woods, woodland borders, and thickets. Rare. Anderson (MEW); Fayette (MEW).

Robinia pseudoacacia L. BLACK LOCUST
Abundant in fencerows, thickets, woodland borders, and old fields.

Strophostyles leiosperma (Torr. & Gray) Piper
WILD BEAN
A single record, Anderson (Pal).

Strophostyles umbellata (Muhl.) Britt. WILD BEAN
Climbing over box elder seedlings in rich bottomland. A single record, Fayette (JBV).

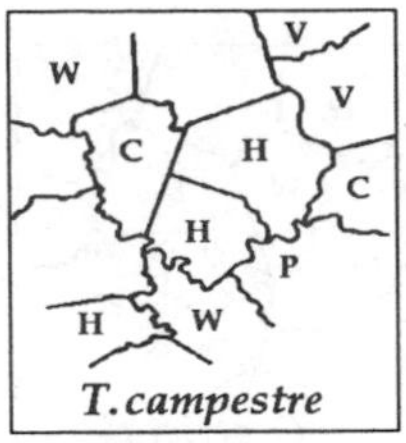

T. campestre

Trifolium arvense L. RABBIT-FOOT CLOVER
On dry roadsides and in fields. Infrequent. Jessamine (McF); Woodford (EC). Introduced.

Trifolium campestre Schreb.
[= *T. procumbens* of authors, not L.] HOP CLOVER
Frequent in fields and on roadsides. Introduced.

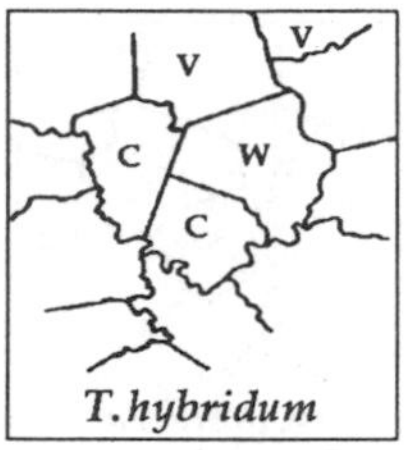

T. hybridum

Trifolium dubium Sibth. LOW HOP CLOVER
A single record, Madison (Pal.). Introduced.

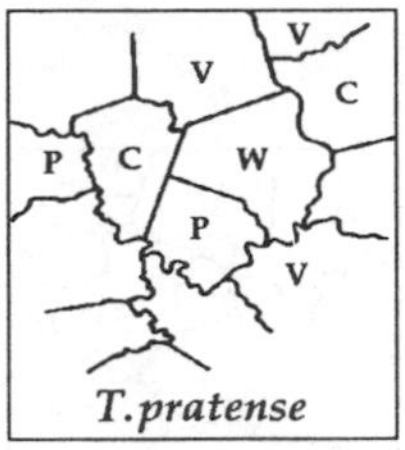

T. pratense

Trifolium hybridum L. ALSIKE CLOVER
In old fields and on roadsides. Infrequent. Introduced.

Trifolium pratense L. RED CLOVER
Common in fields and on roadsides. Introduced.

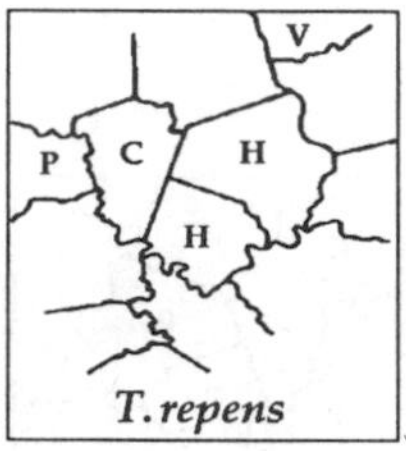

T. repens

Trifolium reflexum L. BUFFALO CLOVER
In openings in woods and on roadsides. Rare. Bourbon (EG); Fayette (UK); Harrison (JBV).

Trifolium repens Roth WHITE CLOVER
Common in lawns, in pastures, and on roadsides. Introduced.

Trifolium stoloniferum Muhl.
RUNNING BUFFALO CLOVER
A prominent component of the original Bluegrass flora and long thought to be extinct in Kentucky, it has recently been rediscovered in lawns of old homes in both the Inner and the Outer Bluegrass. Rare. Fayette (NP).

V. caroliniana

Vicia caroliniana Walt. CAROLINA VETCH
Fairly frequent on wooded cliffs and ravine sides.

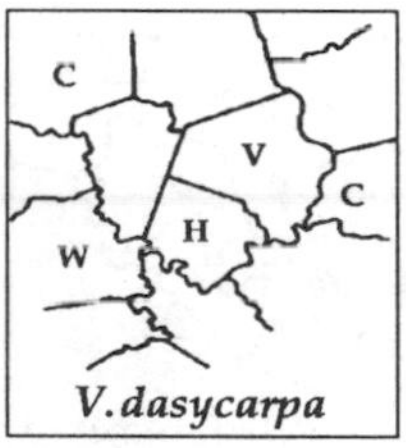

V. dasycarpa

Vicia dasycarpa Ten. SMOOTH VETCH
Frequent in fields and on roadsides. Introduced.

Vicia grandiflora Scop. LARGE-FLOWERED VETCH
In waste ground. A single record, Fayette (UK). Introduced.

V. villosa

Vicia sativa L. SPRING VETCH
In fields. Infrequent. Fayette (MEW), Mercer (Pal). Introduced.

Vicia villosa Roth HAIRY VETCH
Common in fields and on roadsides. Introduced.

Linaceae: Flax Family

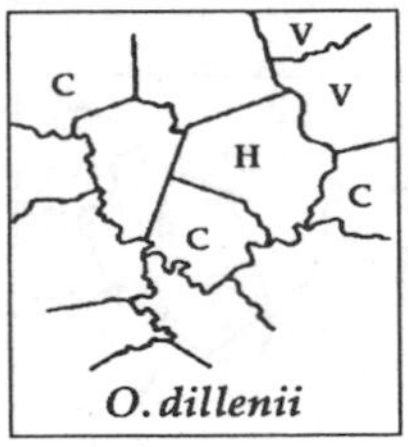

O. dillenii

Linum usitatissimum L. FLAX
On roadsides. Rare. Fayette (UK). Introduced.

Oxalidaceae: Wood-sorrel Family

Oxalis dillenii Jacq.
[= *O. stricta* of authors, not L.] WOOD-SORREL
In fields, thickets, and woodland borders. Frequent.

O. grandis

Oxalis grandis Small — GREAT WOOD-SORREL
On wooded slopes. Frequent.

O. stricta

Oxalis stricta L.
[= *O. europea* Jord.] — WOOD-SORREL
A common weed in cultivated ground and along roadsides.

O. violacea

Oxalis violacea L. — VIOLET WOOD-SORREL
In dry open woods, usually in thin, rocky soil. Fairly frequent.

Geraniaceae: Geranium Family, Crane's-bill Family

G. carolinianum

Geranium carolinianum L. — CRANE'S-BILL
In borders of woods and fields. Frequent.

G. carolinianum var. *confertiflorum* Fernald
Harrison (JBV); Mercer (MEW).

Geraninum columbinum L.
LONG-STALKED CRANE'S-BILL
In fields and on roadsides. Infrequent. Clark (MRB); Harrison (JBV). Introduced.

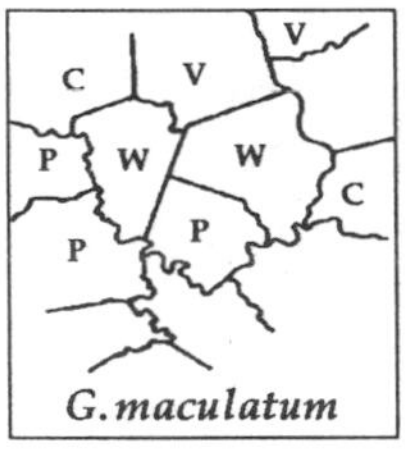
G. maculatum

Geranium maculatum L. — WILD GERANIUM
Frequent on wooded slopes.

Geranium molle L.
A single record, from a roadside. Mercer (MEW). Introduced.

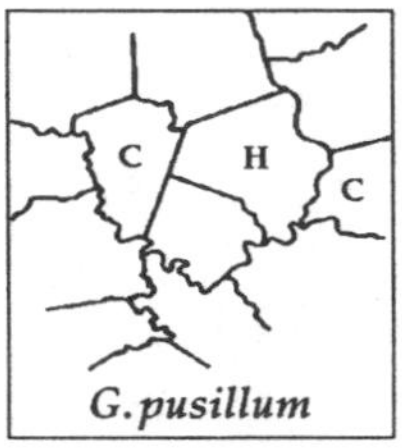
G. pusillum

Geranium pusillum L.
In fields and on roadsides. Infrequent. Introduced.

Rutaceae: Rue Family

P. trifoliata

Ptelea trifoliata L. — HOP-TREE, WAFER ASH
On creek banks and floodplains and in thickets in mesic or moist ground. Frequent.

X. americanum

Xanthoxylum americanum Mill. — PRICKLY ASH
Dry woods. Infrequent.

Simaroubaceae: Quassia Family

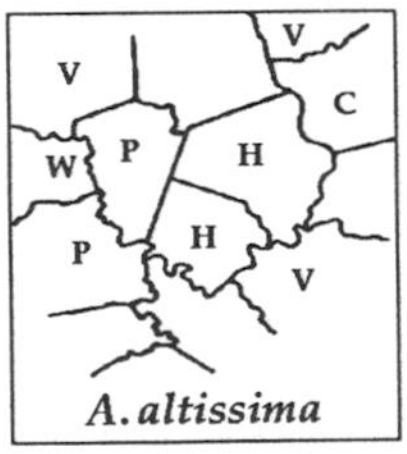
A. altissima

Ailanthus altissima (Mill.) Swingle — TREE-OF-HEAVEN
In waste places, especially in towns. Frequent. Introduced.

Polygalaceae: Milkwort Family

P. senega

Polygala senega L. var. *latifolia* T. & G.
SENECA SNAKEROOT
Frequent in dry, open upland woods, especially in the vicinity of the Kentucky River.

Euphorbiaceae: Spurge Family

A. ostryaefolia

Acalypha ostryaefolia Riddell
THREE-SEEDED MERCURY
A fairly common weed in fields and on roadsides.

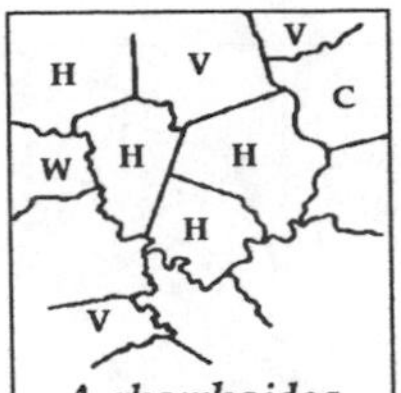

A. rhomboidea

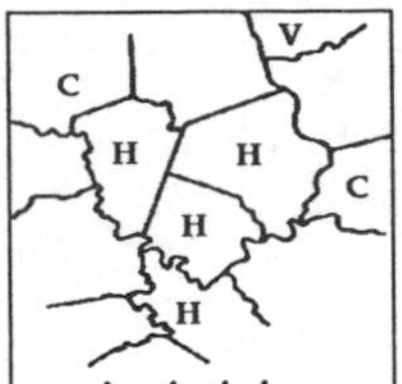

A. virginica

Acalypha rhomboidea Raf. THREE-SEEDED MERCURY
A common weed.

Acalypha virginica L. THREE-SEEDED MERCURY
In fields and other open areas. Frequent.

Croton capitatus Michx. WOOLLY CROTON
In fields. Infrequent.

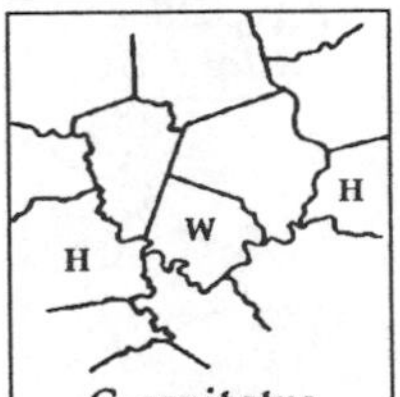

C. capitatus

C. monanthogynus

Croton monanthogynus Michx. PRAIRIE-TEA
Common in dry open situations.

Euphorbia chamaesyce L.
A single record, Bourbon (EG).

Euphorbia commutata Engelm. WOOD SPURGE
Frequent in dry open woods.

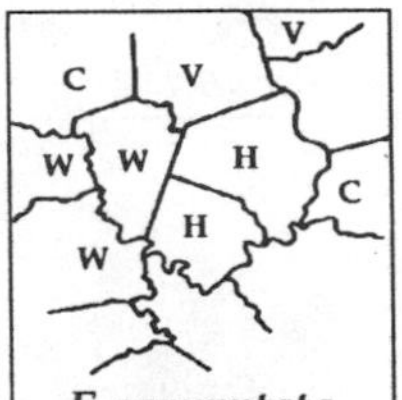

E. commutata

E. corollata

Euphorbia corollata L. FLOWERING SPURGE
Frequent on open, wooded south-facing slopes and cliffs, especially above Kentucky River.

Euphorbia dentata Michx. TOOTHED SPURGE
Frequent on roadsides and in other open situations.

Euphorbia heterophylla L. PAINTED LEAF, FIRE-ON-THE-MOUNTAIN
In moist ground. Infrequent.

E. dentata

E. heterophylla

Euphorbia maculata L. EYEBANE, SPOTTED SPURGE
On roadsides and in gravelly creekbeds. Frequent.

Euphorbia marginata Pursh SNOW-ON-THE-MOUNTAIN
Spread from cultivation to roadsides and waste places. Infrequent.

E. maculata

E. marginata

Euphorbia supina Raf. MILK-PURSLANE
A weed, in cultivated ground and other open areas. Frequent.

Phyllanthus caroliniensis Walt.
A weed, in gardens. Fayette (UK).

E. supina

Tragia cordata Michx.
In dry open woods. Rare. Anderson (MEW); Franklin (C&M).

Buxaceae: Boxwood Family

Pachysandra procumbens Michx. MOUNTAIN SPURGE
In mesic woods. Rare. Fayette (JBV); Jessamine (JBV noted too few to collect).

Limnanthaceae: False Mermaid Family

Floerkea proserpinacoides Willd. FALSE MERMAID
In moist woods. Rare. Fayette (NP).

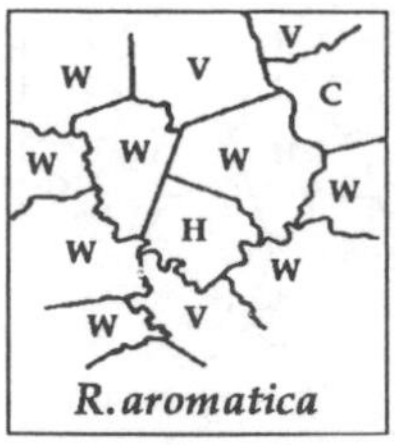

R. aromatica

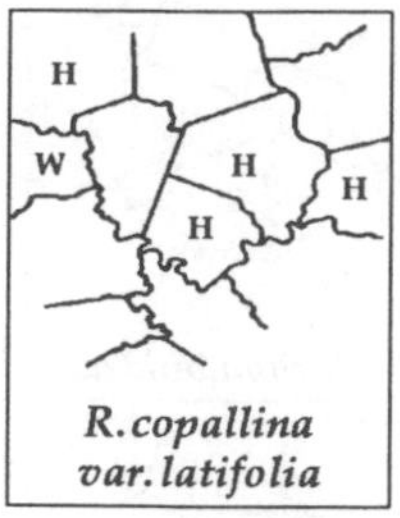

R. copallina var. latifolia

Anacardiaceae: Cashew Family

Rhus aromatica Ait. AROMATIC SUMAC
Common in dry open woods and woodland borders, and on sunny ridgetops.

Rhus copallina L. var. *latifolia* Engler DWARF SUMAC, WINGED SUMAC
In old fields, thickets, and edges of woods. Infrequent.

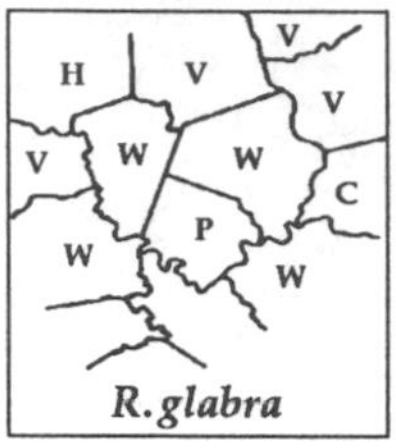

R. glabra

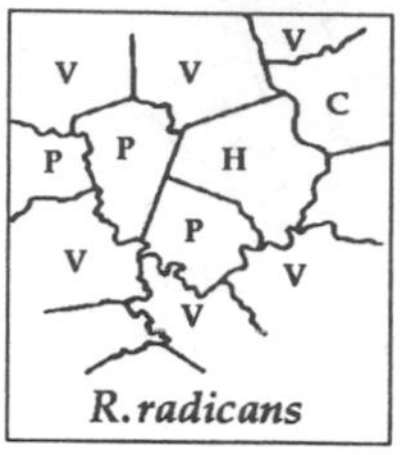

R. radicans

Rhus glabra L. SMOOTH SUMAC
Common in thickets, old fields, fencerows, and woodland borders.

Rhus radicans L. POISON IVY
Abundant in a variety of situations, including woods, fencerows, and roadsides.

Rhus toxicodendron L. POISON OAK
A single record of this erect, pubescent species, Fayette (MEW).

Rhus typhina L. STAGHORN SUMAC
On cliff edges and floodplains. Rare in the region. Garrard (UK); Jessamine (JBV).

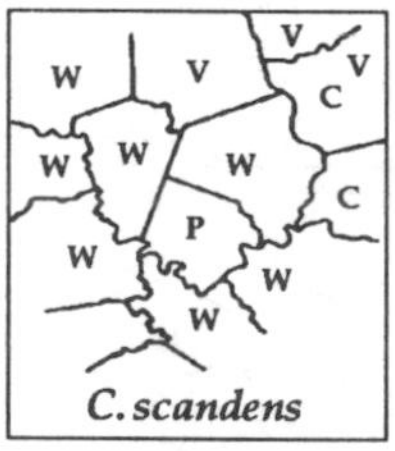

C. scandens

Celastraceae: Staff-tree Family

Celastrus scandens L. BITTTERSWEET
Frequent at the edges of woods and in fencerows.

E. americanus

Euonymus alatus Regel. WINGED EUONYMUS
An escape from cultivation. Jessamine (PAL). Introduced.

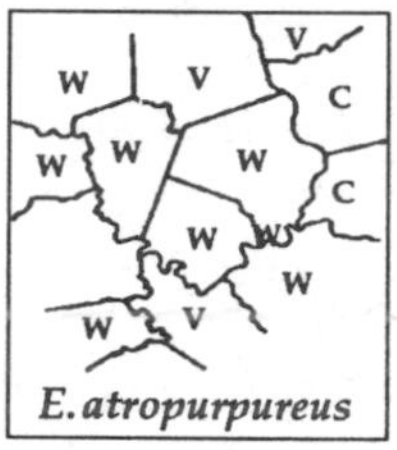

E. atropurpureus

Euonymus americanus L. STRAWBERRY-BUSH
In woods. Infrequent.

Euonymus atropurpureus Jacq. WAHOO
Very frequent in open woods and at edges of woods.

Euonymus kiautschovicus Laes.
[= *E. fortunei* (Turez.) Hand.-Maz.] WINTER CREEPER
An escape from cultivation, now established in woodland borders and rapidly spreading. Fayette (MEW); Franklin (SR); Jessamine (C&M). Introduced.

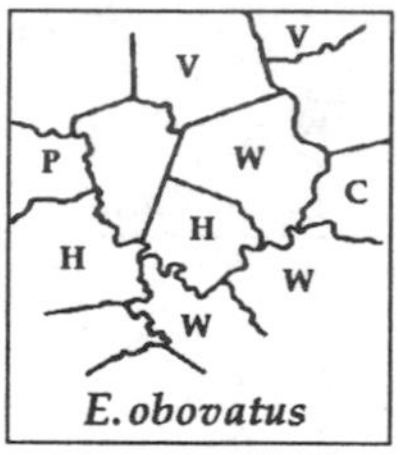

E. obovatus

S. trifolia

Euonymus obovatus Nutt. RUNNING STRAWBERRY-BUSH
Frequent on rich wooded slopes.

Pachystoma canbyi Gray MOUNTAIN-LOVER
On rocky cliffs. Rare. Jessamine (C&M).

Staphyleaceae: Bladdernut Family

Staphylea trifolia L. BLADDERNUT
Frequent on steep wooded slopes and floodplains.

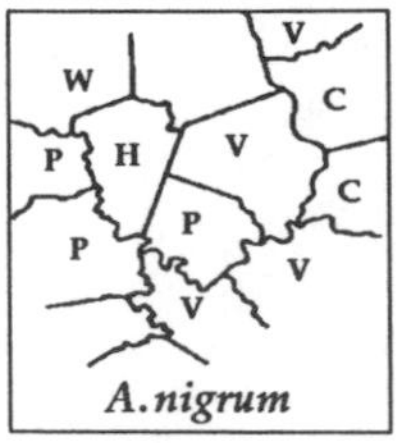

A. nigrum

A. negundo

Aceraceae: Maple Family

Acer negundo L. BOX ELDER
Common on stream margins and floodplains; fairly frequent on uplands.

Acer nigrum Michx. f. BLACK SUGAR MAPLE
Frequent on mesophytic wooded slopes.

A. rubrum

A. saccharinum

Acer rubrum L. RED MAPLE
In both wet and somewhat dry situations but infrequent.

Acer saccharinum L. SILVER MAPLE, WATER MAPLE
Common on stream margins and floodplains.

Acer saccharum Marsh. SUGAR MAPLE
Common in mesic habitats.

A. saccharum

Ae. glabra

Hippocastanaceae: Horse-chestnut Family

Aesculus glabra Willd. OHIO BUCKEYE
Common in woods, especially near edges.

Aesculus octandra Marsh. YELLOW BUCKEYE
In mesophytic woods in the vicinity of the Kentucky River. Infrequent.

Ae. octandra

I. capensis

Balsaminaceae: Touch-me-not Family

Impatiens capensis Meerb. JEWELWEED, TOUCH-ME-NOT
Common in wet ground, usually shaded.

Impatiens pallida Nutt. PALE JEWELWEED, PALE TOUCH-ME-NOT
Along shaded streams and wet banks and in seepage areas in woods. Fairly common.

I. pallida

C. americanus

Rhamnaceae: Buckthorn Family

Ceanothus americanus L. NEW JERSEY TEA
On cliffs and sunny, rocky creek banks. Infrequent.

Rhamnus caroliniana Walt. CAROLINA BUCKTHORN
Frequent at the edges of woods.

R. caroliniana

R. lanceolata

R. caroliniana var. *mollis* Fernald
Less frequent than the typical variety. Fayette (MEW); Garrard (MEW); Scott (MEW).

Rhamnus lanceolata Pursh LANCE-LEAF BUCKTHORN
Frequent at the edges of woods.

Vitaceae: Grape Family

Ampelopsis arborea (L.) Koehne PEPPER-VINE
An escape from cultivation. Introduced.

A. arborea

A. cordata

Ampelopsis cordata Michx.
In moist ground. Infrequent.

Parthenocissus quinquefolia (L.) Planch. VIRGINIA CREEPER
Abundant in woods and thickets.

Vitis aestivalis Michx. SUMMER GRAPE
In dry thickets. Infrequent.

P. quinquefolia

V. aestivalis

V. cinerea

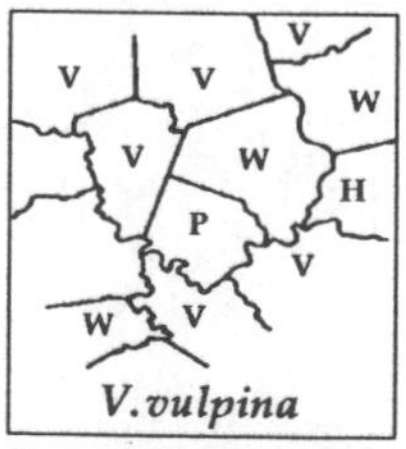

V. vulpina

Vitis cinerea Engelm. PIGEON GRAPE
In moist thickets. Rare.

Vitis rotundifolia Michx. MUSCADINE
In moist thickets. Rare. Anderson (Pal); Fayette (UK)

Vitis vulpina L. FROST GRAPE
Very common in woods and thickets.

T. americana

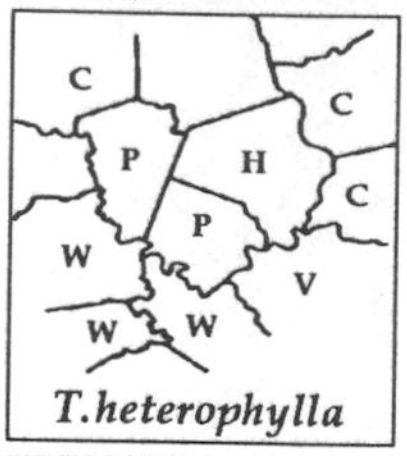

T. heterophylla

T. neglecta

Tiliaceae: Linden Family

Tilia americana L. and the "*T. americana*" species complex BASSWOOD, AMERICAN LINDEN
(Some of these records might be referred to *T. neglecta* Spach). Frequent in mesophytic woods.

Tilia floridana (V. Engler) Small BASSWOOD
In mesophytic woods. Probably more frequent than the records indicate. Bourbon (EG); Fayette (JBV).

Tilia heterophylla Vent. WHITE BASSWOOD
Fairly frequent in mesophytic woods.

Tilia neglecta Spach. BASSWOOD
Fairly frequent in mesophytic woods.

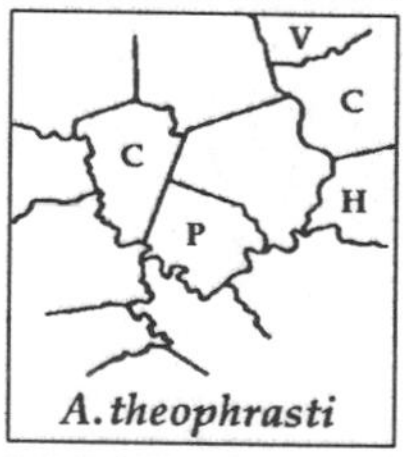

A. theophrasti

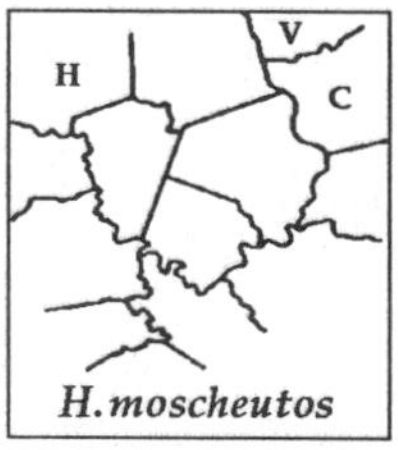

H. moscheutos

M. neglecta

Malvaceae: Mallow Family

Abutilon theophrasti Medic. VELVET-LEAF
A weed in fields and barnyards. Frequent. Introduced.

Hibiscus moscheutos L.
[=*H. palustris* Walt., not L., and *H. oculiroseus* Britt.] SWAMP ROSE MALLOW
In sinks and on margins of small sluggish streams. Infrequent.

M. rotundifolia

S. spinosa

Malva neglecta Wallr. CHEESES, COMMON MALLOW
A weed near barns and dwellings. Frequent. Introduced.

Malva rotundifolia L. ROUND-LEAVED MALLOW
In barnyards and waste places. Infrequent. Introduced.

Malva sylvestris L. HIGH MALLOW
An escape from cultivation. Fayette (UK). Introduced.

S. angusta

H. dolabriforme

Sida spinosa L. PRICKLY MALLOW
A common weed in fields and on roadsides. Introduced.

Sphaeralcea angusta (Gray) Fernald
[=*Malvastrum angustrum* Gray] FALSE MALLOW
A weed in fields. Frequent.

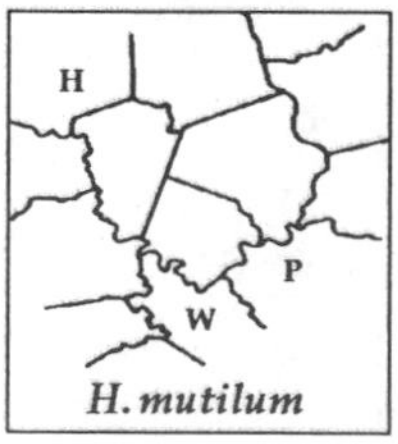

H. mutilum

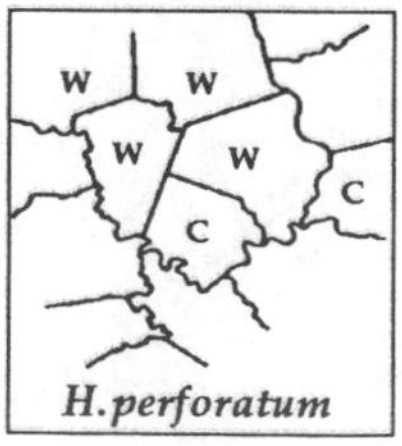

H. perforatum

Hypericaceae: St. John's-wort Family

Hypericum dolabriforme Vent.
On rocky bluffs. Infrequent.

Hypericum mutilum L.
On pond margins. Infrequent.

Hypericum perforatum L. COMMON ST. JOHN'S-WORT
In fields, meadows, and roadsides. Frequent. Introduced.

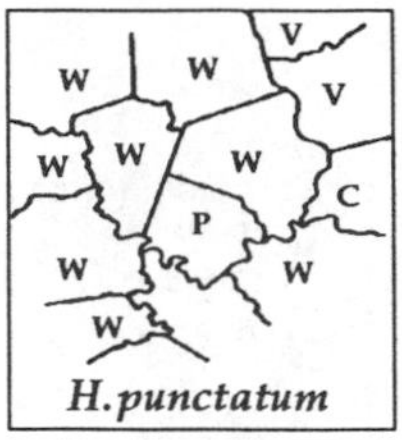

H. punctatum

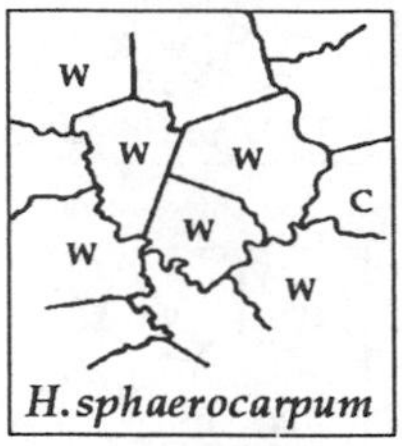

H. sphaerocarpum

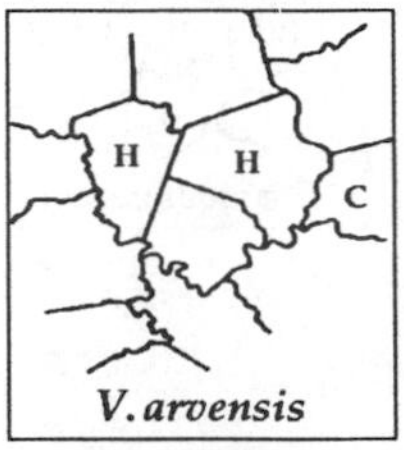

V. arvensis

V. cucullata

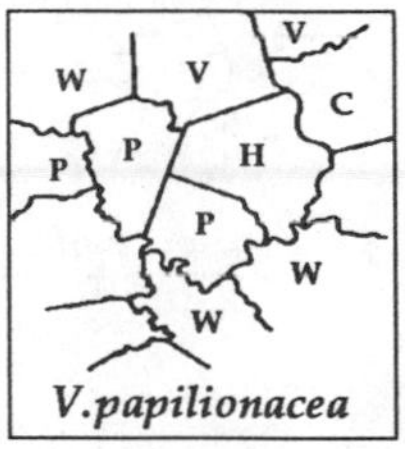

V. papilionacea

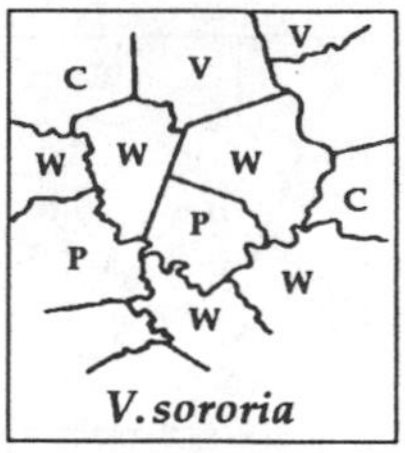

V. sororia

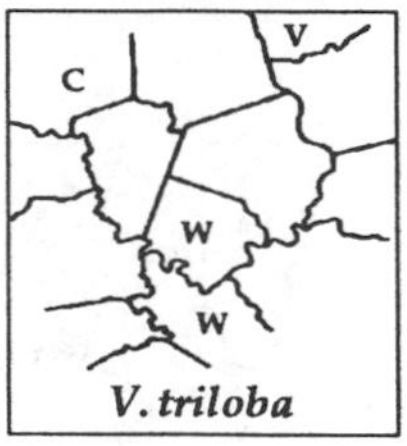

V. triloba

Hypericum punctatum Lam.
Very frequent in thickets and borders of woods.

Hypericum prolificum L. SHRUBBY ST. JOHN'S-WORT
On creek banks and wooded bluffs. Infrequent.

Hypericum sphaerocarpum Michx.
Fairly frequent on sunny limestone ledges and other dry, sunny rocky situations.

Violaceae: Violet Family

Hybanthus concolor (Forst.) Spreng. GREEN VIOLET
Frequent in rich woods.

Viola arvensis Murr. WILD PANSY
In pastures and on roadsides. Infrequent. Introduced.

Viola canadensis L. CANADA VIOLET
In rich mesophytic woods on lower slopes. Infrequent.

Viola cucullata Ait. MARSH BLUE VIOLET
In moist ground. Infrequent.

Viola eriocarpa Schw.
[= *V. pensylvanica* Michx.] SMOOTH YELLOW VIOLET
Frequent in woods.

Viola palmata L.
Infrequent. Mercer (UK).

Viola papilionacea Pursh COMMON BLUE VIOLET
Species among the stemless blue violets are in a state of being revised, with species delineations shifted. However, for the present we are retaining the name *V. papilionacea* for the common violet of lawns, meadows, and roadsides, which is abundant in this region.

Viola pubescens Ait.
In woods. Infrequent. Fayette (UK); Jessamine (C&M), Woodford (UK).

Viola rafinesquii Greene RAFINESQUE'S VIOLET, FIELD PANSY
In meadows and fields, at edges of woods, and on roadsides. Common.

Viola sororia Willd. WOOLLY BLUE VIOLET
Frequent in dry open woods.

Viola striata Ait. WHITE VIOLET, STRIPED VIOLET
Common in moist thickets, on creek banks, and on floodplains.

Viola triloba Schw. THREE-LOBED VIOLET
In dry open woods on cliffs, often with red cedar. Infrequent.

V. triloba var. *dilatata* Elliott & Brainerd
A single record, Mercer (MEW).

Viola walteri House
On rocky cliffs. Rare. Jessamine (C&M).

Passifloraceae: Passion-flower Family

Passiflora incarnata L. PASSION-FLOWER
Along fencerows and in old pastures. Fairly frequent.

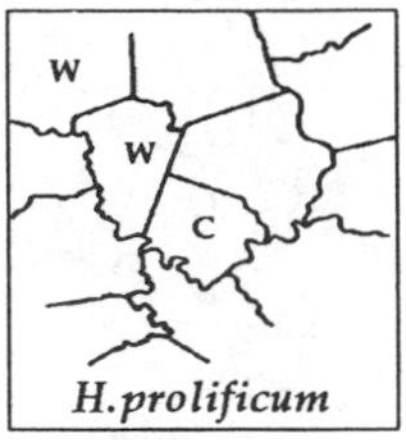

H. prolificum

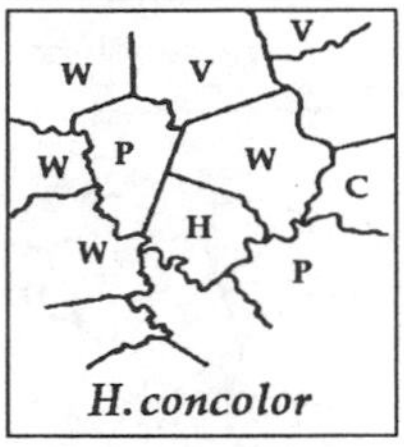

H. concolor

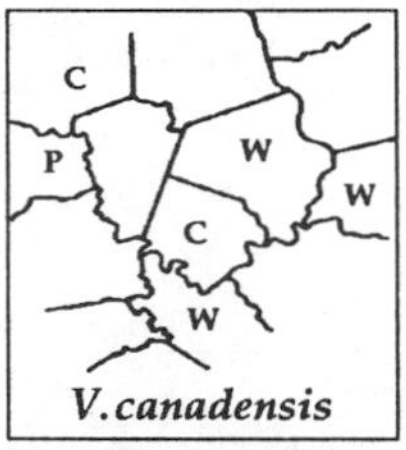

V. canadensis

V. eriocarpa

V. rafinesquii

V. striata

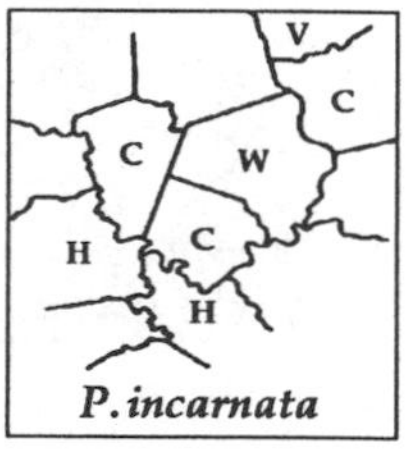

P. incarnata

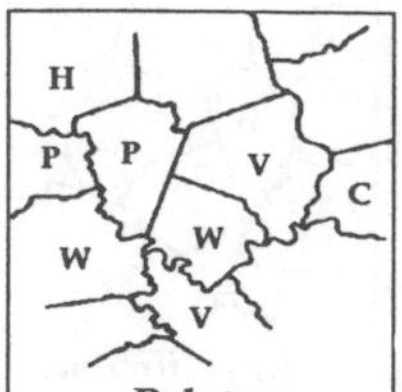

P. lutea var. glabriflora

Passiflora lutea L. var. *glabriflora* Fernald
YELLOW PASSION-FLOWER
In open woods. Fairly frequent.

Cactaceae: Cactus Family

O. humifusa

Opuntia humifusa Raf. PRICKLY PEAR
Frequent on dry, exposed limestone, or in very thin soil, in full sunlight.

Thymelaeaceae: Mezereum Family

D. palustris

Dirca palustris L. LEATHERWOOD
On sides of wooded ravines. Infrequent.

Lythraceae: Loosestrife Family

C. viscosissima

Cuphea viscosissima Jacq.
[= *C. petiolata* (L.) Koehne] CLAMMY CUPHEA
In fields, pastures, and roadsides. Frequent.

Lythrum salicaria L. LOOSESTRIFE
In wet ground. A single record, Woodford (UK). Introduced.

Rotala ramosior (L.) Koehne var. *interior* Fern. & Grisc.
TOOTH-CUP
On mud flats of the Kentucky River. A single record, Jessamine (UK). Introduced.

Onagraceae: Evening Primrose Family

C. lutetiana ssp. canadensis

Circaea lutetiana L. ssp. *canadensis* (L.) Asch. & Magn.
[= *C. quadrisulcata* (Maxim.) Franch. and Sav.]
ENCHANTER'S NIGHTSHADE
Frequent in woods.

E. coloratum

Epilobium coloratum Biehl. WILLOW-HERB
In swamps, creek margins, and creek beds. Infrequent.

Epilobium hirsutum L. GREAT HAIRY WILLOW-HERB
On margin of creek by quarry. A single record, Fayette (JBV). Introduced.

G. biennis

Gaura biennis L.
In low, moist sunny ground. Infrequent.

Ludwigia alternifolia L. SEEDBOX
In wet ground. Infrequent. Fayette (UK); Jessamine (UK).

L. decurrens

Ludwigia decurrens Walt.
[= *Jussiaea decurrens* (Walt.) DC.] PRIMOSE-WILLOW
In wet ground. Infrequent.

L. peploides ssp. glabrescens

Ludwigia peploides (HBK) Raven ssp. *glabrescens* (Kuntz) Raven
[= *Jussiaea repens* L. var. *glabrescens* Kuntz]
Fairly frequent in water at edges of ponds and slow streams.

L. palustris

Ludwigia palustris (L.) Ell. var. *americana* (DC.) Fern. & Grisc. MARSH PURSLANE
On pond borders. Infrequent.

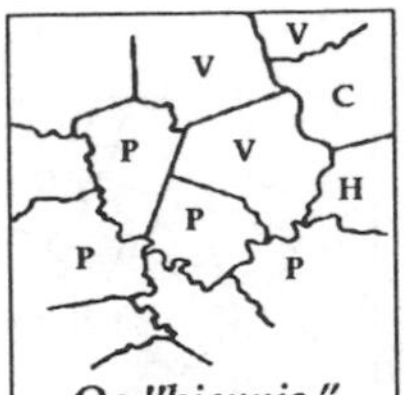

Oe. "biennis," the species complex

Oenothera biennis L. and the *O. biennis* complex
EVENING PRIMROSE
In fields and on roadsides. Frequent.

Oenothera speciosa Nutt. WHITE EVENING PRIMROSE
In fields and on roadsides. Harrison (JBV).

Araliaceae: Ginseng Family

Aralia racemosa L. SPIKENARD
A single record, from a rich, mesophytic wooded slope; Woodford (MEW).

Panax quinquefolium L. GINSENG
In rich mesophytic woods. Becoming rare.

P. quinquefolium

Hedera helix L. ENGLISH IVY
On cliffs above creeks; an escape from cultivation. Fayette (MEW); Franklin (SR). Introduced.

Apiaceae: Parsley Family

Aethusa cynapium L. FOOL'S PARSLEY
In waste ground. A single record, Fayette (MEW). Introduced.

B. rotundifolium

Bupleurum rotundifolium L. HARE'S-EAR
On dry, sunny ledges at the edge of woods. Infrequent.

C. procumbens

Chaerophyllum procumbens (L.) Crantz CHERVIL
Frequent in thickets in low ground.

C. tainturieri

Chaerophyllum tainturieri Hook. CHERVIL
Frequent in woodland borders and on roadsides.

Cicuta maculata

Cicuta maculata L. WATER HEMLOCK
Frequent on floodplains and in swamp thickets.

Conium maculatum

Conium maculatum L. POISON HEMLOCK
Common in fields and on roadsides, especially in moist ground. Introduced.

C. canadensis

Cryptotaenia canadensis (L.) DC.
Frequent in woods.

D. carota

Daucus carota L. QUEEN ANNE'S-LACE, WILD CARROT
Common in fields and on roadsides.

E. bulbosa

Erigenia bulbosa (Michx.) Nutt.
HARBINGER-OF-SPRING
Frequent in rich mesophytic woods on creek banks and ravine slopes.

Ligusticum canadense L. Britt. ANGELICO
In moist woods. Rare. Anderson (Pal); Madison (Pal).

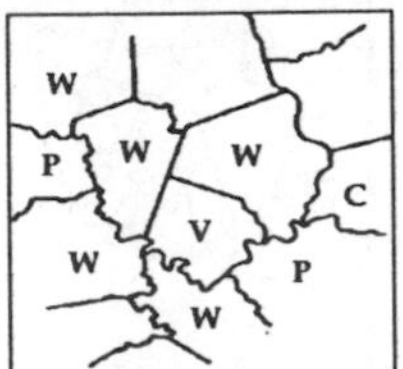

O. claytoni

Osmorhiza claytoni (Michx.) Clarke
HAIRY SWEET CICELY
Frequent on mesophytic wooded slopes.

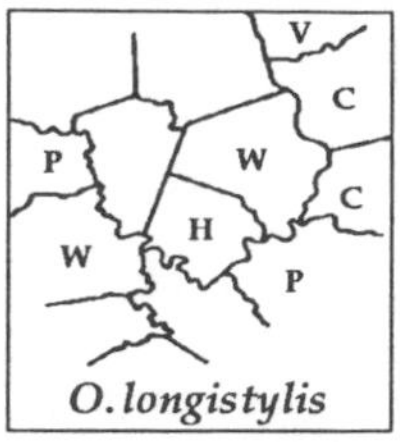

O. longistylis

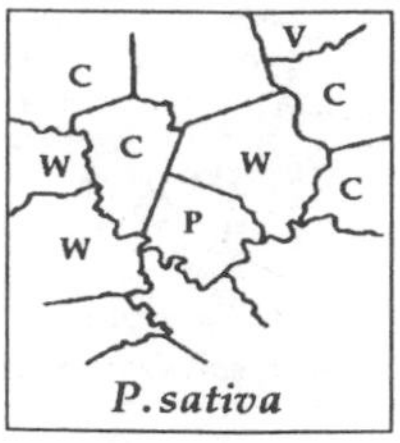

P. sativa

Osmorhiza longistylis (Torr.) DC. SWEET CICELY, SWEET ANISE
Frequent in woods.

Pastinaca sativa L. WILD PARSNIP
A fairly common weed along roadsides and in waste places. Introduced.

S. canadensis

Perideridia americana (Nutt.) Reichenb.
In moist woods. Rare. Jessamine (McF, Mei).

Sanicula canadensis L. (typical) SANICLE
Fairly frequent in woods.

S. canadensis var. *grandis* Fernald
Franklin (MEW).

S. gregaria

S. trifoliata

Sanicula gregaria Bickn.
In woods. Rare.

Sanicula trifoliata Bickn.
In woods. Infrequent.

T. integerrima

Taenidia integerrima (L.) Drude YELLOW PIMPERNEL
In dry woods. Infrequent.

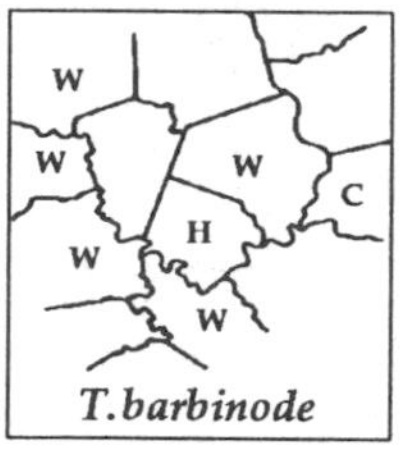

T. barbinode

Thaspium barbinode (Michx.) Nutt. MEADOW PARSNIP
Frequent in woods.

Thaspium trifoliatum (L.) Gray (typical) MEADOW PARSNIP
A single record, Anderson (MEW).

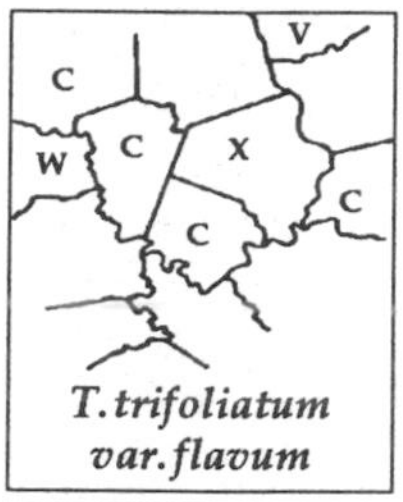

T. trifoliatum var. flavum

T. trifoliatum var. *flavum* Blake
In woods. Infrequent.

T. arvensis

Torilis arvensis (Huds.) Link
[= *T. japonica* (Houtt.) DC.] HEDGE-PARSLEY
Abundant along roadsides and in fields and thickets. Introduced.

Z. aptera

Zizia aptera (Gray) Fernald GOLDEN ALEXANDERS
Frequent in woods.

Zizia aurea L. GOLDEN ALEXANDERS
In moist woods. Rare. Fayette (UK); Woodford (UK).

Zizia trifoliata (Michx.) Fernald
A single record, Clark (UK).

N. sylvatica

Nyssaceae: Sour Gum Family

Nyssa sylvatica Marsh. SOUR GUM, BLACK GUM
Rare in the region.

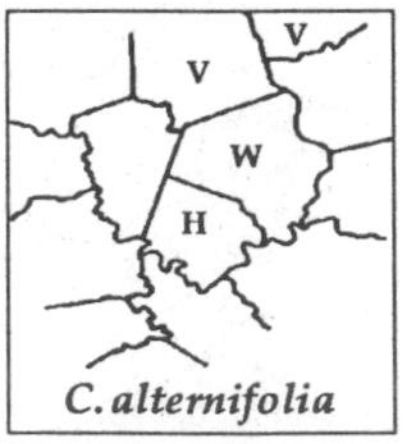

C. alternifolia

Cornaceae: Dogwood Family

Cornus alternifolia L. f. ALTERNATE-LEAF DOGWOOD
On creek banks and rich, wooded slopes. Infrequent.

Cornus amomum Mill. SILKY DOGWOOD
In wet ground. Rare in the region. Jessamine (UK).

C. drummondi

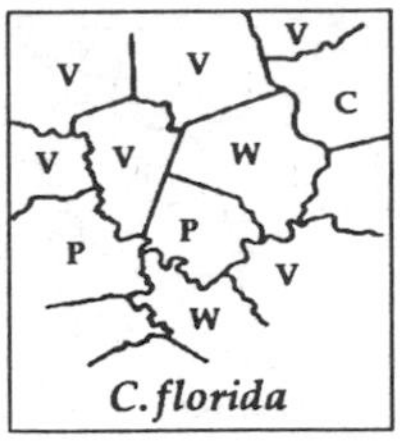

C. florida

Cornus drummondi Meyer ROUGH-LEAF DOGWOOD
Common at the edges of woods.

Cornus florida L. FLOWERING DOGWOOD
Frequent in woods.

Cornus obliqua Raf. PALE DOGWOOD
In wet ground. Rare. Franklin (SR); Jessamine (JBV); Woodford (MEW).

Pyrolaceae: Wintergreen Family

Chimaphila maculata (L.) Pursh.
SPOTTED WINTERGREEN
In the vicinity of the Kentucky River. Very rare. Fayette (UK) (now gone from this location); Jessamine (UK).

Ericaceae: Heath Family

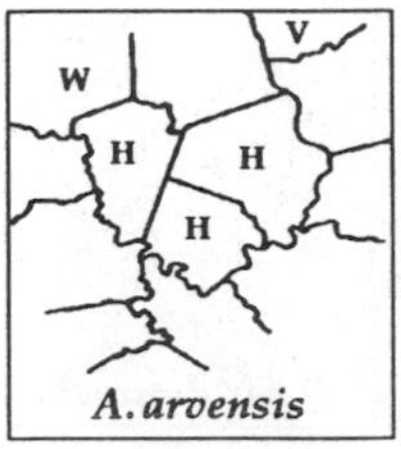

A. arvensis

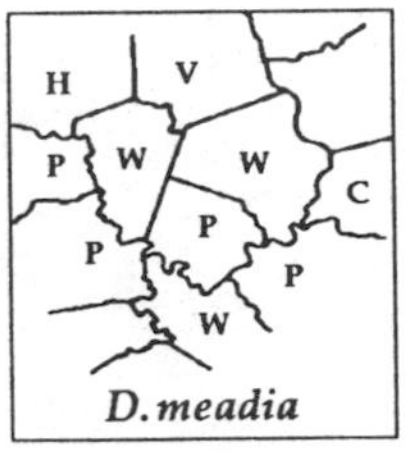

D. meadia

Vaccinium stamineum L. DEERBERRY
Kentucky River cliffs. A single record, Jessamine (UK).

Primulaceae: Primrose Family

Anagallis arvensis L. SCARLET PIMPERNEL
In fields and lawns. Fairly frequent. Introduced.

L. ciliata

L. lanceolata

Dodecatheon meadia L. SHOOTING STAR
Frequent on moist or dripping ledges in woods.

Lysimachia ciliata L. FRINGED LOOSESTRIFE
In swampy ground and stream borders. Infrequent.

Lysimachia lanceolata Walt. LANCE-LEAF LOOSESTRIFE
In moist soil. Infrequent.

L. nummularia

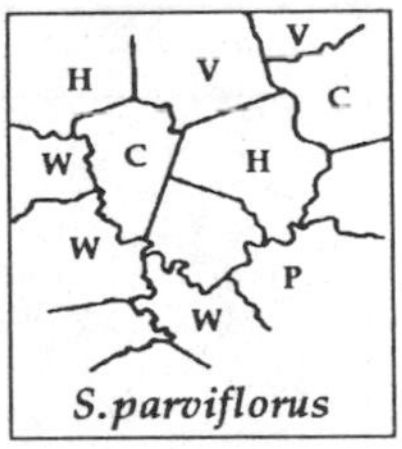

S. parviflorus

Lysimachia nummularia L. MONEYWORT
On creek banks and in ditches. Infrequent. Introduced.

Lysimachia quadrifolia L.
On dry upland. A single record. Jessamine (C&M).

Samolus parviflorus Raf. WATER PIMPERNEL
Fairly frequent on river floodplains and creek banks.

Ebenaceae: Ebony Family

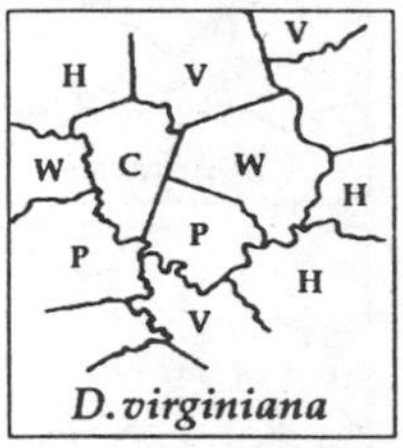

D. virginiana

F. americana

Diospyros virginiana Raf. PERSIMMON
Common in old fields and woodland borders.

Oleaceae: Olive Family

Fraxinus americana L. WHITE ASH
Common on mesic slopes and found in a variety of habitats.

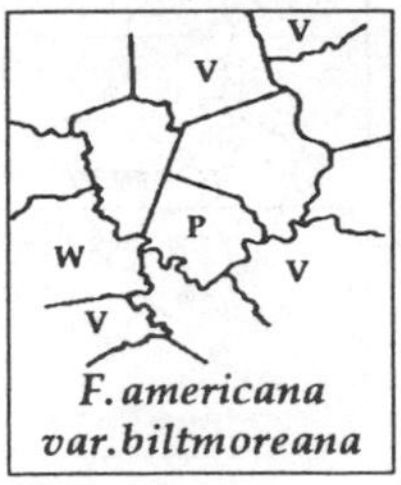

F. americana var. biltmoreana

F. pennsylvanica

F. americana var. *biltmoreana* (Beadle) Wright
Less frequent than the typical variety.

Fraxinus pennsylvanica Marsh RED ASH
Fairly frequent in moist ground.

F.pennsylvanica var.subintegerrima

F. pennsylvanica var. *subintegerrima* (Vahl) Fernald
GREEN ASH
Frequent in moist ground: creek banks, floodplains, and sinks.

F.quadrangulata

Fraxinus quadrangulata Michx. BLUE ASH
A common and characteristic tree of the region. On wooded cliffs. Old trees occur in long-established pastures.

Ligustrum ibota Sieb. IBOTA PRIVET
An escape from cultivation. Fayette (MEW). Introduced.

Gentianaceae: Gentian Family

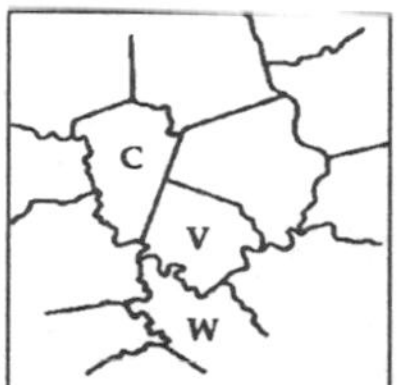

S.angularis

Obolaria virginica L. PENNYWORT
With red cedar and oaks on limestone ledges. Infrequent. Garrard (MEW); Woodford (UK).

Sabatia angularis (L.) Pursh
In cedar glades and other open, rocky areas. Rare in the region.

S.caroliniensis

Swertia caroliniensis (Walt.) Ktze. AMERICAN COLUMBO
Fairly frequent on dry, open wooded slopes and cliff summits.

Apocynaceae: Dogbane Family

A.cannabinum

Apocynum androsaemifolium L. DOGBANE
A single record, from a bluff of the Kentucky River; Fayette (MEW).

Apocynum cannabinum L. INDIAN HEMP
At the edge of woodlands and old fields. Common.

V.minor

Vinca minor L. MYRTLE, PERIWINKLE
An escape from cultivation, at old homesites, old cemeteries, and sometimes on roadsides. Introduced.

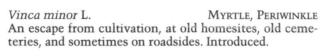

A.incarnata

Asclepiadaceae: Milkweed Family

Asclepias incarnata L. SWAMP MILKWEED
Frequent in moist, usually sunny, situations such as creek banks and swamps.

A.quadrifolia

Asclepias quadrifolia Jacq. FOUR-LEAVED MILKWEED
Frequent on wooded hillsides.

A.syriaca

Asclepias syriaca L. COMMON MILKWEED
Abundant in old fields and along roadsides.

A.tuberosa

Asclepias tuberosa L. BUTTERFLY-WEED
In sunny borders of woodlands and old fields. Infrequent.

Asclepias verticillata L.
In dry open areas. Rare. Anderson (Pal); Jessamine (McF).

A.viridis

Asclepias viridis Walt.
[=*Asclepiodora viridis* (Walt.) Gray] SPIDER-MILKWEED
On dry sunny slopes, old fields, and roadsides. Infrequent.

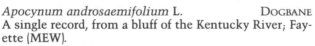

C. laeve

Cynanchum laeve (Michx.) Pers.
[=*Ampelamus albidus* (Nutt.) Britt.] SANDVINE, HONEYVINE
Frequent in fencerows and thickets, especially in moist ground.

Matelea gonocarpa (Walt.) Shinners
[=*Gonolobus gonocarpos* (Walt.) Pers.] ANGLE-POD
A single record, from a grassy field; Mercer (JBV).

M. obliqua

Matelea obliqua (Jacq.) Woodson
[=*Gonolobus obliquus* (Jacq.) Schultes] ANGLE-POD
In open woods, borders of woods, and thickets. Infrequent.

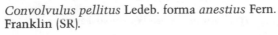

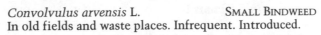

Convolvulaceae: Morning-glory Family

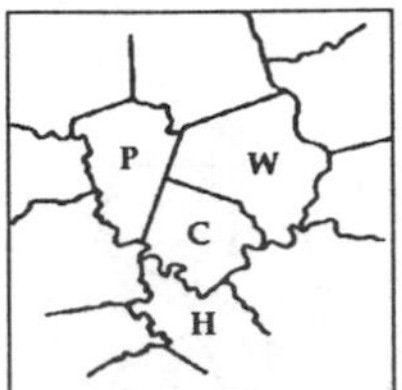

C. sepium

Calystegia sepium (L.) R. Brown
[=*Convolvulus sepium* L.] HEDGE BINDWEED
Fairly frequent in fields and thickets and on roadsides.

Calystegia spithamaea (L.) R. Brown
[=*Convolvulus spithamaeus* L.]
In dry open woods. A single record, Boyle (UK).

C. arvensis

Convolvulus arvensis L. SMALL BINDWEED
In old fields and waste places. Infrequent. Introduced.

Convolvulus pellitus Ledeb. forma *anestius* Fern.
Franklin (SR).

Cuscuta campestris Yuncker DODDER
Parasitic on weeds. Infrequent. Franklin (MEW); Mercer (MEW).

C. gronovii

Cuscuta epithymum Murr. DODDER
Parastic on clover and other legumes. A single record, Woodford (UK). Introduced.

Cuscuta gronovii Willd. ex R. & S DODDER
Parasitic on various old field species. Frequent.

C. pentagona

Cuscuta pentagona Engelm. DODDER
Parasitic on many species. Fairly frequent.

I. coccinea

Cuscuta polygonorum Engelm. DODDER
Parasitic on lowland plants. Infrequent. Scott (UK); Woodford (EC).

Ipomoea coccinea L. RED MORNING-GLORY
On river banks and roadsides, an escape from cultivation. Infrequent. Introduced.

I. hederacea

Ipomoea hederacea (L.) Jacq.
IVY-LEAF MORNING-GLORY
A common weed in cultivated ground. Introduced.

I. lacunosa

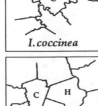

Ipomoea lacunosa L. SMALL WHITE MORNING-GLORY
Fairly frequent in cultivated fields, meadows, and thickets.

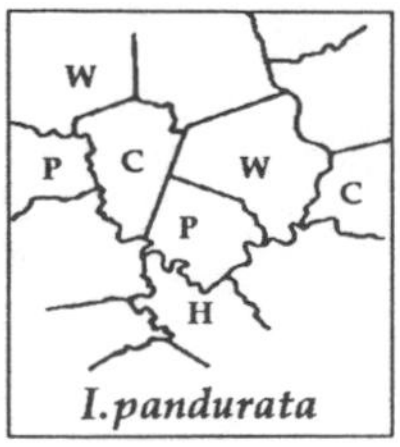

I.pandurata

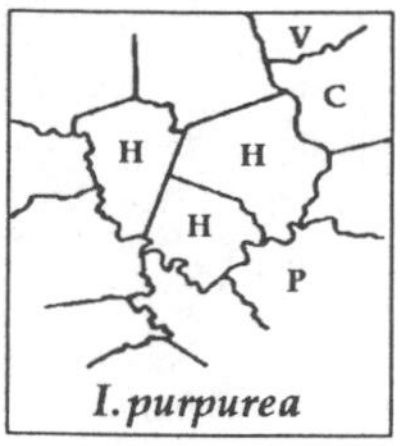

I.purpurea

Ipomoea pandurata (L.) G.F.W. Mey. WILD POTATO-VINE
Common in fields, fencerows, and thickets.

Ipomoea purpurea (L.) Roth COMMON MORNING-GLORY
Common in fields and borders of cultivated ground. Introduced.

Polemoniaceae: Phlox Family

Phlox amplifolia Britt. BROADLEAF PHLOX
On creek banks and other moist wooded slopes. Infrequent. Frankfort (MEW); Woodford (MEW).

P.divaricata

Phlox bifida Beck. [including var. *cedaria* (Brand) Fern.] SAND PHLOX
Dry sunny limestone ledges and cliffs. Rare. Garrard (MEW); Jessamine (UK).

P.paniculata

Phlox divaricata L. BLUE PHLOX
Common in rich woods.

P.reptans

Phlox paniculata L. SUMMER PHLOX, PANICLED PHLOX
On wooded creek banks, alluvial bottoms, and seepage areas. Frequent.

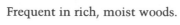

Polemonium reptans L. JACOB'S-LADDER, GREEK VALERIAN
Frequent in rich, moist woods.

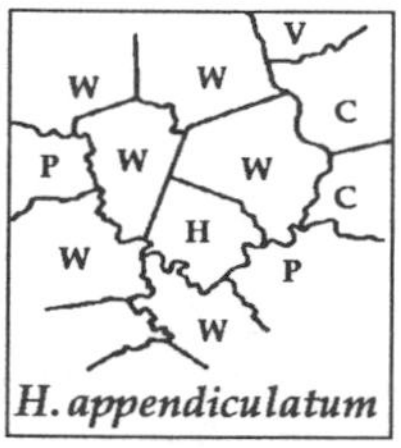

H.appendiculatum

Hydrophyllaceae: Waterleaf Family

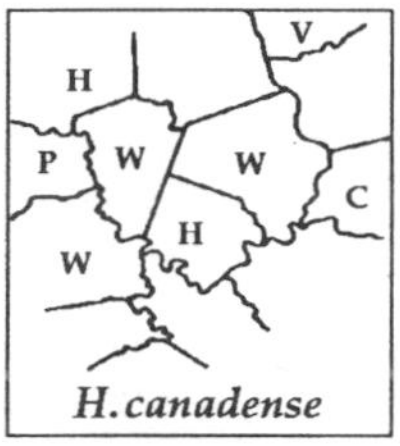

H.canadense

Hydrophyllum appendiculatum Michx. APPENDAGED WATERLEAF
Frequent in moist woods on creek banks and at bases of cliffs.

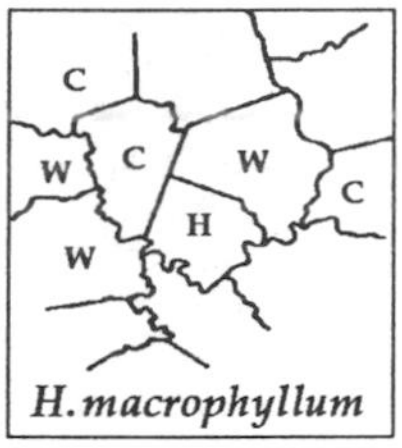

H.macrophyllum

Hydrophyllum canadense L. BROAD-LEAF WATERLEAF
Fairly frequent in ravines in mesophytic woods.

Hydrophyllum macrophyllum Nutt. LARGE-LEAF WATERLEAF
Very frequent in woods.

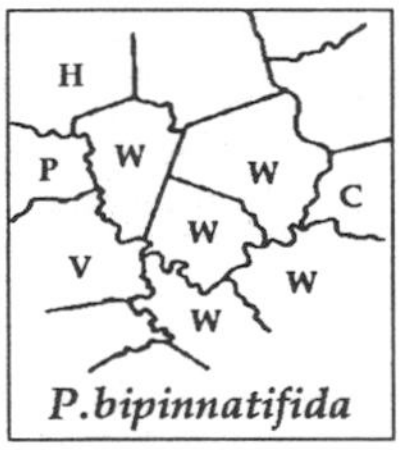

P.bipinnatifida

Hydrophyllum virginianum L.
In rich woods. Rare. Anderson (Pal); Fayette (UK); Woodford (EC).

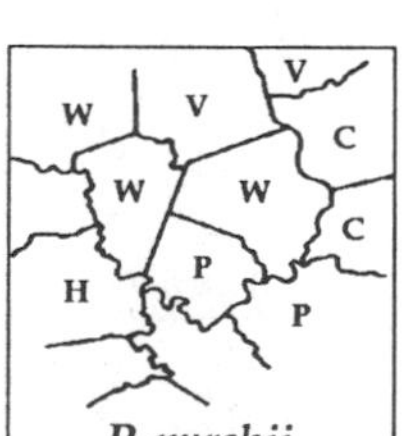

P.purshii

Phacelia bipinnatifida Michx. PURPLE PHACELIA
Very frequent in leaf mold on ledges of cliffs.

Phacelia purshii Buckl. MIAMI MIST
Common in alluvial woods, on sunny creek banks, and along small roads.

C.virginianum

Boraginaceae: Borage Family

Cynoglossum officinale L. HOUNDS-TONGUE
A single record, Fayette (UK). Introduced.

Cynoglossum virginianum L. WILD COMFREY
On dry wooded slopes. Infrequent.

E. vulgare

H. virginiana

Echium vulgare L. BLUEWEED
On bluffs and other sunny, rocky situations. Infrequent. Introduced.

Hackelia virginiana (L.) I. M. Johnston STICKSEED, BEGGAR'S-LICE
Frequent in open woods and thickets.

L. arvense

Lithospermum arvense L. CORN GROMWELL
Common on roadsides. Introduced.

M. virginica

Lithospermum latifolium Michx. GROMWELL
In dry open woods. Infrequent. Clark (MRB); Jessamine (McF).

Mertensia virginica (L.) Pers. VIRGINIA BLUEBELLS
Frequent in shady alluvial ground and on moist wooded slopes.

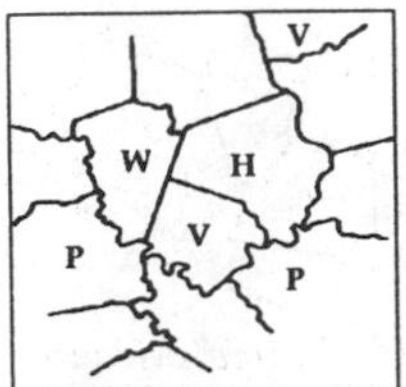

M. macrosperma

Myosotis arvensis (L.) Hill FORGET-ME-NOT
In fields and on roadsides. Infrequent. Clark (MRB); Fayette (MEW). Introduced.

M. verna

Myosotis macrosperma Engelm. FORGET-ME-NOT
Fairly frequent in moist woods and thickets on bottomlands.

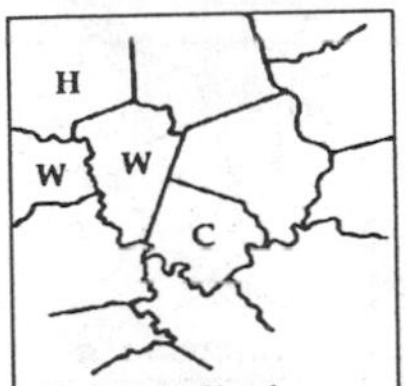

O. hispidissimum

Myosotis verna Nutt. FORGET-ME-NOT
In open rocky woods. Infrequent.

Onosmodium hispidissimum Mackenz. FALSE GROMWELL
In dry rocky ground. Infrequent.

L. lanceolata

Verbenaceae: Verbena Family

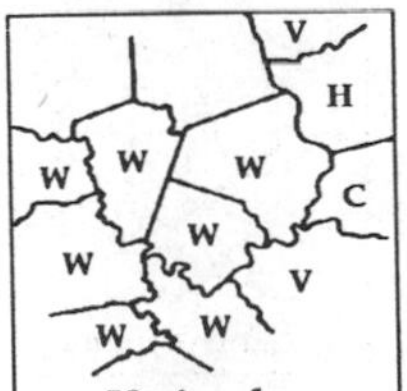

V. simplex

Lippia lanceolata Michx. FOG-FRUIT
On floodplains, creek margins, and in creek beds. Frequent.

Verbena hastata L. BLUE VERVAIN
In wet ground. Rare. Anderson (MEW); Boyle (MEW).

V. urticifolia

Verbena simplex Lehm. NARROW-LEAVED VERVAIN
Frequent in thin soil on ridges and sunny cliffs.

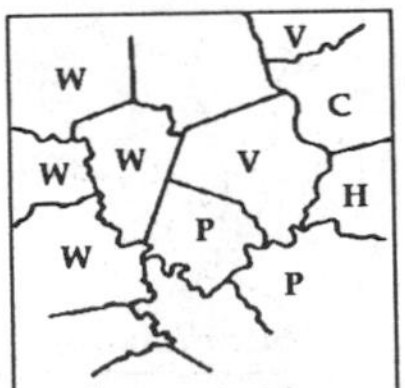

A. nepetoides

Verbena urticifolia L. WHITE VERVAIN
Frequent in borders of woods and openings in woods; also in waste places.

Lamiaceae: Mint Family

Agastache nepetoides (L.) Ktze. GIANT HYSSOP
Frequent in woods.

B. ciliata

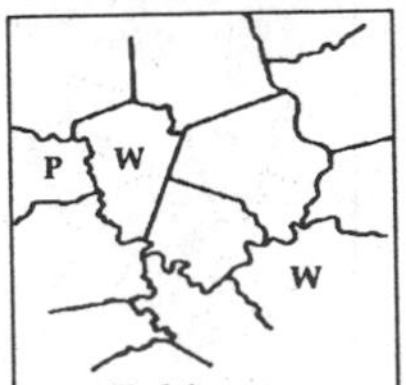

B. hirsuta

Blephilia ciliata (L.) Benth. WOOD-MINT
Frequent in open woods on uplands.

Blephilia hirsuta (Pursh) Benth. WOOD-MINT
On creek banks and in seepage areas. Infrequent.

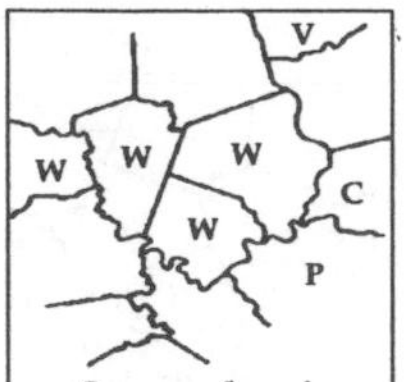

C. canadensis

G. hederacea

Collinsonia canadensis L. CITRONELLA
Fairly frequent on rich mesophytic wooded slopes.

Glechoma hederacea L. LARGE-FLOWERED GROUND-IVY
Frequent in moist, shady places.

G. hederacea var. *micrantha* Moric. SMALL-FLOWERED GROUND-IVY
Common in lawns, in gardens, and on roadsides.

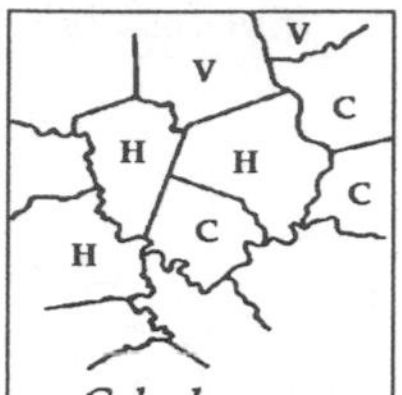

G. hederacea var. micrantha

H. pulegioides

Hedeoma pulegioides (L.) Pers. PENNYROYAL
Frequent in dry open woods on uplands; also in old fields and pastures.

Isanthus brachiatus (L.) BSP. FALSE PENNYROYAL
On dry slopes. Infrequent.

I. brachiatus

L. amplexicaule

Lamium amplexicaule L. HENBIT
A common weed in gardens and other cultivated areas. Introduced.

Lamium purpureum L. PURPLE DEAD-NETTLE
Common on roadsides and in woodland borders. Introduced.

L. purpureum

L. cardiaca

Leonurus cardiaca L. MOTHERWORT
Frequent in barnyards and waste places. Introduced.

Lycopus americanus Muhl. BUGLE-WEED
On creek and pond margins, in swamps, and on floodplains. Infrequent.

L. americanus

L. virginicus

Lycopus virginicus L. BUGLE-WEED
On creek and pond margins, in swamps, and on floodplains. Fairly frequent.

Marrubium vulgare L. HOREHOUND
On roadsides, in waste places, and in borders of dry woods. Infrequent. Introduced.

Meehania cordata (Nutt.) Britt.
In ravine in mesophytic woods. A single record, Jessamine (UK).

M. vulgare

M. officinalis

Melissa officinalis L. LEMON BALM
On roadsides and in waste places; an escape from cultivation. Infrequent. Introduced.

Mentha longifolia (L.) Huds. HORSEMINT
A rare escape. Fayette (UK); Jessamine (McF). Introduced.

Mentha piperita L. PEPPERMINT
Near springs. Infrequent. Introduced.

Mentha rotundifolia L. ROUND-LEAVED MINT
A rare escape. Fayette (UK). Introduced.

Mentha spicata L. SPEARMINT
Frequent near springs and on creek margins. Introduced.

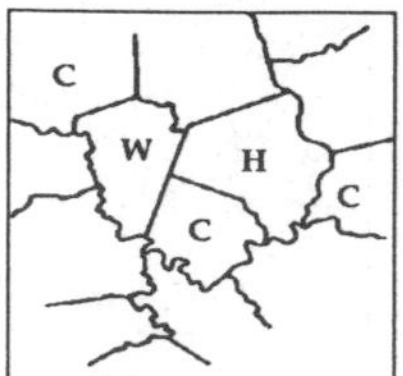

M. piperita

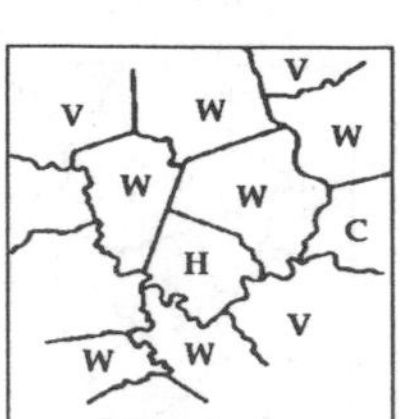

M. spicata

Monarda clinopodia L.
A single record, Jessamine (UK).

M. fistulosa var. mollis

Monarda fistulosa L. (typical) WILD BERGAMOT
Infrequent. Fayette (UK), Franklin (UK).

M. fistulosa L. var. *mollis* (L.) Benth. WILD BERGAMOT
Frequent in old fields with shrubs and at the edges of woods.

N. cataria

Nepeta cataria L. CATNIP
Frequent near dwellings, on roadsides, and in waste places. Introduced.

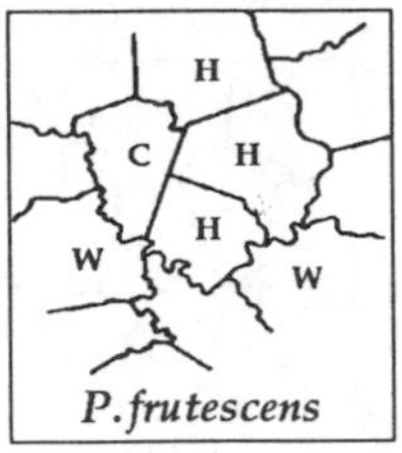

P. frutescens

Perilla frutescens (L.) Britt.
Frequent on roadsides and in barnyards. Introduced.

Physostegia virginiana (L) Benth. FALSE DRAGONHEAD
A single record, from Clay's Ferry (Fayette or Madison County); collected in 1893 (UK).

P. vulgaris

P. vulgaris var. lanceolata

Prunella vulgaris L. (typical) SELF-HEAL, HEAL-ALL
Infrequent. Introduced.

P. vulgaris L. var. *lanceolata* (Bart.) Fernald SELF-HEAL, HEAL-ALL
Very frequent in thickets, old fields, and borders of woods.

Pycnanthemum pycnanthemoides (Leavenw.) Fernald HOARY MOUNTAIN-MINT
In open woods. A single record, Clark (MRB).

S. lyrata

Salvia lyrata L. LYRE-LEAVED SAGE
Frequent in open grassy woods and woodland borders.

Satureja glabella (Michx.) Briquet
On creek banks. Recorded only from Franklin (MEW), (UK), (SR).

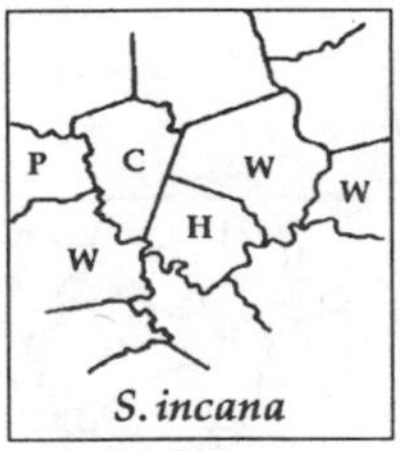

S. incana

Satureja vulgaris (L.) Fritsch var. *neogaea* Fernald WILD BASIL
A single record, from a dry open woods; Fayette (MEW).

S. lateriflora

Scutellaria incana Biehler DOWNY SKULLCAP
Frequent in woods, in thickets, and on creek banks.

Scutellaria lateriflora L. MAD-DOG SKULLCAP
On creek margins, in gravelly creek beds and swamps, and on floodplains. Frequent.

S. nervosa

Scutellaria nervosa Pursh VEINY SKULLCAP
In dry open woods. Infrequent.

S. ovalifolia ssp. hirsuta

Scutellaria ovalifolia Pers. ssp. *hirsuta* (Short & Peter) Epl.
[= *S. elliptica* Muhl.] HAIRY SKULLCAP
In open woods. Infrequent.

Scutellaria ovata Hill ssp. *calcarea* Epl.
A single record, Fayette (Epling).

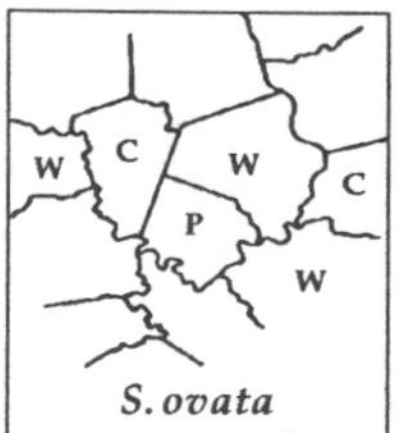

S. ovata ssp. versicolor

S. ovata ssp. *pseudovenosa* Epl.
A single record, Jessamine (Epling).

S. ovata (ssp. not distinguished)

S. ovata ssp. *versicolor* (Nutt.) Epl. HEART-LEAF SKULLCAP
Frequent in woods.

S. ovata (subspecies not distinguished)
Frequent in woods.

S. parvula

Scutellaria parvula Michx. SMALL SKULLCAP
On dry, sunny limestone. Infrequent.

Scutellaria saxatilis Riddell
A single record, Fayette (Epling).

S. riddellii

Stachys riddellii House HEDGE-NETTLE
In woods. Rare.

S. tenuifolia

Stachys tenuifolia Willd. HEDGE-NETTLE
On creek banks and the Kentucky River floodplain. Infrequent.

S. hispidula

Synandra hispidula (Michx.) Baill.
Fairly frequent in rich moist woods on lower slopes.

T. canadense

Teucrium canadense L. [including var. *virginicum* (L.) Eat.] GERMANDER
In thickets and fencerows; on sunny creek banks and river floodplains. Frequent.

Solanaceae: Nightshade Family

D. stramonium

Datura stramonium L. JIMSONWEED
A common weed along borders of cultivated fields and roadsides and in barnyards. Introduced.

N. physalodes

Lycium halimifolium Mill. MATRIMONY VINE
An infrequent escape from cultivation. Clark (UK); Fayette (UK). Introduced.

Nicandra physalodes (L.) Pers. APPLE-OF-PERU
On borders of cultivated fields, especially in alluvial soils. Infrequent. Introduced.

P. pubescens

P. heterophylla

Physalis angulata L. GROUND-CHERRY
A single record, from a grassy floodplain of the Kentucky River; Jessamine (Pal).

Physalis heterophylla Nees GROUND-CHERRY
Frequent in fields, especially in moist soil.

P. virginiana

P. subglabrata

Physalis pubescens L. GROUND-CHERRY
In fields and on roadsides. Infrequent.

Physalis subglabrata Mack. & Bush GROUND-CHERRY
Frequent in fields and meadows.

Physalis virginiana Mill. GROUND-CHERRY
In open woods, fields, and roadsides. Infrequent.

S. americanum

Solanum americanum Mill.
[=*S. nigrum* L.] NIGHTSHADE
A common weed in cultivated ground.

S. carolinense

Solanum carolinense L. HORSE-NETTLE
A common weed in pastures.

S. dulcamara

Solanum dulcamara L. BITTERSWEET NIGHTSHADE
In woodland borders, thickets, and waste places. Infrequent. Introduced.

Solanum rostratum Dunal BUFFALO-BUR
A weed in gardens. Infrequent. Fayette (UK); Clark (UK). Introduced.

Scrophulariaceae: Figwort Family

Aureolaria virginica (L.) Pennell FALSE FOXGLOVE
On wooded rocky slopes. Rare. Fayette (MEW); Jessamine (McF).

Chaenorrhinum minus (L.) Lange
DWARF SNAPDRAGON
Along railroad tracks. Infrequent. Fayette (UK); Franklin (MEW).

Chelone glabra L. TURTLEHEAD
In swamps. Rare. Fayette (MEW); Woodford (UK).

C. verna

Collinsia verna Nutt. BLUE-EYED MARY
Frequent, locally profuse, in rich open woods.

C. multifida

Conobea multifida (Michx.) Benth.
On creek margins, creek beds, and mud flats of the Kentucky River. Infrequent.

Cymbalaria muralis (Gaertn.) Mey. & Scherb.
KENILWORTH IVY
An infrequent escape from cultivation. Fayette (UK); Franklin (UK).

D. macrophylla

Dasistoma macrophylla (Nutt.) Raf. MULLEIN FOXGLOVE
Frequent in open woods.

Gerardia tenuifolia Vahl GERARDIA
On limestone ledge under cedars. A single record, Jessamine (UK).

Gratiola neglecta Torr. HEDGE HYSSOP
Muddy bank of stream. Rare. Fayette (UK); Franklin (SR).

L. vulgaris

Gratiola virginiana L. HEDGE HYSSOP
On muddy banks of creeks. Fayette (UK).

Gratiola viscidula Pennell HEDGE HYSSOP
On muddy banks of small streams. Fayette (UK).

Linaria vulgaris Hill BUTTER-AND-EGGS
Fairly frequent on grassy roadsides; infrequent in fields. Introduced.

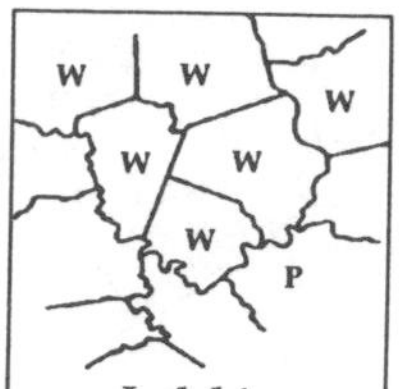

L. dubia

Lindernia anagallidea (Michx.) Pennell FALSE PIMPERNEL
In creek beds and on mud flats of the Kentucky River. Infrequent. Jessamine (UK), Scott (UK).

Lindernia dubia (L.) Pennell
Frequent on margins of ponds and small, quiet streams.

M. alatus

Mimulus alatus Ait. MONKEY-FLOWER
Frequent on margins of ponds and creeks and on river floodplains.

Mimulus ringens L. MONKEY-FLOWER
A single record, from floodplain of the Kentucky River; Mercer (MEW).

P. calycosus

Paulonia tomentosa (Thunb.) Steud. EMPRESS-TREE
On roadsides. An escape from cultivation. Anderson (JBV). Introduced.

Pedicularis canadensis L. WOOD-BETONY
On rocky ridges. Rare in the region. Garrard (UK).

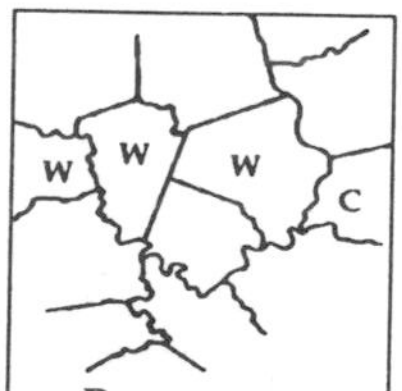

P. canescens

Penstemon calycosus Small BEARD-TONGUE
Fairly frequent in open woods, borders of woods, and meadows.

P. digitalis

Penstemon canescens Britt. BEARD-TONGUE
In dry open woods, on rocky banks, and in old fields. Infrequent.

P. hirsutus

Penstemon digitalis Nutt. BEARD-TONGUE
Fairly frequent in open woods.

P. laevigatus

Penstemon hirsutus (L.) Willd. BEARD-TONGUE
Common on sunny rocky banks and cliffs.

Penstemon laevigatus Soland BEARD-TONGUE
In open woods and meadows. Infrequent.

S. marilandica

Penstemon pallidus Small BEARD-TONGUE
A single record, Fayette (UK).

V. blattaria

Scrophularia marilandica L. FIGWORT
Frequent in open woods.

Verbascum blattaria L. MOTH MULLEIN
On roadsides and in fields and waste places. Common. Introduced.

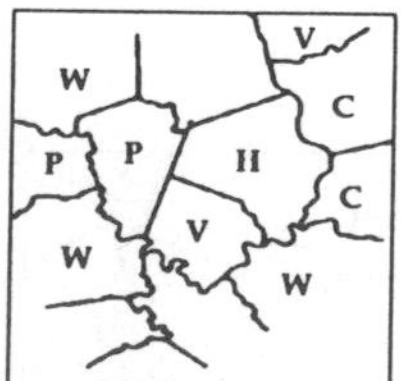

V. thapsus

Verbascum thapsus L. MULLEIN
Common on dry sunny banks and roadsides. Introduced.

V. anagallis-aquatica

Veronica agrestis L. FIELD SPEEDWELL
A single record, Jessamine (UK). Introduced.

Veronica anagallis-aquatica L. var. *anagalliformis* (Boreau) G. Beck. WATER PIMPERNEL
In small streams and on river margins. Infrequent.

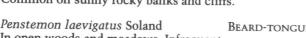

V. arvensis

V. hederaefolia

Veronica arvensis L. CORN SPEEDWELL
A common weed in lawns and fields. Introduced.

Veronica hederaefolia L. IVY-LEAVED SPEEDWELL
On grassy roadsides and in fields. Infrequent. Introduced.

Veronica officinalis L. COMMON SPEEDWELL
On dry, open wooded slopes. Infrequent.

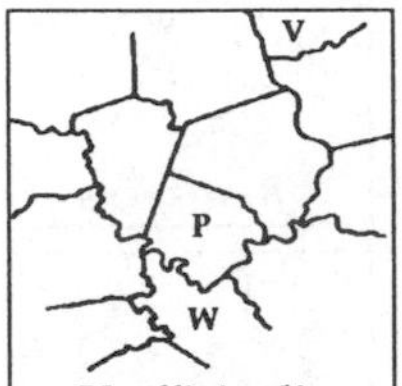

V. officinalis

V. peregrina

Veronica peregrina L. PURSLANE-SPEEDWELL
A fairly frequent weed in lawns and gardens. Introduced.

Veronica serpyllifolia L. THYME-LEAVED SPEEDWELL
On creek banks. Rare. Fayette (UK); Franklin (SR); Jessamine (McF). Introduced.

Bignoniaceae: Trumpet-creeper Family

B. capreolata

C. radicans

Bignonia capreolata L. CROSS-VINE
Frequent on wooded slopes and cliffs.

Campsis radicans (L.) Seem. TRUMPET-VINE
Abundant in thickets, fencerows, and old fields.

Catalpa bignonioides Walt. CATALPA
On edges of woods and creek banks. Infrequent.

C. bignonioides

C. speciosa

Catalpa speciosa Warder CATALPA
An infrequent escape from cultivation.

Martyniaceae: Martynia Family

Proboscidea louisianica (Mill.) Thell UNICORN-PLANT
A single record, Jessamine (Pal).

Orobanchaceae: Broom-rape Family

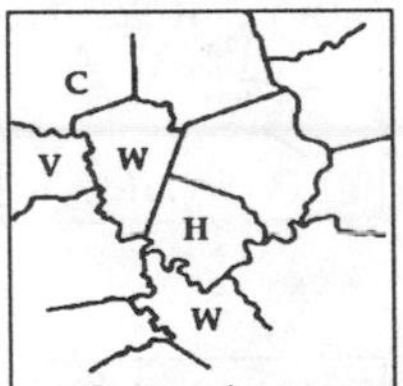

C. americana

E. virginiana

Conopholis americana (L.) Wallr. SQUAWROOT
Parasitic on roots of maple, elm, and oak. Infrequent.

Epifagus virginiana (L.) Bart. BEECH-DROPS
Parasitic on roots of beech. Infrequent.

Orobanche ludoviciana Nutt. BROOM-RAPE
Parasitic on composites. A single record, Jessamine (McF).

O. ramosa

O. uniflora

Orobanche ramosa L. BROOM-RAPE
Currently an infrequent parasite on roots of tobacco; prior to 1910, on hemp also.

Orobanche uniflora L. CANCER-ROOT
Parasitic on roots of various plants. Infrequent.

Acanthaceae: Acanthus Family

J. americana

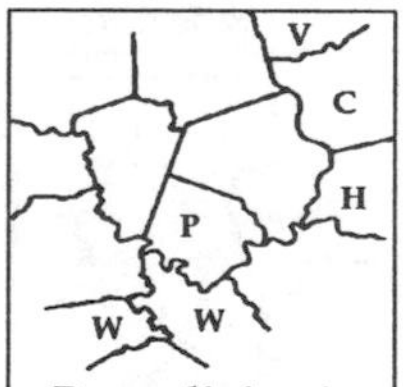

R. caroliniensis

Justicia americana (L.) Vahl WATER-WILLOW
Frequent in shallow, quiet water in creeks.

Ruellia caroliniensis (Walt.) Steud. (typical variety, and variety not distinguished)
At edges of woods and in openings in woods. Infrequent.

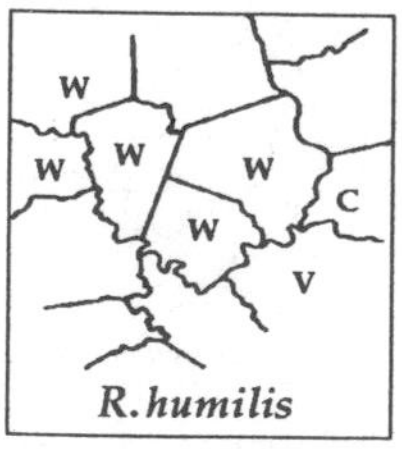

R. humilis

R. caroliniensis var. *membranacea* Fernald.
Boyle (MEW).

Ruellia humilis Nutt.
Frequent on sunny limestone ledges and other dry sunny situations.

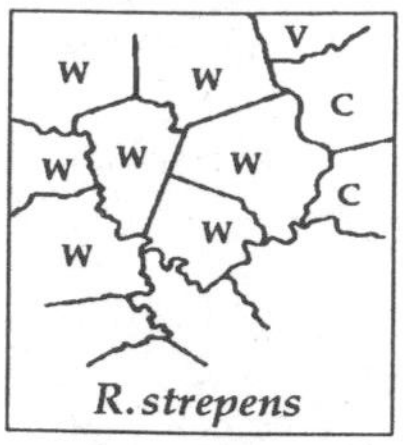

R. strepens

Ruellia strepens L. [including forma *cleistantha* (Gray) S. McCoy]
Frequent in open woods and at edges of woods.

Phrymaceae: Lopseed Family

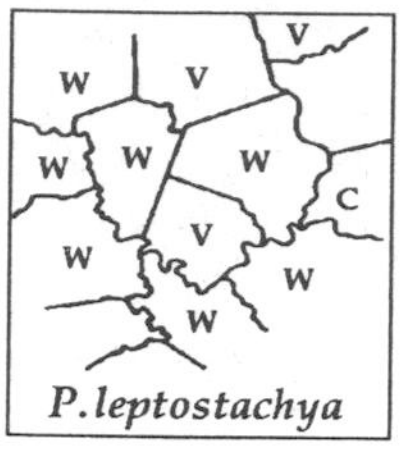

P. leptostachya

Phryma leptostachya L. LOPSEED
Frequent in woods.

Plantaginaceae: Plantain Family

P. aristata

Plantago aristata Michx. BRACTED PLANTAIN
Frequent in thin, rocky soil on dry sunny uplands.

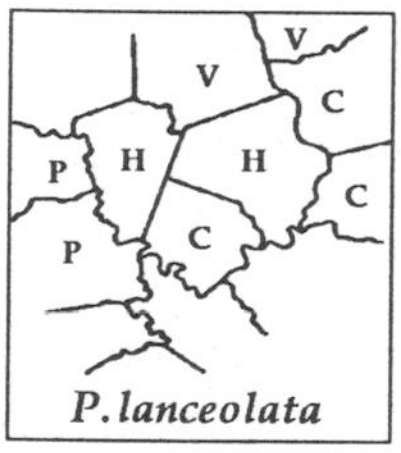

P. lanceolata

Plantago lanceolata L. BUCKHORN, ENGLISH PLANTAIN
A common weed in lawns and pastures and along roadsides. Introduced.

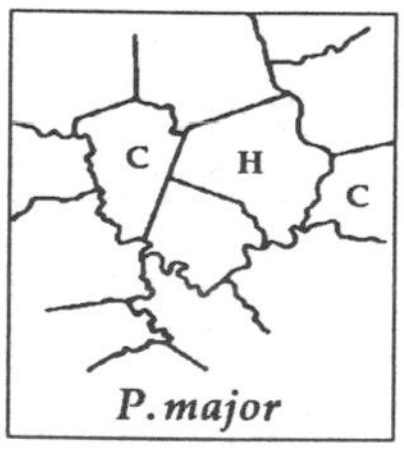

P. major

Plantago major L. COMMON PLANTAIN
A common weed in lawns and on roadsides. Introduced.

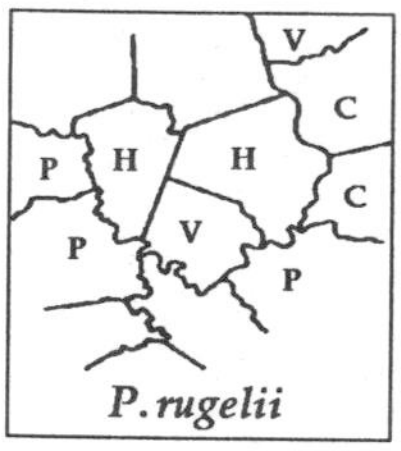

P. rugelii

Plantago rugellii Dcne.
In lawns, gardens, and roadsides. Frequent.

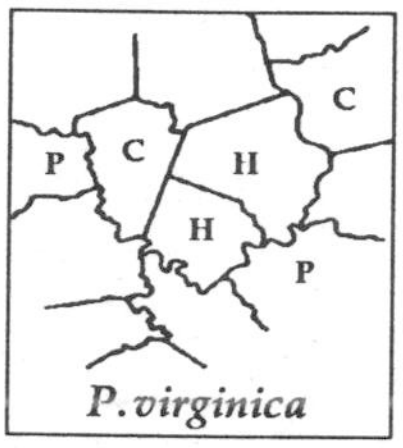

P. virginica

Plantago virginica L. HOARY PLANTAIN
Frequent in thin soil in dry sunny areas.

Rubiaceae: Madder Family

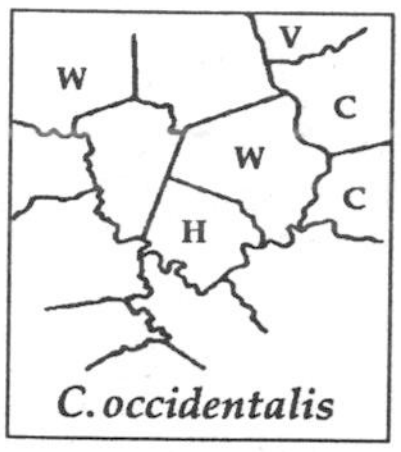

C. occidentalis

Cephalanthus occidentalis L. BUTTONBUSH
Fairly frequent on creek and pond margins.

Diodia teres Walt. BUTTONWEED
In thin, dry soil. Rare in the region. Fayette (MEW), Woodford (EC).

Diodia virginiana L. BUTTONWEED
In wet ground. A single record, Madison (Pal).

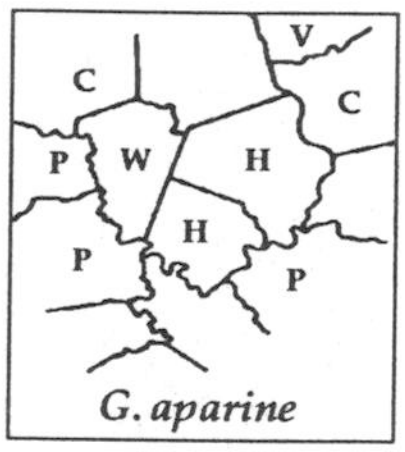

G. aparine

Galium aparine L. BEDSTRAW
Abundant in thickets and disturbed woodlands. Introduced.

G. circaezans

Galium circaezans Michx. (including the typical variety, var. *hypomalacum* Fernald, and intermediates between them) CROSS CLEAVERS
Frequent in woods.

G. concinnum

Galium concinnum T. & G. SHINING BEDSTRAW
Frequent in woods.

G. lanceolatum

Galium lanceolatum Torr. WILD LICORICE
In open woods. Infrequent.

Galium obtusum Bigel.
In wet ground. Rare. Franklin (SR); Jessamine (McF); Woodford (UK).

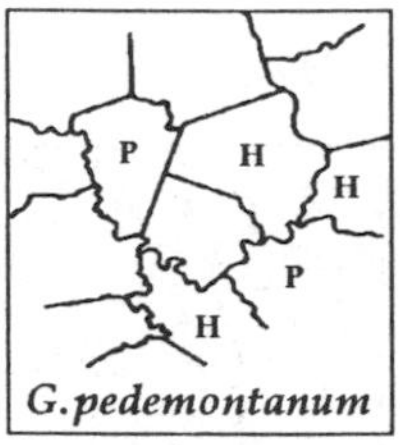

G. pedemontanum

Galium pedemontanum (Bellardi) All.
A common weed in pastures. Introduced.

Galium pilosum Ait. HAIRY BEDSTRAW
In dry open woods. A single record, Anderson (Pal).

Galium tinctorium L.
In wet ground. A single record, Woodford (UK).

G. triflorum

Galium triflorum Michx. SWEET-SCENTED BEDSTRAW
Frequent on mesophytic wooded cliffs and in other mesic sites.

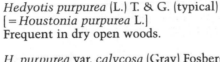

Hedyotis longifolia (Gaertn.) Hook.
[=Houstonia canadensis Willd.]
In dry open woods. Rare in the region. Jessamine (UK); Mercer (MEW).

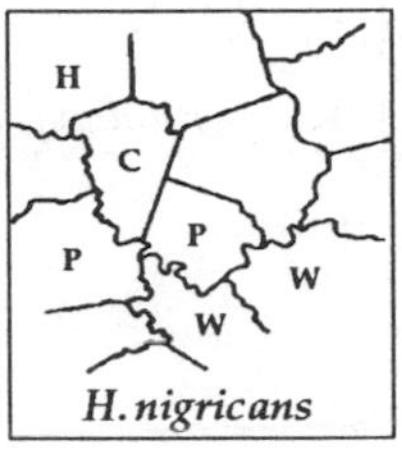

H. nigricans

Hedyotis nigricans (Lam.) Fosberg
[=*Houstonia nigricans* (Lam.) Fernald]
Frequent on exposed limestone cliffs and ledges.

H. purpurea (typical)

Hedyotis purpurea (L.) T. & G. (typical)
[=*Houstonia purpurea* L.]
Frequent in dry open woods.

H. purpurea var. calycosa

H. purpurea var. *calycosa* (Gray) Fosberg
[=*Houstonia lanceolata* (Poir.) Britt.]
Fairly frequent in dry open woods.

Hedyotis nuttalliana Fosberg
[=*Houstonia tenuifolia* Nutt.]
A single record. Fayette (UK).

Spermacoce glabra Michx. BUTTONWEED
In Kentucky River alluvium. Rare. Fayette (UK); Jessamine (McF).

Caprifoliaceae: Honeysuckle Family

L. dioica

Lonicera dioica L. WILD HONEYSUCKLE
Fairly frequent on steep wooded banks, especially hanging over ledges above creeks.

L. japonica

Lonicera japonica Thunb. JAPANESE HONEYSUCKLE
Abundant in thickets and disturbed woodlands. Introduced.

L. maackii var. podocarpa

Lonicera maackii Maxim. var. *podocarpa* Franch.
BUSH HONEYSUCKLE
Common and increasing rapidly in woods and thickets. Introduced.

Lonicera prolifera (Kirchner) Rehd. GRAPE HONEYSUCKLE
On bluff above creek. Rare, Franklin (MEW).

L. sempervirens

Lonicera sempervirens L. TRUMPET HONEYSUCKLE
In thickets; probably an escape from cultivation. Infrequent.

Lonicera standishii Jacq. BUSH HONEYSUCKLE
An escape from cultivation. A single record, Bourbon (EG). Introduced.

S. canadensis

Sambucus canadensis L. ELDERBERRY
Common on river floodplains and creek margins; also occurring in other moist situations.

S. orbiculatus

Symphoricarpos orbiculatus Moench BUCKBERRY
Abundant in old fields, fencerows, and woodland borders and on roadsides.

T. angustifolium

Triosteum angustifolium L. YELLOW HORSE-GENTIAN
Fairly frequent on cliffs and other rocky wooded slopes.

Triosteum aurantiacum Bickn. (typical) HORSE-GENTIAN
On south-facing cliffs. Infrequent. Garrard (MEW); Mercer (MEW).

T. aurantiacum var. *illinoense* (Wieg.) Palm & Steyerm.
On south-facing cliffs. Infrequent. Anderson (MEW); Madison (MEW).

T. aurantiacum (variety not distinguished)
Fayette (UK); Franklin (SR); Jessamine (UK).

Viburnum dentatum L. (typical) ARROW-WOOD
On steep sides of wooded ravines. Infrequent. Clark (MEW); Jessamine (UK).

V. dentatum var. *deamii* (Rehd.) Fernald.
Clark (UK).

V. molle

Viburnum molle Michx. KENTUCKY VIBURNUM
On wooded slopes. Fairly frequent.

V. prunifolium

Viburnum prunifolium L. BLACK HAW
Very frequent on wooded slopes.

V. rafinesquianum

Viburnum rafinesquianum Schult. (typical)
DOWNY ARROW-WOOD
Fairly frequent on wooded cliffs.

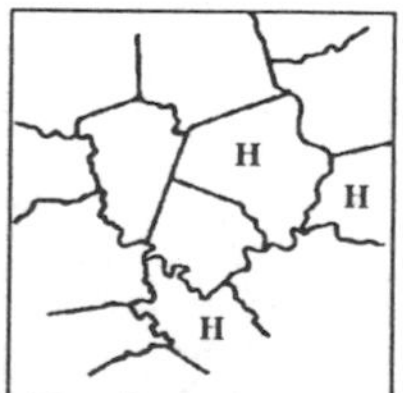

V. rafinesquianum var. affine

V. rafinesquianum var. *affine* (Bush) House
On wooded cliffs. Infrequent.

Viburnum recognitum Fernald ARROW-WOOD
In moist ground. Woodford (UK).

V. rufidulum

Viburnum rufidulum Raf. SOUTHERN BLACK HAW
Very frequent in woods and thickets.

Valerianaceae: Valerian Family

V. pauciflora

Valeriana pauciflora Michx. VALERIAN
Frequent on rich, moist wooded creek banks.

V.chenopodifolia

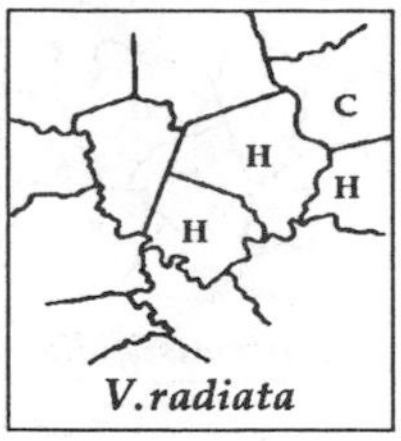

V.radiata

Valerianella chenopodifolia (Pursh) DC. CORN SALAD
In moist meadows and on alluvial flats. Fairly frequent.

Valerianella radiata L. CORN SALAD
In meadows and other open areas. Fairly frequent.

V.umbilicata

Valerianella umbilicata (Sull.) Wood [including *V. patellaria* (Sull.) Wood and *V. intermedia* Dyal.]
CORN SALAD
Common in wet sunny ground at the edges of creeks and on alluvial flats.

Dipsacaceae: Teasel Family

D.fullonum

Dipsacus fullonum L.
[=*D. sylvestris* Huds.] TEASEL
Common on weedy roadsides. Introduced.

Cucurbitaceae: Gourd Family

Echinocystis lobata Michx. WILD BALSAM-APPLE
On alluvial banks. A single record, Fayette (UK).

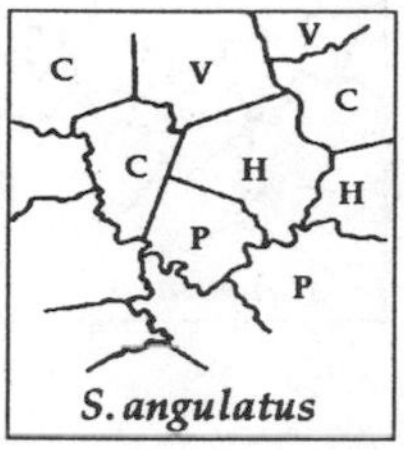

S.angulatus

Melothria pendula MELONETTE
In damp thickets. A single record, Scott (JBV).

Sicyos angulatus L. BUR-CUCUMBER
Frequent on alluvial flats. Introduced.

Campanulaceae: Bluebell Family, Bellflower Family

C.americana

Campanula americana L. [including the typical variety and var. *illinoensis* (Fresn.) Farw.] TALL BELLFLOWER
Very frequent in open woods and borders of woods in mesic situations.

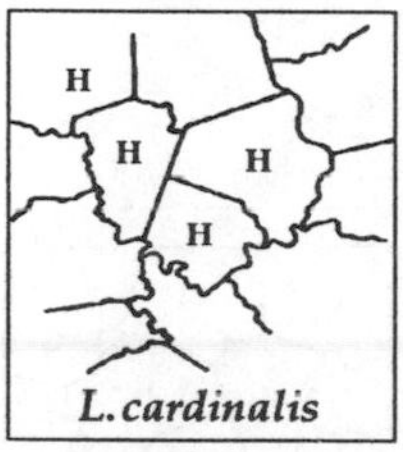

L.cardinalis

Lobelia cardinalis L. CARDINAL FLOWER
In swampy woods and areas of sinking creeks. Infrequent.

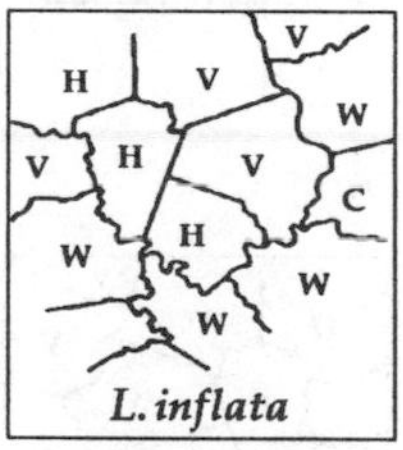

L.inflata

Lobelia inflata L. INDIAN TOBACCO
Frequent in open woods, thickets, and old fields.

L.siphilitica

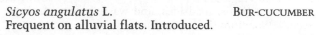

Lobelia siphilitica L. GREAT BLUE LOBELIA
Very frequent in wet places: creek margins, creek beds, spring areas, swamps, and floodplains.

Lobelia spicata Lam.
A single record. Jessamine (C&M).

T.perfoliata

Triodanis perfoliata (L.) Nieuwl.
[=*Specularia perfoliata* (L.) A. DC.]
VENUS' LOOKING-GLASS
Frequent in woodland borders, openings in woods, and fields.

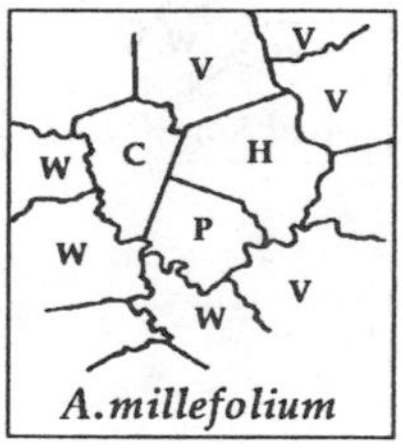

A.millefolium

Asteraceae: Composite Family

Achillea millefolium L. [including forma *rosea* Rand & Redf.] YARROW, MILFOIL
In fields, roadsides, and waste areas. Introduced.

A. artemisiifolia

Ambrosia artemisiifolia L. [including var. *elatior* (L.) DC. and var. *paniculata* (Michx.) Blankenship]
COMMON RAGWEED
Common in fields and on roadsides.

A. trifida

Ambrosia trifida L. GIANT RAGWEED, HORSEWEED
Abundant in moist ground in open situations.

A. plantaginifolia

Antennaria plantaginifolia (L.) Hook. [including var. *ambigens* (Greene) Cronq.] PUSSY-TOES
Fairly frequent on south-facing cliffs with cedars and oaks.

A. cotula

Anthemis cotula L. DOGFENNEL
Fairly common in weedy pastures, barnyards, and waste places. Introduced.

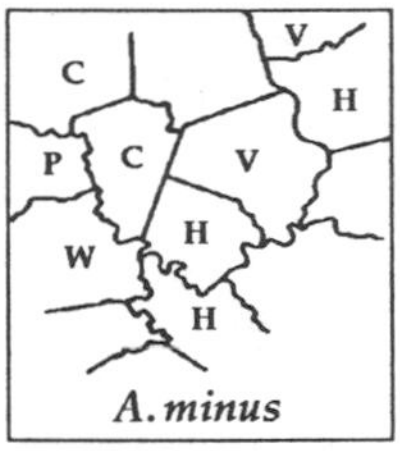

A. minus

Arctium minus (Hill) Bernh. BURDOCK
Common in weedy pastures, barnyards, and waste places. Introduced.

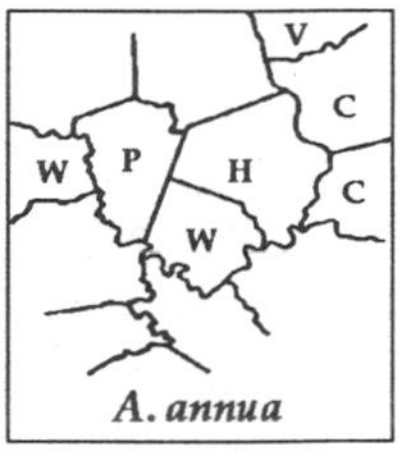

A. annua

Artemisia annua L. WORMWOOD, SWEET FERN
Frequent in fields and waste places. Introduced.

Artemisia vulgaris L. MUGWORT
A weed of fields, roadsides, and waste places. A single record, Woodford (EC). Introduced.

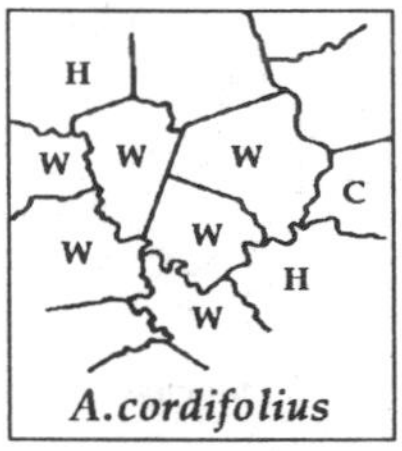

A. cordifolius

Aster cordifolius L. HEART-LEAVED ASTER
Frequent in woods.

Aster divaricata L.
A single record. Jessamine (C&M).

Aster drummondii Lindl.
On wooded rocky bank of creek. A single record, Woodford (MEW).

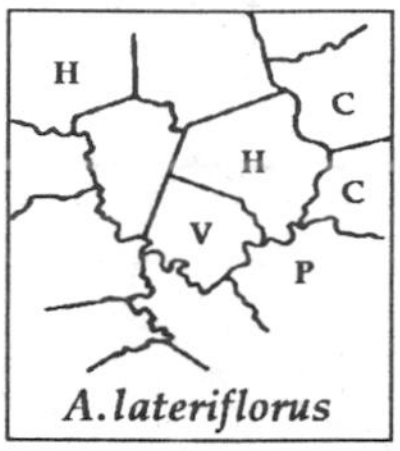

A. lateriflorus

Aster lateriflorus (L.) Britt. CALICO ASTER
Fairly frequent in open woods, thickets, and meadows.

Aster macrophyllus L.
A single record. Jessamine (C&M).

A. novae-angliae

Aster novae-angliae L. NEW ENGLAND ASTER
Fairly frequent in moist ground in meadows and on floodplains.

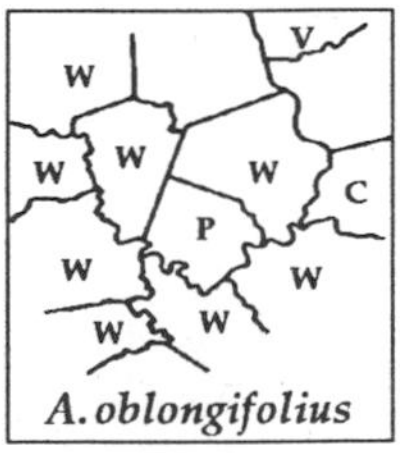

A. oblongifolius

Aster oblongifolius L. AROMATIC ASTER
Abundant on sunny limestone cliffs.

A. ontarionis

Aster ontarionis Wieg.
On river bottoms and creek banks, and in moist meadows. Infrequent.

Aster patens Ait. SPREADING ASTER
On wooded south-facing cliffs. Infrequent. Fayette (MEW); Garrard (JBV); Madison (JBV).

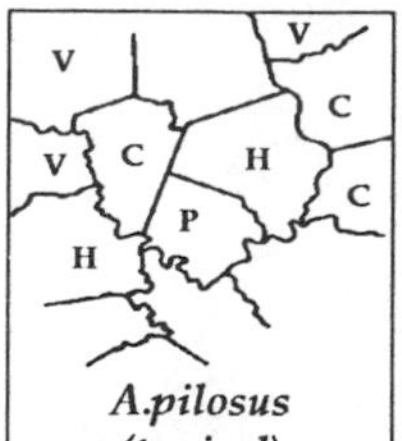

A.pilosus (typical)

A.pilosus var.demotus

Aster pilosus Willd. (typical and var. *demotus* Blake) FROST-WEED ASTER
Common in old fields.

Aster prenanthoides Muhl. CROOKED-STEM ASTER
Common on creek margins.

Aster shortii Lindl. SHORT'S ASTER
Common in open woods.

A.prenanthoides

A.shortii

Aster schreberi Nees
A single record, Madison (Pal).

Aster tataricus L. f.
An escape from cultivation. Bourbon (NP). Introduced.

Astranthium integrifolium (Michx.) Nutt. WESTERN DAISY
Fairly frequent on creek banks and other moist places.

A.integrifolium

B.aristosa

Bidens aristosa (Michx.) Britt [typical and var. *retrorsa* (Sherff) Wunderlin]
[= *B. polylepis* Blake] TICKSEED SUNFLOWER
On pond borders and floodplains. Frequent; locally profuse.

B.bipinnata

B.cernua

Bidens bipinnata L. SPANISH NEEDLES
A common weed in open places. Introduced.

Bidens cernua L. NODDING BUR-MARIGOLD
On pond and stream margins, in swamps, and in ditches. Frequent.

Bidens discoidea Britt.
A single record, collected in 1887 near Dix River; either Garrard or Mercer County (UK).

B.frondosa

Bidens frondosa L. BEGGAR-TICKS
Frequent on stream and pond margins and floodplains.

B.tripartita

Bidens laevis (L.) BSP. SMOOTH BUR-MARIGOLD
A single record, collected in 1901 at Clay's Ferry; either Fayette or Madison County (UK).

Bidens tripartita L.
[= *B. connata* Muhl. and *B. comosa* (Gray) Wieg.] SWAMP BEGGAR-TICKS
On creek and pond margins.

B.eupatorioides

Bidens vulgata Greene BEGGAR-TICKS
In wet places. Infrequent. Anderson (MEW); Jessamine (McF).

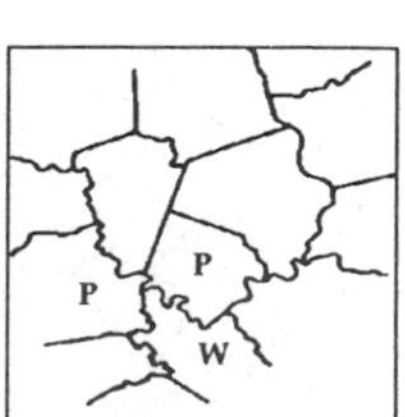

B.eupatorioides var.corymbulosa

Brickellia eupatorioides (L.) Shinners (typical)
[= *Kuhnia eupatorioides* L.] FALSE BONESET
Frequent on dry hillsides, especially in borders between open woodland and old fields.

B. eupatorioides var. *corymbulosa* (Torr. & Gray) Shinners.
Same habitat and frequency as the typical variety.

Cacalia atriplicifolia L. PALE INDIAN-PLANTAIN
In open woods. Infrequent. Fayette (UK); Madison (MEW).

Cacalia muhlenbergii (Sch.) Fernald
A single record, Jessamine (McF).

Carduus acanthoides L.
On roadsides. Infrequent. Scott (MEW); Woodford (MEW). Introduced.

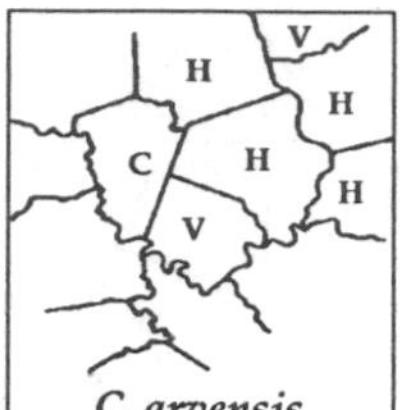

C. arvensis

Carduus arvensis (L.) Robson
[=*Cirsium arvense* (L.) Scop.] CANADA THISTLE
Fields and waste places. Fairly frequent. Introduced.

C. discolor

Carduus discolor (Muhl. ex Willd.) Nutt.
[=*Cirsium discolor* (Muhl.) Spreng.] FIELD THISTLE
Frequent in fields and pastures.

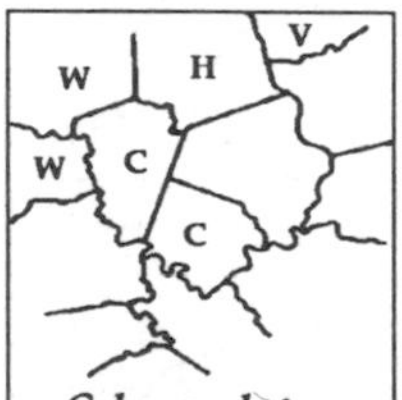

C. lanceolatus

Carduus lanceolatus L.
[=*Cirsium vulgare* (Savi) Tenore.] BULL THISTLE
On roadsides and in waste places. Fairly frequent. Introduced.

C. nutans

Carduus nutans L. NODDING THISTLE
On roadsides and in fields and waste places. Now an abundant weed, having spread rapidly. Introduced.

C. maculosa

Centaurea maculosa L. STAR-THISTLE
On roadsides. Infrequent. Introduced.

Centaurea nigra L. KNAPWEED
In fields and roadsides. A single record, Fayette (UK). Introduced.

Centaurea solstitialis L. ST. BARNABY'S THISTLE
Collected from alfalfa fields. Fayette (UK); Woodford (UK). Introduced.

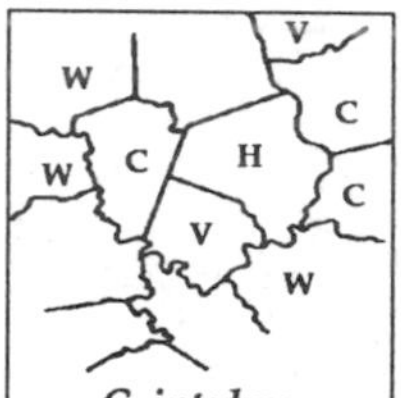

C. intybus

Cichorium intybus L. CHICORY
Abundant on roadsides. Introduced.

C. canadensis

Conyza canadensis (L.) Cronq.
[=*Erigeron canadensis* L.] HORSEWEED, HOGWEED
Common in weedy fields, roadsides, and waste places.

Crepis capillaris L. HAWK-BEARD
In fields and waste places. A single record, Fayette (UK). Introduced.

C. pulchra

Crepis pulchra L. HAWK-BEARD
In fields and waste places. Infrequent. Introduced.

Echinacea purpurea (L.) Moench PURPLE CONEFLOWER
In dry ground. Rare. Franklin (NP).

E. alba

Eclipta alba (L.) Hassk. YERBA DE TAGO
Frequent in borders of ponds and streams and in creek beds.

E. carolinianus

Elephantopus carolinianus Willd. ELEPHANT'S-FOOT
Frequent in open woods, especially in low ground.

E. hieracifolia

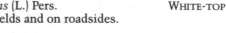

Erectites hieracifolia (L.) Raf. FIREWEED
In clearings and burned-over areas. Infrequent.

E. annuus

Erigeron annuus (L.) Pers. WHITE-TOP
Abundant in fields and on roadsides.

E. philadelphicus

Erigeron philadelphicus L. FLEABANE
Common in various open situations.

Erigeron pulchellus Michx. ROBIN'S-PLANTAIN
A single record, from a south-facing, oak-wooded cliff; Fayette (MEW).

Erigeron strigosus Muhl. FLEABANE
In open areas. Infrequent. Anderson (Pal); Boyle (MEW); Jessamine (McF); Woodford (EC).

E. altissimum

Eupatorium altissimum L. TALL THOROUGHWORT
On dry sunny slopes, in openings in woods, and with red cedar on bluffs. Fairly frequent.

Eupatorium aromaticum Walt. SMALL WHITE SNAKEROOT
In dry open woods. A single record, Clark (UK).

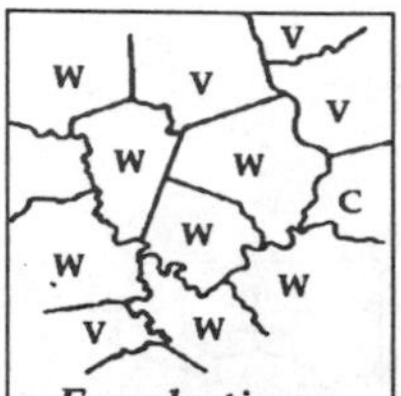

E. coelestinum

Eupatorium coelestinum L. MISTFLOWER
Common in moist ground, usually sunny and often grassy.

E. fistulosum

Eupatorium fistulosum Barratt JOE-PYE-WEED
Grassy floodplain of the Kentucky River and other low, moist places. Infrequent.

E. incarnatum

Eupatorium incarnatum Walt. PINK THOROUGHWORT
In rocky thickets and at the edges of cliffside woods. Fairly frequent.

E. perfoliatum

Eupatorium perfoliatum L. BONESET
Frequent on pond and creek margins, floodplains, and other moist places.

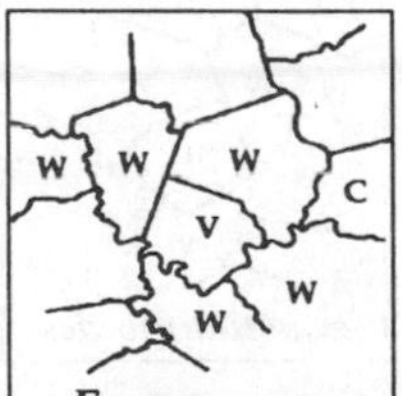

E. purpureum

Eupatorium purpureum L. JOE-PYE-WEED
Frequent in woods.

E. rugosum

Eupatorium rugosum Houtt. WHITE SNAKEROOT
Common in woods and thickets.

E. serotinum

Eupatorium serotinum Michx. THOROUGHWORT
Fairly frequent in old fields and on creek banks.

E. sessilifolium

Eupatorium sessilifolium L. UPLAND BONESET
In open woods. Infrequent.

G. ciliata

Galinsoga ciliata (Raf.) Blake PERUVIAN DAISY
A weed in fields and gardens; frequent in low ground. Introduced.

G. obtusifolium

Gnaphalium obtusifolium L.
[including var. *praecox* Fernald.] EVERLASTING
Frequent in open woods, clearings, and old fields.

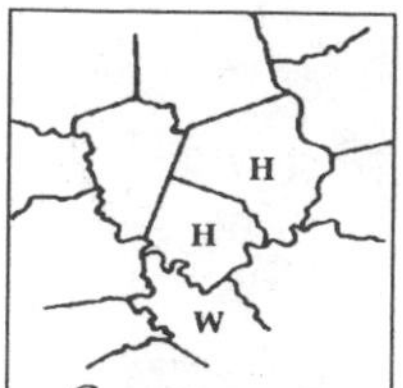

G. purpureum

H. autumnale

Gnaphalium purpureum L. PURPLE CUDWEED
In old fields and open cedar-oak woods on bluffs. Rare.

Helenium autumnale L. SNEEZEWEED
Frequent on creek margins and in other wet places.

Helianthus annuus L. ANNUAL SUNFLOWER
An occasional escape from cultivation. Jessamine (McF); Woodford (EC).

H. decapetalus

H. divaricatus

Helianthus decapetalus L. THIN-LEAVED SUNFLOWER
Fairly frequent at the edges of woods in moist ground.

Helianthus divaricatus L. WOODLAND SUNFLOWER
In dry open woods. Infrequent.

Helianthus grosseserratus Martens
A single record, Fayette (MEW).

H. hirsutus

Helianthus hirsutus Raf. STIFF-HAIRED SUNFLOWER
In open woods and thickets. Infrequent.

Helianthus maximiliani Martens
In old fields and on roadsides. Probably an escape from cultivation. Fayette (MEW); Madison (JBV).

H. microcephalus

Helianthus microcephalus T. & G.
SMALL WOOD-SUNFLOWER
Frequent in open woods and at the edges of woods.

H. tuberosus

Helianthus strumosus L.
A single record, Woodford (Pal).

Helianthus tuberosus L. JERUSALEM ARTICHOKE
Common in moist soil in open places.

H. helianthoides

Heliopsis helianthoides (L.) Sweet [including var. *scabra* (Dunal) Fernald] FALSE SUNFLOWER
In fencerows and woodland borders in moist ground and on sunny creek banks. Frequent.

Inula helenium L. ELECAMPANE
On weedy roadsides and in fencerows. Fayette (UK). Introduced.

Iva annua L.
[= *I. ciliata* Willd.] MARSH-ELDER
In pastures. Rare. Clark (MRB); Scott (UK).

L. biennis

Iva xanthifolia Nutt. MARSH-ELDER
An adventive weed from the West. Woodford (UK).

Lactuca biennis (Moench) Fernald
TALL BLUE LETTUCE
In woodland borders. Rare.

L. canadensis

Lactuca canadensis L. [including var. *latifolia* Ktze., var. *longifolia* (Michx.) Farw., and var. *obovata* Wieg.]
WILD LETTUCE
Fairly frequent in woodland borders and thickets.

L. floridana

Lactuca floridana (L.) Gaertn. [including var. *villosa* (Jacq.) Cronq.] WILD LETTUCE
Frequent at the edges of woods, in openings in woods, and in thickets.

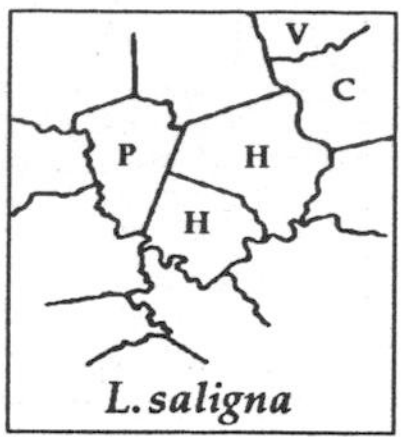

L. saligna

Lactuca saligna L. WILLOW-LEAVED LETTUCE
In waste places. Introduced.

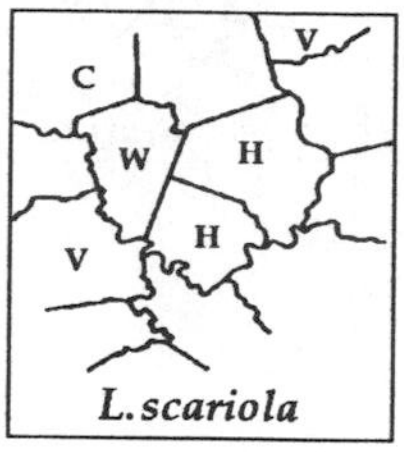

L. scariola

Lactuca scariola L. PRICKLY LETTUCE
A common weed of fields, roadsides, and waste places. Introduced.

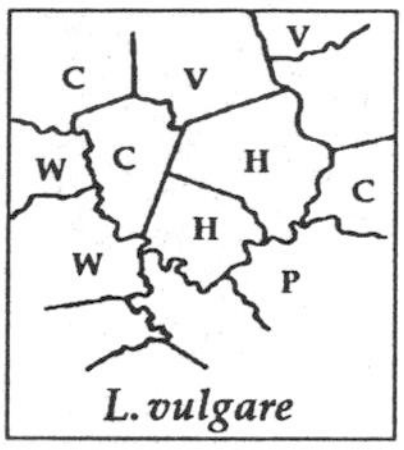

L. vulgare

Leucanthemum vulgare Lam.
[= *Chrysanthemum leucanthemum* L. var. *pinnatifidum* Lecoq & Lamotte] OXEYE DAISY
Abundant in fields and meadows and along roadsides. Introduced.

O. acanthium

Liatris squarrosa (L.) Michx. BLAZING STAR
A single record, from thin soil on rock ledges in full sun; Jessamine (Pal).

Onopordum acanthium L. COTTON THISTLE
On roadsides and in waste places. Infrequent. Introduced.

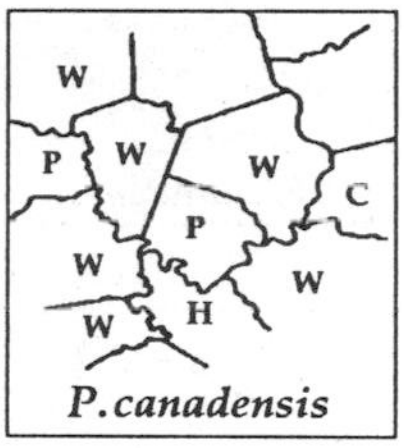

P. canadensis

Parthenium integrifolium L. WILD QUININE
A single record, Woodford (Pal).

P. uvedalia

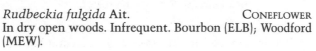

Polymnia canadensis L. LEAF-CUP
Abundant in rich woods.

Polymnia uvedalia L. YELLOW LEAF-CUP
Frequent in openings in woods and at edges of woods, usually in moist ground.

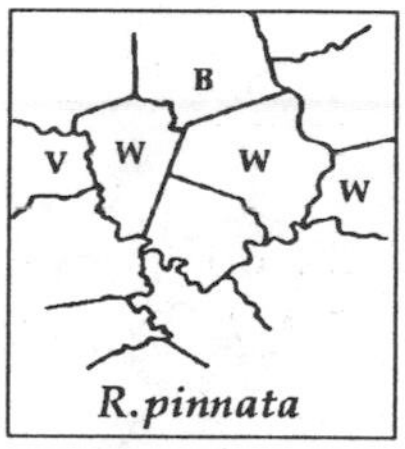

R. pinnata

Prenanthes altissima L. RATTLESNAKE-ROOT
In woods. Rare. Anderson (MEW); Jessamine (JBV).

Ratibida pinnata (Vent.) Barnh. PRAIRIE CONEFLOWER
In sunny grassy areas. Fairly frequent.

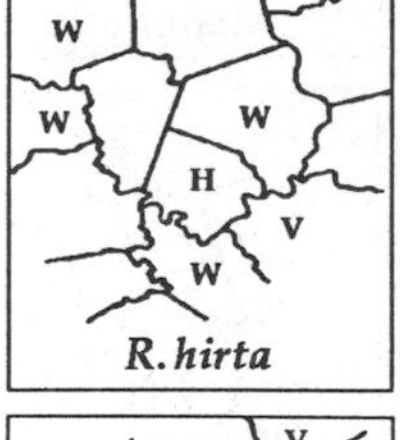

R. hirta

Rudbeckia fulgida Ait. CONEFLOWER
In dry open woods. Infrequent. Bourbon (ELB); Woodford (MEW).

Rudbeckia hirta L. BLACK-EYED SUSAN
In grassy fields and meadows. Fairly frequent.

R. laciniata

Rudbeckia laciniata L. WILD GOLDEN-GLOW
Fairly frequent on wooded creek banks.

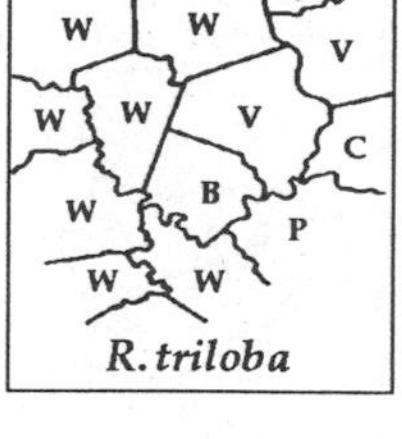

R. triloba

Rudbeckia triloba L. CONEFLOWER
Abundant in woodland borders, thickets, and old fields.

Senecio anonymus Wood
[= *S. smallii* Britt.] SQUAW-WEED
In dry ground at the edges of woods, in clearings, and in dry grassy fields. Rare. Fayette (JBV); Jessamine (JBV).

S. obovatus

Senecio glabellus Poir. BUTTERWEED
In moist ground. Rare. Fayette (UK); Franklin (SR); Woodford (EC).

S. perfoliatum

Senecio obovatus Muhl. RAGWORT
Very frequent in woods.

Silphium perfoliatum L. INDIAN-CUP
Frequent on sunny creek banks and floodplains.

S. altissima

Silphium trifoliatum L. ROSINWEED
In dry open woods. A single record, Fayette (JBV).

Solidago altissima L. TALL GOLDENROD
Abundant in old fields.

Solidago arguta Ait.
[= *S. bootii* Hook.]
A single record, Fayette (UK).

S. caesia

S. canadensis

Solidago caesia L. WREATH GOLDENROD
Fairly frequent in woods.

Solidago canadensis L. CANADA GOLDENROD
Fairly frequent in clearings and thickets, especially on dry slopes.

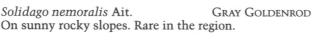

S. flexicaulis

Solidago flexicaulis L. BROAD-LEAF GOLDENROD, ZIGZAG GOLDENROD
Very frequent in mesophytic woods.

S. gigantia

Solidago gigantea Ait. [including var. *serotina* (Ktze.) Cronq.] LATE GOLDENROD
In moist soil in open situations. Infrequent.

S. graminifolia

Solidago graminifolia (L.) Salisb. GRASS-LEAVED GOLDENROD
In swamps and other moist ground. Rare in the region.

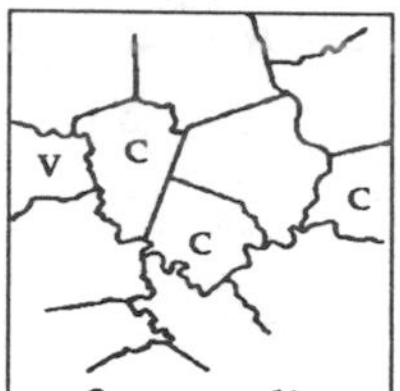

S. nemoralis

Solidago nemoralis Ait. GRAY GOLDENROD
On sunny rocky slopes. Rare in the region.

Solidago rugosa Mill. VEINY-LEAVED GOLDENROD
In low, wet ground in meadows and woodland borders. Rare. Jessamine (Pal); Madison (Pal).

S. sphacelata

Solidago rupestris Raf.
On river banks. Rare. Jessamine (C&M). Woodford (UK).

S. ulmifolia

Solidago sphacelata Raf. FALSE GOLDENROD
Frequent in dry open woods, especially on rocky south slopes and cliffs.

Solidago ulmifolia Muhl. ELM-LEAVED GOLDENROD
Frequent in open woods on dry slopes.

S. asper

Sonchus asper (L.) Hill SPINY SOW-THISTLE
A weed on roadsides and in waste places. Introduced.

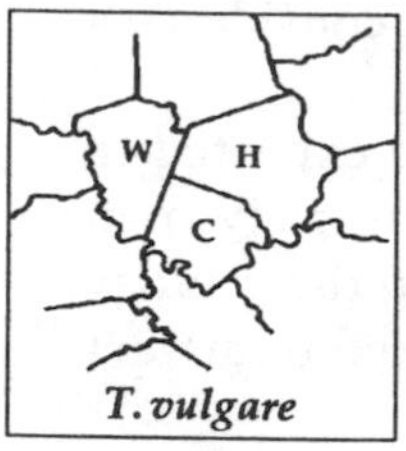

T. vulgare

Sonchus oleraceus L. COMMON SOW-THISTLE
A single record, Fayette (UK). Introduced.

Tanacetum vulgare L. TANSY
An infrequent escape from former cultivation. Introduced.

Taraxacum erythrospermum Andrz.
RED-SEEDED DANDELION
A single record, Fayette (UK). Introduced.

T. officinale

Taraxacum officinale Weber COMMON DANDELION
Abundant in lawns and pastures and on roadsides. Introduced.

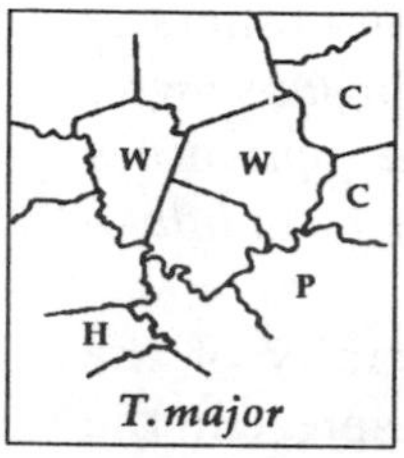

T. major

Tragopogon major Jacq.
[= *T. dubius* of authors, not Scop.] GOAT'S-BEARD
A common weed of roadsides and fields. Introduced.

V. alternifolia

Tragopogon pratensis L. GOAT'S-BEARD
Infrequent. Fayette (UK); Franklin (SR). Introduced.

Verbesina alternifolia (L.) Britt.
[= *Actinomeris alternifolia* (L.) DC.] WINGSTEM
Common in thickets and woodland borders, especially in moist ground.

V. helianthoides

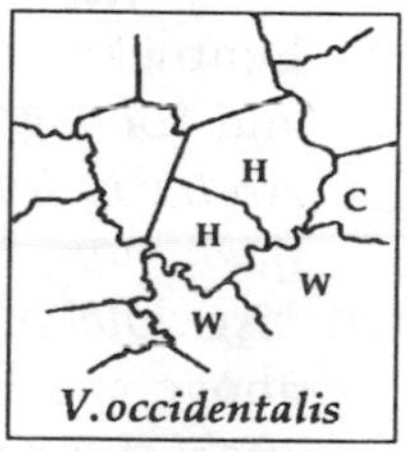

V. occidentalis

Verbesina helianthoides Michx. CROWN-BEARD
In old fields and open woods. Infrequent.

Verbesina occidentalis (L.) Wats. CROWN-BEARD
Fairly frequent in old fields, clearings, and rocky open woods.

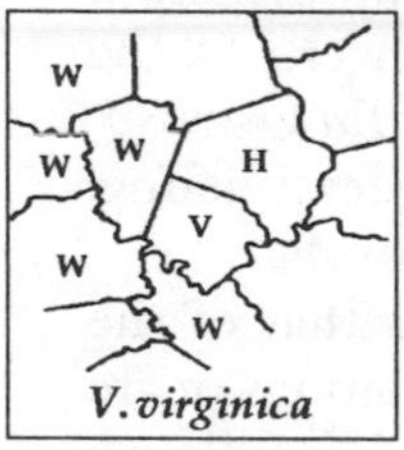

V. virginica

Verbesina virginica L. WHITE CROWN-BEARD
Frequent at the edges of woods, in old fields with shrubs, and in clearings on steep slopes.

V. gigantea

Vernonia gigantea (Walt.) Trel.
[= *V. altissima* Nutt.] IRONWEED
In old fields, pastures, and roadsides. Common.

Xanthium globosum Shull COCKLEBUR
A single record, Bourbon (EG).

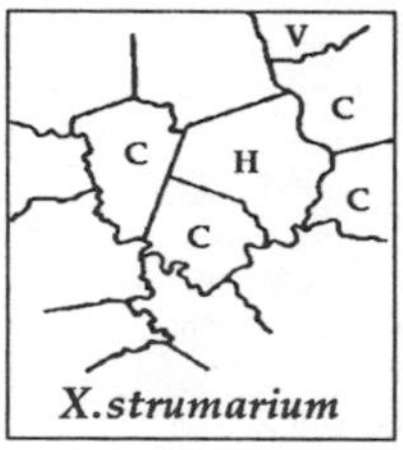

X. strumarium

Xanthium italicum Moretti COCKLEBUR
A single record, Harrison (JBV).

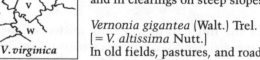

Xanthium strumarium L. var. *glabratum* (DC.) Conq.
[= *X. pensylvanicum* Wallr.] COCKLEBUR
A common weed in cultivated and waste ground. Introduced.

FLORISTIC SUMMARY

In view of the fact that such a small percentage of the total Inner Bluegrass region is in natural areas (probably no more than 4 percent), the flora of 1,149 species (plus 52 varieties, subspecies, and forms, making 1,201 taxa) may be considered a relatively rich and varied one.

An area in which farmland and towns predominate would be expected to have a goodly share of introduced weeds, those species that accompany man wherever he goes. This element of the flora bears no relationship to the geology that determines the region, except insofar as the geology has helped to attract inhabitants for over 200 years.

Many species occurring here are more or less widespread in deciduous forests of eastern United States, such as *Sanguinarea canadensis, Phlox divaricata, Claytonia virginica, Dentaria laciniata, Adiantum pedatum,* and many others of the forest floor, as well as many trees, such as *Acer saccharum* and *Juglans nigra.* Some species that are rare throughout their range—as, for example, *Spiranthes ovalis, Hydrastis canadensis, Panax quinquefolium,* and *Synandra hispidula*—occur here, the last with considerable frequency.

A few species occur in the Inner Bluegrass only in the vicinity of the Kentucky River and are rare even there, although common and widespread in the Cumberland Plateau, where the river rises. The river valley has probably served as a migration route for these species, which include *Aesculus octandra, Alnus serrulata, Amelanchier arborea, Vaccinium stamineum,* and *Iris cristata.*

A few species in Kentucky seem to be restricted to the Inner Bluegrass: *Trillium nivale, Draba ramosissima,* and *Phlox bifida.*

The following species in the Inner Bluegrass are listed as endangered in Kentucky: *Trillium nivale, Arabis perstellata, Pachystima canbyi, Viola walteri,* and *Solidago rupestris.* Those threatened in Kentucky are *Oryzopsis racemosa, Arenaria fontinalis, Lesquerella globosa, Cladrastis kentukea, Panax quinquefolium, Perideridia americana, Onosmodium hispidissimum,* and *Synandra hispidula.* Also *Hydrastis canadensis* is in the category for special concern. Of the above species, *Arabis perstellata, Arenaria fontinalis, Lesquerella globosa, Pachystima canbyi,* and *Synandra hispidula* are under review for federal listing. (Branson et al. 1981.)

The most significant element of the Inner Bluegrass flora is that of the calciphiles, those species that are either restricted to calcareous situations or are much more frequent there than elsewhere. Some of these are listed as follows:

Ferns

Asplenium resiliens
Asplenium rhizophyllum
Asplenium ruta-muraria
Cystopteris bulbifera
Cystopteris tennesseense
Pellaea atropurpurea
Pellaea glabra

Monocotyledons

Carex aggregata
Carex davisii
Carex eburnea
Carex muhlenbergii
Carex oligocarpa
Carex woodii
Camassia scilloides
Erythronium albidum
Nothoscordum bivalve
Agave virginica
Belamcanda chinensis
Sisyrinchium albidum

Herbaceous Dicotyledons

Arenaria patula
Isophrum biternatum
Aquilegia canadensis
Anemone virginiana
Jeffersonia diphylla
Sedum pulchellum
Hypericum dolabriforme
Opuntia humifusa
Scutellaria parvula
Agastache nepetoides
Blephilia ciliata
Satureja glabella
Ruellia humilis
Hedyotis nigricans
Eupatorium incarnatum
Brickellia eupatorioides
Aster oblongifolius
Solidago sphacelata

Shrubs and Woody Vines

Physocarpus opulifolius
Rhus aromatica
Pachysandra procumbens
Cornus drummondi
Campsis capreolata
Lonicera dioica var. *glaucescens*
Lonicera prolifera
Viburnum molle
Viburnum rafinesquianum

Trees

Juniperus virginiana
Quercus macrocarpa
Quercus muehlenbergii
Ulmus thomasi
Cladrastis kentukea
Gymnocladus dioica
Fraxinus quadrangulata

EXCLUDED SPECIES

In a paper published in the *Transactions of the Kentucky Academy of Science* (37 [1976]: 78-79), it is claimed that "the bald cypress [*Taxodium distichum*] grew in the Inner Bluegrass before the arrival of the first white settlers." The circumferences and diameters are listed for several old bald cypress trees, and the estimates of age are based on the rate of growth as reported for that species in Maryland and Louisiana.

Three of the trees mentioned as occurring on a Woodford County farm had diameters of 63, 45.8, and 38 inches, respectively. Two of these were claimed to be over 200 years old. However, increment borings by Dr. William McComb of the College of Forestry at the University of Kentucky showed the three trees to be the same age, all dating back to about 1820, certainly no earlier than 1810 and no later than 1830. The smallest tree had many years ago suffered severe lightning damage, which would have retarded its growth more than that of its contemporaries. The tree with a diameter of 45.8 inches was very tall. The one with a diameter of 63 inches was much shorter, with ponderous low branches, not a characteristic growth habit for this species; its situation had noticeably more moisture (but was well drained) and probably had extremely high levels of mineral nutrients. Furthermore, a check into the history of the farm indicates that the residence was built in 1820, and an analysis of the spacing of the trees with respect to the house shows the two largest ones to be in line and the same distance from each front corner. The lightning-damaged tree is at the side and approximately the same distance from the house. The conclusion is that these trees were planted about the time the house was built

An old bald cypress tree in a water-logged area in Fayette County was also cited. Much of the heartwood in its large trunk has rotted, resulting in mushy increment borings which are difficult to interpret. Hence, to conclude that this specimen is over 200 years old and that bald cypress was part of the original native flora of the Inner Bluegrass is risky.

Future researchers should note that growth rates determined for a species in one locality are not necessarily applicable to a distant locality that may differ in ecological factors. Neither can the diameter and age of one species be used to indicate the age of a different species with the same diameter in the same habitat.

A paper published in *Castanea* in 1978 (43: 129-37) reported new records of several species of plants and one species of salamander supposedly in the Inner Bluegrass. The study area was "at the edge of the Inner Bluegrass region" and was indicated by a circle on a map. The author also stated that the area was an abandoned Pliocene channel of the Kentucky River, a flat valley with little relief, and that the poorly drained soil is composed of old fluvial deposits.

However, a geologic map of the Lawrenceburg quadrangle shows the study area to be in the Clay's Ferry Formation ("Eden Shale"), not in the middle Ordovician limestone, which determines the Inner Bluegrass. Even if some of the study area extended to land underlain by limestone, the soil in which the plants are growing is not derived from limestone. Any species found only in fluvial deposits derived principally from material other than High Bridge or Lexington Limestone is not considered to be among the Inner Bluegrass flora.

Quercus montana Willd. and *Q. michauxii* Nutt. have been reported in the region but are probably misidentifications of *Q. muehlenbergii* Engelm. (Specimens on which the reports were based were lost in a fire.) A sterile specimen called *Quercus coccinea* Muench is questionable; it is more likely *Q. shumardii* Buckl., which it strongly resembles.

Vertebrate Animals

OF THE approximately 717 described species of vertebrates occurring in Kentucky at the present time, 474 (66 percent) have been recorded or may reasonably be expected to occur in the Inner Bluegrass. Some groups are much better represented than others; for example, 80 percent of the bird species in the state are represented, 70 percent of the mammals, 53 percent of the amphibians, 52 percent of the fishes, and 50 percent of the reptiles.

These variances are perhaps due in part to the geography of the state, with the highest mountains at one end harboring our most northern animals, and coastal plain cypress swamps at the other end harboring our most southern species. The majority of the birds, with their great mobility and their propensity to migrate, can be expected to occur, at least periodically, over a large area and in a wide variety of habitats. Some habitats may be completely unsuitable for a protracted stay but serve well for short-term food and shelter.

With a few exceptions, species occurring in the Inner Bluegrass also occur in the Outer Bluegrass and in the Knobs: in equally good habitats, they occur in about the same abundance. As for vertebrates, there is little difference in representation between the Inner and the Outer Bluegrass, save perhaps in population density in some cases. The Knobs, however, show some interesting variations.

Several species of amphibians, reptiles, and mammals range into the Knobs but do not ordinarily reach the Outer Bluegrass. The mountain chorus frog, *Pseudacris brachyphona*, for example, occurs throughout the mountains of eastern Kentucky, westward down the Green River drainage to below Mammoth Cave National Park, and in the Salt River drainage northward at least into Jefferson County. In this whole circuit, the species extends into the Knobs in many places but apparently never into the Outer Bluegrass. Surely some must be carried down the Kentucky and Licking rivers into the Bluegrass, but they have not yet been discovered.

Another species of chorus frog, *Pseudacris triseriata triseriata*, has a huge range, covering most of eastern and midwestern United States and much of central Canada. It is absent in the higher Appalachians but occurs throughout Kentucky save in the mountains, the Inner Bluegrass, the eastern Knobs, and east of a line roughly from Berea to Middlesboro. There must be some valid reason for this pattern, but it is not obvious.

The timber rattlesnake probably inhabited the Bluegrass region in earlier times, but there have been no valid records for many years. Surely an individual must occasionally float down the rivers accidentally in flood time to lodge somewhere along the river bluffs, but the possibility of their establishing a breeding population is remote.

The hairy-tailed mole, *Parascalops breweri*, is a woodland species, ranging from New England southward into southern North Carolina and Tennessee. It occurs throughout the Kentucky mountains and westward into the eastern Knobs but has not been recorded in either the Outer or the Inner Bluegrass, or even along the river bluffs, where a refugee from a flood might land.

A sort of reverse situation to all of these occurs with the queen snake, *Regina septemvittata*, which is one of the commonest snakes in the Inner and Outer Bluegrass and occurs sparingly throughout the Knobs. Frequenting rocky streams, it feeds to a large extent on crayfish. It extends into the eastern Knobs but does not appear to occur anywhere in the Kentucky mountains save along the Ohio River and up the Big Sandy at least to Tug Fork. To the west it ranges into western Kentucky, and southward it occurs almost as far as the Gulf of Mexico.

Species names used in this list have been updated through 1989.

FISHES

Class *Petromyzones* LAMPREYS

Petromyzontidae: Lamprey Family

Ichthyomyzon bdellium (Jordan) OHIO LAMPREY
Common. Length to 160 mm; parasitic. Favors larger rivers but ascends smaller streams to breed. Immatures develop in creeks, then descend to larger streams, where they parasitize fish.

Ichthyomyzon greeleyi Hubbs & Trautman ALLEGHENY BROOK LAMPREY
Uncommon. Length to 175 mm; essentially nonparasitic but does feed in part on living fishes. Favors large to medium-size streams.

Ichthyomyzon unicuspis Hubbs & Trautman SILVER LAMPREY
Uncommon. Length to 330 mm; parasitic on fishes. In spring, adults ascend clear creeks, spawn over riffles, and die. Immatures spend up to six years in U-shaped burrows in mud banks, feeding on minute organic matter that drifts by. After transformation into adults, they live for about three years, feeding on the soft parts of fishes.

Lampetra aepyptera (Abbott) LEAST BROOK LAMPREY
Uncommon. Length to 130 mm; nonparasitic. Occurs in rivers and larger creeks but requires soft muddy areas with much organic debris along the stream banks. Adults ascend small streams in March or April to breed in shallow, clear riffles and then die. Immatures burrow into the muddy banks and feed on organic matter. The young, commonly known as "mud eels" by fisherman, are used in some places as live bait, particularly for bass.

Lampetra lamottei (Le Sueur) AMERICAN BROOK LAMPREY
Rare. Length to 7 inches; nonparasitic. Similar to the preceding species in appearance and habits.

Class *Osteichthyes* BONY FISHES

Acipenseridae: Sturgeon Family

Acipenser fulvescens Rafinesque LAKE STURGEON
Formerly present in this area but not recorded for many years. Now probably absent.

Scaphirhynchus platorhynchus (Rafinesque) SHOVELNOSE STURGEON
Formerly common in Kentucky and Licking rivers; not recorded in recent years and probably no longer present.

Polyodontidae: Paddlefish Family

Polyodon spathula (Walbaum) PADDLEFISH
Formerly present in the larger streams of this area but not recorded for more than 20 years; probably no longer present.

Lepisosteidae: Gar Family

Lepisosteus osseus (Linnaeus) LONGNOSE GAR
Common. Length to 4.5 feet. Favors rivers and larger creeks, where it feeds on fishes.

Lepisosteus platostomus Rafinesque SHORTNOSE GAR
Uncommon. Length to 2 feet common, to 3 feet rare. Inhabits larger rivers, where it feeds on fishes.

Clupeidae: Herring and Shad Family

Dorosoma cepedianum (LeSueur) GIZZARD SHAD
Abundant. Length to 20 inches. Favors rivers, larger creeks, and impoundments. Travels in schools. Adults feed largely on algae and organic debris.

Dorosoma petenense (Günther) THREADFIN SHAD
Rare. Length to 6 inches. Favors largest streams, but commonly stocked in reservoirs as a forage fish. More subject to winter kill than the gizzard shad. Since it has been stocked in Buckhorn Reservoir, strays may be expected in the Kentucky River and perhaps its larger tributaries in the Inner Bluegrass.

Salmonidae: Salmon and Trout Family:

Salmo gairdneri Richardson RAINBOW TROUT
Rare. Length to 30 inches. Although not native, this species is stocked in the Inner Bluegrass on a put-and-take basis for fishermen. It does not reproduce here.

Esocidae: Pike and Pickerel Family

Esox americanus vermiculatus LeSueur GRASS PICKEREL
Uncommon. Length to 14 inches. Favors ponds or quiet pools of streams with clear water and dense aquatic vegetation. Carnivorous, feeding on a wide variety of animals.

Esox lucius (Linnaeus) NORTHERN PIKE
Rare. Length to 48 inches. Not known to be native to Kentucky but introduced into various impoundments. Has been caught in the Kentucky River, and an occasional individual may be expected in the Inner Bluegrass.

Esox masquinongy (Mitchill) MUSKELLUNGE
Rare. Length to 50 inches; Kentucky record weight is 42 pounds. Native and formerly occurring in abundance, this magnificent fish is now rare or perhaps absent in the Inner Bluegrass. It favors larger rivers and creeks, but many other-

wise suitable streams are now so polluted and silted in that they no longer support the species.

Hiodontidae: Mooneye and Goldeye Family

Hiodon tergisus LeSueur MOONEYE
Common. Length to 15 inches. Limited to larger streams, this species occurs in the Kentucky River and in the lower reaches of its major tributaries.

Catostomidae: Sucker Family

Ictiobus bubalus (Rafinesque) SMALLMOUTH BUFFALO
Common. Length to 33 inches, weight to 20 pounds. Favors rivers and larger tributaries, where it frequents deeper, swifter channels.

Ictiobus cyprinellus (Valenciennes) BIGMOUTH BUFFALO
Uncommon. Length to 40 inches, weight to 40 pounds or more. Favors larger rivers and their major tributaries. This is one of the better "rough fish" for table use.

Carpiodes carpio (Rafinesque) RIVER CARPSUCKER
Common. Length to 24 inches. Favors larger rivers and major creeks. Frequents deep water, often over silt-laden bottoms.

Carpiodes cyprinus (LeSueur) QUILLBACK
Common. Length to 26 inches, weight rarely to 6 pounds. Adults favor larger streams but ascend to smaller creeks to breed. Young remain for some time in smaller tributaries.

Carpiodes velifer (Rafinesque) HIGHFIN CARPSUCKER
Uncommon. Length to 14 inches or so. Adults favor larger rivers and major tributaries but ascend creeks to breed, where the young may remain for some time.

Catostomus commersoni (Lacépède) WHITE SUCKER
Abundant. Length to 24 inches, weight rarely to 5 pounds or more. Favors rivers and creeks; adults winter in rivers and larger pools, then ascend to smaller waters in spring to spawn in rocky rapids. The young remain in small streams for some time.

Hypentelium nigricans (LeSueur) NORTHERN HOGSUCKER
Common. Length to about 24 inches. Favors riffles of small to moderate-sized streams but also occurs in the largest rivers.

Minytrema melanops (Rafinesque) SPOTTED SUCKER
Formerly common, now rare. Length to 18 inches. Favors larger rivers but is sometimes found in creeks. It is basically a lowland species and may now be essentially absent from the Inner Bluegrass.

Moxostoma anisurum (Rafinesque) SILVER REDHORSE
Uncommon. Length to 20 inches. Occurs in rivers and larger creeks.

Moxostoma carinatum (Cope) RIVER REDHORSE
Uncommon. Length to 30 inches. Favors rivers and larger creeks, where it frequents the deeper holes.

Moxostoma duquesnei (LeSueur) BLACK REDHORSE
Rare. Length to 18 inches. Favors rivers and creeks.

Moxostoma erythrurum (Rafinesque) GOLDEN REDHORSE
Common. Length rarely to more than 20 inches. Occurs in rivers and creeks; in

spring ascends small creeks to breed in riffles. Appears more tolerant of siltation and pollution than the other species of Moxostoma.

Moxostoma macrolepidotum breviceps (Cope) SHORTHEAD REDHORSE
Uncommon. Length usually 10 to 14 inches. Favors rivers and large creeks.

Cyprinidae: Carp and Minnow Family

Cyprinus carpio Linnaeus CARP
Common. Length to 3.5 feet, weight to about 60 pounds. Indigenous to Asia but now widely introduced into other parts of the world. Occurs in all rivers and larger creeks in the Inner Bluegrass as well as in reservoirs and many ponds; prefers areas of sluggish water with rooted vegetation. Although taken commercially, the flesh is not greatly esteemed.

Carassius auratus (Linnaeus) GOLDFISH
Rare. Length to 20 inches. Native to Asia and Europe, now widely introduced into other parts of the world. Feral individuals are usually dark olive with a golden tinge but often show brown, black, gray, red, yellow, or some combination of these, as in aquarium specimens. Favors quiet waters with rooted vegetation; may be expected in almost any water save the smallest streams.

Phoxinus erythrogaster Rafinesque SOUTHERN REDBELLY DACE
Common. Length to about 3 inches. Favors headwater streams having small, clear pools with gravel bottoms; does not tolerate pollution and is thus absent from many small streams where it once surely occurred. Gregarious, traveling usually in small schools.

Notemigonus crysoleucas (Mitchill) GOLDEN SHINER
Rare. Length to about 10 inches. Favors quiet water, whether ponds or streams. There are apparently no native populations in the Inner Bluegrass, but the species is stocked in local ponds and sold as bait minnows. Consequently, individuals may be expected almost anywhere as escapees from a bait bucket.

Semotilus atromaculatus (Mitchill) CREEK CHUB
Common. Length to about 12 inches. Favors headwater streams, and in many of them this is the last fish upstream.

Rhinichythys atratulus (Hermann) BLACK-NOSED DACE
Rare but locally common. Favors headwater streams. Quite intolerant of pollution, it is now essentially restricted in the Inner Bluegrass to spring-fed or small high-gradient steams adjacent to the Kentucky River.

Nocomis biguttatus (Kirtland) HORNYHEAD CHUB
Rare. Length to about 7 inches. In the Inner Bluegrass this species has been collected only in Elkhorn Creek in Franklin County.

Nocomis micropogon (Cope) RIVER CHUB
Uncommon. Length to 10 inches. Favors rapidly flowing creeks.

Hybopsis aestivalis (Girard) SPECKLED CHUB
Common. Length to about 3 inches. Favors lower portions of larger streams.

Hybopsis amblops (Rafinesque) BIGEYE CHUB
Common. Length to about 4 inches. Favors moderate-sized streams with moderate gradient. Seems absent from the larger rivers and headwater streams.

Hybopsis dissimilis (Kirtland) STREAMLINE CHUB
Rare. Length to about 4 inches. Usually found in clear rivers and large creeks, but may persist in the Kentucky River.

Hybopsis storeriana (Kirtland) SILVER CHUB
Rare. Length to 10 inches. Favors larger rivers and is generally absent from creeks. Frequents sandy bottoms and can tolerate considerable silt.

Notropis ardens Cope ROSEFIN SHINER
Common. Length to about 4 inches. Favors creeks and headwater streams.

Notropis ariommus (Cope) POPEYE SHINER
Rare. Length to about 4 inches. Favors fast-flowing, gravel-bottomed streams of large size; frequents pools.

Notropis atherinoides Rafinesque EMERALD SHINER
Uncommon. Length to about 5 inches. Favors rivers and larger creeks but often ascends into smaller creeks, where it frequents areas with clean, firm bottoms.

Notropis blennius (Girard) RIVER SHINER
Rare. Length to 5 inches. Favors larger rivers, seldom entering creeks. Recorded from the Kentucky River.

Notropis boops Gilbert BIGEYE SHINER
Common. Length to about 3.5 inches. Seems partial to limestone creeks of moderate gradient.

Notropis buchanani Meek GHOST SHINER
Rare. Length to about 3 inches. Favors rivers; seems to enter creeks only rarely.

Notropis chrysocephalus (Rafinesque) STRIPED SHINER
Abundant. Length to about 9 inches. Favors small streams of moderately high gradient with alternating pools and riffles with firm bottoms. It is not confined to such habitats, however, for it occurs sparingly in large streams.

Notropis fumeus Evermann RIBBON SHINER
Rare. Length to about 3 inches. Favors rivers of moderate gradient. Although not recorded in the Inner Bluegrass, it has been taken in the Kentucky River at Jackson in Breathitt County and may be expected in the Kentucky River as it traverses this area.

Notropis photogenis (Cope) SILVER SHINER
Common. Length to about 5 inches. Favors creeks of moderate gradient; avoids both small streams and larger rivers.

Notropis rubellus (Agassiz) ROSYFACE SHINER
Common. Length to about 4 inches. Prefers high-gradient streams. It was formerly common in larger rivers, but since it shows a decided preference for swift water, it is now rare or even absent from the larger streams, such as the Kentucky River, that bear successive dams along their length.

Notropis spilopterus (Cope) SPOTFIN SHINER
Common. Length to about 4.5 inches. Occurs in a variety of habitats, from sluggish water to moderately swift streams of moderate to large size.

Notropis stramineus (Cope) SAND SHINER
Uncommon. Length to about 3 inches. Favors moderately swift streams with clean gravel and sand bottoms.

Notropis umbratilis (Girard) REDFIN SHINER
Uncommon. Length to about 3 inches. Occurs in many types of streams with clean gravel and sand bottoms.

Notropis volucellus (Cope) MIMIC SHINER
Uncommon. Length usually less than 2.5 inches. Occurs in a variety of waters,

from the largest rivers to small headwater streams. Seems to prefer pools or gently flowing riffles; avoids marked turbulence.

Notropis whipplei (Girard) STEELCOLOR SHINER
Uncommon. Length usually less than 5 inches. Occurs in larger creeks and rivers.

Phenacobius mirabilis (Girard) SUCKERMOUTH MINNOW
Rare. Rarely attains a length greater than 4 inches. Favors larger creeks and rivers.

Pimephales notatus (Rafinesque) BLUNTNOSE MINNOW
Common. Length rarely more than 3.5 inches. Occurs from shallower parts of rivers to the smallest headwater streams. It even invades semipermanent streams for breeding and retreats downstream in dry weather.

Pimephales promelas (Rafinesque) FATHEAD MINNOW
Common. Rarely longer than 3 inches. Described originally in 1820 by C.S. Rafinesque from a pond near Lexington. Quite tolerant of turbidity, it favors quiet waters of ponds and slow-flowing portions of streams. Easily propagated in ponds and commonly used as bait by fishermen.

Pimephales vigilax Baird & Girard BULLHEAD MINNOW
Rare. Length rarely to 3.5 inches. Seems most abundant in larger bodies of semi-stagnant water, such as backwaters of larger streams and sluggish pools.

Ericymba buccata Cope SILVERJAW MINNOW
Uncommon. Length to about 3 inches. Prefers clear, silt-free streams with gravel or sandy bottoms, but occurs over shelf rock at 3- to 12-inch depths.

Campostoma anomalum (Rafinesque) STONEROLLER
Common. Length commonly to 4 inches, rarely to 6 inches. Probably occurs in every permanent stream in the Inner Bluegrass; most abundant in riffles and flowing pools. It is unique among our fishes in that the intestine is spirally wound about the airbladder.

Ictaluridae: Catfish Family

Ameiurus melas (Rafinesque) BLACK BULLHEAD
Common. Length to 10 inches, rarely more. Tolerant of silty, sluggish water and present in every major stream and many farm ponds in the Inner Bluegrass.

Ameiurus natalis (LeSueur) YELLOW BULLHEAD
Common. Length to 15 inches, rarely larger. Probably still occurs in every major stream in the Bluegrass region but is apparently being replaced by the more pollution-tolerant black bullhead.

Ameiurus nebulosus (LeSueur) BROWN BULLHEAD
Rare. Length commonly 8–12 inches, rarely to 16 inches. Recorded from Jessamine Creek and the Licking River.

Ictalurus furcatus (LeSueur) BLUE CATFISH
Rare. Length commonly to 30 inches and rarely exceeding 40 inches; weight to 250 pounds. Occurs only in our largest streams and then only in the lower reaches.

Ictalurus punctatus Rafinesque CHANNEL CATFISH
Common. Length frequently to 20 inches, rarely over 30 inches. Weight to 58 pounds. Favors rivers and larger creeks, but introduced into many farm ponds.

Pylodictis olivaris (Rafinesque) FLATHEAD CATFISH
Uncommon. Length usually less than 35 inches and rarely exceeds 48 inches. Weight commonly to 25 pounds; record weight in Kentucky is 108 pounds. Favors

larger rivers and their major tributaries, where it inhabits sluggish pools with relatively little silt and much shelter in the form of logs, drifts, or large rocks.

Noturus eleutherus Jordan MOUNTAIN MADTOM
Rare. Length rarely exceeds 2.5 inches. Favors larger rivers and creeks where the current is relatively rapid and the bottom is of sand, gravel, or rubble.

Noturus flavus Rafinesque STONECAT
Uncommon. Length commonly to 6 inches, rarely exceeding 12 inches. Frequents riffles of rivers and large creeks.

Noturus miurus Jordan BRINDLED MADTOM
Uncommon. Length usually to 3 inches, rarely to 4 inches. Frequents riffle areas in larger creeks and rivers.

Noturus nocturnus Jordan & Gilbert FRECKLED MADTOM
Rare. Length 3–4 inches, rarely 5 inches. Favors riffles in streams of moderate to large size. Perhaps exterminated in the Inner Bluegrass but still occurs in the lower sections of the Kentucky River.

Anguilladae: Freshwater Eel Family

Anguilla rostrata (LeSueur) AMERICAN EEL
Uncommon. Maximum length about 5 feet. Inhabits rivers and larger creeks; migratory. Sexually mature adults go downstream to the Gulf, thence into the Atlantic, where they breed in or near the Sargasso Sea and die. Young move to the coast, then upstream to smaller rivers and larger creeks, where they mature in five to 20 years, then go downstream to complete the cycle. Movements are impeded by high dams.

Gadidae: Cod and Burbot Family

Lota lota (Linnaeus) AMERICAN BURBOT
Rare. Length commonly to 30 inches, weight to 7 pounds. Frequents larger rivers; recorded rarely from both the Kentucky and Licking rivers.

Fundulidae: Killifish Family

Fundulus catenatus (Storer) NORTHERN STUDFISH
Rare. Length to 7 inches. Introduced into Dix River but otherwise not known in the Kentucky and Licking River basins.

Fundulus notatus (Rafinesque) BLACKSTRIPE TOPMINNOW
Rare. Length usually less than 3 inches. Frequents small creeks, sloughs, drainage ditches, and the quiet margins of pools in lowland portions of the Kentucky and Licking River basins.

Poeciliidae: Livebearer Family

Gambusia affinis (Baird & Girard) MOSQUITOFISH
Common. Length of females to about 3 inches, males to about 1 inch or less. Native to western Kentucky and the South, introduced into the Bluegrass region. Favors calm shallow water of any size, from ditches to impoundments. Young are born alive, up to 30 or more per litter, with several litters per season.

Percopsidae: Troutperch Family

Percopsis omiscomaycus (Walbaum) TROUTPERCH
Rare. Length to 5 inches. Favors larger rivers and their major tributaries.

Atherinidae: Silverside Family

Labiesthes sicculus (Cope) BROOK SILVERSIDE
Common. Length to about 3.5 inches. Prefers clean, clear water with little current. Formerly common in larger streams, but pollution and siltation have now essentially limited it to smaller streams and some impoundments.

Serranidae (Percichthyidae): True Bass Family

Morone chrysops (Rafinesque) WHITE BASS ("STRIPED BASS")
Common. Length often to 15 inches, rarely more than 18 inches. Frequents medium to large streams and impoundments.

Morone saxatilis (Walbaum) STRIPED BASS ("ROCKFISH")
Rare. Length to over 4 feet; weight to 125 pounds. Introduced into Herrington Lake, where it surely persists, but it is not known to breed there.

Centrarchidae: Sunfish and Black Bass Family

Micropterus dolomieui Lacépède SMALLMOUTH BASS
Uncommon. Length commonly 10 to 18 inches; maximum known weight about 12 pounds. Favors clear streams of medium gradient with clean bottoms and alternating swift riffles and pools.

Micropterus punctulatus (Rafinesque) SPOTTED BASS
Common. Length often to 15 inches; maximum known weight in Kentucky 7 pounds 10 ounces. Occurs in both flowing streams and impoundments but prefers larger streams than the smallmouth bass. Frequents long flowing pools of low gradient.

Micropterus salmoides (Lacépède) LARGEMOUTH BASS
Common. Length commonly to 18 inches; rarely exceeds 24 inches or 10 pounds in Kentucky. Favors larger, sluggish streams and impoundments. Introduced into many, farm ponds in the Inner Bluegrass.

Lepomis gulosus (Cuvier) WARMOUTH
Rare. Length to about 10 inches. Frequents sluggish streams and bayous. Introduced sparingly into farm ponds.

Lepomis auritus (Linnaeus) REDBREAST SUNFISH
Rare. Length to 8 inches. Introduced into a few farm ponds.

Lepomis cyanellus (Rafinesque) GREEN SUNFISH
Common. Length rarely to 10 inches. Occurs in many types of waters, from the largest rivers to small creeks; does well in farm ponds. Rare in the main channel of the Kentucky River.

Lepomis humilis (Girard) ORANGESPOTTED SUNFISH
Rare. Length rarely to 5 inches. Favors slow-flowing streams with silted bottoms.

Lepomis macrochirus Rafinesque BLUEGILL
Abundant. Length rarely to 11 inches. Favors ponded or sluggishly flowing waters of larger streams. Stocked in many, perhaps most, farm ponds, where it thrives.

Lepomis megalotis (Rafinesque) LONGEAR SUNFISH
Common. Length to 10 inches. Favors clear pools in moderate-sized streams but is also present in impoundments.

Lepomis microlophus (Günther) REDEAR SUNFISH
Common. Length to 10 inches. Formerly rare, now present in some farm ponds and many streams due to stocking. Does best in clear ponds and impoundments with emergent vegetation.

Ambloplites rupestris (Rafinesque) ROCK BASS
Common. Length to 12 inches, weight to 1.5 pounds. Favors creeks with rocky bottoms, either loose boulders or limestone ledges.

Pomoxis annularis Rafinesque WHITE CRAPPIE
Common. Length to about 12 inches. Favors larger creeks and rivers but does well in impoundments and farm ponds.

Pomoxis nigromaculatus (LeSueur) BLACK CRAPPIE
Rare. Length to about 12 inches. Occurs in larger creeks and rivers, impoundments, and some farm ponds.

Percidae: Perch and Darter Family

Stizostedion canadense (Smith) SAUGER
Uncommon. Length to about 30 inches, weight to about 7 pounds. Inhabits rivers and larger impoundments and avoids smaller waters except to breed in tributaries.

Stizostedion vitreum (Mitchill) WALLEYE
Uncommon. Length to 34 inches, weight to 19.25 pounds. Frequents larger rivers and impoundments and, where no dams intrude, runs upstream in spring to smaller streams and shallower waters to breed.

Percina caprodes (Rafinesque) LOGPERCH
Common. Length to about 8 inches. This, the largest of the Kentucky darters, inhabits riffles and adjacent pools of rivers and larger creeks. The first named darter, the Logperch was described by Rafinesque from Kentucky specimens.

Percina copelandi (Jordan) CHANNEL DARTER
Rare. Length to about 2.5 inches. Frequents quiet, sandy-bottomed reaches of rivers and creeks but often enters gravelly riffles.

Percina cymatotaenia (Gilbert & Meek) BLUESTRIPE DARTER
Rare. Length to about 5 inches. Although not recorded in the Inner Bluegrass, it may well occur sparingly in the Kentucky River, as it is known in a number of localities farther upstream.

Percina evides (Jordan & Copeland) GILT DARTER
Rare. Length to about 3 inches. Inhabits larger rivers and creeks.

Percina macrocephala (Cope) LONGHEAD DARTER
Rare, perhaps extinct in the Inner Bluegrass. Length to 4 inches. Inhabits rivers and larger creeks.

Percina maculata (Girard) BLACKSIDE DARTER
Uncommon. Length to about 4 inches. Inhabits small streams in both pools and riffles.

Percina phoxocephala (Nelson) SLENDERHEAD DARTER
Rare. Length to about 4 inches. Frequents gravelly riffles in medium-sized streams, usually in water less than a foot deep.

Percina sciera (Swain) DUSKY DARTER
Rare. Length to 5 inches. Inhabits rivers and creeks of larger to medium size.

Percina shumardi (Girard) RIVER DARTER
Rare. Length to about 3 inches. Inhabits our larger rivers, frequenting riffle or chute areas with sandy or gravelly bottoms.

Ammocrypta pellucida (Putnam) EASTERN SAND DARTER
Formerly rare, now probably extinct in the Inner Bluegrass. Length to 3 inches.

Frequents sandy bottoms in medium-size streams, and such habitats are rare in the Inner Bluegrass.

Ethoestoma baileyi Page & Burr — EMERALD DARTER
Rare. Length to about 4 inches. This darter is widespread in streams in the upper Kentucky drainage and may well occur erratically in the Kentucky River as it traverses the Inner Bluegrass.

Etheostoma blennioides Rafinesque — GREENSIDE DARTER
Common. Length to 4.5 inches. This is a riffle species, often frequenting mats of algae on shelving limestone ledges in the Inner Bluegrass. Occurs in both large and small streams.

Etheostoma caeruleum Storer — RAINBOW DARTER
Uncommon (locally common). Length to about 3 inches. Inhabits moderate-size streams with alternating pools and riffles.

Etheostoma flabellare Rafinesque — FANTAIL DARTER
Common. Length to about 3 inches. Inhabits flowing water of many sizes, from rivers to tiny tributary streams. Frequents shallow riffles with gravelly or rocky bottoms.

Etheostoma maculatum Kirtland — SPOTTED DARTER
Formerly rare, now probably absent from the Inner Bluegrass. Length to about 2.5 inches. Inhabits medium-size streams with gravelly or rocky bottoms.

Etheostoma nigrum Rafinesque — JOHNNY DARTER
Common. Length to about 2.5 inches. Favors small to medium-size streams, frequenting shallow pools with gravel, sand, or rubble bottoms.

Etheostoma spectabile (Agassiz) — ORANGETHROAT DARTER
Common. Length to about 3 inches. This handsome species, probably the commonest darter in the Inner Bluegrass, inhabits small to moderate streams of low gradient. It frequents rocky riffles, often in water depths of only a few inches.

Etheostoma tippecanoe Jordan & Evermann — TIPPECANOE DARTER
Rare. Length to 1.75 inches. Although not recorded in the Inner Bluegrass, this extremely rare species may still occur in the Licking and Kentucky rivers as they traverse the area. It has been recorded in both streams nearer their headwaters. Frequents long riffles with shaley, sandy, or gravelly bottoms and a depth of about 2 feet.

Etheostoma variatum Kirtland — VARIEGATE DARTER
Rare. Length to about 4 inches. Inhabits large creeks and small rivers, frequenting riffles, often where the bottom is sandy or gravelly.

Etheostoma zonale (Cope) — BANDED DARTER
Common. Length to about 3 inches. Inhabits streams of moderate size.

Sciaenidae: Drum Family

Aplodinotus grunniens (Rafinesque) — FRESHWATER DRUM ("WHITE PERCH")
Common. Length commonly to 2 feet, rarely to about 30 inches. Weight commonly to 5 pounds; a 35-pound specimen was caught in the Kentucky River. Inhabits rivers and large creeks.

Cottidae: Sculpin Family

Cottus bairdi Girard — MOTTLED SCULPIN
Rare. Length to 4 inches, rarely more. Apparently, this species reaches the Inner Bluegrass only in the Licking drainage. It frequents gravelly riffles or pools at the foot of such riffles.

Cottus carolinae (Gill) BANDED SCULPIN
Common. Length to about 6 inches. Inhabits creeks and their tributaries, well up into headwater streams. Often found in springs and in streams in caves. Frequents riffle areas. Rarely seen in summer, when most individuals migrate into cooler water, such as underground streams or deep pools.

AMPHIBIANS

Class *Amphibia:* AMPHIBIANS

Cryptobranchidae: Giant Salamander Family

Cryptobranchus alleganiensis alleganiensis (Daudin) EASTERN HELLBENDER
Common. Permanently aquatic, inhabiting the largest streams; occasionally caught by fishermen. This is the only salamander in the Inner Bluegrass that practices external fertilization. The eggs, deposited in a cavity dug by the male under a submerged rock or log, are guarded by him until they hatch.

Ambystomatidae: Mole Salamander Family

Ambystoma jeffersonianum (Green) JEFFERSON SALAMANDER
Widespread and common; occurs in and about some farm ponds along the river bluffs. Inhabits ponds in winter and early spring, and woodlands in late spring, summer, and early fall, where it hides under rocks or logs, or burrows into the earth.

Ambystoma barbouri Kraus and Petranka
BLUEGRASS SMALL-MOUTHED SALAMANDER
Common in and about small streams with rocky bottoms. Winters in small streams, breeds there in January, February, and sometimes March. The adults then leave the stream to summer under rocks, logs, or burrows in the earth, reentering the streams in late fall or early winter.

Ambystoma maculatum (Shaw) SPOTTED SALAMANDER
Favors wooded areas. Most often encountered in late winter or early spring in or about woodland pools where they congregate to mate and lay eggs.

Plethodontidae: Lungless Salamander Family

Desmognathus fuscus fuscus (Green) NORTHERN DUSKY SALAMANDER
Locally uncommon. Inhabits small, clear woodland streams feeding the Kentucky and Ohio rivers. Although it frequently enters the water, it generally spends most of its time in hiding under stones, logs, or debris along the stream margin, rarely venturing more than a few feet from the water's edge.

Plethodon dorsalis dorsalis Cope EASTERN ZIGZAG SALAMANDER
Abundant. For many years this species was extremely abundant in early spring under stones on rocky wooded slopes in the southern and western portions of the Inner Bluegrass. The population in 1978 was at a very low ebb, presumably because of the extremely cold winters of 1976–77 and 1977–78. The population has substantially recovered since that time.

Plethodon richmondi Netting & Mittleman RAVINE SALAMANDER
Locally common. Normally it can be found abundantly in early spring under stones on rocky wooded slopes throughout the Inner Bluegrass. The population in 1978 was at a low ebb, likely because of the two extremely severe winters in succession. Unlike the zigzag salamander, this species apparently has been slow to recover.

Plethodon glutinosus glutinosus (Green) SLIMY SALAMANDER
Widespread and common. Frequents wooded areas, seeking shelter under stones, logs, or other cover. Most often seen March or April, as it avoids the hot dry weather of summer and early fall by going underground.

Gyrinophilus porphyriticus duryi (Weller) KENTUCKY SPRING SALAMANDER
Locally rare. Favors springs or small, clear, rocky streams. Most often encountered under a flat rock partially in the water. However, they sometimes wander a considerable distance from a stream to frequent wet places, such as roadside ditches, and woodlands; sometimes enter caves.

Pseudotriton montanus diastictus Bishop MIDLAND MUD SALAMANDER
Widespread and uncommon. Inhabits muddy areas. Most often encountered under rocks or logs along a shallow sluggish stream or spring run. Although not limited to wooded areas, it seems more abundant along woodland streams.

Pseudotriton ruber ruber (Latreille) NORTHERN RED SALAMANDER
Local and rare. Inhabits cold, clear rocky streams and spring runs, either in open areas or in woods. Most often found under a flat stone at or near the water's edge. Sometimes quite terrestrial, especially in summer, when it may be encountered under a sheltering rock or log at a considerable distance from any open water.

Eurycea bislineata bislineata (Green) NORTHERN TWO-LINED SALAMANDER
Widespread and common. A brookside species, often seen perched on a rock jutting from the water in a moist, shaded area along a small woodland stream. It is not, however, limited to such streams, as it often occurs in streams flowing through sunny pastures. In rainy weather it often wanders considerable distances from streams.

Eurycea longicauda longicauda (Green) LONGTAIL SALAMANDER
Local and rare. Seems particularly fond of moist, shaded cliff faces with an abundance of thin, flat rocks. Also encountered often under stones or logs along woodland streams.

Eurycea lucifuga Rafinesque CAVE SALAMANDER
Widespread and common. Most often encountered in wet limestone caves. However, it often frequents areas far from caves, finding shelter under logs or stones in wooded areas or along streams. Formerly a common inhabitant of spring-houses, it is now scarce there.

Proteidae: Mudpuppy Family

Necturus maculosus maculosus (Rafinesque) MUDPUPPY
Widespread and common. Inhabits rivers and larger creeks. This is a permanently aquatic, gill-breathing creatue whose gills are external. It is often taken on trot lines, in fish traps, or by still fishermen.

Salamandridae: Newt Family

Notophthalmus viridescens viridescens (Rafinesque) RED-SPOTTED NEWT
Widespread and uncommon. Historically, this has been a creature of wooded areas; it is highly adaptable, however, and may now be found in farm ponds considerably removed from wooded areas. In addition to the expected larval period, this creature goes through two distinct stages in its life cycle. The larval form metamorphoses into a rough, red, lung-breathing creature that inhabits moist woodlands for a year or so and then goes into woodland pools, where it normally remains as an aquatic, lung-breathing creature for the rest of its life.

Ranidae: True Frog Family

Rana catesbeiana Shaw BULLFROG
Widespread and abundant. Inhabits margins of rivers and larger creeks, and especially farm ponds. More often heard than seen, as its bellowing call, "jug-o'-rum," can be heard almost nightly from May to August.

Rana clamitans clamitans Latreille BRONZE FROG
Widespread and common. Inhabits ponds, swamps, rivers, creeks, brooks, and springs, both in woodlands and in open areas. The explosive, banjo-like "pung" call is usually repeated a few times in measured succession, each note lower in pitch and volume than the preceding.

Rana pipiens Schreber NORTHERN LEOPARD FROG
Widespread and rare. Inhabits wet areas and shores, from small creeks to rivers and small ponds to large impoundments. In summer often wanders into meadows or woodlands. Voice similar to the sounds made by rubbing the fingers over a tightly inflated balloon; most frequently heard from late March into May.

Rana sphenocephala Cope SOUTHERN LEOPARD FROG
Locally uncommon. Inhabits wet areas and shores, from small creeks to rivers and small ponds to large impoundments. In summer, it often wanders into meadows or woodlands. The voice is of higher pitch and shorter duration than the northern species.

Rana palustris Le Conte PICKEREL FROG
Widespread and uncommon. Frequents the edges of cool, clear waters, small or large, quiet or flowing. However, in summer they often wander into grassy fields or woodlands. In winter they may be encountered in caves. The grating, snore-like call is most often heard about quiet water in late March and April and is sometimes emitted under water.

Bufonidae: True Toad Family

Bufo americanus americanus Holbrook AMERICAN TOAD
Widespread and common. Usually encountered about homes and gardens, but also occurs in deep woodlands. During the day it usually remains secreted under a board, rock, clump of vegetation, or other shelter, emerging at night to feed. The long-drawn-out high-pitched musical trill of the male is often heard about farm ponds from early March into May.

Bufo woodhousii fowleri Hinckley FOWLER'S TOAD
Widespread and common. Often encountered about homes and gardens, but also frequents fields and woodlands where there is shelter and some quiet water suitable as a breeding site nearby. The male, often heard at night from May to July, utters a loud, nasal scream of 1 to 3 seconds' duration, repeated over and over.

Hylidae: Treefrog Family

Acris crepitans blanchardi Harper BLANCHARD'S CRICKET FROG
Local and common. Favors shallow-water areas with mud flats and vegetated areas, either emergent or along the shore. Often lives about farm ponds but also occurs about other quiet waters, in rivers, creeks, and impoundments. The voice is an oft-repeated "gick, gick, gick" resembling the clicking of two rounded pebbles shaken in a loosely closed fist. Calling begins about the last of April and continues sporadically into summer.

Hyla crucifer crucifer Wied NORTHERN SPRING PEEPER
Widespread and common. Occurring in many woodland pools throughout the Inner Bluegrass, this species is frequently encountered in and about shallow pools

in wooded areas along the major watercourses. From March into June, choruses may be heard in such areas; the individual call is a single clear piping whistle emitted at intervals of about a second.

Hyla chrysoscelis Cope — COPE'S GRAY TREEFROG
Widespread and common. These woodland creatures inhabit trees and brush except when in hibernation and during the breeding season. They begin to congregate in late April about shallow woodland pools to mate and lay their eggs, with a peak of this activity in late May. Rainy periods may bring them back to the breeding pools as late as August. The voice is a loud, coarse trill.

REPTILES

Class *Reptilia* — REPTILES

Chelydridae: Snapping Turtle Family

Chelydra serpentina serpentina (Linnaeus) — COMMON SNAPPING TURTLE
Widespread and common. Occurs in rivers, creeks, impoundments, and farm ponds. They seem to prefer larger, quiet waters. Individuals sometimes make surprisingly long overland journeys, and it is not uncommon to encounter one some distance from the nearest water. This animal will bite viciously if handled incautiously.

Emydidae: Freshwater and Marsh Turtle Family

Terrapene carolina carolina (Linnaeus) — EASTERN BOX TURTLE
Locally common. Inhabits woodlands and woodland edges, from low, swampy woods to high, dry uplands. In hot weather, they often congregate in shallow pools in woodland streams.

Graptemys geographica (LeSueur) — MAP TURTLE
Widespread and common. Inhabits larger rivers and creeks and large impoundments. Rarely found in ponds or small, swift-flowing streams. Often seen basking in the sun on a grassy shore or a stranded log.

Chrysemys picta marginata Agassiz — MIDLAND PAINTED TURTLE
Local and uncommon. Occurs in quiet, shallow water such as ponds and sloughs and prefers areas with much aquatic vegetation.

Trachemys scripta elegans (Wied) — RED-EARED SLIDER
Widespread and common. Favors larger bodies of quiet water but often occurs in farm ponds. May often be seen basking on floating or stranded logs but is seldom seen on land.

Kinosternidae: Musk and Mud Turtle Family

Sternotherus odoratus (Latreille) — STINKPOT
Widespread and uncommon. Found in permanent waters, from rivers and creeks to ponds and swamps. Prefers shallow, muddy-bottomed waters. When disturbed, this creature emits a yellowish fluid with a strong, musky odor from a pair of glands on either side of the carapace. Handled recklessly, a stinkpot may inflict a painful bite.

Kinosternon subrubrum subrubrum (Lacepede) — EASTERN MUD TURTLE
Local and rare. It is found in permanent waters, from rivers and creeks to ponds and swamps. This turtle prefers shallow, muddy-bottomed waters. It can be observed most easily at night as it walks leisurely along the bottom of a pond or stream in search of food.

Trionychidae: Softshell Turtle Family

Trionyx spiniferus spiniferus LeSueur EASTERN SPINY SOFTSHELL
Widespread and common. Favors clean, flowing streams and rivers but also occurs in impoundments and larger ponds. It may sometimes be seen basking on a mud flat near the water's edge. Although appearing quite innocuous, this animal has sharp jaws and will bite viciously.

Iguanidae: Iguana Family

Sceloporus undulatus hyacinthinus (Green) NORTHERN FENCE LIZARD
Local and uncommon. Prefers dry, open, sunny woodlands but may be found in a variety of other sites—about old houses and barns, fence posts, piles of logs or scrap lumber, and rock piles. Males are usually brown-backed and blue-bellied, females usually gray-backed and light-bellied.

Scincidae: Skink Family

Scincella lateralis (Say) GROUND SKINK
Local and rare. Apparently occurring only along the wooded bluffs of the Kentucky River and its tributaries. Occurs in woodlands, most frequently in the vicinity of small streams. Prefers a moist but not wet environment. This animal is quite secretive, scurrying about in the leaf litter and only rarely appearing on the surface of the forest floor.

Eumeces fasciatus (Linnaeus) FIVE-LINED SKINK
Local and uncommon. Occurs about old houses and barns, overgrown piles of rocks, and in cut-over woods with an abundance of rotting stumps. Juveniles and younger adults have bright blue tails.

Eumeces laticeps (Schneider) BROAD-HEAD SKINK
Widespread and uncommon. Recorded only on the wooded bluffs along the Kentucky River in Fayette and Mercer counties. This is the largest of our skinks; any red-headed lizard more than 9 inches long is almost surely this species.

Colubridae: Harmless Snake Family

Carphophis amoenus helenae (Kennicott) MIDWEST WORM SNAKE
Local and uncommon. Length to 13 inches, usually 6–10 inches. Occurs in woodlands, woodland edges, and rocky fields nearby. Generally found in hiding under rocks, logs, or debris on the forest floor.

Diadophis punctatus edwardsii (Merrem) NORTHERN RINGNECK SNAKE
Locally uncommon. Length to 23 inches, usually 10–16. Occurs in woodlands, rarely venturing more than a few yards from the sheltering trees. Usually found secreted beneath a rock or log, sometimes beneath the loose bark of a dead tree.

Heterodon platyrhinos Latreille EASTERN HOGNOSE SNAKE
Widespread and common. Length to 43 inches, usually 16–30. Occurs in both woodlands and open fields but seems to favor woodland edges. When disturbed, it will often hiss and strike repeatedly, then writhe about and roll over on its back as though dead. Left undisturbed, it will soon recover.

Opheodrys aestivus (Linnaeus) EASTERN ROUGH GREEN SNAKE
Uncommon. Length to 42 inches, usually 24–36. Occurs in woodlands, woodland edges, and particularly along overgrown fence rows. This is a particularly handsome and perfectly innocuous snake.

Coluber constrictor constrictor Linnaeus NORTHERN BLACK RACER
Widespread and common. Length to 73 inches, usually 30–60. Inhabits a variety

of situations, from woodlands through brushy areas to pastures and cultivated fields, but is most commonly found along woodland edges or brushy fence rows.

Coluber constrictor priapus Dunn & Wood SOUTHERN BLACK RACER
Widespread and common. This subspecies differs from the northern in having a distinctly white chin and throat. The two subspecies occur sympatrically (together) in the Inner Bluegrass. The name for the species is a misnomer, since racers do not constrict their prey.

Elaphe obsoleta obsoleta (Say) BLACK RAT SNAKE
Widespread and common. Length to 102 inches, usually 30–72. Inhabits a variety of situations—woodlands, meadows, fencerows, gardens, and occasionally barns or houses. An excellent climber, it is frequently seen in trees or along narrow ledges in houses or barns. In this area the snake is purported to take milk from cows, but it does not do so.

Lampropeltis getulus niger (Yarrow) BLACK KINGSNAKE
Local and rare. Length to 56 inches, usually 36–48. Occurs in woods, woodland edges, and weedy or brushy fields, where it often secretes itself beneath a log, stone, or other form of shelter. This species often feeds on other snakes, including venomous ones.

Lampropeltis triangulum triangulum (Lacépède) EASTERN MILK SNAKE
Locally common. Length to 48 inches, usually 20–36. Occurs in a variety of habitats, from woodlands to open fields, and often enters buildings, including those occupied by humans. Usually spends the day secreted under some type of cover, emerging to feed by night. They are excellent climbers, often resting along ledges in buildings.

Thamnophis sirtalis sirtalis (Linnaeus) EASTERN GARTER SNAKE
Widespread and common but becoming less so. Length to 48 inches, usually 16–30. Occupies a wide range of habitats, from deep woodlands through open farmland to city lots. The great majority of snakes seen in towns and suburbs are of this species.

Storeria dekayi dekayi (Holbrook) NORTHERN BROWN SNAKE
Local and rare. Length to about 18 inches, usually 3–14. Occurs in a variety of situations, from woodlands through open farmlands to lowland swamps and marshes. Highly secretive and seldom seen; spends much of the time in hiding beneath a rock or other shelter.

Regina septemvittata. (Say) QUEEN SNAKE
Widespread and common. Length to 36 inches, usually 16–30 inches. Occurs in rocky streams in woodlands, as well as those in open fields. Usually in hiding beneath a flat rock by day, emerging at night to feed, mostly on crayfish. Although most water snakes will bite savagely on slight provocation, this species rarely, if ever, bites a human.

Nerodia sipedon sipedon (Linnaeus) NORTHERN WATER SNAKE
Widespread and common. Length to 58 inches, usually 24–48. Occurs in or about nearly any body of water, from farm ponds to the largest reservoirs, and from small streams to rivers. Seems most common about flowing water and is often seen basking on overhanging trees or brush or on piles of debris along the banks. If mishandled, it will bite savagely. It is sometimes misidentified as a venomous cottonmouth moccasin, which is not known to occur within a hundred miles of the Inner Bluegrass.

Viperidae: Viper and Pit Viper Family

Agkistrodon contortrix mokeson (Daudin) NORTHERN COPPERHEAD
Widespread and uncommon. Length to 53 inches, usually 20-36. Occurs in woodlands, especially on wooded hillsides or bluffs with rocky outcrops. Sometimes found about old houses and barns.

Crotalus horridus horridus Linnaeus TIMBER RATTLESNAKE
Local and extremely rare. There have been few positive records over the last few years. An individual is apparently deposited along the river bluffs by floods from time to time; the few records from those areas add credence to that assertion.

BIRDS

Class *Aves* BIRDS

Gaviidae: Loon Family

Gavia immer (Brunnich) COMMON LOON
Migrant. Generally uncommon, but flocks of as many as 145 have been encountered in fall. Found on larger bodies of open water from late March to mid-May and from October to early December.

Podicipedidae: Grebe Family

Podiceps grisegena (Boddaert) RED-NECKED GREBE
Migrant. Rare; only a very few records. Has been observed on larger bodies of open water in March, April, October, and November.

Podiceps auritus (Linnaeus) HORNED GREBE
Migrant. Uncommon. Favors larger bodies of water. May be expected from March to mid-May and from October to December. May occasionally spend the winter in a mild season.

Podilymbus podiceps (Linnaeus) PIED-BILLED GREBE
Migrant. Common on larger streams, reservoirs, and farm ponds from February to mid-May and from late September to mid-November. May occasionally overwinter in mild seasons, and a pair may sometimes spend the summer.

Pelecanidae: Pelican Family

Pelecanus erythrorhynchos Gmelin AMERICAN WHITE PELICAN
Accidental. One individual was seen and photographed on Herrington Lake, near the dam, in the autumn of 1979.

Phalacrocoracidae: Cormorant Family

Phalacrocorax auritus (Lesson) DOUBLE-CRESTED CORMORANT
Migrant. Rare. Occasionally seen near larger bodies of water, usually in April.

Ardeidae: Heron, Egret, and Bittern Family

Ixobrychus exilis (Gmelin) LEAST BITTERN
Summer resident. Rare. Inhabits patches of cattails or other emergent vegetation in shallow marshes. Arrives in early April or a bit later; departs by early October. Nests usually in a dense clump of cattails or a small shrub, 1–3 feet above water, from mid-May into July.

Botaurus lentiginosus (Rackett) AMERICAN BITTERN
Migrant. Uncommon. Favors marshy areas and wet meadows with dense stands of tall vegetation. Most often seen from late March to mid-May or in October and November. This species formerly spent the summer here; perhaps an occasional pair does so now.

Nycticorax nycticorax (Linnaeus) BLACK-CROWNED NIGHT HERON
Summer resident. Rare except near breeding colonies. Frequents marshes, farm ponds, and streams. Arrives by late March, usually gone by mid-October. Nests in the tops of trees near streams or sloughs from April to September. May occasionally overwinter in mild seasons.

Nycticorax violaceus (Linnaeus) YELLOW-CROWNED NIGHT HERON
Summer resident. Uncommon, but may be locally common. Frequents mature woods, usually near streams, ponds, or sloughs. Arrives in late March or early April; usually departs by mid-October. Nests in the tops of trees near water or in park-like woods from April to July.

Butorides striatus (Linnaeus) GREEN-BACKED HERON
Summer resident. Common. Frequents farm ponds, marshes, streams, and impoundments. Arrives in late March or early April; departs usually by mid-October, but may linger on into November. Nests from late April to July in trees sometimes over water, sometimes up to a mile or so distant; sometimes nests in loose colonies but usually singly. May occasionally overwinter in mild seasons.

Bubulcus ibis Linnaeus CATTLE EGRET
Vagrant; becoming more common. Often associated with cattle, feeding on insects stirred up by their feet. Frequently inhabits the borders of farm ponds.

Egretta caerulea (Linnaeus) LITTLE BLUE HERON
Vagrant. In some years, locally common about wet open areas and upland meadows; sometimes about farm ponds, impoundments, or streams. Although it may appear in April or May, its appearance is most likely between late June and late September.

Egretta thula (Molina) SNOWY EGRET
Vagrant. Uncommon. Frequents wet meadows and shallow water of streams, ponds, and reservoirs. Sometimes seen as early as mid-April; most common between mid-August and early September.

Casmerodius albus (Linnaeus) GREAT EGRET
Vagrant. Rare in spring and an uncommon post-breeding visitor in fall; inhabits shores of streams, ponds, and reservoirs and often frequents wet meadows. Most often seen between late August and late October.

Ardea herodias Linnaeus GREAT BLUE HERON
Migrant. Uncommon. Frequents farm ponds, reservoirs, and larger watercourses from late March to early May and from September to mid-November. An occasional post-breeding adult wanders by in summer, and a rare individual may spend the winter.

Ciconiidae: Stork Family

Mycteria americana Linnaeus WOOD STORK
Vagrant. A rare post-breeding vagrant, favoring low wet country with swamps and open areas. Sometimes seen perched in unlikely places, as on a television antenna atop a house. May appear in late summer or early fall.

Gruidae: Crane Family

Grus canadensis (Linnaeus) SANDHILL CRANE
Migrant. A rare transient, formerly regular in appearance, now quite irregular. This is a bird of open fields but is most frequently seen in Kentucky as it flies high overhead with neck and legs extended, uttering its vibrant honking cry. Most

often seen from mid-September to mid-February. Spring records are irregular, from early March to early May.

Anatidae: Duck, Goose, and Swan Family

Chen caerulescens (Linnaeus) SNOW GOOSE
Migrant. Rare and irregular. Usually seen flying high overhead. Sometimes alights on larger bodies of water or in open fields. Usually seen between mid-March and early May or mid-October and late December. Not seen in many (most?) years.

Branta canadensis (Linnaeus) CANADA GOOSE
Migrant. An uncommon transient. Usually seen flying high overhead; sometimes alights on larger bodies of water or, more rarely, in open fields. Most often seen from late February to mid-April and from mid-October to late November.

Anas platyrhynchos Linnaeus MALLARD
Migrant. Common about larger bodies of water. Usually seen between late February and early April and from mid-October to early December. May occasionally overwinter in mild seasons.

Anas rubripes Brewster AMERICAN BLACK DUCK
Migrant. Common about larger bodies of water from late February to early May and between early October and mid-December. A few may overwinter in mild seasons.

Anas strepera Linnaeus GADWALL
Migrant. Rare on farm ponds, reservoirs, and larger streams from late February to late April and from late October to early December. May occasionally overwinter in mild seasons.

Anas crecca Gmelin GREEN-WINGED TEAL
Migrant. Uncommon. Frequents open water, from farm ponds and small streams to the largest reservoirs and rivers. Most abundant from late February to early May and from mid-September to early December.

Anas americana Gmelin AMERICAN WIDGEON
Migrant. Common in spring, less common in fall, on farm ponds, reservoirs, and larger rivers. Most abundant from late February to mid-April and from mid-October to late December.

Anas acuta Linnaeus NORTHERN PINTAIL
Migrant. Common about shallow marshes, ponds, and flooded fields, especially in spring. Less common in fall. Most often seen between late January and late April and from late September to late November.

Anas clypeata Linnaeus NORTHERN SHOVELER
Migrant. Common in spring, rare in fall. Favors ponds and reservoirs but also occurs on larger streams. Most abundant from February to early May and in October or November.

Anas discors Linnaeus BLUE-WINGED TEAL
Migrant. Common on farm ponds, reservoirs, creeks, mud flats, and marshes. Most abundant from mid-March to early May and from late August to early November.

Oxyura jamaicensis (Gmelin) RUDDY DUCK
Migrant. Uncommon in spring, common in fall on ponds and streams, as well as larger bodies of water. Most common from late February to May and from late October to mid-December. May occasionally overwinter in mild seasons.

Aix sponsa (Linnaeus) WOOD DUCK
Summer resident. Common. Frequents wooded streams and farm ponds. Arrives in early March, is usually gone by November. Nests in hollows of trees (to 50 feet above ground) from mid-March to late June; will accept nest boxes. May occasionally overwinter in mild seasons.

Aythya valisineria (Wilson) CANVASBACK
Migrant. Rare. Frequents larger bodies of water but sometimes alights on farm ponds. Most common from late February to mid-April, and from late October to early December. Perhaps overwinters on occasion.

Aythya americana (Eyton) REDHEAD
Migrant. Rare. Favors larger bodies of water but sometimes alights on farm ponds. Most frequent from late February to late April and from late October to late November.

Aythya collaris (Donovan) RING-NECKED DUCK
Migrant. Common on larger rivers and impoundments. Seen mainly from late February to early May and between late October and late November. May occasionally overwinter in mild seasons.

Aythya marila (Linnaeus) GREATER SCAUP
Migant. Rare. Partial to larger bodies of water but frequently alights on small ponds. Present from mid-March to mid-May and from late September to early December. Perhaps occasionally overwinters in mild seasons.

Aythya affinis (Eyton) LESSER SCAUP
Migrant. Common in quiet water, from puddles to the largest rivers and impoundments. Most abundant from mid-March to mid-May and from late September to early December. Occasionally overwinters in mild seasons.

Clangula hyemalis (Linnaeus) OLDSQUAW
Vagrant. A rare transient and sometimes a winter resident on large bodies of water. In the Inner Bluegrass it must be considered a rare vagrant indeed; there is but one record, in late March.

Bucephala clangula (Linnaeus) COMMON GOLDENEYE
Migrant. Uncommon. May be seen on larger bodies of water from February to mid-April and in late November and early December. Sometimes overwinters in mild seasons.

Bucephala albeola (Linnaeus) BUFFLEHEAD
Migrant. Uncommon. Seen on farm ponds and reservoirs in March and April and from late October to early December. May overwinter in mild seasons.

Mergus merganser Linnaeus COMMON MERGANSER
Migrant. Uncommon. Seen on larger bodies of water, mostly from late February to early April and from October to December. Perhaps occasionally winters in mild seasons.

Mergus serrator Linnaeus RED-BREASTED MERGANSER
Migrant. Uncommon in spring, rare in fall on ponds and streams. Present from late March to early May and from late September to early November.

Lophodytes cucullatus (Linnaeus) HOODED MERGANSER
Migrant. Uncommon. Seen on farm ponds, reservoirs, and streams. Most abundant in March and early April and from mid-October to mid-December. Perhaps overwinters in mild seasons.

Rallidae: Rail, Coot, and Gallinule Family

Rallus elegans Audubon KING RAIL
Vagrant. Rare. There are records of this species' occurrence around Lexington Reservoir Number 4 in 1969, 1973,and 1975.

Rallus limicola Vieillot VIRGINIA RAIL
Migrant. Rare, frequenting dense marshes. Present in April and May and from late September through November.

Porzana carolina (Linnaeus) SORA
Migrant. Uncommon. Frequents marshes and wet weed patches; sometimes feeds in grain fields. Most numerous from late March to early May and from late August to late October.

Porphyrula martinica (Linnaeus) PURPLE GALLINULE
Accidental. The only record is an individual found in a backyard in Lexington in the late 1960s.

Gallinula chloropus (Linnaeus) COMMON MOORHEN
Migrant. Rare. Favors marshes with open leads of water. May be expected in April and May and from late August through October.

Fulica americana Gmelin AMERICAN COOT
Migrant. Abundant. Partial to larger bodies of water, but also occurs on farm ponds and creeks. Most abundant from late February to June and from mid-September to late November. May occasionally overwinter in mild seasons.

Charadriidae: Plover and Turnstone Family

Charadrius semipalmatus Bonaparte SEMIPALMATED PLOVER
Migrant. Rare. Prefers sandbars, mud flats, and flooded fields. Spring records are mostly in early and middle May; in fall, may be expected from August to mid-October.

Charadrius vociferus Linnaeus KILLDEER
Resident. Common. Frequents open areas with sparse ground cover. Nests on bare ground in open areas. Clutches are completed from mid-March to late June.

Pluvialis squatarola (Linnaeus) BLACK-BELLIED PLOVER
Migrant. Rare. Sometimes seen, usually in fields with killdeer, in May or from mid-September to mid-October.

Pluvialis dominica (Müller) LESSER GOLDEN PLOVER
Migrant. Rare. Frequents upland fields in spring, and mud flats, sand bars, and wet rocks in fall. May be expected from mid-March to mid-May and from early August to mid-November.

Scolopacidae: Sandpiper, Snipe, and Woodcock Family

Tringa melanoleuca (Gmelin) GREATER YELLOWLEGS
Migrant. Uncommon. Frequents sandbars, mud flats, and shallow water about the margins of reservoirs and farm ponds. May be expected from mid-March to mid-May and from late July or early August to mid-November.

Tringa flavipes (Gmelin) LESSER YELLOWLEGS
Migrant. Common. Frequents sandbars, mud flats, and shallow water about the shores of reservoirs and farm ponds. May be expected from mid-March to late May and from early August to late October.

Tringa solitaria Wilson SOLITARY SANDPIPER
Migrant. Common about the shores of streams and ponds. Most often seen from early April to late May and from mid-July to mid-October.

Actitis macularia (Linnaeus) SPOTTED SANDPIPER
Migrant. Common. Frequents borders of streams, ponds, and impoundments. May be expected in spring from late March or early April to early June; fall migrants begin to arrive in early July, become common in late July, and are essentially gone by November. Perhaps an occasional pair breeds here.

Phalaropus tricolor (Vieillot) WILSON'S PHALAROPE
Migrant. Very rare. Frequents shores and shallow waters. There are only two records, one each in Fayette and Woodford counties, both in the first week of May, 1978 and 1979.

Phalaropus fulicarius (Linnaeus) RED PHALAROPE
Migrant. Very rare. Frequents shallow water and muddy or grassy shores. May be expected from early September to mid-November.

Limnodromus griseus (Gmelin) SHORT-BILLED DOWITCHER
Migrant. Rare. Frequents mud flats and grassy or rocky shores. Most often seen from mid-March to mid-May and from late July to late October.

Gallinago gallinago (Linnaeus) COMMON SNIPE
Migrant. Common in wet places, such as drainage ditches, stream and pond margins, and marshes. May be expected from late February to early May and from late August or early September until December.

Scolopax minor Gmelin AMERICAN WOODCOCK
Summer resident. Rare in summer, more common in spring and fall. Frequents wet thickets along meandering streams but also found in upland thickets and woodland edges. Arrives in February or March, departs by early December. Nests on the ground, usually in a moist thicket, but sometimes in relatively dry second growth woods. Courtship begins as soon as the birds arrive; clutches are complete by mid-April. May occasionally overwinter in mild seasons.

Arenaria interpres (Linnaeus) RUDDY TURNSTONE
Migrant. Rare. Sometimes encountered on sandbars and mud flats about larger bodies of water. Most common in late May and from August to October.

Calidris alpina (Linnaeus) DUNLIN
Migrant. Rare. Frequents mud flats and essentially bare fields. Usually encountered in May or from early September to mid-December.

Calidris himantopus (Bonaparte) STILT SANDPIPER
Migrant. Rare to uncommon in fall; very rare in spring. Frequents mud flats and rocky or sandy shores. Expected from mid-March to mid-May and from mid-July to mid-October.

Calidris pusilla (Linnaeus) SEMIPALMATED SANDPIPER
Migrant. Rare in spring, uncommon in fall. Frequents rocky or sandy shores. May be expected in May and from late July to late October.

Calidris mauri (Cabanis) WESTERN SANDPIPER
Migrant. Rare. Sometimes encountered on mud flats or sandbars about larger bodies of water. Most often seen in March or April, or from mid-August through September.

Calidris minutilla (Vieillot) LEAST SANDPIPER
Migrant. Rare in spring, more numerous in fall about grassy or muddy shores.

May be expected from mid-April to late May and from late July to late October; a few may linger on as late as December.

Calidris fuscicollis (Vieillot) WHITE-RUMPED SANDPIPER
Migrant. Rare. Frequents mud flats, sandbars, and rocky areas about larger bodies of water. Usually encountered from late March to mid-June and from late August to mid-October.

Calidris melanotos (Vieillot) PECTORAL SANDPIPER
Migrant. Uncommon; frequents mud flats and grassy or rocky shores. May be expected from mid-March to late May and from mid-July to mid-December.

Philomachus pugnax (Linnaeus) RUFF
Accidental. This Old World shorebird has been recorded in Boyle County in early May.

Bartramia longicauda (Bechstein) UPLAND SANDPIPER
Migrant. Rare; frequents open grassy country, where it often perches on fence-posts. May be expected from late March to early May and from late July to mid-October.

Laridae: Gull and Tern Family

Larus pipixcan Wagler FRANKLIN'S GULL
Vagrant. Rare; present about larger bodies of water. Usually seen between late October and mid-May.

Larus philadelphia Ord BONAPARTE'S GULL
Vagrant. Rare. Frequents larger bodies of water. Although it may appear as early as October, it seems of more likely occurrence in March or April. It may be seen in most years around the Lexington reservoirs.

Larus delawarensis (Ord) RING-BILLED GULL
Vagrant. Uncommon, though this is the gull most frequently seen in the Inner Bluegrass. Frequents fields or parking lots. May be expected at any time from September to May.

Larus argentatus Pontoppidan HERRING GULL
Vagrant. Uncommon. Frequents larger bodies of water. Usually seen between early October and late April.

Larus hyperboreus Gunnerus GLAUCOUS GULL
Vagrant. Rare. Occasionally seen about large bodies of water from November to March.

Sterna hirundo Linnaeus COMMON TERN
Vagrant. Rare. Most often seen about larger streams and reservoirs between early July and late October or from mid-April to mid-May.

Sterna forsteri Nuttall FORSTER'S TERN
Vagrant. Rare. Occurs about larger bodies of water. Sometimes seen between late July and October but most commonly from late April to early May.

Sterna antillarum (Lesson) LEAST TERN
Vagrant. Rare. Seen about larger streams and reservoirs. Most likely occurrences are in April or May or from late July to early October.

Chlidonias niger (Linnaeus) BLACK TERN
Migrant. Rare in spring, uncommon in fall. Favors larger bodies of shallow water and marshes, but often feeds over open fields. May be expected from early May to early June and from late July to mid-October.

Cathartidae: American Vulture Family

Cathartes aura (Linnaeus) TURKEY VULTURE
Resident. Uncommon in summer, rare in winter. Roosts on cliffs or in larger trees in secluded areas. Often associates with herons in their rookeries. No nests are constructed, and the eggs are laid in a sheltered place, such as a hollow log, rock pile, abandoned building, or a cavity in a cliff face. Clutches completed between late March and mid-May.

Coragyps atratus (Bechstein) BLACK VULTURE
Resident. Rare except along the Kentucky River bluffs. Roosts on rocky ledges, cliffs, and large secluded trees. Often congregates about heron rookeries. No nest is constructed, and the eggs are laid in a hollow log, a cavity in a cliff face, or some similar secluded spot. Clutches are completed between late February and mid-May.

Accipitridae: Kite, Hawk, Eagle, and Harrier Family

Haliaeetus leucocephalus (Linnaeus) BALD EAGLE
Vagrant. Rare. Frequents larger streams and impoundments. May be seen at any time, but more likely between mid-October and early May.

Circus cyaneus (Linnaeus) NORTHERN HARRIER
Winter resident. Uncommon. Usually seen flying low across open fields or marshes. Arrives in late August or early September, is usually gone by mid-April.

Accipiter striatus Vieillot SHARP-SHINNED HAWK
Resident. Rare. Frequents woods and woodland edges. Nests 10 to 60 feet up in a crotch or against the trunk of a forest tree, usually a conifer. Clutches are completed in April or May.

Accipiter cooperii (Bonaparte) COOPER'S HAWK
Resident. Uncommon. Frequents woods and woodland edges. One of the species usually winters in the Lexington Cemetery. Nests up to 60 feet high on a limb or in the crotch of a forest tree. Clutches are completed from mid-April to June.

Accipiter gentilis (Linnaeus) NORTHERN GOSHAWK
Accidental. This northern species occurs only occasionally in Kentucky. One of the species took a bird from a feeding station in Lexington on 29 December 1979 and devoured it while perched on a nearby post. (The description of the hawk left no doubt as to its identity.)

Buteo lineatus (Gmelin) RED-SHOULDERED HAWK
Resident. Rare. Frequents woodlands in the larger stream valleys. Nests about 50 feet high in a large tree in open woods. Clutches are completed from late February to early April.

Buteo platypterus (Vieillot) BROAD-WINGED HAWK
Summer resident. Rare. Favors rough country with extensive oak-hickory or pine-oak-hickory associations. Arrives in March or early April, departs by early October. Nests in woodlands, 15–70 feet up, in a main crotch or against the trunk of a tree, from late April to mid-July.

Buteo jamaicensis (Gmelin) RED-TAILED HAWK
Resident. Rare in summer, common in migration, and fairly common in winter. Frequents woodlands and park-like areas, where it often perches in isolated trees. Nests usually up to 75 feet high in a woodland tree. Clutches completed March to June.

Buteo lagopus (Pontoppidan) ROUGH-LEGGED HAWK
Winter resident. A locally common winter resident. Frequents relatively flat, open farm country; most often seen perched at the top of some large tree. Arrives about mid-October, departs usually by March but may linger on to early May.

Pandion haliaetus (Linnaeus) OSPREY
Migrant. Uncommon. Occurs about larger bodies of water from late March to mid-May and from late August to mid-October.

Falconidae: Falcon Family

Falco sparverius Linnaeus AMERICAN KESTREL
Resident. Common in summer, more abundant in winter. Frequents open agricultural land; usually avoids dense woods. Nests in a cavity, such as a woodpecker hole, a cranny in a building, or a nest box. Clutches completed from about mid-March to late April.

Falco columbarius Linnaeus MERLIN
Migrant. Rare, favoring open country. May be expected from late March to early May and less commonly from late September to mid-December.

Falco peregrinus Tunstall PEREGRINE FALCON
Accidental. Extremely rare or perhaps absent. Bob Morris, an avid bird-watcher, saw an individual perched on a power pole in east Lexington about 1970.

Phasianidae: Grouse, Ptarmigan, Quail, and Pheasant Family

Bonasa unbellus (Linnaeus) RUFFED GROUSE
Accidental. Rare. This woodland species may sometimes be encountered along the Kentucky River cliffs of the Inner Bluegrass area.

Colinus virginianus (Linnaeus) NORTHERN BOBWHITE
Resident. Uncommon, increasingly so the last few years. Frequents various habitats, from open woods and woodland edges to cultivated fields and fencerows; prefers brushy edges. Nests on the ground in grassy cover. Clutches are completed from about early May to mid-August.

Phasianus colchicus Linnaeus RING-NECKED PHEASANT
Resident. This introduced species is a rare resident, inhabiting farm land, fencerows, and open brushland. Escapees sometimes survive for some time, and the species may be encountered any place.

Columbidae: Pigeon and Dove Family

Columba livia Gmelin ROCK DOVE
Resident. This introduced species is firmly established in cities and towns and often about farmsteads.

Zenaidura macroura (Linnaeus) MOURNING DOVE
Resident. Abundant; least numerous in winter. Frequents farmlands, feeding in fields, drinking at ponds, and resting on trees and wires. Nests some 5 to 25 feet above ground, usually on a horizontal limb, often in a conifer; the nest is typically little more than a platform of sticks with a shallow depression. Clutch completion occurs as early as mid-February to as late as late September.

Cuculidae: Cuckoo and Ani Family

Crotophaga sulcirostris Swainson GROOVE-BILLED ANI
Accidental. One individual was seen in Lexington between Bob-O-Link Drive and Lafayette High School in 1982.

Coccyzus americanus (Linnaeus) YELLOW-BILLED CUCKOO
Summer resident. Common. Favors forest edges and open woodlands. Arrives usually in early May, departs by mid-October. Nests are rather low, in a thicket or tangle of vines. Nesting occurs from mid-May to early September, with a peak in early June.

Coccyzus erythropthalmus (Wilson) BLACK-BILLED CUCKOO
Summer resident. Rare, but more common in migration. Frequents woodlands. Arrives in mid-April, usually gone by mid-October. Nests a few feet off the ground in dense brush; most clutches are complete by May.

Tytonidae: Barn Owl Family

Tyto alba (Scopoli) COMMON BARN OWL
Resident. Uncommon. Frequents open country, spending the day in barns, old buildings, and sometimes hollow trees. Nests in almost any dark, secluded spot, most often in a haymow or deserted building. Clutches probably completed in April and May.

Strigidae: Typical Owl Family

Asio flammeus (Pontoppidan) SHORT-EARED OWL
Winter resident. Uncommon. Flies by day in open grasslands but is generally seen sitting on a fencepost or in a tree. About 25 individuals spent the winter of 1979–80 near the intersection of Huffman Mill and Lemon's Mill roads in Fayette County.

Bubo virginianus (Gmelin) GREAT HORNED OWL
Resident. Rare. Favors mature woodlands, but sometimes occurs in second-growth woodlots. There are at least two pairs residing within the Urban Service Area of Fayette County at this writing. Nest usually in a crotch or hollow in some large forest tree, often using the old nest of a hawk or crow as a foundation. Most clutches are complete by late February.

Strix varia Barton BARRED OWL
Resident. Rare. Favors woodlands in stream valleys and swamps. Nests usually in the hollow of a large forest tree but sometimes in the deserted nest of a squirrel, hawk, or crow. Clutches are completed from late February through March.

Nyctea scandiaca (Linnaeus) SNOWY OWL
Vagrant. Rare. Partial to open country. May appear from late October to mid-March.

Otus asio (Linnaeus) EASTERN SCREECH OWL
Resident. Common. Favors woodland edges in farmland but sometimes occurs in cities or in dense woodlands. Nests in a natural cavity in a hollow tree, a woodpecker hole, or a nest box. Most clutches are complete by late March or early April.

Caprimulgidae: Nightjar Family

Caprimulgus carolinensis Gmelin CHUCK-WILL'S-WIDOW
Summer resident. Rare. Inhabits relatively dry areas, such as farm woodlots, oak-hickory groves, and the margins of old fields. Arrives about mid-April, departs probably in late August or September. Eggs are laid directly on the forest floor, usually in May.

Caprimulgus vociferus Wilson WHIP-POOR-WILL
Summer resident. Rare. Favors moist woodlands. Arrives late March to mid-

April, departs in late September or October. Eggs are laid directly on the forest floor, from late April to mid-June.

Chordeiles minor (Forster) COMMON NIGHTHAWK
Summer resident. Common. Frequents open country and towns. Arrives from mid-April to mid-May; becomes rare by early October and is gone by November. Eggs are laid directly on a gravel rooftop or on the ground, usually in May but sometimes as late as mid-July.

Apodidae: Swift Family

Chaetura pelagica (Linnaeus) CHIMNEY SWIFT
Summer resident. Abundant. Frequents cleared and settled places. Sometimes arrives in late March but usually in early April. Departs usually by late October. Nest a bracket of twigs cemented with saliva, normally in chimneys but sometimes in hollow trees and rarely on a sheltered internal wall of an open, little-used building. Nesting occurs between early June and mid-July.

Trochilidae: Hummingbird Family

Archilochus colubris (Linnaeus) RUBY-THROATED HUMMINGBIRD
Summer resident. Common. Frequents many habitats—woodlands, farmlands, gardens. Usually appears about mid-May and departs beginning in September; most are gone by October. Nest a tiny cup of bud scales, plant down, spider silk, and lichens atop a horizontal branch. Nesting occurs from eary April to mid-July.

Alcedinidae: Kingfisher Family

Ceryle alcyon (Linnaeus) BELTED KINGFISHER
Resident. Uncommon in summer, rare in winter. Frequents streams, ponds, and reservoirs; often seen perched on a limb overhanging the water. Nest is at the end of a horizontal hole dug 2 to 3 feet deep in a stream bank, river bluff, or road cut. Clutches are completed from early April to late May.

Picidae: Woodpecker Family

Melanerpes erythrocephalus (Linnaeus) RED-HEADED WOODPECKER
Resident. Rare. Favors open country, forest edges, and park-like environments. Nests in holes dug from 10 to 60 feet up, usually in dead trees. Clutches are completed from the start of May to as late as mid-August. Formerly abundant (until about the 1930s), nesting in holes dug in telephone and power line poles along highways, with no competition from starlings. Now the poles are treated and no longer suitable for nesting, and the ubiquitous starling competes aggressively for cavities dug by the woodpecker. The future of the red-headed woodpecker in the Inner Bluegrass is grim.

Melanerpes carolinus (Linnaeus) RED-BELLIED WOODPECKER
Resident. Uncommon. Frequents a variety of habitats, from farmland with scattered trees to dense forests. Nests in holes dug in trees, from 15 to 90 feet up. Clutches are completed from about mid-April to mid-May.

Colaptes auratus (Linnaeus) NORTHERN FLICKER
Resident. Common. Occupies a variety of habitats, from cities and towns to farms, woodland edges, and open woods. Digs a nest cavity in a fencepost or forest tree, from 4 to 60 feet above the ground. Clutches are completed from mid-April to mid-June.

Sphyrapicus varius (Linnaeus) YELLOW-BELLIED SAPSUCKER
Winter resident. Common in orchards and fairly open deciduous woodlands, especially in spring and fall. Less common in winter. Some arrive in late Sep-

tember, but the fall population peaks in October, then drops to the winter level. In late March or early April an influx of north-bound migrants swells the population. Most are gone by mid-April, but a few stragglers may linger on into early May.

Picoides pubescens (Linnaeus) DOWNY WOODPECKER
Resident. Common. Occurs wherever trees are present, from dense woodlands to parklike pastures. Nest cavity dug in a dead tree at heights of 10–40 feet. Clutches are completed from late April to late May.

Picoides villosus (Linnaeus) HAIRY WOODPECKER
Resident. Uncommon. Favors extensive woodlands but is sometimes found in woodlots and along forested streams. Nests are usually dug in a dead snag, 15 to 20 feet up. Clutches are completed in April and May.

Dryocopus pileatus (Linnaeus) PILEATED WOODPECKER
Resident. Rare; favors dense forests. Nests in cavities dug in large trees, at heights of 20 to 70 feet; the opening is usually elliptical and vertically oriented. Clutches are completed from early April to mid-May.

Tyrannidae: Tyrant Flycatcher Family

Tyrannus tyrannus (Linnaeus) EASTERN KINGBIRD
Summer resident. Common. Favors open country with widely spaced trees. Usually arrives about 20 April, becomes rare by early September, and is gone by October. Nests located near the tip of a horizontal branch up to 75 feet high, averaging about 30 feet. Breeding season is from early May to late July.

Tyrannus verticalis Say WESTERN KINGBIRD
Vagrant. Rare; autumn. Prefers open country. May occur from mid-September to mid-October.

Tyrannus forficatas (Gmelin) SCISSOR-TAILED FLYCATCHER
Accidental. Inhabits fencerows and semi-open countryside. There are but two records, in May 1966 and August 1924.

Myiarchus crinitus (Linnaeus) GREAT CRESTED FLYCATCHER
Summer resident. Common. Frequents open sunny woods. Arrives from late March to late April; most are gone by mid-September. Nests in a cavity in a tree or post, 4–15 feet up; often hangs a cast snake skin from the opening. Clutches are completed from early May to late June.

Contopus borealis (Swanson) OLIVE-SIDED FLYCATCHER
Migrant. Rare. Favors woodland edges and open areas with large trees. May be expected from late April to early June and from mid-August to mid-October.

Contopus virens (Linnaeus) EASTERN WOOD PEEWEE
Summer resident. Common. Inhabits forests and forest edges but seems to prefer drier woods. Arrives in late April and early May, departs from late September to mid-October. Nests from 15 to 50 feet up, on a horizontal limb or fork, in June and July.

Sayornis phoebe (Latham) EASTERN PHOEBE
Summer resident. Common. Frequents many habitats. Arrives generally in March, departs from late October to late November. Nests are usually located under a bridge, culvert, porch, or other manmade site, but often on a sheltered cliff face. Clutch completion ranges from late March to early July. A few individuals overwinter in mild seasons.

Empidonax minimus (Baird and Baird) LEAST FLYCATCHER
Migrant. Uncommon. Inhabits rather open country with large trees. May be expected from early April to early June and from late August to mid-October.

Empidonax virescens (Vieillot) ACADIAN FLYCATCHER
Summer resident. Uncommon. Favors woodlands, especially near water. Arrives from mid-April to early May; departs from mid-September to mid-October. Nest suspended in a horizontal fork near the tip of a branch at heights of up to 30 feet. Clutches completed from early May to late July, peaking in early July.

Empidonax flaviventris (Baird and Baird) YELLOW-BELLIED FLYCATCHER
Migrant. Rare in spring, uncommon in fall. Frequents a variety of habitats, from deep woods to thickets. Most spring records are in May. In fall, most likely to be seen from late August to early October.

Alaudidae: Lark Family

Eremophila alpestris (Linnaeus) HORNED LARK
Resident. Uncommon. Inhabits extensive barren and close-cropped fields and requires bare soil. In winter, flocks of 25–30 and sometimes more are occasionally encountered. Nests on the ground near the shelter of a tuft of grass or weeds. Clutches are completed from late February to mid-June.

Hirundinidae: Swallow Family

Tachycineta bicolor (Vieillot) TREE SWALLOW
Migrant. Uncommon. Favors open water, sometimes in large flocks, especially in fall. Appearance is erratic; may appear in mid-March, but sometimes not until mid-April. Most abundant in late April and rare by late May. In fall, may be expected from late July to late October.

Progne subis (Linnaeus) PURPLE MARTIN
Summer resident. Uncommon. Frequents open areas in towns and about rural residences. Arrives sometimes as early as mid-March but usually in late March or early April; begins departure by mid-August and is gone by mid-September. Formerly nested in cavities; now nests only in artificial shelters ("martin houses"). Clutches completed between late April and early June.

Riparia riparia (Linnaeus) BANK SWALLOW
Migrant. Rare. Favors streams, quiet waters, and open fields. Usually appears first in mid- to late April, with a peak in early May; essentially gone by late May. Fall migrants appear in mid-August, and most are gone by late September.

Stelgidopteryx serripennis (Audubon) NORTHERN ROUGH-WINGED SWALLOW
Summer resident. Common in open areas where there are bare vertical exposures—road cuts, cliffs, bridge abutments, or earthern banks. Arrives from late March to mid-April; departs from late August through mid-September or sometimes into early October. Nests in a cavity in a cliff or road cut, a weep hole in an abutment or wall, or a hole excavated in an earthen bank. Clutches are completed in May and early June.

Hirundo pyrrhonota Vieillot CLIFF SWALLOW
Migrant. Until 1886 a fairly common summer resident; presently an uncommon migrant. Frequents larger streams and impoundments; formerly nested about buildings on farmsteads. May be expected from late March to late May, and from late July or early August to mid-September.

Hirundo rustica Linnaeus BARN SWALLOW
Summer resident. Common in open farmlands; especially numerous about ponds

and reservoirs. Arrives usually in early or mid-April, departs in September. One individual lingered about the lagoons of the Lexington sewage disposal plant and survived at least to mid-January. Nests communally or sometimes singly, in barns and outbuildings or under bridges. Clutches are completed from early May to mid-July or sometimes into August. Two and sometimes three broods are reared, often in the same nest.

Corvidae: Crow and Jay Family

Cyanocitta cristata (Linnaeus) BLUE JAY
Resident. Common. Occurs in a variety of habitats, from deep woods to parklike areas. Often occurs about farmsteads and in towns. Nests from 6 to 45 feet up in a tree. Clutches are completed from late March to late June.

Corvus brachyrhynchos Brehm AMERICAN CROW
Resident. Common in summer, abundant in winter. Favors regions with a mixture of woodland and farmland. Nests 15–60 feet up in the crotch of a tree, either within the woods or at a woodland edge. Clutches are completed from late March to mid-May. Presently much less abundant than in the early 1960s, but the population seems to be steadily increasing.

Paridae: Titmouse and Chickadee Family

Parus bicolor Linnaeus TUFTED TITMOUSE
Resident. Common. Frequents woodlands of many kinds; often occurs in well-wooded areas in towns, cities, and suburbs. Nests in a cavity 8–35 feet up in a tree; readily accepts bird boxes. Clutches are completed from early April to early June.

Parus carolinensis Audubon CAROLINA CHICKADEE
Resident. Common. Favors forests and forest edges but occurs also in suburban and city areas where trees and shrubs abound. Nests in a cavity, such as a hole in a fencepost, tree, or bird box, from 2 to 12 feet above the ground. Clutches are completed from early April to late May.

Certhiidae: Creeper Family

Certhia americana Bonaparte BROWN CREEPER
Winter resident. Uncommon to common. Usually seen climbing spirally about tree trunks and larger branches in mature forests, especially in sheltered valleys. Most often arrives in early October and departs in late April or early May.

Sittidae: Nuthatch Family

Sitta carolinensis Latham WHITE-BREASTED NUTHATCH
Resident. Uncommon, and the population has been decreasing for the last several years. Occurs in a variety of forests. Nests in a cavity in a tree at almost any height. Clutches are probably completed from March to April.

Sitta canadensis Linnaeus RED-BREASTED NUTHATCH
Winter resident. Rare. Most often encountered in dry upland forests. Sometimes appears by late August but in most years is not seen before late September. Usually is gone by mid-May.

Troglodytidae: Wren Family

Troglodytes aedon Vieillot HOUSE WREN
Summer resident. Generally uncommon but common in some sections of Lexington. Favors suburban areas and farmsteads. Arrives sometimes by early March but usually in early April; departs from September to mid-October. Nests in a

cavity, often a bird box. Clutches completed from early April to mid-July, with a peak about mid-May and another in late June.

Troglodytes troglodytes (Linnaeus) WINTER WREN
Winter resident. Uncommon. Favors thick tangles of Japanese honeysuckle, underbrush in bottomland forests, and piles of rotting brush or logs. Normally arrives by early October and is usually gone by late March or early April.

Thryothorus ludovicianus (Latham) CAROLINA WREN
Resident. Rare. Formerly more common, but the particularly severe winters of 1976 and '77 decimated the population. The population is now increasing, however. Occurs in a wide variety of habitats, from deep forests to farmsteads and suburbs. Nests in a great variety of artificial sites—shelves, door jambs, sills, and other flat projections in sheds, barns, and various other little-used outbuildings—but also nests in natural cavities, such as stumps or posts. Clutches are completed from late March to mid-July.

Thryomanes bewickii (Audubon) BEWICK'S WREN
Summer resident. Rare; formerly common in clearings, farmlands, small towns, and suburbs. Usually appears in mid-March, departs by late October. Nests in a variety of cavities—nest boxes, old hats, tires, shelves, mailboxes, tin cans, and farm machinery. Clutch completion from late March to late June. Occasionally (perhaps often) overwinters in mild seasons.

Cistothorus palustris (Wilson) MARSH WREN
Migrant. Rare. Favors cattail marshes but also occurs in wet places in densely grown fields or thickets. May be expected from late March or early April to mid-May and from mid-September to mid-November.

Cistothorus platensis (Latham) SEDGE WREN
Summer resident. Rare, favoring marshes and wet grassy places. Usually appears in late April or early May and is normally gone by late October. May overwinter in some years.

Muscicapidae: Kinglet, Gnatcatcher, and Thrush Family

Regulus satrapa Lichtenstein GOLDEN-CROWNED KINGLET
Winter resident. Common in woodlands, particulary those with conifers. Sometimes arrives as early as late August, but the main influx usually occurs in late October or early November. Most are gone by mid-April.

Regulus calendula (Linnaeus) RUBY-CROWNED KINGLET
Migrant. Common. Favors forested areas but is commonly encountered in trees or shrubs in gardens or similar open areas. May be expected from late March to mid-May and from early September (rarely) to early November. Occasionally overwinters in mild seasons.

Polioptila caerulea (Linnaeus) BLUE-GRAY GNATCATCHER
Summer resident. Common. Favors open woods and woodland edges. Arrives in late March or early April; usually departs in September, but a few may linger as late as November. Nest is 9 to 40 feet above ground, in a crotch or fork of a small tree in open woods. Clutches are completed from mid-April to late June.

Sialia sialis (Linnaeus) EASTERN BLUEBIRD
Resident. Uncommon in summer, a little more so in winter. Favors open country but occurs in clearings in extensively wooded areas. Nests in open areas in cavities, from 4 to 11 feet up, in a post or tree; readily accepts nest boxes. Clutches are completed from late March to early July.

Hylocichla mustelina (Gmelin) WOOD THRUSH
Summer resident. Common. Favors woodlands. Arrives in late April; most are gone by late October. Nests low (3–30 feet) above the ground in a vine, shrub, or small tree in woods or woodland edges. Clutches are completed from early May to late July.

Catharus fuscescens (Stephens) VEERY
Migrant. Uncommon. Favors woodland or brushland edges. May be expected from mid-April to late May and from early September to mid-October.

Catharus ustulata (Nuttall) SWAINSON'S THRUSH
Migrant. Common. Favors woodlands but is often encountered in wooded lawns and gardens. May be expected from early April to early June and from late August to mid-October.

Catharus minimas (Lafresnaye) GRAY-CHEEKED THRUSH
Migrant. Uncommon. Favors brushy cover on wooded hillsides. May be expected from mid-April to early June and from early September to late October.

Catharus guttatus (Pallas) HERMIT THRUSH
Migrant. Common. Favors wooded hillsides and ravines. May be expected from late March or early April to mid-May and from early September to mid-November. Occasionally overwinters in mild seasons.

Turdus migratorius (Linnaeus) AMERICAN ROBIN
Resident. Abundant in summer, uncommon in winter, but may be locally abundant. Prefers open settled country with scattered trees and shrubs. Nests usually built in a crotch or on a horizontal limb of a tree, up to 50 feet off the ground; it may, however, be built in some artificial site, as on a shelf, porch, or windowsill. Clutches are completed from early March to late July.

Laniidae: Shrike Family

Lanius ludovicianus Linnaeus LOGGERHEAD SHRIKE
Resident. Rare. Favors broad expanses of open country interspersed with hedgerows and scattered trees. The bulky nest is 5–12 feet up in a low, dense shrub or tree located in a fencerow or other relatively open place. Clutches are completed from early April to mid-June.

Mimidae: Mimic Thrush Family

Dumatella carolinensis Linnaeus GRAY CATBIRD
Summer resident. Common. Prefers dense shrubbery of medium height, wherever it may occur. Usually appears first in mid-April and becomes common by May. Departure begins in early October, and most are gone by late October. Nests low (2–15 feet) in a shrub or shrubby section of a vine or a small tree. Clutches are completed from early May to late June. Occasionally overwinters in mild seasons.

Mimus polyglottos (Linnaeus) NORTHERN MOCKINGBIRD
Resident. Common in summer, somewhat less common in winter. Favors open places with some trees and dense shrubbery. Avoids woods and seems completely absent from extensive forests. Nests low, 1–15 feet up in a shrub, vine, or small tree, in a rather open site, such as a suburban garden. Clutches are completed from early April to late July.

Toxostoma rufum (Linnaeus) BROWN THRASHER
Summer resident. Common. Prefers brushy areas, such as fencerows, forest edges, overgrown fields, and thick residential plantings. Some usually arrive by early March, most by late March. Departure begins in late September, and nearly

all are gone by November. Nest is low (1½–10 feet), in a shrub, small tree, or vine. Clutches are completed from late March to early June. Occasionally overwinters in mild seasons.

Motacillidae: Pipit Family

Anthus spinoletta (Linnaeus) WATER PIPIT
Migrant. Rare. Found on the ground in open places, such as mud flats, fallow fields, thin pastures, and airfields. Irregular in migration, both in numbers and dates. May appear as early as late February or as late as mid-May. Fall dates range from late August to late November. May occasionally overwinter in mild seasons.

Bombycillidae: Waxwing Family

Bombycilla cedrorum Vieillot CEDAR WAXWING
Resident. Common to rare; this species is quite irregular in its movements and numbers, and on occasion probably is completely absent from this region. It occurs in all seasons but is most numerous in spring and fall, least numerous in winter. Favors relatively open country with scattered trees and shrubs but sometimes is found in open woods. Nests on a horizontal branch, from 8 to 50 feet up in a tree. Clutches are completed from early June to late August.

Sturnidae: Starling Family

Sturnus vulgaris Linnaeus EUROPEAN STARLING
Resident. Abundant. Favors extensively cleared and cultivated land, from cities to farms. Nests 10–40 feet above ground in a variety of cavities, both natural and artificial. They have begun to nest recently in cavities in high, rocky road cuts. Clutches are completed from late March to late May. This introduced species was first recorded in Kentucky in 1919 and by 1932 had become common; it is now a serious pest.

Vireonidae: Vireo Family

Vireo griseus (Boddaert) WHITE-EYED VIREO
Summer resident. Common. Frequents shrubby areas in forests, forest edges, and along streams. Arrives in early or mid-April; is usually gone by mid-October. Nest is usually concealed in a dense shrub at a forest edge. Clutches are completed from mid-May to mid-July.

Vireo flavifrons Vieillot YELLOW-THROATED VIREO
Summer resident. Rare. Favors mature woodlands. Arrives about mid-April, begins to depart in September, and is usually gone by mid-October. Nest is 10-40 feet high in the fork of a small branch, near the trunk of a tree. Clutches are completed from early May to mid-June.

Vireo solitarius (Wilson) SOLITARY VIREO
Migrant. Rare. Frequents dry open woods and woodland edges. May be expected from early April to early June and from early September to early November.

Vireo olivaceus (Linnaeus) RED-EYED VIREO
Summer resident. Common in forested areas; probably our most abundant woodland bird. Arrives in mid-April, departs in September and early October. Nest is usually suspended near the tip of a small branch 5–40 feet above the ground, most often in a woodland edge but sometimes deep in the woods or around residences with many trees. Clutches completed from early May to late June.

Vireo gilvus (Vieillot) WARBLING VIREO
Summer resident. Uncommon. Favors tall, well-spaced trees with little understory, as in pastures and gardens. Usually arrives from mid-April to early May.

Departure begins in late August; most are gone by mid-September, but some linger into October. Nests 10–35 feet up, suspended near the tip of a twig in a solitary tree. Clutches are completed from early May to about mid-June.

Vireo philadelphicus (Cassin) PHILADELPHIA VIREO
Migrant. Uncommon. Frequents brushy hillsides and second-growth woodland. May be expected from mid-April to late May and from late August to early October.

Emberizidae, I: Warbler Family

Protonotaria citrea (Boddaert) PROTHONOTARY WARBLER
Summer resident. Rare. Favors woodlands along streams or other wet areas. Usually arrives in mid- to late April and departs beginning in late August or early September; most have left by October. Nests in a cavity, usually a woodpecker hole or crevice in a stump or snag, 3–18 feet up, and often over water; occasionally uses an artificial cavity, such as a bird box. Clutches are completed from early May to early July.

Vermivora pinus (Linnaeus) BLUE-WINGED WARBLER
Summer resident. Uncommon. Favors dry weedy or brush hillsides. Arrives in April; departs in September and October. Nests on the ground in dense vegetation; most clutches are completed in May.

Vermivora chrysoptera (Linnaeus) GOLDEN-WINGED WARBLER
Migrant. Rare. Favors brushy or weedy clearings in deciduous forests. May be expected from mid-April to late May and from late August to early October.

Vermivora peregrina (Wilson) TENNESSEE WARBLER
Migrant. Common. In spring, favors tops of forest trees; in fall, often feeds low in brushy areas. May be expected from early or mid-April through May and from mid-August through October.

Vermivora celata (Say) ORANGE-CROWNED WARBLER
Migrant. Rare. Favors thickets and brushy woodlands. May be expected from early April to mid-May and from mid-September to early November. Occasionally overwinters in mild seasons.

Vermivora ruficapilla (Wilson) NASHVILLE WARBLER
Migrant. Common. Favors thickets up to 15 feet high. During migration often feeds high in forest trees. May be expected from mid-April to late May and from late August or early September to mid-October.

Parula americana (Linnaeus) NORTHERN PARULA
Summer resident. Uncommon. Favors mature woods in wet lowlands. Arrives usually in April, departs in September and October. Nests are 3–30 feet high, woven into twigs at the end of a horizontal branch of a large tree. Clutches are usually completed in May.

Myiotilta varia (Linnaeus) BLACK-AND-WHITE WARBLER
Summer resident. Rare. Favors dense, moist woodlands. Arrives in late March to mid-April, departs from late July to mid-October. Nests on sloping ground in the forest, in a shallow cavity sheltered by overhanging vegetation. Clutches are completed from early May into early June.

Dendroica caerulescens (Gmelin) BLACK-THROATED BLUE WARBLER
Migrant. Rare. Frequents brushy borders of mixed woodlands. May be expected from mid-April to late May and from early September to late October.

Dendroica cerulea (Wilson) CERULEAN WARBLER
Summer resident. Rare. Favors forested watercourses. Usually arrives in mid-April; most are gone by early September, but some may linger into October. Nests 18–60 feet off the ground, on a thin horizontal branch of a large tree. Clutches are completed from early May to late June.

Dendroica fusca (Müller) BLACKBURNIAN WARBLER
Migrant. Uncommon in spring, common in fall; favors tops of woodland trees. May be expected from mid-April to late May and from mid-August to late October.

Dendroica pensylvanica (Linnaeus) CHESTNUT-SIDED WARBLER
Migrant. Common. Favors brushy fields or overgrown clearings in open woodlands. May be expected from mid-April to late May and from late August to mid-October.

Dendroica tigrina (Gmelin) CAPE MAY WARBLER
Migrant. Uncommon. Sometimes locally abundant for short periods. Frequents tops of large trees. May be expected from late April to late May and from mid-September to mid-October.

Dendroica magnolia (Wilson) MAGNOLIA WARBLER
Migrant. Common. Frequents many kinds of wooded habitats. May be expected from early April to mid-May and from mid-August to mid-October.

Dendroica coronata (Linnaeus) YELLOW-RUMPED WARBLER
Migrant. Common. Occurs almost anywhere, from open woods to weedy tangles. Most often present from late March to mid-May and from early September to mid-November. Occasionally overwinters in mild seasons.

Dendroica virens (Gmelin) BLACK-THROATED GREEN WARBLER
Migrant. Common. Frequents woodlands. May be expected from about mid-April to late May and from mid-August to early October. This species may be a rare summer resident and may breed in the Inner Bluegrass, but it has not been recorded.

Dendroica dominica (Linnaeus) YELLOW-THROATED WARBLER
Summer resident. Rare. Frequents upper parts of tall trees, from suburban shade trees to the giants of the forest; often associated with large sycamore trees. Arrives generally in April, departs in late September and early October. Nests high in large trees, on horizontal limbs. Nesting activity begins in April and on occasion continues into August.

Dendroica discolor (Vieillot) PRAIRIE WARBLER
Summer resident. Uncommon. Frequents shrubby cover, open woodlands, and woodland edges, where much sunlight reaches the ground. Usually arrives in the last half of April and departs by mid-October, but a few may linger even into early December. Nests in a small sapling at a height up to 3 feet, characteristically in an old overgrown field or woodland edge. Clutches are completed from early May to early July.

Dendroica castanea (Wilson) BAY-BREASTED WARBLER
Migrant. Uncommon in spring, common in fall; occurs in woodlands and woodland edges. May be expected from late April to late May and from late August to late October.

Dendroica striata (Forster) BLACKPOLL WARBLER
Migrant. Common in spring, rare in fall. Favors treetops in woodlands. May be expected from late April to late May and from late September to mid-October.

Dendroica pinus (Wilson) PINE WARBLER
Migrant. Rare. Usually found in stands of pine. May be expected from mid-March to mid-May and from late August to mid-October.

Dendroica palmarum (Gmelin) PALM WARBLER
Migrant. Uncommon to common. Favors forest clearings, lawns, and other open ground. May be expected from late March to late May and from late September to late October. May occasionally overwinter in thick tangles in mild seasons.

Dendroica petechia (Linnaeus) YELLOW WARBLER
Summer resident. Common. Frequents rather open situations, often near water, that are grown up in willows, alders, sycamores, and the like. Often found in orchards, well-planted farmsteads, and suburban gardens. Arrives usually in mid- or late April; fall migration begins in late August, and all birds are gone by mid-October. Nests 4–20 feet off the ground in the crotch of a shrub or small tree. Egg laying occurs from about the middle of May into early June.

Oporornis philadelphia (Wilson) MOURNING WARBLER
Migrant. Rare. Favors brush or high weeds, especially in lowlands. May be expected from late April to early June and from late August to late October.

Oporornis agilis (Wilson) CONNECTICUT WARBLER
Migrant. Rare in spring; even less numerous in fall. Frequents brushy or weedy open ground, sometimes brushy areas in open woods. May be expected in May and sometimes from late September to mid-October.

Oporornis formosus (Wilson) KENTUCKY WARBLER
Summer resident. Common. This is a ground-dwelling bird of moist, shady, mature woodlands where there is abundant undergrowth. Usually appears about mid-April; most are gone by late September, but a few linger even into November. Nests often on the ground, sheltered by an overhanging clump of vegetation, or a few inches off the ground, tucked among the stems of a clump of vegetation. Clutches are completed from early May to mid-June.

Wilsonia canadensis (Linnaeus) CANADA WARBLER
Migrant. Uncommon in spring, more common in fall; favors the dense understory of fairly open woods, or dense herbaceous growth along woodland edges. May be expected any time in May and from late August to early October.

Wilsonia pusilla (Wilson) WILSON'S WARBLER
Migrant. Uncommon. Frequents open woods, thickets, and overgrown fencerows. May be expected from late April to late May and from late August to late October.

Wilsonia citrina (Boddaert) HOODED WARBLER
Summer resident. Rare. Inhabits mature forests, favoring more mesic habitats while avoiding both the wetter and the drier situations. Usually arrives about mid-April; is generally gone by mid-September but may sometimes linger on into October. Nests no more than a few feet off the ground, in the fork of a bush or small tree. Clutches are completed from early May to mid-June.

Helmitheros vermivorus (Gmelin) WORM-EATING WARBLER
Summer resident. Rare. Prefers steep, heavily forested slopes. Usually arrives in April; gone by late October. Nests on the ground, in a shallow cavity sheltered by fallen leaves or overhanging vegetation, usually on the steeply sloping side of a forested ravine. Clutches are completed from early May to mid-June.

Seiurus aurocapillus (Linnaeus) OVENBIRD
Summer resident. Rare. Favors woodlands of assorted types but seems to avoid

both the wetter and the drier associations. Arrives in April and early May; begins to depart in late August or early September and is essentially gone by mid-October. The domed nest is on the ground on a steep slope, often tucked under a log. The opening faces downhill and is frequently sheltered by a clump of overhanging vegetation. Clutches are completed from mid-May to mid-June.

Seiurus motacilla (Vieillot) LOUISIANA WATERTHRUSH
Summer resident. Common. Frequents the heavily shaded margins of rocky, rushing streams in woodlands. Arrives from late March to late April; departs usually in August and early September, but individuals occasionally linger on into mid-October. The nest is on a steep bank, usually facing a small stream. Clutches are completed between late April and early June.

Seiurus noveboracensis (Gmelin) NORTHERN WATERTHRUSH
Migrant. Uncommon in spring, common in fall. Prefers moist, well-shaded habitats, such as woodland streams and flooded lowland forests. May be expected from early or mid-April to late May and from late August to mid-October.

Geothlypis trichas (Linnaeus) COMMON YELLOWTHROAT
Summer resident. Common. Frequents thickets and high weeds in marshes, forest edges, overgrown fields, and pond and stream banks. Arrives in late April or early May; begins to depart in late September and is rare by mid-October. The nest is hidden in dense vegetation, often near the edge of a thicket or weed patch. Clutches are completed in May and June.

Icteria virens (Linnaeus) YELLOW-BREASTED CHAT
Summer resident. Common. Frequents woodland edges, brushy clearings, overgrown pastures, and the like. Arrives in late April or early May and begins to depart in late September; most are gone by mid-October. Nests 2–4 feet above the ground, usually in a dense tangle of brush, but sometimes in quite open situations. Clutches are completed from late April to mid-July.

Setophaga ruticilla (Linnaeus) AMERICAN REDSTART
Summer resident. Rare. Frequents woodland edges and overgrown clearings in forests. Usually arrives from mid-April to mid-May; departs from early September to mid-October. Nests are 10–30 feet up in an upright crotch of a tree or on a horizontal limb. Clutches are completed from mid-May to early June.

Emberizidae, II: Grosbeak, Bunting, and Sparrow Family

Pheucticus ludovicianus (Linnaeus) ROSE-BREASTED GROSBEAK
Migrant. Uncommon. Frequents mature forests but in migration is sometimes found in low trees and bushes, especially in wet places. May be expected from late April to late May (has been recorded in Fayette County as late as June 11) and from early or mid-September to late October.

Cardinalis cardinalis (Linnaeus) NORTHERN CARDINAL
Resident. Abundant. Frequents weedy or brushy fields and woodland edges. Occurs commonly in shrubby plantings about residences, even in cities. Nests 2–20 feet up, usually in thick shrubbery. Clutches are completed from early April to late August.

Guiraca caerulea (Linnaeus) BLUE GROSBEAK
Summer resident. Rare. Favors tangles of weeds and shrubbery, preferably streamside. Arrives in late April. Little information is available, but a few pairs have nested every year at least since 1971 along Kearney Road in Fayette County.

Passerina cyanea (Linnaeus) INDIGO BUNTING
Summer resident. Abundant. Found nearly everywhere except in closely cropped

or cultivated fields or in deep woods. Arrives in mid- to late April; usually departs from mid-September to mid-October. Nests from a few inches to about 6 feet off the ground in a shrub or sturdy weed in an overgrown field or woodland edge. Clutches are completed from mid-May to late July. May occasionally overwinter in mild seasons.

Pipilo erythrophthalmus (Linnaeus) RUFOUS-SIDED TOWHEE
Resident. Uncommon. Frequents brushlands and second-growth woodlands. Nests on the ground or up to 15 feet up in a thick tangle of brush and vines. Early nests are characteristically on the ground, later ones successively higher. Clutches are completed from early April to early August.

Ammodramus savannarum (Gmelin) GRASSHOPPER SPARROW
Summer resident. Uncommon. A grassland species, it frequents meadows, pastures, and weedy fields. Arrives in March or early April, departs from early September to mid-November. Nests on the ground in the shelter of dense vegetation. Clutches are probably completed in May and June. Not known to nest in this area, but singing males are present all summer.

Ammodramus henslowii (Audubon) HENSLOW'S SPARROW
Summer resident. Rare, but several pairs nest in Masterson Station Park near Lexington. Frequents grasslands, apparently favoring orchard-grass meadows. Arrives in March or April, departs usually in September and October. Nests on the ground under a clump of grass. Clutches are completed from May to July.

Ammodramus leconteii (Audubon) LECONTE'S SPARROW
Migrant. Rare. Favors grasslands, particularly areas of matted grass, whence it seems reluctant to fly. May be expected from mid-March to early May and from mid-October to late December. Perhaps occasionally overwinters in mild seasons.

Pooecetes gramineus (Gmelin) VESPER SPARROW
Summer resident. Rare in summer; common in migration. Nests at least in Woodford County most years. Favors open areas with sparse ground cover. Arrives mid-March to early May; departs from early October through mid-November. Nests on the ground, under a clump of grass in areas of sparse cover. Clutches completed from May to July.

Passerculus sandwichensis (Gmelin) SAVANNAH SPARROW
Summer resident. Rare, but 25 to 30 pairs have nested in the grasslands just northeast of Lexington for the last 10 years or so. Favors open grasslands but frequents weedy fields and similar situations in migration. Arrives in March; departs from early September to November. Nests on the ground in the shelter of dense vegetation. Clutches are completed in May and June.

Melospiza melodia (Wilson) SONG SPARROW
Resident. Common. Frequents a wide variety of brushy habitats—swampy ground and stream borders, forest edges, overgrown fencerows, and shrubby lawns and gardens. Nests in dense grass or shrubby growth at the edge of an open space, either on the ground or up to about 5 feet up in low shrubbery. Clutches are completed from early April to mid-August.

Chondestes grammacus (Say) LARK SPARROW
Summer resident. Extremely rare in summer; uncommon in migration. Favors sparse grassland interspersed with areas of bare soil or rock. Usually appears in April; departs in September and October, but some may linger into December. Nests usually on the ground under a clump of vegetation. Clutches are presumably completed in May and June.

Spizella arborea (Wilson) AMERICAN TREE SPARROW
Winter resident. Common. Frequents weedy fields, fencerows, and woodland edges. Although some may arrive as early as October, they rarely become common before December. Departures may begin as early as late February or early March, and most are gone by early April.

Spizella pusilla (Wilson) FIELD SPARROW
Resident. Common; less numerous in winter. Frequents shrubby meadows and clearings; avoids dense woodlands and pure stands of grasses or other crops. Nests usually near the edge of a field supporting scattered brush and small trees. The nest is on the ground at the base of a woody plant or in thick grass, or not more than about 5 feet from the ground in a bush, vine, small tree, or robust weed. Clutches are completed from late April to early August.

Spizella passerina (Bechstein) CHIPPING SPARROW
Summer resident. Uncommon. Favors brushy areas, rocky, overgrown pastures, open woodlands, and suburban lawns and gardens. Arrives from mid-March to mid-April; departs usually from late October to early December. Nests 2–15 feet up in a shrub or small tree (evergreens are favored) situated in an overgrown field, woodland edge, overgrown fencerow, or residential lawn or garden. Clutches are completed from mid-April to late July. Sometimes overwinters in mild seasons.

Spizella pallida (Swainson) CLAY-COLORED SPARROW
Vagrant. Extremely rare inhabitant of grassy, brushy areas along streams; also favors brushy areas in open woods. Recorded only on May 7, 1978. This species may be a rare transient, but there is no solid evidence of this.

Junco hyemalis (Linnaeus) DARK-EYED JUNCO
Winter resident. Abundant in brushy fencerows and fields, dry standing corn, and brushy woodlands. Arrives from late September to late October; departs from late March to early May.

Zonotrichia querula (Nuttall) HARRIS'S SPARROW
Winter resident. Rare; absent in some winters. Frequents weed patches, thickets, and brush piles in open woods. Records are few but range from early December to mid-March; one record in early May.

Zonotrichia albicollis (Gmelin) WHITE-THROATED SPARROW
Winter resident. Commonly encountered in open woods, forest edges, and brushy or weedy fields near woodlands. Arrives in late September or October; begins to depart in late April, and most are gone by mid-May.

Zonotrichia leucophrys (Forster) WHITE-CROWNED SPARROW
Winter resident. Common inhabitant of brushy situations in fairly open country, such as thickets and rows of trees along country lanes. Often appears at bird-feeding stations. A few may arrive in late September, but most appear about mid-October; departure begins in early April, and most are gone by May.

Passerella iliaca (Merrem) FOX SPARROW
Winter resident. Uncommon. Prefers dense stands of tall weeds or shrubby growth near forest edges, often near water. Arrives from late September to late October; departs from late March to early May, but most are gone by mid-April.

Melospiza lincolnii (Audubon) LINCOLN'S SPARROW
Migrant. Uncommon. Inhabits weeds and brush, usually in old fields and woodland edges, but often in suburban gardens. May be expected from about mid-April to late May and from early September to mid-November.

Melospiza georgiana (Latham) SWAMP SPARROW
Winter resident. Uncommon winter resident but a common transient. Favors wet, overgrown fields and brushy growth along streams and drainage ditches. Sometimes found in low growth, such as blackberry vines, in upland fields. Arrives in late September or early October, and is essentially gone by mid-May.

Calcarius lapponicus (Linnaeus) LAPLAND LONGSPUR
Winter resident. Rare; absent in some winters. Favors open ground, such as around airports and in bare fields, where it often associates with prairie horned larks. May arrive by late November and becomes increasingly rare after January; there is a single record as late as May.

Plectrophenax nivalis (Linnaeus) SNOW BUNTING
Vagrant. Rare winter visitant, frequenting open fields. Absent in some, perhaps most, winters; in the winter of 1977–78, however, it was recorded both in the Lexington Cemetery and along U.S. Highway 460 in Bourbon County.

Spiza americana (Gmelin) DICKCISSEL
Summer resident. Uncommon; formerly common to abundant, but the population in this area has declined precipitously in the last 15–20 years. This is a grassland species, favoring luxuriant growths of grasses, weeds, clover, alfalfa, and the like. Arrives from mid-April to early May; departs in September or October but may occasionally linger on into December. Nests a few inches off the ground in grass, weeds, blackberry canes, and the like in open fields. Clutches are completed from mid-May to late June.

Emberizidae, III: Blackbird, Oriole, and Tanager Family

Dolichonyx oryzivorus (Linnaeus) BOBOLINK
Summer resident. Rare. Frequents open country, favoring areas with thick high grass and weeds. Arrives in April and May; departs from August to mid-October. The few nests found here were in knee-high grasses in open fields. Clutches completed from May to late June.

Sturnella magna (Linnaeus) EASTERN MEADOWLARK
Resident. Common in summer, less so in winter. Favors grasslands, whether meadows or the edges of cultivated fields. Nests on the ground, usually beneath the shelter of a clump of grass. Clutches are completed from late April to late July.

Xanthocephalus xanthocephalus Bonaparte YELLOW-HEADED BLACKBIRD
Accidental. Rare. There is a record of this species along U.S. Highway 68 between Lexington and Paris in 1976.

Agelaius phoeniceus (Linnaeus) RED-WINGED BLACKBIRD
Resident. Common in summer; rare to uncommon in winter. Favors more or less open country, usually about the margins of ponds and marshes, but also occurs in upland meadows. In fall and winter they assemble in flocks and can be expected nearly anywhere. Nests commonly in marshes, the nests located from a few inches to several feet off the ground, often in cattails. Nests are sometimes located in weeds or high grass in upland meadows. Clutches are completed from mid-April to mid-July.

Euphagus carolinus (Müller) RUSTY BLACKBIRD
Migrant. Uncommon. Frequents farmsteads and dense cover, especially near swamps and marshes. In spring may be expected from early March to early May; sometimes appears in fall by late August, but usually not before late October; remains often through November. May sometimes overwinter in mild seasons.

Euphagus cyanocephalus (Wagler) BREWER'S BLACKBIRD
Migrant. Rare. Frequents open country, especially about wet areas. Often feeds about farmsteads and roosts with other blackbirds and starlings in groves. May be expected from late March to early May, and from early September to mid-November. May occasionally overwinter in mild seasons.

Molothrus ater (Boddaert) BROWN-HEADED COWBIRD
Resident. Common. Favors open agricultural lands, shunning forested areas. No nest is built; instead, the female lays her eggs in the nest of another species of birds (25 recorded in Kentucky). Most likely hosts are the red-eyed vireo, indigo bunting, wood thrush, cardinal, rufous-sided towhee, and field sparrow.

Quiscalus quiscula (Linnaeus) COMMON GRACKLE
Resident. Common. Favors open agricultural country and suburban or city parks and gardens. Nests 6–60 feet up in a crotch or on a horizontal limb of a tree, usually a conifer. Sometimes nests in an artificial site, such as a girder under a bridge. Clutches are completed from mid-April to late May. In late fall and early winter this species congregates nightly with assorted other blackbirds and starlings, forming huge roosting flocks numbering into the thousands. During the last few years our winter population has been declining.

Icterus spurius (Linnaeus) ORCHARD ORIOLE
Summer resident. Uncommon. Favors farmyards, forest edges, shady roadsides, and groves of trees. Arrives in late April and May; departs in August and September. Nests 10–60 feet up, on a forked branch of a tree in a rather open environment; a tree about a farm home is often chosen. Clutches are completed from mid-May to mid-June.

Icterus galbula (Linnaeus) NORTHERN ORIOLE
Summer resident. Rare. Favors large trees in a rather open environment. Arrives from late April to mid-May; departs usually from late August through Sepember, with a few birds lingering into late October. The nest is a hanging basket, 25–40 feet up near the tip of a limb of a large tree located usually in a rather open area. The few records of nests in this area all cite the vicinity of the Kentucky River. Clutches are completed in May and June.

Piranga olivacea (Gmelin) SCARLET TANAGER
Summer resident. Rare in summer; uncommon in migration. Favors open woods. Arrives in mid-April and is usually gone by October, but a few may linger into November. Nests 10–50 feet up, well out on the horizontal limb of a forest tree. Clutches are completed from early May to mid-July.

Piranga rubra (Linnaeus) SUMMER TANAGER
Summer resident. Uncommon; favors moderately open woodlands of many kinds, including cemeteries and suburban parks and gardens. Arrives about mid-April; departure begins in late August or early September, and all are gone by late October. Nests 5–45 feet up near the end of a horizontal branch, often over a clearing, such as a country road or lawn. Clutches are completed from early May to late July.

Passeridae: Weaver Family

Passer domesticus (Linnaeus) HOUSE SPARROW
Resident. Abundant. Found wherever human habitations occur, as well as in open farm country, woodlots, and even open woodlands. Usually nests in a cavity, such as a hole in a building, a woodpecker hole, or a bird box, but often constructs a

bulky nest among the branches of a tree or shrub. Clutches are completed from early March to late August. This introduced species was released in Kentucky about 1865–70 and was common by about 1890.

Fringillidae: Finch Family

Loxia curvirostra Linnaeus RED CROSSBILL
Winter resident. Casual winter resident, not present in some, perhaps most, years. Frequents groves of conifers. May be expected between late October and mid-March.

Loxia leucoptera Gmelin WHITE-WINGED CROSSBILL
Winter resident. Casual resident; not present in some, perhaps most, years, but more common than the red crossbill. Frequents groves of conifers but also feeds on alder and sweet-gum fruits. May be expected from late November to late March.

Carduelis flammea (Linnaeus) COMMON REDPOLL
Winter resident. Rare; absent in some, perhaps most, years. Frequents forest openings, brush, and second-growth timber. Arrives by early December; is usually gone by early March but some have lingered on to early May.

Carduelis pinus (Wilson) PINE SISKIN
Winter resident. Irregular in abundance, from rare to common; absent in some years. Occasional flocks of 75 or more have been seen. Favors open woodlands but is most often recorded in cemeteries, parks, golf courses, and the like. May appear in early October or at any time thereafter until their departure, in late April or May.

Carduelis tristis (Linnaeus) AMERICAN GOLDFINCH
Resident. Common. Favors weedy open country with scattered brushy growth. Nests in weeds, shrubbery, or small trees, 3–25 feet above the ground. Clutch completion ranges from late July to early September.

Carpodacus purpureus (Gmelin) PURPLE FINCH
Winter resident. Common. Frequents thickly weeded fields, overgrown fencerows, cedar thickets, and dense undergrowth in open woods. In early spring often seen feeding quietly on buds in the tops of deciduous trees. Often visits bird-feeding stations, sometimes in flocks of 50 or more. Arrives in late September or early October but does not become common until November; departs usually in late April or early May.

Carpodacus mexicanus frontalis (Say) HOUSE FINCH
Vagrant. This species is abundant in northern Mexico and the western United States, and is extending its range eastward. It has been introduced along the coast in eastern United States and is now common there in many areas. This coastal population is extending its range westward and was first recorded in the Inner Bluegrass on 21 February 1977 by Robert Morris. In 1979–80 at least 16 individuals wintered in Lexington. The population in the region is growing, and it has become a common breeding bird in this area.

Coccothraustes vespertinus (Cooper) EVENING GROSBEAK
Winter resident. Uncommon; absent in some winters. An inhabitant of woodlands, this species is most often seen in small flocks at bird-feeding stations. May arrive in early November and remain until late May.

MAMMALS

Class: *Mammalia* MAMMALS

Didelphidae: Opossum Family

Didelphis virginia virginiana Kerr VIRGINIA OPOSSUM
Common. Favors woodlands and woodland edges but often occurs around homes and gardens, even in suburban areas. Occasionally encountered on a downtown city street.

Soricidae: Shrew Family

Blarina brevicauda kirtlandi Bole & Moulthrop SHORT-TAILED SHREW
Common. Favors moist woodlands but also occurs commonly in a great variety of other habitats. In short, it occurs wherever there is adequate cover and is one of the most abundant mammals in Kentucky.

Cryptotis parva parva (Say) LEAST SHREW
Common. A creature of grasslands, most abundant in fields and fencerows that have a dense stand of relatively undisturbed grasses.

Sorex longirostris Bachman SOUTHEASTERN SHREW
Rare. Favors moist woodlands and lowland weedy or brushy areas. Known only from the river bluffs in Franklin County.

Sorex fumeus Miller SMOKY SHREW
Rare. Favors moist woodlands. Known only from the river bluffs in Franklin County.

Talpidae: Mole Family

Scalopus aquaticus machrinus (Rafinesque) EASTERN MOLE
Common. Favors loose, well-drained soils wherever they occur—woodlands, pastures, gardens, lawns. May persist for years in housing tracts if the streets do not have curbs. This subspecies was described by C.S. Rafinesque in 1832 from a specimen collected near Lexington.

Vespertilionidae: Vespertilionid Bat Family

Myotis lucifugus lucifugus (Le Conte) LITTLE BROWN BAT
Uncommon. Sometimes encountered in spring and fall in or about caves or buildings, but more common in winter, when they occur sparingly in numerous caves in the Inner Bluegrass. A summer colony is rarely encountered, usually in the attic of a building but occasionally in the rafters of a barn.

Myotis grisescens (Howell) GRAY BAT
Rare. Formerly there were breeding colonies in some of the caves in the Inner Bluegrass, but at present only one remains. Now, other than that colony, only occasional individuals are sometimes encountered in fall, winter, or spring, in or about caves.

Myotis sodalis Miller & Allen INDIANA BAT
Rare. Occasionally encountered in or about caves in fall, winter, or spring. Except for an occasional male, this species apparently does not occur here in summer; most are in Ohio, Indiana, or Michigan, in breeding colonies.

Lasionycteris noctivagans (Le Conte) SILVER-HAIRED BAT
Rare. Migrates through the Inner Bluegrass in both spring and fall, but seems most abundant during the last two weeks of April. During this time, one can occasionally be found during the day hanging under the loose bark of a tree, in a crevice on a rock face, or in a building.

Pipistrellus subflavus subflavus (F. Cuvier) EASTERN PIPISTRELLE
Common. In summer favors woodland edges and wooded streams; in winter retreats into caves to hibernate. Nearly every cave in the Inner Bluegrass harbors a few individuals, almost invariably hanging singly.

Eptesicus fuscus fuscus (Palisot de Beauvois) BIG BROWN BAT
Abundant. This is by far the most common summer bat in the Inner Bluegrass, with breeding colonies in many buildings. Winters in caves, buildings, or other sheltered spots, but much less common in winter than in summer.

Lasiurus borealis borealis (Müller) RED BAT
Uncommon. This is a bat of woodland edges and clearings. It is not colonial and does not regularly enter caves. At least a part of our summer population almost surely winters here, in cavities in large trees.

Lasiurus cinereus cinereus (Palisot de Beauvois) HOARY BAT
Rare. This migratory creature of woodlands and woodland edges is present in the Inner Bluegrass only from spring to fall, and then only sparingly.

Nycticeius humeralis humeralis (Rafinesque) EVENING BAT
Rare. This southern species of colonial bat is known from the Inner Bluegrass by a single specimen found in a residence near Lexington.

Leporidae: Rabbit Family

Sylvilagus floridanus mearnsii (Allen) EASTERN COTTONTAIL
Common. Favors upland thickets and brushy farmland but occupies a variety of habitats—open grasslands, fencerows, brushy areas, suburban lawns and gardens, cemeteries, and woodlands. This is one of Kentucky's major game animals, ranking second to the gray squirrel.

Sciuridae: Squirrel Family

Tamias striatus striatus (Linnaeus) EASTERN CHIPMUNK
Common. Favors woodlands but is found, sometimes abundantly, in parks, cemeteries, suburban gardens, and the like. This is one of the best known small mammals in Kentucky. By late November most are in hibernation. Unlike most hibernators, they awaken every few days to feed on their stores of food and sometimes emerge briefly from their burrows. By mid-March most are active above ground.

Marmota monax monax (Linnaeus) WOODCHUCK, GROUNDHOG
Common. Occupies farmlands, fencerows, roadsides, and forest edges. Occurs in woodlands but is less common there than in more open areas. This is our largest squirrel, notable for its large size, robust body, and short tail. By the end of October, most have disappeared into their underground hibernation chambers, not to appear again with any regularity until March. This species ranks third in the number of game mammals harvested in Kentucky.

Sciurus carolinensis carolinensis Gmelin GRAY SQUIRREL
Common. Favors oak–hickory woodlands but is abundant in cemeteries, parks, and well-wooded areas of cities and towns. This species is active throughout the year and is strictly diurnal. It is the favorite game mammal in Kentucky.

Sciurus niger rufiventer St.-Hilaire FOX SQUIRREL
Common. Favors open country with scattered oak, hickory, and walnut trees. Strictly diurnal, this squirrel spends more time on the ground than in trees when foraging. Active throughout the year.

Glaucomys volans volans (Linnaeus) SOUTHERN FLYING SQUIRREL
Uncommon. Favors woodlands but is sometimes encountered in well-wooded parks, cemeteries, and similar situations. Strictly nocturnal, it remains active throughout the year. Often uses a deserted woodpecker hole as a nest site.

Castoridae: Beaver Family

Castor canadensis carolinensis Rhoads BEAVER
Rare. An occasional individual or pair may sometimes be encountered along a watercourse or large impoundment in this area. They were exterminated in Kentucky by about 1900 but have been restocked and are now common in some areas.

Cricetidae: New World Rat and Mouse Family

Reithrodontomys humulis humulis (Audubon & Bachman)
EASTERN HARVEST MOUSE
Commonly favors fields of dense, tall weeds, but is occasionally encountered along weedy woodland edges or roadsides. Nocturnal, these small mice are rarely seen and less frequently recognized by humans.

Peromyscus maniculatus bairdii (Hoy and Kennicott) PRAIRIE DEER MOUSE
Common. Frequents open weedfields, grasslands, and grassy fencerows. These handsome mice are nocturnal and leave little sign of their presence; they are rarely seen by humans.

Peromyscus leucopus (Rafinesque) WHITE-FOOTED MOUSE
Abundant. Favors woodlands and brushy areas wherever they may occur, including cities and towns. Cliffs and caves are also inhabited, and manmade structures are readily used; this is the common mouse of woodland cabins. They are nocturnal, and active throughout the year. Two subspecies occur in the Inner Bluegrass. The northern race, *Peromyscus leucopus novaboracensis* (Fisher), generally occupies the bluffs along the Kentucky River; the shorter-tailed southern race, *Peromyscus leucopus leucopus* (Rafinesque), occupies the uplands.

Neotoma floridana magister Baird EASTERN WOODRAT
Uncommon. Frequents rocky outcrops, cliffs with deep crevices, and woodland caves. Wherever found, they leave distinctive piles of sticks, leaves, cut pieces of green vegetation, and assorted debris in crevices and on rocky ledges. These handsome creatures are nocturnal, active throughout the year, remarkably docile, and almost as large as a gray squirrel.

Microtus pennsylvanicus pennsylvanicus (Ord) MEADOW VOLE
Common. Favors grasslands, where it shows preference for more moist areas. Occasionally encountered in woodlands or brushy areas. Active both day and night throughout the year. Quite prolific; one captive female produced 17 litters in a year, and one of her daughters produced 13 litters before she was a year old.

Microtus ochrogaster (Wagner) PRAIRIE VOLE
Abundant; the commonest vole in this area. Favors grasslands, and since it will construct underground nests, can survive in heavily grazed or closely mowed grasslands. The well-traveled runways are sometimes readily visible in sparsely vegetated areas. Two subspecies occur in the Inner Bluegrass: west of a north-south line through Lexington, a buff-bellied prairie vole *Microtus ochrogaster ochrogaster* (Wagner); east of the line, a white-bellied prairie vole (*Microtus ochrogaster ohionensis* Bole & Moulthrop. There is a rather narrow zone of intergradation between the two races along the line and for a few miles on either side of it.

Microtus pinetorum auricularis (Bailey) PINE VOLE
Abundant. Found almost everywhere there is adequate food, cover, and friable soil. Often the most abundant small mammal along fencerows and roadsides. Although active by both day and night, there is some evidence that they are more active on the surface at night and restrict their daytime travel essentially to their extensive burrow systems.

Ondatra zibethicus zibethicus (Linnaeus) MUSKRAT
Common. Frequents stream banks, impoundments, and farm ponds. Sometimes damages farm ponds by burrowing into the dam and causing leakage. The houses they build may consist of a hollow heap of vegetation piled up in shallow water, with an underwater entrance; more frequently they dig burrows in banks, starting under water and rising in the bank to an underground nest cavity above water level.

Synaptomys cooperi kentucki Barbour BLUEGRASS BOG LEMMING
Common. Favors thick stands of grasses, especially those with an occasional bush, bit of brush, log, or rock pile. Often occurs about a fallen tree in an otherwise closely grazed pasture. This subspecies was described in 1956 from specimens collected at Sadieville, in Scott County.

Muridae: Old World Rat and Mouse Family

Rattus norvegicus (Berkenhout) NORWAY RAT
Abundant. This introduced animal inhabits homesteads and other buildings, in both the city and the country. In summer some move out into open woods and fields; thus they may be encountered almost anywhere.

Mus musculus Linnaeus HOUSE MOUSE
Abundant. Another introduced species that lives with humans, sharing both shelter and food. In summer individuals are often encountered in open woods and fields, well away from buildings, where they successfully compete with our native mammals.

Zapodidae: Jumping Mouse Family

Zapus hudsonius (Zimmerman) MEADOW JUMPING MOUSE
Rare. Favors moist areas with a rank growth of high weeds and/or grasses. Probably most common in high grasses along the floodplain of the Kentucky River, but also occurs sparingly in and about boggy upland areas. Since it does not make runways, its presence in an area often goes unsuspected.

Canidae: Fox Family

Canis latrans Say COYOTE
Scarce. Favors thickets and woodlands for cover but forages widely in other habitats. May occur almost anywhere, at any time. The first coyote recorded in Kentucky was shot in January 1953 near the Fayette–Clark County line. Since that time, the species has become widespread and common in parts of western Kentucky, and there have been a number of confirmed records from central Kentucky in the last few years. It is likely that the coyote will eventually become quite common in the Inner Bluegrass.

Vulpes vulpes (Linnaeus) RED FOX
Uncommon. A creature of farmlands and other open areas. While the Inner Bluegrass seems near-ideal habitat, this magnificent creature is unfortunately declining in numbers, and the total population in this area is probably not more than a quarter of what it was 25 years ago.

Urocyon cinereoargenteus cinereoargenteus (Schreber) GRAY FOX
Common. Favors hardwood forests and does well along the river bluffs and other wooded areas in this region. Forages at night in essentially all available habitats, even around farmsteads and suburban homes.

Procyonidae: Raccoon Family

Procyon lotor lotor (Linnaeus) RACCOON
Common. Essentially every wooded stream in this area supports a quota of raccoons. They usually den in hollow trees but often den in stored hay or other shelter in barns near wooded areas; they feed about ponds and in vegetable gardens.

Mustelidae: Weasel Family

Mustela nivalis allegheniensis (Rhoads) LEAST WEASEL
Apparently fairly common. The world's smallest carnivore, this circumpolar species has been rapidly extending its range southward. Several specimens have now been collected from Lexington and vicinity.

Mustela frenata noveboracensis (Emmons) LONG-TAILED WEASEL
Rare. Favors woodland edges, brushland, overgrown fencerows, and streambanks. Usually nocturnal but sometimes hunts by day. This creature is strictly carnivorous and seems essentially fearless.

Mustela vison vison Schreber MINK
Uncommon. Frequents stream banks of whatever size, particularly in woodlands or brushy areas. Usually nocturnal, it is carnivorous and will feed on almost any vertebrate animal up to the size of a rabbit or muskrat.

Mephitis mephitis nigra (Peale and Palisot de Beauvois) STRIPED SKUNK
Common. Occurs in a variety of habitats—woodlands, brushlands, cliffs, farmlands, and farmsteads. Essentially nocturnal but sometimes encountered by day, especially during the breeding season in late winter. They seem reluctant to discharge their musk and, if given a quiet chance, will retreat with obvious dignity instead of spraying.

Felidae: Cat Family

Lynx rufus (Schreber) BOBCAT
Rare. Favors woodlands. A single individual was observed at close range in 1982 on the river bluffs near Shakertown, in Mercer County.

Cervidae: Deer Family

Odocoileus virginianis virginianis Zimmermann WHITE-TAILED DEER
Uncommon. Favors woodlands, woodland edges, and brushy areas. For probably a hundred years deer were absent from the Inner Bluegrass, having been killed out soon after the area was well settled. Within the past 30 years or so, restocking and natural reproduction have built up a small population, especially in wooded areas along streams.

Part IV
The Future of the Bluegrass

8. The Bluegrass Region of Tomorrow in Light of Present Trends

"PARADISE" it was called when explorers came upon this land. Wave after wave of pioneer settlers entered what they considered the Promised Land and described as a second Eden. Shortly after 1900 a young man returning to the Bluegrass region said in addressing a class reunion at Georgetown College, "Somewhere in this old world, God planted a garden. In the Book of Books that garden is called Eden. They say it has vanished from the earth. I make no answer save to call them here, that they may cease to search where Eden was, and find where Eden is." Westbrook Pegler a few decades ago called the Bluegrass region of Kentucky "the sweetest countryside on earth." And recently the poet Logan English wrote of it, "No land where I have traveled is more fair."[1]

Throngs are still migrating to this beautiful land, as Table 8 shows. To most of these it does not matter that the soil is extraordinarily rich, for they do not intend to farm. Developers and entrepreneurs, often from faraway places, see the economic advantage of buying farmland to be subdivided into residential lots to accommodate the influx of newcomers and to sell to industries interested in establishing manufacturing plants on the best land. Chambers of Commerce beckon to both executives and workers with the message that the Bluegrass is a pleasant place to live and work, and industries find that the charm of the region enhances personnel recruitment.

Since World War II and the advent of the interstate highways, the Inner Bluegrass region has undergone radical transformation. We confront a question: Can it retain its integrity and its personality in face of massive alteration by industrialization and urbanization? Or will it become like any other fast-growing

1. Warren B. Davis and Leigh Mitchell Hodges, *A Boy from Kentucky* (Philadelphia: n.p., 1938); Logan English, *No Land Where I Have Traveled: A Kentucky Poem* (Louisville: Kentucky Poetry Press, 1979).

Table 8. Population Growth in Selected Bluegrass Counties
(Census figures from 1950-1990)

	1950	1960	1970	1980	1990
Bourbon	17,752	18,178	18,476	19,405	19,236
Clark	18,898	21,075	24,090	28,322	29,496
Fayette	100,746	131,906	174,323	204,165	225,366
Jessamine	12,458	13,625	17,430	26,146	30,508
Scott	15,141	15,376	17,948	21,813	23,867
Woodford	11,212	11,913	14,434	17,778	19,955

locality, losing those qualities that made it so attractive initially? Will it go the way of the bison and elk, which once lived here? If the reasons for its uniqueness are understood, can measures be taken to preserve its distinctive character, individuality, and charm? Or does the following poem by Bettye Lee Mastin describe the future of the Bluegrass?

A Grandfather Speaks to a Child

This was a meadow once,
And there were trees.
I don't know how to tell you about the trees.
They were so big, not like these little ones, that spot the earth;
Your dad and I, we couldn't put our arms
Around the trunks of some that grew.
They were so tall, they stood above the pasture
So high they seemed to tower the way
The biggest bank building holds its head
Above the other buildings down along Main Street.
Oh, I forget.
Your mother never shops downtown. You wouldn't know.

But this was Bluegrass country once.
Bluegrass? That was the name
They gave this land when it was fair and lovely,
That's bluegrass there, in that small plot out front.
I grow it there to help myself remember how it was.[2]

THE REGION'S NATURAL HERITAGE

Since the arrival of the first white explorers, who were startled at what they saw, the Inner Bluegrass region has been recognized as unique. The early settlers interpreted the vast populations of large mammals grazing in gently undulating savanna-woodlands as indicating that the region would favor the best quality in domestic livestock. In this they quickly gained a national reputation for excellence. Springs determined the location of towns and farmsteads, and creeks

2. Unpublished. Used by permission.

provided a source of power for milling. Thus land features determined land use, in contrast to today's pattern in which man decides what he wants and then, with his machinery, alters the land to conform to his wishes regardless of its suitability.

Nature richly endowed Kentucky's Inner Bluegrass region. The natural features of soil, rock type, topography, geologic structure, and vegetation were responsible for its scenic beauty and the course of its cultural development. The source of the charm and elegance of the area has been the land, especially the horse farms, rather than the cities and towns. Part of the attractiveness of living in a Bluegrass town or city is that it is situated in natural parkland. The Bluegrass cultural landscape is one of the most widely known and admired landscape forms in the world.[3] The Bluegrass that we know has been a blend of natural and cultural splendor.

Since the Inner Bluegrass was the first part of the state to be settled, it has deep historic roots. In the early nineteenth century, Lexington was a nationally important center of education, often called the "Athens of the West." Many aspects of the landscape have historic value. The productivity of its rich soil provided prosperity, which permitted the building of many antebellum mansions of architectural and historic significance. Historic stone fences, mortarless and dry-laid, are a special feature of the countryside. In an earlier time there were hundreds of miles of them. Picturesque byways and a few crossroad villages are still with us.

By 1800 Kentucky horses were nationally acclaimed, and from 1840 to the present, Kentucky has led all states in the raising of Thoroughbreds. It is the one thing Kentucky does better than any other area. Although we speak of "Kentucky," horses are raised almost exclusively in the Bluegrass, but the entire Commonwealth basks in the glow. This area's rich limestone land is naturally suited for the raising of horses. It may be noted that the stud farms of England, Ireland, and France are also established in limestone areas.

Nineteenth-century Bluegrass farms were diversified, and those famous for Thoroughbreds also produced other stock and crops. In the antebellum years racing was a sideline, although indeed an important one in this area, and Bluegrass horsemen were intent upon producing a better running horse.

Although the control of racing after the Civil War was in the hands of the North, Kentucky continued its undisputed preeminence in breeding. At this time affluent horsemen from out of the state began buying Bluegrass farmland because this was the location of the best stock with which to breed their winners and because the mineral-rich soil would help to strengthen foals. Since World War II horsemen from several other nations have bought Bluegrass farms. Although Thoroughbreds lead, Standardbreds and Saddlebreds are also important in the Bluegrass picture.

The Bluegrass region is the world's most important area related to the raising of Thoroughbreds, and for many decades has been internationally recognized as "the horse capital of the world." More horse farms are concentrated here

3. "Cultural landscape" refers to how man has adapted land use to the natural attributes, how the natural landscape has been modified by human activities.

than anywhere else in the world, and Lexington is the hub of the international bloodstock business. The world's best stallions stand here; the best horses in America come from Bluegrass farms, although in their racing careers they may be owned by persons elsewhere. For instance, Bluegrass-breds won six of the seven prestigious Breeders' Cup races in 1988. Bluegrass-breds have won the Epsom Derby in England and the Prix de l'Arc de Triomphe in France. The higher quality of Kentucky-breds (essentially Bluegrass-breds) is shown in the percentage of stakes winners in North America. In the racing period 1979-1988, 29 percent of all North American stakes winners were Kentucky bred. The state next behind Kentucky was Florida, with 13.6 percent.[4]

Buyers come from all over the world to the horse sales in Lexington. In 1988 the Thoroughbred auction totals in Lexington plus a few dispersal sales amounted to $416,681,515. In the same year Kentucky sold 46.9 percent of the North American yearling crop and received 76.8 percent of gross sales dollars; of weanlings, Kentucky sold 58.7 percent of the North American total and received 93.3 percent of gross sales; of broodmares auctioned, Kentucky sold 47.4 percent, receiving 94.2 percent of gross sales. The higher prices paid for Kentucky horses reflect the buyers' belief in their higher quality.[5] Of all states, Kentucky produces the largest share of Thoroughbred foals. Over 9,000 of the 1988 foals registered by The Jockey Club are Kentucky-bred; California is second with about 6,000.[6]

The horse is no longer a hobby of gentlemen farmers but is "big business" in the Bluegrass. Besides breeding, training, and racing—with extensive payrolls involved—there are also sales companies, horse transportation companies, bloodstock research, computerized marketing service for breeding seasons and shares, equine insurance, veterinary medicine, horse publications, numerous other services, various supplies, and the Maxwell H. Gluck Equine Research facility at the University of Kentucky.

The horse industry generates much tax revenue for Kentucky, paying every tax that all other segments of agriculture pay plus the following taxes that no other segment pays and some taxes that no other state collects from the horse industry: 6 percent tax on equipment, 6 percent tax on feed, 6 percent tax on stud fees (not taxed in any other state), 6 percent sales tax on all horses sold at auction except breeding stock and except horses less than two years old bought by nonresidents and shipped out of state. (Kentucky residents pay sales tax on these; federal law prohibits sales tax on interstate commerce items.) The horse industry also contributes taxes from the tracks.[7] As a major industry and a major employer, not to mention the many "ripple industries," the horse's contribution to the economic prosperity of the area is enormous.

Tourism is the third largest generator of income in Kentucky and probably the leading one in Fayette County, considering the spin-off into jobs such as those in hotels, restaurants, and gift shops. Kentucky's Department of Tourism says that the two main attractions in the state are horses and scenery. Tourists come to

4. *Blood-Horse.*
5. Auctions Supplement to the *Blood-Horse.*
6. The Jockey Club.
7. Kentucky Thoroughbred Association.

the Bluegrass region to attend events, to visit historic sites, and to admire the area's green, well manicured pastures with their noble trees, the country lanes bordered by historic stone fences, the white-fenced paddocks, the palatial barns, and the sight of frolicking yearlings and, in spring, mares with their long-legged foals.

Tourism is a multimillion-dollar industry with little environmental degradation and relatively little economic cost to the community. For every dollar spent on tourism, it is estimated that nine dollars are collected. In 1987 tourism added approximately $4 billion to Kentucky's economy, including $56.6 million in local tax revenues and $226.6 million in tax revenues to the state government. Also in 1987, tourism supported 114,707 jobs in the state,[8] and three million tourists in Fayette County spent $317.4 million at local businesses.[9] The Kentucky Horse Park, the leading attraction, had 350,000 paid admissions in 1988. In the entire Inner Bluegrass, tourism furnishes $400 million annually in wages and taxes and employs approximately 18,000 persons, 10,000 of them in Fayette County alone.

Besides the horse industry and tourism, the region has had a diversified local economy, including general farming, education (with several independent colleges in the area and the University of Kentucky, Fayette County's largest employer), medical centers and hospitals, numerous professional enterprises, marketing, manufacturing, and others.

A HERITAGE BESIEGED

The Bluegrass region is now under attack. Modern society is oriented toward urbanization and industrialization, and contemporary life is married to the automobile, which demands an extensive roadway system to connect everyone with everything. We live in an industrial culture, and a prevalent view is that farming is not the best use of the land nor the best use of human time and energy. Cities tend to spread into areas of the best farmland, level and well drained; land good for farming is also good for development. The conversion of prime farmland to urban uses causes farming to be shifted to poorer land—land with steeper slopes that increase soil erosion, and with poorer soil quality that requires more human manipulation, resulting in increased cost of products. Natural areas too are taken, with a resulting loss of natural ecosystems and natural species diversity.

Urbanization has been on the march into the Bluegrass countryside, and the fury of its onslaught seems especially keen in view of what has been usurped. Bulldozers, uprooting trees and altering the topography and natural drainage, continue to rumble over pastures where horses and cattle formerly grazed. Early writers described Bluegrass farms as "grazing parks"; today we have "industrial parks." Congressman Larry Hopkins recently estimated that industry has increased here approximately 2,000 percent since 1960. Development pressure is tremendous. The scramble for land in the pioneer period is being repeated in a

8. State Department of Tourism, Frankfort.
9. Lexington Convention and Visitor's Bureau.

different fashion in the late twentieth century. Speculators and developers want to buy land for houses, offices, shopping malls, and factories, and can usually obtain zone changes for their projects. Strong pressure is exerted against local planning and zoning boards. All of this has resulted in phenomenally inflated land prices at a time when the agricultural economy is declining and farm labor is hard to obtain. Hence a landowner can hardly resist the pressure to sell for development.

Each major development—industrial, commercial, or residential—promotes further development. The coming of a mammoth manufacturing plant spawns subsidiary plants and supplying industries in neighboring counties. Although for many years the Bluegrass has had a low rate of unemployment, we constantly hear the outcry for more jobs. Their creation means massive inmigration resulting in more and more residential subdivisions, shopping centers, and highway enlargements. Although communities talk about development increasing the tax base, this increase is nearly offset by capital expense to provide additional storm and sanitary sewers, water mains, schools, and public services such as fire and police protection. Development demands more roads, and new roads invite further development. Roads that were constructed to alleviate traffic congestion, such as beltlines to bypass towns, also stimulate development and ultimately generate more traffic.

A strong effort is being made to attract new industry. Part of the persuasion is the strategic central location, with easy accessibility to the consumer markets of the Northeast, the Midwest, the Southeast, and the Southwest, and to the major industrial areas of the nation. Another bait is to emphasize the beauty and charm of the region. One Chamber of Commerce brochure suggested a ten-acre or twenty-acre bit of Bluegrass countryside as an ideal place for corporate headquarters. The attractiveness of living in horse country is portrayed. What is not mentioned is that a horse farm cannot continue adjacent to a residential subdivision, with its dogs that will chase foals and yearlings, and its children, who may climb fences and throw rocks at million-dollar horses.

The Kentucky Commerce Cabinet also uses "horse power" to entice new industry. Their booklet entitled "Kentucky's Fabulous Bluegrass" presents the region as an ideal place to bring industry or business, an ideal place to live and work. The secretary of the Commerce Cabinet has said in correspondence, "The region's pastoral qualities were, I understand, one of the prime factors in Toyota's decision to locate in Scott County." Another major manufacturing industry stated in its publication that the Bluegrass was the company's first choice because the area was rich in culture and natural beauty and had a reputation for excellence in what it produced.

Shopping malls, factories, and housing are continually creeping farther and farther out into the country. When new office buildings and commercial centers are built farther out, existing ones lose tenants. With more and more exurban housing being built, there is a comparable increase in houses for sale in town. The *Wall Street Journal* of April 5, 1989, caried an article entitled "Bluegrass Country Goes to Shopping Malls" and discussed the demise of much Bluegrass farmland. The Bluegrass image has thus already become tarnished nationally.

Industrialization and urbanization have polluted streams and groundwater, on which many outlying farms depend. Industrial plants may move away, but land paved over and shifted from agriculture to urban uses is irretrievably lost from the agricultural resource base. Even the country of the majestic Kentucky River Palisades—the only extensive natural area remaining in the Inner Bluegrass Section—is under assault. Speculators have started buying large tracts to subdivide for "second homes," targeting especially the Louisville-Cincinnati-Lexington triangle. If the present trend in the Bluegrass continues unabated, the inevitable consequence will be the decline of the horse industry, of tourism, and of general farming.

The family farm is in jeopardy. A farmer today can realize more money by selling his land for nonfarm uses than by continuing to farm it. Young families find it difficult to start a farming career in view of the almost prohibitive initial outlay for land and equipment. In addition, farm labor is scarce. The decline of general farming in the Inner Bluegrass means that farming in Kentucky will be on less productive land.

A decline in the horse industry would be a serious blow to the economic prosperity of the region. Even though it is well established, we cannot take for granted its continuance here. More Kentucky horse farms are for sale now than ever before. Virginia wishes to regain the front rank in horse breeding that it lost to Kentucky 150 years ago. The Virginia Horse Center aims to outdistance the Kentucky Horse Park. Horse breeding and training form a fast-growing industry in New York State. Between 1970 and 1982 it advanced from twelve breeding farms to 450.[10] Between 1976 and 1986 New York state showed a 321 percent increase in the number of foals per year; Louisiana was second, and Illinois third. Kentucky's annual foal crop increased by 107 percent in the same period.[11]

Several states, recognizing the economic benefits of horse breeding and its related businesses, have instituted incentive programs to attract the industry to their states. These programs offer awards to breeders and to owners, plus stallion awards and purses for state-bred winners of restricted races. For Thoroughbreds, New York in 1987 awarded $24,863,665, California $15,333,440, and Illinois $11,490,736, in all categories. Kentucky ranked fourteenth among the twenty-three states with some Thoroughbred incentive programs, awarding $2,401,843 only in the owner category. The only states with less in incentive awards than Kentucky are those with little breeding and little racing. Among Standardbred incentive programs, Illinois led in 1986 with $13,084,613, New Jersey was second, New York third, and Ohio fourth. Kentucky awarded $750,161, only for restricted races. The only pari-mutuel states with smaller incentive programs than Kentucky are those with little harness racing and little Standardbred breeding.[12]

We repeatedly hear, "We must protect the horse farms!" and "We must save the horse farms!" But if we promote conditions and situations unfavorable to the horse farms, if we allow housing developments and industry to advance ever

10. *New York Times*, June 2, 1982.
11. The Jockey Club.
12. American Horse Council.

closer to them, they will not be saved in Kentucky; they will leave the state. Despite ample talk about preserving the horse farms, the prevailing policies are whittling them away. Can Kentucky afford to let its horse industry decline in favor of shopping centers and urban sprawl while other states woo the horses and horsemen? How long can Kentucky withstand the competition?

Kentucky horse farms today number about 1,000, down from about 1,400 less than ten years ago. A horse farm owner whose farm has been in the family for three generations says, "In ten or fifteen years the Bluegrass will be a different kind of place." Another horse breeder says he feels that the horse industry is being undermined by urbanization. The market for horse farms here is depressed; hence many owners end by selling their land for development. A 100-acre horse farm recently sold for $2.7 million for development ($27,000 per acre). The owner sold, he said, because "Development in the area made it difficult to operate a horse farm." Developable residential land in Fayette County is selling for $27,000 to $40,000 or more per acre, whereas horse farm land sold as such usually brings only $10,000 to $20,000 per acre, depending on location and improvements. Recently a prominent Bluegrass horseman moved all his stallions to another state. He said he hated to do so because "this is the best place in the world to raise horses." But it is business, and he must consider profits.

With the present trend, how long will the Bluegrass region remain the horse capital of the world? If the horse farms leave, the region will lose its greatest asset. In addition, any decline in the Bluegrass horse industry will carry tourism down with it. With the preservation of aesthetic and historic values, tourism promotes economic security. But after bulldozers and builders have worked over the Bluegrass landscape, what tourist would come to see residential subdivisions or manufacturing plants or office buildings standing in the countryside? Tourism in the United States is predicted to increase. Will we foster its decline in Kentucky?

That the Bluegrass region of Kentucky is unraveling cannot be denied. But since its character is not yet totally destroyed, there is still hope for wiser planning, for better balance between development and preservation, and for better harmony between industry and the fragile Bluegrass environment. We must have a better understanding of the limitations of the land, as well as its virtues, if we are to continue as a distinct and world-renowned entity. To do so will require work and commitment.

UNDERSTANDING THE CONSEQUENCES

Our twin enemies are ignorance and greed. We must recognize that there are individuals whose selfish objectives are maximum material gain and quick profit for themselves, and who care nothing for what is damaged as they pursue their course. It would be futile to try to convert them. But if among our community leaders and decision-makers there is adequate comprehension of the characteristics, assets, and limitations of the land, there will be little chance for the few who are merely money-hungry to make further inroads. The need, then, is to dispel ignorance and lack of understanding. Few of those living here and even fewer of those currently migrating here understand what made the Bluegrass a treasure or what is causing its integrity to unravel. The region has fragility as well as uniqueness. By analyzing some mistakes of the past, we can hope they will not be repeated. "We have never known what we were doing because we have never known what we were *un*doing," writes Wendell Berry.[13] And so to a better understanding!

Water Quality. The Inner Bluegrass region in general is mildly karst—that is, with sinks and underdrainage—but in some places it is strongly so, with caves and sinking streams. The attractive undulating topography results from the solubility of the limestone and underground drainage. But this means a shortage of readily available water at the surface for immediate use, despite ample rainfall, and it means also the extreme vulnerability of groundwater to pollution.

Vertical cracks in limestone are enlarged by solution, and water moves down with ease. When it reaches a zone of saturation, it moves more or less horizontally along bedding planes, often down the dip of the strata and in general toward a major surface stream. This groundwater becomes a branching conduit system and eventually emerges as springs or as seepage on the banks or in the beds of permanent streams, accounting for the base flow of streams in dry periods. Ninety percent of rural Kentuckians depend on groundwater for drinking water. In karst areas, groundwater base flow, or dry-weather flow, averages 1,444 feet per day, requiring about eighteen days to go five miles, but after heavy rain groundwater may go five miles in a day. By contrast, groundwater moving only through pores, as in sandstone, would move at five feet or less per day.

It needs to be emphasized that no filtration can be counted on in karst land. Limestone is no filter, and soil cover is usually too thin to be an effective filter. In such an area, solution openings provide direct access to the aquifer for any pollutant introduced at the surface. Hence such groundwater is highly susceptible to pollution, whether from industry or from septic fields. Wells miles away from the source of pollution may be contaminated. Unfortunately, the notion "out of sight, out of mind" prevails. Underground pollution is inaccessible for clean-up; only prevention can succeed.

Actually, the Bluegrass area is unsuitable for septic drainfields, and the percolation test is almost meaningless because the drainage may go quickly and directly to an underground channel. For this reason the Fayette County Health Department persuaded the Urban County government to adopt a ten-acre minimum per house in areas not served by city sewers. But some counties have no restriction, and others have a five-acre minimum. Raw sewage in the rural water supply is a health hazard. A twenty- or twenty-five-acre minimum would actually better suit the Bluegrass land. Where there is no sewer system, alternative and innovative types of on-site sewage disposal, not the septic tank and drain field method, should be promoted.

Other types of groundwater pollution can be found today. Urban and suburban runoff from streets and parking areas contains hydrocarbons, suspended

13. Wendell Berry, *Home Economics: Fourteen Essays* (San Francisco: North Point Press, 1987), 147.

solids, fecal bacteria, nitrates and phosphates, pesticides, and often zinc, nickel, and cadmium. Stormwater drainage frequently enters solution openings into an underground system. The rock formations and soils of the Inner Bluegrass are not suitable for sanitary landfills, but the increasing population produces more waste to be disposed of, some of it toxic.

A few blatant examples will demonstrate the dangers of a lack of understanding of the region's limitations.

One of the most astounding of the natural phenomena of the entire region is the Royal Spring, or "Big Spring," at Georgetown, discharging several million gallons of water per day. The average daily pumpage from the spring is 2,000,000 gallons, although in a rainy season much more flows out. The spring was responsible for the settling of Georgetown and has been the community's source of water for two centuries. With the area's population growth in recent years, it must be supplemented occasionally with water from North Elkhorn Creek.

The source of water emanating from the Royal Spring is rainwater falling on a vast watershed that includes virtually all the land between northern Lexington and Georgetown. It consists of a large branching pattern of solution openings collecting water and carrying it to the main trunk lines of the system. This has been demonstrated over many decades by numerous dye tests, including one reported to the author by geologist W.R. Jillson, who placed dye in a sinkhole on the grounds of Eastern State Hospital in Lexington at Fourth Street and Newtown Pike. This dye reappeared in Georgetown's Royal Spring.

One of the main trunk lines of the system lies immediately south of Lemons Mill Road, running west-northwest to Georgetown for several miles, following a line of sinks on the divide between North Elkhorn Creek and the Cane Run drainage basin. Georgetown several years ago zoned for industry an area on the Lemons Mill Road, beginning only one mile from the Royal Spring—precisely on the main trunk of the aquifer.

South of Georgetown the second trunk line, having run north-northwest, joins the first near town, and over it a residential subdivision and shopping centers with extensive parking areas have been built. This trunk carries all the headwaters of Cane Run, which loses most of its water to an underground channel through several sinks in its bed between New Circle Road and Interstates 75 and 64. If one follows the creek here, one can see water flowing, and then suddenly there is little or no flow as most of the water has dropped to an underground channel. Cane Run as a surface creek picks up more water as it continues northwest, entering North Elkhorn downstream from Georgetown. Its underground channel follows the dip of the rock strata and flows north-northwest to the Royal Spring. Political leaders and planners years ago gave no thought to the headwater drainage of Can Run before it drops underground and comes out in Georgetown's drinking water. That area contains the commercial properties along New Circle Road between Georgetown Road and Bryan Avenue, Nandino Boulevard, several industrial plants, including those in the urban portion of Russell Cave Road, and several residential subdivisions.

Of course, the water issuing from the Royal Spring is treated before Georgetonians draw it from the tap. Fecal coliform and other bacteria can be killed by chlorination. But the chemicals in runoff from streets, parking areas, lawns, gardens, and industrial plants—containing heavy metals, hydrocarbons, insecticides, and other harmful substances—are much more difficult to deal with. For several days in December 1989, Georgetown's water consumers had to refrain from using the water for drinking or bathing because of gasoline leaking into a major aquifer.

Information concerning the linkage between the land north of Lexington and Georgetown's water supply has been readily available since the publication in 1968 of *The Hydrology of the Lexington and Fayette County, Kentucky, Area* by the Lexington and Fayette County Planning Commission from a study by the United States Geological Survey. Nevertheless, the Lexington-Fayette Urban County Council recently zoned for industry the corridor between the Georgetown Road and the Southern Railway tracks north to Interstates 64 and 75. Approximately half of this corridor is in the Royal Spring drainage via the upper waters of Cane Run. In this portion every pollutant that is spilled, that runs off the pavement, and that goes into the ground will come out in the drinking water of a neighboring town. A 30-foot screening is to be required along the road, but that cannot be expected to alleviate groundwater pollution. More "out of sight, out of mind"!

A mammoth project in the watershed of the Royal Spring has been proposed, but not yet enacted. It would convert 900 green acres to a many-faceted development. A consulting firm prepared what they called an "economic impact study"—clearly omitting the environmental impact—stating that the development would provide thousands of jobs, generate millions in tax revenue, and open up the north end of Lexington for further development. The initial plans call for a regional shopping mall of at least 500,000 square feet, offices, a conference center, and housing. Requisite to the total proposal is an additional interchange on Interstate 64 and 75.

In view of the state's inaction thus far to construct an additional interchange, the inclusion of a shopping mall has been temporarily dropped and a proposal for approximately half of the 900 acres has been submitted. This includes high-technology firms, light manufacturing, research, a business conference center, residential developments, and a greenspace buffer along Newtown Pike and the interstate. Also it specifies, "The banks of a large stream that runs through the property and later feeds Georgetown's water supply would be developed into a parklike setting." This indicates a lack of understanding of the characteristics of this land. Landscaping the banks of the stream is only sugarcoating. It overlooks the fact that all the land in the development is in the Cane Run watershed and drains into the creek. It is here that Cane Run loses its water underground. Hence all runoff from roadways and parking areas in the development, chemical spills, pesticides in the landscape area—everything that enters the ground—will surface in Georgetown's water supply. At this writing, the shopping mall proposal may not be completely dead.

This proposed development will be the final blow to the quality of water in the Royal Spring, which has been gradually deteriorating for the past 30 or 40 years with development of the north edge of Lexington and the southern and southeastern edge of Georgetown. With increased pollution the millions of gallons flowing daily from the Royal Spring will not be potable at all within a very few years. Such an occurrence would be a colossal waste of a marvelous resource that nature has provided—a true example of "man's inhumanity to man."

Water Supply. Lexington is one of very few cities of its size in the United States not located on a major body of water. It is situated on a plateau, with all drainage flowing away from it. By 1880 it was evident that the springs and wells were becoming inadequate for the population, and in 1884 the first dam was constructed on the headwaters of West Hickman Creek to form Reservoir No. 1. By 1903 two other dams were built, forming Reservoirs No. 2 and No. 3, all in sequence on the same creek. In 1906 the headwaters of East Hickman Creek were dammed to form Reservoir No. 4, which was later enlarged. This was sufficient for the growing city until the severe drought of 1930 made it necessary to pipe water from the Kentucky River into No. 4. With the city's rapid growth following World War II, it became necessary to increase the amount of water brought from the river. In 1958 a treatment plant was put in operation at the river, and this has been enlarged. At present about 75 percent of Lexington's water comes from the Kentucky River. Several other Bluegrass towns—Nicholasville, Wilmore, Versailles, and Frankfort—also obtain their water supply from the Kentucky River.

Using the river for water supply is possible because of the locks and dams constructed between 1836 and 1917 to enable navigation to continue during periods of reduced flow in summer. The pools thus backed up have retained sufficient water to be pumped for water supply. Altogether there are fourteen locks and dams, of which seven (numbers 4 through 9) are in the Inner Bluegrass.

The U.S. Army Corps of Engineers has estimated that, if the area continues to grow at its present rate and if no additional measures are taken, there will be insufficient water by the year 2000 should another drought occur as severe as that of 1930, the worst in our history. The only serious problems regarding water supply from the Kentucky River in the 1988 drought were in Pool 9, from which Lexington withdrew a large amount of water, and Pool 8, which had a deficit inconveniencing Nicholasville because of the amount withdrawn from Pool 9 upstream.

All regional economic studies concerning new industry state that one drawback of the Lexington area is a shortage of water. If we provide for the water demands of an ever-increasing industrial expansion, beyond the limits nature has given us, the environmental impact will be enormous. A high dam with a large impoundment in the Palisades of the Kentucky River—one proposed solution—would damage much of the only natural area remaining in the Inner Bluegrass Constructing a large dam and impoundment upstream in the Eastern Kentucky hills would inundate valley farms and is opposed by residents of that area.

Most of the existing locks and dams now need repair to prevent leakage; two of them (numbers 5 and 12) need to be rebuilt, and these could be made higher. In case of drought there could be drawdown from Pools 12 and 13, which are not used for local community water supply. This step, plus some measures planned by the Kentucky-American Water Company in Lexington, would provide for the city's water requirements for several decades, even in drought periods, if we do not admit intensive water-demanding industries. In promoting industrial growth statewide, it would be wiser for the state to site excessive water-consuming industries near a large water supply rather than bring them to the Bluegrass region and pipe water to them from many miles away.

Drainage Patterns. Disregarding natural drainage brings about serious consequences from the standpoint of both pollution and flooding. To develop former pastureland requires some grading for new streets, and runoff with soil erosion will occur during building. But that is not all. The usual procedure is for the developer to send bulldozers in to smooth down the undulations, a procedure that results in uprooting most of the trees and overlooks the fact that the undulations are part of the normal drainage pattern. Moving soil from the high places leaves them with a shallow cover—and no topsoil—above bedrock. Adding soil to the low places, which lead to joints in the limestone enlarged by solution, either partially or totally obstructs this normal pathway for underdrainage, allowing rainwater to stand too long in some spots. Sinkhole grading and filling reduces underground water; paving and roofing increase stormwater runoff. All too often the result is flooded basements.

A cardinal example of disrupting the normal drainage pattern lies in northwest Jessamine County just south of the Fayette line. Land speculators and developers have targeted land close to the Fayette County line in all adjoining counties because it is less costly than Fayette land, regulations are less strict, taxes are lower, the distance from Lexington is not great, and the planning and zoning boards are easily persuaded to approve development. This Jessamine County area is one of the largest and most notable of the strongly karst regions of the Inner Bluegrass, and this feature has been ignored. Here the area of the Sinking Creek system has been built up in seven residential developments. Another large subdivision nearby occupies a second karst drainage system, and still another has been planned in the Cave Spring drainage system south of the Sinking Creek system. Many of these residences are on one-acre or half-acre tracts, although some are on five acres. All have septic tanks and drainfields, and sewage contamination in groundwater is excessive downstream from the built-up areas.

In this section of several square miles, the natural and inevitable habits of sinking creeks have been disregarded. The developer, the planning and zoning board, the fiscal court, the purchasers of homesites—all should have known. Sinking Creek in its course alternates four times between coming into the light of the day and sinking underground, and the system includes several tributaries with springs. Following torrential rains an ordinary surface stream will overflow its banks but an underground stream is confined and unable to overflow laterally. Its velocity is increased, and, when issuing under pressure, it will rapidly flood low-lying land far and wide. Since the points where it would go underground again cannot accommodate much of the increased volume, water may stand for several weeks.

This land formerly was in several large farms. Dry seasons provided good grazing because the high water table maintained green pasturage; in wet seasons the farmers moved their cattle to higher ground. But houses and roads cannot be so moved. Several roads were impassable due to flooding in 1989. In the subdivision most affected, water stood five feet deep over the causeway, despite its having been raised eight feet since the 1978 flooding. Many fields had water twelve feet deep. Basements were flooded, and one house had water to the top of the first floor. Two or three dozen houses carefully situated could have been accommodated in these drainage systems, but hundreds of houses cannot. A natural phenomenon was ignored and will recur.

HOW CAN WE SAFEGUARD THE REGION'S CHARACTER?

All Kentuckians would like to see a boost to our state's economy. Statewide we have a low per capita income, a high unemployment rate, and too much illiteracy in comparison with other states. Yet there are areas in the state with high per capita income, low unemployment, and high educational levels; other areas bring down the state averages. Officials of the Commonwealth, in promoting economic development, seem to be concentrating merely on improving statistics for the state as a whole, not on promoting economic development where it is most needed. Often new industries are being placed where there is virtually no unemployment (3 or 4 percent), rather than where unemployment is 10 to 15 percent. That means a great in-migration to the already prosperous sections from other states and from skilled workers and technicians formerly living in the more depressed areas of Kentucky, where jobs are most needed. Between 1984 and 1986, 66 of the state's 120 counties lost population. That should be compared with the statistics on page 208 concerning population growth in the Bluegrass section.

Officials in Frankfort must come to realize that today's economy is knowledge-intensive and is built on technological innovation. Sustained economic growth will necessitate improvement in mathematics and science education in our poorer schools, as well as in higher education. Kentucky must face these demands, must improve the skills and educational levels of the work force in the so-called depressed areas, must provide more job training and reduce school dropout rates—in other words, build the work capacities of people in those areas. Computer and telecommunication technology could, for example, expand the number of jobs in Eastern Kentucky, since many such jobs can be done anywhere if the work force is trained to perform complex jobs. An example is the Appalachian Computer Services in London, Kentucky, which employs 1,400 persons and furnishes record-keeping and computer services to many companies nationwide.

Poor schools make poor counties, and poor counties make poor schools. The cycle must be broken and the populace better educated, but the remedy will not be easy. Funding for schools comes from property taxes. Basic to the disease is considerable lack of fairness and honesty regarding property assessment and inefficient collection of property taxes. Curing this deep-seated malady will require legislative reform to restructure the system.

There is another aspect to economic development. Quality of life is increasingly important in decisions of business and industry concerning where they choose to locate. An executive of a major manufacturing enterprise in the

Bluegrass section said that he and other executives would refuse to go to areas lacking economic development; good quality of life in a beautiful environment with many cultural amenities would be a necessity. Local governments need to be concerned about schools, environmental protection, parks, physical infrastructure, hospitals, sewage treatment, trash disposal, and safe drinking water if they are not to remain at the bottom. To prepare depressed areas for economic development will require more time than to usurp prime Bluegrass farmland for industry. The state Commerce Cabinet would be wise to encourage industry in places that need economic growth. The result will be more long-term benefits to all concerned.

The state government makes sizable grants to industries to entice them to Kentucky. Before making such an offer, however, a careful study should be made, analyzing strengths and weaknesses, to decide where such investment of public funds will bring the most benefits. For instance, industry requiring large amounts of water should be placed near an adequate source of water, not where water is scarce and will have to be brought to them. At times the state has superimposed an industry on a county (with payment to the industry) contrary to the county's Comprehensive Plan, which then must be changed with considerable rezoning.

When state agencies place large manufacturing industries in the Inner Bluegrass, which has the least unemployment in the state, they do not comprehend what they are doing (to paraphrase Wendell Berry) because they do not realize what they are undoing. They are ignoring the area's natural limitations and undermining what has been established for two centuries and has brought economic prosperity and fame: the horse industry, farming on some of the richest land in the United States, and, more recently, tourism. We seem to be afflicted, both locally and statewide, with blindness to the consequences of destroying the values we now possess.

Local planning and zoning boards or commissions are made up of responsible citizens, many of them with legal and business expertise, often trained in finance, economics, and political science. One other qualification is needed, however. Since these persons are making decisions regarding land use, they need to know the character of the land they are dealing with—its limitations as well as its assets. They need to know the impact a zone change is likely to have on other land and other people. They need to know that much Inner Bluegrass land has underground solution channels. They should know whether or not a rezoning for housing or industry is likely to affect the quality of drinking water of people on other land. They should know that disaster is bound to follow the zoning of natural wetland for residential development. The effectiveness of a county's Comprehensive Plan depends on the wisdom of the planners and their resistance to pressure from special interest groups. Unfortunately, some counties have no countywide zoning; here, urban sprawl, rural subdivisions, and leap-frog development can proliferate without zone changes or public hearings.

Land use patterns should be designed in harmony with the natural systems of soil, water, and topography. Decision-makers should understand an area's geology, physiography, drainage systems, and native vegetation, including a recognition of the significance of certain plant communities. Through the National

Environmental Policy Act, the Clean Water Act, the Clean Air Act, the Endangered Species Act, and others, the federal government has said that the natural environment can no longer be ignored. Something that appears economically or technologically feasible may not be environmentally feasible. Any prospective developer should be required to prepare a study similar to the Environmental Impact Statement required of public agencies in federal programs. He should have to prove that his plan is altogether beneficial and has no adverse impact, that it is environmentally sound. No decision should be made until all side-effects have been evaluated. Environmentally sensitive areas should be identified, listed, and removed from consideration for development. Actually, the Commonwealth should enact legislation requiring an EIS for any project affecting the environment.

Planning and zoning boards in the Bluegrass are under tremendous pressure to provide land for industry and a rapidly growing population. When there is a wide disparity between the price of land for agriculture and that of the same land for development, there is pressure for a zone change. An attorney representing property owners desiring to sell to industry argued that the change from agricultural to industrial zoning "would bring badly needed industry to Lexington and create more jobs." Lexington is not "badly" in need of more industry, and "more jobs" would mean more in-migration and more housing development on more agricultural land. Bad decisions made today regarding zone changes and development are irrevocable.

One of the great needs in maintaining the character of the Inner Bluegrass is a regional approach, not just county planning, and more communication between counties. County separations are artificial and political; we should consider how the region fits together naturally. Without an overall understanding, many far-reaching decisions concerning the area tend to be disjointed. Piecemeal planning does not adequately consider long-range goals and the well-being of the entire community. Where one county has stricter zoning regulations than an adjoining county, problems arise near the county boundary—water pollution, traffic congestion, and others.

Very specifically, there needs to be coordinated regional planning for transportation. Too often highway construction is planned in response to local demands: wider roads from point to point, designed on a corridor-by-corridor basis, instead of a long-range, overall regional consideration. Road planning to provide traffic movement should also be sensitive to our priceless landscape and cultural heritage. When the Department of Transportation plans a bypass around a town to facilitate through traffic, there needs to be cooperation with local planners, who should restrict development along the bypass lest it become a commercial corridor, bringing townspeople out and defeating the original purpose. A recent candidate for local political office favored a proposed bypass around a town because of the development it would generate.

The Bluegrass is a region, not a ring of towns around Lexington with each town wanting its "slice" of the economic development "pie." To maintain any Bluegrass distinctiveness, a serious, conscientious, regional growth management plan to guide economic development must be adopted before it is too late.

Without regional direction, county and municipal jurisdictions will compete for the short-term benefits of industrialization without regard for the long-term negative side-effects.

A regional approach to development would involve the cooperation of different local government agencies, environmental organizations, and knowledgeable private individuals. Ideally a regional land-use commission would review all new development and construction projects. In Kentucky this would be advisory to local decision-making boards, but such advice should carry weight. An example from another state would be the Cape Cod land-use commission, which, by a large voting majority, was empowered to act for all the Cape instead of dispersing approval for development in 15 separate town governments. Our present Bluegrass Area Development District is good and helpful, but we need more. We need some inter-county conferences immediately.

One area requiring regional control is the gorge of the Kentucky River, with its majestic cliffs, often referred to as the Palisades. It is an area of outstanding scenic grandeur, and, together with its tributaries, which are characterized by waterfalls and forested slopes that are blanketed by wildflowers in spring, is the only area of the Inner Bluegrass still in an almost natural state. Recently it has been labeled as underutilized, and its potential for development, tourism, and recreation is receiving attention. Since the gorge lies in parts of several counties, its development needs state and regional as well as county planning.

Both economic opportunity and recreational enhancement of the Palisades can be provided in a framework of preservation and protection. Because the gorge is an aesthetic, historic, geological, and biological treasure, any development here should be done with great care and sensitivity lest the natural values be diminished. Recreational development should fit the place, and visitor attractions should not disrupt the natural assets. As a natural area it has value for scientific research and also for passive recreation.

In a world dominated by technology we need places where nature is in charge, places that man did not create. In the rush and stress of modern life we need to experience the dignity and peace of nature in order to keep our thinking straight, to maintain a balanced perspective. The tremendous visitor-load at Fayette County's Raven Run Nature Sanctuary indicates the need for more similar places offering nature trails. The Kentucky River Palisades can serve that purpose. But Palisades planning should be aimed toward the maximum enjoyment for the most persons—"the greatest good for the greatest number of people, for the longest period of time." To be publicly accessible, some portions should be acquired by government. A state resort park could be established, and possibly other state-owned parks without hotel facilities. A paddlewheeler, such as the popular Dixie Belle owned by Shakertown, could be purchased by the state for river cruises. Canoeing could be encouraged. The use of speed boats should be discouraged; the gorge is too narrow for them, since their speed tends to erode the banks.

For any development, public or private, a comprehensive environmental assessment should be required. For any building, there should be a mandatory setback from the ridge line, with trails leading to scenic overlooks. Views from a river cruise are too beautiful to be marred by buildings at the crestline. A similar example is New York's greenway system in the Palisades of the Hudson River, which prohibits any future structures that could obstruct panoramic views.

The Kentucky River Palisades area should not be left to speculators who see chiefly a chance for financial gain for themselves. Any extensive development of "second homes" would reduce the area's value for scientific research, general aesthetics, and passive recreation for more persons.

The greatest detraction to the scenic beauty of the Kentucky River is the water itself. A stream is the offspring of its watershed, and the Kentucky carries silt and garbage from far upstream. There needs to be better watershed management in the headwater region, but that is beyond the scope of a book on the Bluegrass region.

Protection for the Bluegrass area's precious natural heritage is needed immediately, for each year we have less and less to be protected. Several methods of land preservation are already available in Kentucky, and still others have been proposed. For a number of years, for example, Kentucky has had legislation enabling landowners to contribute conservation easements, but it has not been widely publicized and the value to the landowner has not been appreciated. The landowner places in a conservation easement whatever restrictions—many or few—he wishes his land to have in perpetuity and deeds the easement to a government agency or a private foundation. The landowner continues to own the land and may sell it with the restrictions he has designated. The land must be worthy of preservation, and the grantee must be willing to accept and enforce the designated restrictions. The difference between the value of the land unrestricted and its value with the restrictions constitutes a charitable contribution which is deductible from federal and state income tax. This deduction can be carried over for five years beyond the initial year. There is also saving in state and federal estate tax. The total saving is considerable and should appeal to any owner of special land who wishes to see the character of his land and the integrity of the Bluegrass perpetuated. Conservation easements can also be purchased by the county.

The contribution of farmland to maintaining environmental quality is usually not appreciated, and we are faced with the need to restore profitability to agriculture. According to the Sierra Club book *Soil and Survival,* only 11 percent of the earth's land surface is rich, productive farmland. The Bluegrass country is in that 11 percent. If we are to save rich agricultural land and persuade the farmer to continue farming when there is financial pressure to convert the most productive land to nonfarm use, we must act, not just sit and hope. One method that might be tried is property tax incentive.

Bluegrass land to be developed sells for far more than it would bring as farmland per se. Our present differential assessment for agricultural land is helpful, but a stronger incentive is needed to keep farmers farming. The present agricultural assessment for an individual farm is based on that farm's potential income from farming. Income from farming is insufficient to resist the pressure to sell for development. Since some degree of tax exemption is used to lure new industry, why could there not be a similar inducement to retain farming on rich land and to channel other land uses to less productive land? In exchange for low property taxation on developable but undeveloped land, the landowner could be assessed a charge at the time he sells his farm for development. The government would then partially or totally recoup the taxes excused. If the landowner has received a rebate of 50-80 percent of the property tax, that would have to be returned if the land is sold for development. (The minimum acreage for a home site in an agricultural zone needs to be increased throughout the Bluegrass. To receive the maximum tax rebate, the minimum should be 50 acres per dwelling unit.)

Another possible method is purchase of development rights. To insure permanent green space, a county could purchase development rights to land that could be sold for industrial, commercial, or housing uses. This would necessitate purchasing development rights to at least a hundred contiguous acres, either from one landowner or from neighboring owners all willing to sell such rights. In such a transaction the county would pay the landowner the difference between the price as farmland and what a developer would be willing to pay. The landowner's agreement never to develop the land would apply also to future owners. Land to be preserved can also be purchased outright by the county.

Another tool for preservation is the establishment of conservation districts as a zoning category for unique and environmentally sensitive areas. The zoning restrictions here would exceed those in an agricultural zone. In addition, Kentucky has an Agricultural District Law, and contiguous farmers wishing to continue farming should be encouraged to establish Agricultural Districts wherever possible. Finally, much value can come from the clustering of building sites, leaving open green spaces. Developers of industrial and housing areas should be required to contribute open space.

Other states have taken a number of steps that could be emulated here. Oregon has had a statewide growth-management plan since 1973. Maine, Vermont, New Jersey, and other states have more recently established regional growth-management plans. Rhode Island in 1987 approved a bond act for buying land to protect it as open space. Later that state passed a bill permitting cities and towns to approve open space bond acts of their own, and 34 out of 39 have done so. Enabling legislation in Massachusetts has permitted the islands of Nantucket and Martha's Vineyard each to have a land bank commission. In this there is a 2 percent tax on the sale of real estate or land transfer, paid by the seller, with the proceeds used to acquire land for preservation. In 1988 a conference of New England governors agreed to assemble a list of special places that give distinctiveness to their corner of the country. This list, essentially a catalog of regional assets that should be preserved, is useful as a guide to future development and nondevelopment.[14] In California an Environmental Impact Statement is required for any significant private as well as public development, and a regulatory agency controls development along the coastline of San Francisco Bay.

In order that the special Bluegrass character not be lost in the economic and

14. Tony Hiss, "Reflections Encountering the Countryside," *New Yorker,* August 21 and 28, 1989.

population growth occurring in Fayette County, a Greenspace Conservancy Ordinance has been proposed. It would establish a Greenspace Conservancy Commission charged with developing and implementing plans for the preservation and enhancement of the special quality of life in Lexington and Fayette County. It recognizes that the natural resources here are finite and are threatened by unmanaged growth. To safeguard the county's scenic beauty, historic and cultural heritage, agriculture, ecological environment, and tourism, concurrent with economic development and growth, the commission would apply several of the preservation tools listed in the preceding paragraphs. It would be responsible to the Lexington-Fayette Urban County Council and would be aided by a citizens' advisory board. The commission could expend appropriated funds to carry out the purposes of the ordinance. This is a wise step—although late, since we have already lost much. We must hope that it will be enacted and that other counties will follow with similar efforts.

Anyone observing present trends in the Bluegrass is forced to recognize that if we continue with no more sensitive and responsible planning than what we have had, within less than two decades the region will no longer be the "horse capital of the world." It will have no special personality but will resemble any bustling, growing metropolis. All groundwater will be contaminated, and our air will be hazy with pollution from automobile traffic. But it is not yet too late—if we take immediate steps—to insure a worthwhile legacy for future generations. With knowledge and wise planning, we can protect what is most valuable in the environmental, cultural, scenic, and historic character of the Bluegrass and at the same time meet the needs of the population with housing, roads, business, and industry. But to do so will require, in every Bluegrass county, effort, caring, commitment, dedication, and a sense of stewardship, since our use of the land is borrowed from our children. We must begin now, for soon it will be too late.

Appendixes

A. Glossary of Geologic Terms

anticline: An upward fold in rock strata, in the form of an arch.
aquifer: A body of earth material, rock or sand or gravel, which will yield water in usable quantity.
argillaceous: Pertaining to or containing clay.
base level: The lowest level to which a stream can cut its valley by mechanical wear, or the lowest level to which a land area can be eroded.
cycle of erosion: The reduction of a land area to a base level.
dip: The inclination of a rock layer tilted from the horizontal.
dolomite: A rock composed predominantly of the mineral dolomite, a calcium magnesium carbonate, CaMg(CO3)2; it is slightly harder than limestone.
dome: An uplift in which the strata dip away in all directions from a more or less circular center, a feature of bedrock structure, not of surface topography.
fault: A fracture in which rocks on one side have been displaced relative to those on the opposite side.
geanticline: An anticline or structural arch on a large scale.
karst: Of or relating to land characterized by numerous caverns, sinks, solution valleys, and disappearing streams.
limestone: A rock in which the predominant mineral is calcite (calcium carbonate, CaCO3). A **bioclastic limestone** is one in which most of the calcium carbonate is derived from shells. A **lithographic limestone** is a very fine-grained limestone in which the calcium carbonate is either chemically precipitated or formed by algal or bacterial processes.
peneplain or **peneplane:** A land surface of low relief and wide extent reduced by erosion to a base level.
shale: A fine-grained rock formed from consolidated, hardened, compacted mud or clay.
sink: A surface depression made in either of two ways: by collapse of a cavern roof, or by solution from the surface downward whereby the dissolving action of the descending water enlarges cracks.
stratigraphy: The age relation of rocks, with the oldest at the bottom and the youngest at the top.
structure: The architectural feature of rocks resulting from deformational movements within the earth's crust.

B. The Geologic Time Scale

Geologic time is divided into eras, which in turn are divided into periods, and periods are divided into epochs. The periods and epochs pertaining directly to the Bluegrass region of Kentucky are in boldface, and the time span involved in these periods and epochs is included. The Ordovician is the period in which the rock was formed. Features of land surface result from geologic events or physiographic history from the Miocene epoch of the Tertiary to Recent times, except for the Kentucky River, which dates back over 100,000,000 years into the Mesozoic era, although its course has changed since then.

THE GEOLOGIC TIME SCALE

CENOZOIC ERA From 70,000,000 years ago to the present	**QUATERNARY PERIOD** From 1,000,000 years ago to the present	**RECENT** From 12,000 years ago to the present
		PLEISTOCENE EPOCH From 1,000,000 to 12,000 years ago
	TERTIARY PERIOD From 70,000,000 to 1,000,000 years ago	**PLIOCENE EPOCH** From 12,000,000 to 1,000,000 years ago
		MIOCENE EPOCH From 25,000,000 to 12,000,000 years ago
		OLIGOCENE EPOCH
		EOCENE EPOCH
		PALEOCENE EPOCH
MESOZOIC ERA From 200,000,000 to 70,000,000 years ago	CRETACEOUS PERIOD JURASSIC PERIOD TRIASSIC PERIOD	
PALEOZOIC ERA From 550,000,000 to 200,000,000 years ago	PERMIAN PERIOD PENNSYLVANIAN PERIOD MISSISSIPPIAN PERIOD DEVONIAN PERIOD SILURIAN PERIOD **ORDOVICIAN PERIOD** From 460,000,000 to 400,000,000 years ago CAMBRIAN PERIOD	
PROTEROZOIC AND ARCHEOZOIC, the PRE-CAMBRIAN ERAS, From 3,000,000,000 to 550,000,000 years ago		

C. Plant Communities and Succession: A Basic Explanation

Populations of plants and animals living together in complementary relationships and interacting with each other and with their environment form a **biotic community.** A biotic community and all factors of the physical environment constitute an **ecosystem.** An ecosystem includes the transfer and circulation of energy and matter. The vegetational component of a biotic community is known as a **plant community,** which may be defined as an assemblage of plant populations living together and organized to the extent that it has group characteristics in addition to those of its component parts. (A **population** is a group of individuals of the same species occupying the same area.) The **dominant** species are those which control and characterize the community; subordinate species must be able to live with the dominants.

Plant communities are not static, and the accompanying animal populations change as the plant community changes. When a plant community occupies an area, its presence and life processes may modify the area to the extent that it becomes more suitable for a different plant community, which therefore succeeds the previous one. This is called **plant succession,** which, when undisturbed, proceeds in an orderly sequence, often for centuries or even thousands of years until it becomes somewhat stabilized. As succession proceeds, there is an increase in species diversity, in biomass (all living matter taken collectively), and in the complexity of the ecosystem. A relatively stabilized plant community is called a **climax.** This is the culmination of vegetational development where species reproduce within the community and exclude others, especially potential dominants, from becoming established; therefore the community tends to be followed by the same type instead of being succeeded by a different one.

There are four types of climax or somewhat stabilized situations in the Inner Bluegrass region: climatic, relic, physiographic, and edaphic. A **climatic climax** is the maximum natural vegetational production of which the present climate is capable and is not restricted by local conditions. A **relic climax** is a remnant of a former climax when conditions (for example, climate) were different from the present conditions. A **physiographic climax** is a stabilized plant community restricted by topographic features such as cliff faces or narrow ridgetops. An **edaphic climax** is a stabilized plant community restricted by peculiarities of soil different from that of the area as a whole.

Primary succession begins where plants have never previously grown (such as bare rock surface); it is **secondary succession** if it is initiated after destruction of previous vegetation due to fire, cultivation, or other disturbance. Plants beginning in a wet or **hydric** situation (such as a pond or swamp), called **hydrophytes,** will gradually cause a reduction in wetness and a progression through intermediate stages toward a **mesic** situation, which is neither wet nor dry, the "golden mean" of soil moisture. Plants beginning in a dry, or **xeric** situation, called **xerophytes,** increase moisture-holding capacity, and plant occupancy proceeds through mid-successional stages toward a mesic situation, occupied by plants called **mesophytes** with medium moisture requirements. When vegetation becomes somewhat stabilized, it is the most nearly mesophytic possible in the area.

Bibliography

Allen, James Lane. 1900. *The Bluegrass Region of Kentucky.* 1892; reprint: New York: Macmillan.

Anderson, William A., Jr. 1924. "The Graminales of Kentucky." Master's thesis, University of Kentucky.

Appleton, Thomas H., Jr. 1981. "The Journal of Thomas Smith, Jr., of Lincolnshire." *Register of the Kentucky Historical Society* 79: 57-62.

Audubon, John James. 1926. *Delineations of American Scenery and Character,* intro. by Francis Hobart Herrick. New York: G.A. Baker.

Axton, William F. 1975. *Tobacco in Kentucky.* Lexington: Univ. Press of Kentucky.

Bailey, H.H., and J.H. Winsor. 1964. *Kentucky Soils.* Lexington: Kentucky Agricultural Experiment Station. Miscellaneous Publication 308.

Bakeless, John. 1939. *Daniel Boone.* New York: William Morrow.

Banks, Richard C., Roy W. McDiarmid, and Alfred L. Gardner. 1987. *Checklist of Vertebrates of the United States, the U.S. Territories, and Canada.* Washington, D.C.: U.S. Department of the Interior.

Barbour, Roger W. 1970. *Amphibians and Reptiles of Kentucky.* Lexington: Univ. Press of Kentucky.

———, and Wayne H. Davis. 1969. *Bats of America.* Lexington: Univ. Press of Kentucky.

———, Clell T. Peterson, Delbert Rust, Herbert E. Shadowen, and A.L. Whitt, Jr. 1973. *Kentucky Birds: A Finding Guide.* Lexington: Univ. Press of Kentucky.

———, and Wayne H. Davis. 1974. *Mammals of Kentucky.* Lexington: Univ. Press of Kentucky.

Beckett, Mary R. 1956. "The Flora of Clark County, Kentucky, in Relation to Geologic Regions." Master's thesis, University of Kentucky.

Black, Douglas F.B., E.R. Cressman, and W.C. MacQuown, Jr. 1965. *The Lexington Limestone (Middle Ordovician) of Central Kentucky.* Geological Survey Bulletin 1224-C. Washington, D.C.: U.S. Government Printing Office.

Bradbury, John. 1819. *Travels in the Interior of America in the Years 1809, 1810, and 1811.* London: Sherwood, Neely, and Jones.

Branson, Branley A., et al. 1981. "Endangered, Threatened, and Rare Animals and Plants of Kentucky." *Transactions of the Kentucky Academy of Science* 42, nos. 3-4 (Sept.): 77-89.

Braun, E. Lucy. 1943. *An Annotated Catalog of Spermatophytes of Kentucky.* Cincinnati: John F. Swift.

———. 1950. *Deciduous Forests of Eastern North America.* Philadelphia: Blakiston Co.

Bromfield, Louis. 1947. *Malabar Farm.* New York: Harper & Bros.

Brooks, R.E. 1983. "*Trifolium stoloniferum,* Running Buffalo Clover." *Rhodora* 85: 343-54.

Brown, Samuel. 1817. *Western Gazeteer; or Emigrant's Directory.* Auburn, N.Y. 91-95.

Bryant, William S. 1978. "An Unusual Forest Type, Hydromesophytic, for the Inner Bluegrass Region of Kentucky." *Castanea* 43: 129-37.

______, Mary E. Wharton, William H. Martin, and Johnnie B. Varner. 1980. "The Blue Ash–Oak Savanna–Woodland: A Remnant of Presettlement Vegetation in the Inner Bluegrass of Kentucky." *Castanea* 45: 149-53.

Castleman, John B. 1917. *Active Service.* Louisville: Courier-Journal Job Printing Co.

Chinn, George M. 1975. *Kentucky: Settlement and Statehood, 1750-1800.* Frankfort: Kentucky Historical Society.

Clark, Thomas D. 1929A. "The Antebellum Hemp Trade of Kentucky with the Cotton Belt." *Register of the Kentucky Historical Society* 27: 538-44.

______. 1929B. "Livestock Trade between Kentucky and the South, 1840-1860." *Register of the Kentucky Historical Society* 27: 569-81.

______. 1942. *The Kentucky.* New York: Farrar and Rinehart.

______. 1950. *A History of Kentucky.* Lexington: John Bradford Press.

______. 1977. *Agrarian Kentucky.* Lexington: Univ. Press of Kentucky.

Clay, William M. 1977. *The Fishes of Kentucky.* Frankfort: Kentucky Department of Fish and Wildlife Resources.

Clotfelter, Elizabeth R. 1953. "Agricultural History of Bourbon County prior to 1900." Master's thesis, University of Kentucky.

Collins, Richard H. 1966. *History of Kentucky.* 2 vols. 1874; reprint: Frankfort: Kentucky Historical Society.

Cranfill, Ray. 1980. *Ferns and Fern Allies of Kentucky.* Frankfort: Kentucky Nature Preserves Commission, Scientific and Technical Series No. 1.

Cressman, Earle R. 1973. *Lithostratigraphy and Depositional Environments of the Lexington Limestone (Ordovician) of Central Kentucky.* Geological Survey Professional Paper 768. Washington, D.C.: U.S. Government Printing Office.

______, and M.C. Noger. 1976. *Tidal-Flat Carbonate Environments in the High Bridge Group (Middle Ordovician) of Central Kentucky.* Kentucky Geological Survey, Series X.

Davidson, Ursula M. 1950. "The Original Vegetation of Lexington, Ky., and Vicinity." Master's thesis, University of Kentucky.

Davis, Darrell Haug. 1927. *The Geography of the Blue Grass Region of Kentucky: A Reconnaissance of the Distribution and Activities of Man in the Area of Ordovician Outcrop Embraced by the Commonwealth.* Frankfort: Kentucky Geological Survey.

Denbo, Bruce, Mary Wharton, and Clyde Burke. 1980. *The Horse World of the Bluegrass.* Lexington: John Bradford Press.

Drake, Daniel. 1948 [1870]. *Pioneer Life in Kentucky, 1785-1800.* E.F. Horine, ed. New York: Henry Schuman.

Draper, Lyman C. Manuscript Collection. Madison, Wisconsin, Historical Society. The following are journal entries or interviews by Draper or by John D. Shane. They are available on microfilm at the Department of Special Collections, Margaret I. King Library, University of Kentucky.

Barrow, David	12 CC 163-86	Hanson, Thomas	24 CC 1-54
Clinkenbeard, William	11 CC 54-66	Hedge, John	11 CC 19-23
Collins, Josiah	12 CC 64-78	Matthew, Samuel	11 CC 157-58
Falconer, Joice Craig	11 CC 130-38	Records, Spencer	23 CC 1-108
Farrar, Asa	13 CC 1-6	Scholl, Septimus	11 CC 51
Graddy, Jesse	13 CC 130-34	Todd, Levi	15 CC 157-62
Guyn, Robert	11 CC 216-17	Wymore, Martin	11 CC 128-32, 159

Duke, Basil W. 1911. *Reminiscences.* New York: Doubleday, Page.

Ernst, Carl H., and Roger W. Barbour. 1972. *Turtles of the United States.* Lexington: Univ. Press of Kentucky.

Faust, Robert J. 1977. "Ground Water Resources of the Lexington, Kentucky, Area." *Water Resources Investigations,* 76-113. Washington, D.C.: U.S. Geological Survey.

Fenneman, Nevin M. 1938. *Physiography of Eastern United States.* New York: McGraw-Hill.

Fernald, Merritt L. 1950. *Gray's Manual of Botany, Eighth Edition.* New York: American Book Co.

Filson, John. 1784. *The Discovery, Settlement, and Present State of Kentucke.* Wilmington: John Adams.

Finley, James B. 1853. *Autobiography.* Cincinnati: Cranston and Curtis.

Flint, Timothy. 1832. *The History and Geography of the Mississippi Valley,* 2nd ed., vol. 1. Cincinnati: E.H. Flint and L.R. Lincoln.

Funkhouser, W.D. 1925. *Wild Life in Kentucky.* Frankfort: Kentucky Geological Survey, Ser. VI.

Gray, Lewis C. 1941. *History of Agriculture in the Southern United States to 1860.* 2 vols. New York: P. Smith.

Guharja, Edi. 1962. "The Flora of Bourbon County, Kentucky." Master's thesis, University of Kentucky.

Guilday, J.E., H.W. Hamilton, and A.D. McCrady. 1971. "The Welsh Cave Peccaries (Platygonus) and Associated Fauna, Kentucky Pleistocene." *Annals of the Carnegie Museum* 43: 249-320.

Hall, James. 1834, 1835. "Travels in Hot Weather." *Western Monthly Magazine* 2: 528-39; 3: 29-38. Reprinted in Schwaab, *Travels in the Old South,* 266-72.

Hammon, Neil O. 1980. "Land Acquisition on the Kentucky Frontier." *Register of the Kentucky Historical Society* 78: 297-321.

Hardin, Martin D. 1810. Kentucky Court of Appeals. *Reports of Cases Argued and Adjudged in the Court of Appeals of Kentucky, from Spring Term 1805, to Spring Term 1808, Inclusive.* Frankfort: Johnston and Pleasants.

Hendrickson, G.E., and R.A. Krieger. 1964. *Geochemistry of Natural Waters of the Blue Grass Region, Kentucky.* Geological Survey Water-Supply Paper 1700. Washington, D.C.: U.S. Government Printing Office.

Henlein, Paul C. 1959. *Cattle Kingdom in the Ohio Valley.* Lexington: Univ. of Kentucky Press.

Herrick, Francis H. 1917. *Audubon the Naturalist: A History of His Life and Times.* 2 vols. New York: D. Appleton.

Hervey, John. 1944. *Racing in America, 1665-1865.* 2 vols. New York: Jockey Club.

Hockensmith, Charles D. 1980. "Fort Ancient Settlement Patterns in the Bluegrass Region of Kentucky." In *Fort Ancient Tradition of the Middle Ohio Valley. Proceedings of the 45th Annual Meeting of the Society of American Archeology.*

Hopkins, James F. 1951. *A History of the Hemp Industry in Kentucky.* Lexington: Univ. of Kentucky Press.

Hughes, R.E. 1966. "Fire Ecology of Canebrakes." *Proceedings of Fifth Tall Timbers Fire Ecology Conference,* 148-58.

Hutchens, Thomas. 1788. *A Topographical Description of Virginia, Pennsylvania, and North Carolina.* London.

Hyland, Peggy. 1979. *On Site Sewage Disposal in Rural Kentucky.* Research Report No. 155, Frankfort: Legislative Research Commission.

Imlay, Gilbert. 1797. *A Topographical Description of the Western Territory of North America,* 3rd ed. London: J. DeBrett.

Jakle, John A. 1968. "The American Bison and Human Occupance of the Ohio Valley." *Proceedings of the American Philosophical Society* 112: 299-305.

James, James A., ed. 1912. *George Rogers Clark Papers, 1771-1781.* Springfield: Illinois Historical Society Collections VIII, Virginia Series.

Jillson, Willard R. 1925. *Kentucky Land Grants.* Filson Club Publication No. 33. Louisville: Standard Printing Co.

______. 1926. *Old Kentucky Entries and Deeds.* Louisville: Standard Printing Co.

______. 1927. *The Topography of Kentucky.* Frankfort: Kentucky Geological Survey.

______, ed. 1931. *The Palaeontology of Kentucky.* Frankfort: Kentucky Geological Survey, Ser. VI, vol. 36.

______. 1934. *Pioneer Kentucky.* Frankfort: State Journal Co.

______. 1945. "The Kentucky River: An Outline of the Drainage Modification of a Master Stream during Geologic Time." *State Journal* 14: 1-104.

______. 1946. *The Nonesuch Abandoned Channel of the Kentucky River.* Frankfort: Roberts Printing Co.

______. 1947. *The Warwick Abandoned Channel of the Kentucky River near Clover Bottom.* Frankfort: Roberts Printing Co.

______. 1961. *Erosion Cycles in Central Kentucky.* Frankfort: Roberts Printing Co.

______. 1963. *Deliniations of the Mesozoic Course of the Kentucky River across the Inner Bluegrass Region of the State.* Frankfort: Roberts Printing Co.

______. 1968A. *The Extinct Vertebrata of the Pleistocene in Kentucky.* Frankfort: Roberts Printing Co.

______. 1968B. *Geology of Fayette County, Kentucky.* Frankfort: Roberts Printing Co.

Johnston, J. Stoddard. 1898. *First Explorations of Kentucky.* Filson Club Publication No. 13. Louisville: J.P. Morton.

Karan, P.P., and Cotton Mather, eds. 1977. *Atlas of Kentucky.* Lexington: Univ. Press of Kentucky.

Kartez, J.T., and R. Kartez. 1980. *A Synchronized Checklist of the Vascular Flora of the United States, Canada, and Greenland.* vol. 2, *The Biota of North America.* Chapel Hill: Univ. of North Carolina Press.

Kenton, Edna. 1930. *Simon Kenton, His Life and Period, 1755-1836.* New York: Doubleday, Doran.

Knight, Thomas A., and Nancy L. Greene. 1904. *Country Estates of the Bluegrass.* Lexington: Henry Clay Press. [Reprinted 1973.]

Kuehne, Robert A., and Roger W. Barbour. 1983. *The American Darters.* Lexington: Univ. Press of Kentucky.

Marsh, George. 1965. *Man and Nature,* ed. D. Lowenthal. Cambridge: Belknap Press of Harvard University Press.

Marshall, Humphrey. 1812. *The History of Kentucky,* vol. 1. Frankfort: Henry Gore.

Martin, W.H., W.S. Bryant, S.G. Lassiter, and J.B. Varner. 1979. *The Kentucky River Palisades: Flora and Vegetation.* Kentucky Chapter of the Nature Conservancy.

Mastin, Bettye Lee. 1979. *Lexington 1779.* Lexington: Lexington-Fayette County Historic Commission.

McClung, John Alexander. *Sketches of Western Adventure.* Maysville, Ky.: L. Collins, 1832.

McCoy, Thomas N. 1936. "The Ferns of Kentucky." Master's thesis, University of Kentucky.

McFarlan, Arthur C. 1943. *Geology of Kentucky.* Lexington: University of Kentucky.

———. 1958. *Behind the Scenery in Kentucky.* Lexington: Kentucky Geological Survey. Series IX, Special Publication no. 10.
McFarland, James. 1946. "The Vascular Plants of Jessamine County, Kentucky." Master's thesis, University of Kentucky.
McGrain, Preston, and James C. Currens. 1989. *Topography of Kentucky.* Lexington: Kentucky Geological Survey. Series X, Special Publication no. 25
McHargue, J.S. 1926. "Kentucky Bluegrass: Whence Did It Come?" *Transactions of the Kentucky Academy of Science* 2: 179-90.
———. 1941. "Canebrakes in Prehistoric and Pioneer Times in Kentucky." *Annals of Kentucky Natural History* 1: 1-13.
McInteer, B.B. 1941. "Distribution of the Woody Plants of Kentucky in Relation to Geologic Regions." Frankfort: Kentucky Department of Mines and Minerals, Geology Division, Series VIII, Bulletin 6.
———. 1946. "A Change from Grassland to Forest Vegetation in the 'Big Barrens' of Kentucky." *American Midland Naturalist* 35: 153-282.
———. 1952. "Original Vegetation in the Bluegrass Region of Kentucky." *Castanea* 17: 153-56.
McMurtrie, Henry. 1819. *Sketches of Louisville and Its Environs.* Louisville.
Meijer, Willem. 1972. *Compositae Family (Asteraceae) in Kentucky.* Lexington: Thomas Hunt Morgan School of Biological Sciences, University of Kentucky.
———. 1976. "Notes on the Flora of the Sinking Creek System and Elkhorn Source Areas in the Inner Bluegrass Region of Kentucky." *Transactions of the Kentucky Academy of Science* 37: 77-84.
Melish, John. 1812. *Travels in the United States of America.* Vol. 2. Philadelphia.
Michaux, François. 1805. *Travels to the Westward of the Alleghany Mountains.* London: J. Mawman.
———. 1871. *The North American Sylva,* 3 vols. 1819; reprint: Philadelphia: W.M. Rutter.
Miller, A.M. 1919. *The Geology of Kentucky.* Frankfort: Kentucky Department of Geology and Forestry, Ser. V, Bull. 2.
Moore, Arthur K. 1957. *The Frontier Mind: A Cultural Analysis of the Kentucky Frontiersman.* Lexington: Univ. of Kentucky Press.
Morse, Jedidiah. 1789. *The American Geography.* Elizabethtown, N.J.: Shepherd Pollock, Printer.
Mull, D.S. 1968. *The Hydrology of the Lexington and Fayette County Area.* U.S. Geological Survey. Lexington: Lexington and Fayette County Planning Commission.
Nosow, Edmund, and A.C. McFarlan. 1960. *Geology of the Central Bluegrass Area.* Lexington: Kentucky Geological Survey and the University of Kentucky.
Nourse, James. 1925. "Journal, 1775." *Journal of American History* 19: 251-52.
Owen, D.D. 1857. *Report of the Geological Survey in Kentucky, Second and Third Reports.* Frankfort.
Palmquist, W.N., Jr., and F.R. Hall. 1961. *Reconnaissance of Groundwater Resources in the Blue Grass Region, Kentucky.* Kentucky Geological Survey Water Supply Paper 1533. Washington, D.C.: U.S. Government Printing Office.
Parry, Needham. 1948. "Diary of a Trip Westward in 1794," ed. L. Beckner, *Filson Club Quarterly* 22:232-37.
Peattie, Donald C., ed. 1940. *Audubon's America.* Boston: Houghton Mifflin Co.
———. 1950. *A Natural History of the Trees of Eastern and Central North America.* Boston: Houghton Mifflin Co.
Perrin, W.H. 1882A. *History of Fayette County, Kentucky.* Chicago: O.L. Baskin.

______. 1882B. *History of Bourbon, Scott, Harrison, and Nicholas Counties, Kentucky.* Chicago: O.L. Baskin.

Peter, Robert. 1882. "Synopsis of the Blue Grass Region." In W. H. Perrin, *History of Fayette County, Kentucky.* Chicago: O. L. Baskin.

Rafinesque, C.S. 1819. "Botany of Kentucky: On Its Principal Features." *Western Review and Miscellaneous Magazine* 1:92-95.

______. 1824. "Florula Kentuckiensis." *First Catalogs and Circulars of the Botanical Garden of Transylvania University in Kentucky,* 12-16. [Lexington, Ky.: Transylvania University.]

Ranck, George W. 1901. *Boonesborough.* Filson Club Publication No. 16. Louisville: John P. Morton.

Sargent, Charles S. 1896. *The Silva of North America,* vol. 8. Boston: Houghton Mifflin.

Schwaab, Eugene L., ed. 1973. *Travels in the Old South.* 2 vols. Lexington: Univ. Press of Kentucky.

Sears, Paul. 1942. "Xerothermic Theory." *Botanical Review* 8:708-36.

Short, Charles Wilkins. 1828-29. "Florula Lexingtoniensis . . . or a Descriptive Catalog of the Phanerogamous Plants Indigenous to This Portion of Kentucky." *Transylvania Journal of Medicine* 1:250-65, 407-22, 560-75; 2: 438-53.

Smith, J. Soule. 1898. *Art Work of the Blue Grass Region of Kentucky.* Oshkosh, Wis.: Art Photogravure Co.

Smith, Leland. 1950. "A History of the Tobacco Industry in Kentucky from 1783 to 1860." Master's thesis, University of Kentucky.

Speed, Thomas. 1886. *The Wilderness Road.* Filson Club. Louisville: John P. Morton.

Spraker, Hazel A. 1922. *The Boone Family.* Rutland, Vt.: Tuttle Co.

Staples, Charles R. 1932. "History in Circuit Court Records, Fayette County." [Record Book A, 1805, abstracted.] *Register of the Kentucky Historical Society* 30:281-92.

______. 1939. *The History of Pioneer Lexington, 1779-1806.* Lexington: Transylvania Press.

Taylor, Philip F. 1975. *A Calendar of the Warrants for Land in Kentucky, Granted for Service in the French and Indian War.* Baltimore: Genealogical Publishing Co.

Thornbury, W.D. 1965. *Regional Geomorphology of the United States.* New York: John Wiley and Sons.

Tinling, Marion, and Godfrey Davies, eds. 1948. *The Western Country in 1793: Reports on Kentucky and Virginia by Harry Toulmin.* San Marino, Calif.: Henry E. Huntington Library.

Townsend, J.W. 1932. *Bradford's Notes on Kentucky.* San Francisco: Grabhorn Press.

Transeau, E.N. 1935. "The Prairie Peninsula." *Ecology* 16:423-37.

Troutman, Richard. 1957. "Stock Raising in the Antebellum Bluegrass." *Register of the Kentucky Historical Society* 55:15-28.

______. 1968. "The Physical Setting of the Bluegrass Planter." *Register of the Kentucky Historical Society* 66:367-77.

______. 1971. "Aspects of Agriculture in the Antebellum Bluegrass." *Filson Club History Quarterly* 45:163-73.

U.S.D.A., Soil Conservation Service. 1968A. *Soil Survey, Fayette County, Kentucky.* Washington, D.C.: U.S. Government Printing Office.

______. 1968B. *Soil Survey, Harrison County, Kentucky.* Washington, D.C.: U.S. Government Printing Office.

———. 1977. *Soil Survey, Scott County, Kentucky.* Washington, D.C.: U.S. Government Printing Office.

Van Couvering, J.A. 1962. *Characteristics of Large Springs in Kentucky.* Frankfort: Kentucky Geological Survey, Ser. X.

Verhoeff, Mary. 1917. *The Kentucky River Navigation.* Filson Club Publication No. 28. Louisville: John P. Morton.

Walker, Felix. 1854. "Journey with the Transylvania Company to Boonesborough in 1775." *DeBow's Review* 2:150-55. [Reprinted by George Ranck in *Boonesborough.* Filson Club Publication No. 16, Louisville: John P. Morton, 1901.]

Webb, W.S., and W.D. Funkhouser. 1928. *Ancient Life in Kentucky.* Frankfort: Kentucky Geological Survey, Ser. VI.

Weir, Gordon W., and Robert C. Greene. 1965. *Clay's Ferry (Ordovician)—A New Map Unit in South-central Kentucky.* U.S. Geological Survey Bulletin 1224-B. Washington, D.C.: U.S. Government Printing Office.

Wharton, Mary E., and Roger W. Barbour. 1971. *A Guide to the Wildflowers and Ferns of Kentucky.* Lexington: Univ. Press of Kentucky.

———. 1973. *Trees and Shrubs of Kentucky.* Lexington: Univ. Press of Kentucky.

Wilson, Alexander. 1832. *American Ornithology,* vols. 1-3. London: Whitaker and Co.; Edinburgh: Stirling and Kenney.

Woods, Neander M., ed. 1905. *The Woods-McAfee Memorial, Containing James and Robert McAfee's Journals, 1773.* Louisville: Courier-Journal Job Printing Co.

Young, Bennett. 1898. *History of Jessamine County from Earliest Settlement to 1898.* Louisville: Courier-Journal Job Printing Co.

Young, Chester R., ed. 1981. *Westward into Kentucky: The Narrative of Daniel Trabue.* Lexington: Univ. Press of Kentucky.

Index of Species

Abutilon theophrasti, 128
Acalypha ostryaefolia, 124; *rhomboidea*, 125; *virginica*, 125
Acanthaceae, 143-44
Accipiter cooperii, 183; *gentilis*, 183; *striatus*, 183
Accipitridae, 183-84
Aceraceae, 126-27
Acer negundo, 51, 52, 54, 58, 61, 126; *nigrum*, 52, 54, 55, 56, 126; *rubrum*, 61, 127; *saccharinum*, 51, 52, 61, 127; *saccharum*, 52, 53, 54, 55, 56, 58, 60, 127, 156
Achillea millefolium, 147
Acipenser fulvescens, 161
Acipenseridae, 161
Acorus americanus, 96; *calamus*, 96
Acris crepitans blanchardi, 172
Actaea pachypoda, 110
Acticis macularia, 181
Actinomeris alternifolia, 155
Adiantum pedatum, 57, 81, 156
Aegilops cylindrica, 84
Aesculus glabra, 22, 52, 53, 54, 56, 58, 127; *octandra*, 22, 53, 54, 127, 156
Aethusa cynapium, 131
Agastache nepetoides, 137, 157
Agave virginica, 54, 100, 156
Agelaius phoeniceus, 199
Agkistrodon contortrix mokeson, 176
Agrimonia parviflora, 117; *pubescens*, 117; *rostellata*, 117
agrimony, 117
Agropyron repens, 84; *smithii*, 84
Agrostemma githago, 108
Agrostis alba, 84; *alba* var. *palustris*, 84; *elliottiana*, 84; *hyemalis*, 84; *perennans*, 84
Ailanthus altissima, 124
Aix sponsa, 179
Aizoaceae, 108
Alaudidae, 188
Alcedinidae, 186
alder, 102
alfalfa, 122
Alisma subcordatum, 83
Alismataceae, 83-84
Alliaria officinalis, 113; *petiolata*, 58, 59, 113
Allium canadense, 97; *cernuum*, 97; *tricoccum*, 57, 98; *vineale*, 58, 98
Alnus serrulata, 102, 156
aloe, false, 100
Alopecurus myosuroides, 84; *pratensis*, 84
alum-root, 116
Alyssum alyssoides, 113
amaranth, purple, 107; thorny, 107
Amaranthaceae, 107
Amaranthus albus, 107; *cruentus*, 107; *graecizans*, 107; *hybridus*, 107; *retroflexus*, 107; *spinosus*, 107; *tuberculatus*, 107
Amaryllidaceae, 100
Ambloplites rupestris, 168
Ambrosia artemisiifolia, 148; *trifida*, 148
Ambystoma barbouri, 67, 170; *jeffersonianum*, 170; *maculatum*, 170; *texanum*, 68
Ambystomatidae, 170
Ameiurus melas, 165; *natalis*, 165; *nebulosus*, 165
Amelanchier arborea, 117, 156
Ammocrypta pellucida, 168-69
Ammodramus henslowii, 197; *leconteii*, 197; *savannarum*, 197
Ampelopsis arborea, 127; *cordata*, 127
Amphibia, 170-73
amphibians, 74-75, 159, 170-73
Amphicarpa bracteata, 26, 120
Anacardiaceae, 126
Anagallis arvensis, 133
Anas acuta, 178; *americana*, 178; *clypeata*, 178; *crecca*, 178; *discors*, 178; *platyrhynchos*, 178; *rubripes*, 178; *strepera*, 178
Anatidae, 178-79
Andropogon elliottii, 84; *gerardii*, 84; *saccharoides*, 85; *scoparius*, 91; *virginicus*, 85
anemone, false rue, 111; rue, 112; tall, 110
Anemonella thalictroides, 112
Anemone virginiana, 110, 157
angelico, 131
Angiospermae, 83-155
angiosperms, 83-155
angle-pod, 135
Anguilladae, 166
Anguilla rostrata, 166
ani, groove-billed, 184
anise, sweet, 132
Annonaceae, 112
Annona triloba, 20
Antennaria plantaginifolia, 148
Anthemis cotula, 148
Anthoxanthum odoratum, 85
Anthus spinoletta, 182
Apiaceae, 131-32
Apios americana, 120
Aplectrum hyemale, 100
Aplodinotus grunniens, 169
Apocynaceae, 134
Apocynum androsaemifolium, 134; *cannabinum*, 134
Apodidae, 186
apple, 119; crab, 22
apple-of-Peru, 140
Aquilegia canadensis, 55, 110, 157
Arabidopsis thaliana, 113
Arabis canadensis, 113; *hirsuta*, 113; *laevigata*, 113; *perstellata*, 113, 156

Araceae, 96
Araliaceae, 131
Aralia racemosa, 131
Archilochus colubris, 186
Arctium minus, 148
Ardea herodias, 177
Ardeidae, 176-77
Arenaria fontinalis, 108, 156; *interpres*, 181; *patula*, 55, 108, 157; *patula* var. *robusta*, 108; *serpyllifolia*, 108
Argenome alba, 112
Arisaema atrorubens, 57, 96; *dracontium*, 96
Aristida oligantha, 85
Aristolochiaceae, 105
Aristolochia serpentaria, 105
Arrhenatherum elatius, 85
arrowhead, 83, 84
arrow-wood, 146
Artemisia annua, 148; *vulgaris*, 148
artichoke, Jerusalem, 152
Aruncus dioicus, 117
Arundinaria gigantea, 26, 52, 85
Asarum canadense, 57, 105; var. *acuminata*, 105
Asclepiadaceae, 134-35
Asclepias incarnata, 61, 134; *quadrifolia*, 134; *syriaca*, 134; *tuberosa*, 134; *verticillata*, 134; *viridis*, 134
Asclepiodora viridis, 134
ash, 19, 20, 23, 27, 28, 52, 53, 54, 55, 56; "black," 19, 20, 22; blue, 19, 20, 21, 22, 26, 28, 29, 30, 31, 52, 53, 54, 58, 59, 60, 134; green, 19, 61, 134; red, 133; white, 19, 20, 22, 28, 29, 30, 52, 53, 54, 57, 58, 59, 61, 133
Asimina triloba, 52, 112
Asio flammeus, 185
asparagus, 98
Asparagus officinalis, 98
Aspidiaceae, 82-83
Aspleniaceae, 82
Asplenium X *ebenoides*, 82; *platyneuron*, 82; *resiliens*, 82, 156; *rhizophyllum*, 55, 82; *ruta-muraria*, 56, 82, 156; *trichomanes*, 82
asters, 148-49
Asteraceae, 147-56
Aster cordifolius, 148; *divaricatus*, 148; *drummondii*, 148; *lateriflorus*, 148; *macrophyllus*, 148; *novae-angliae*, 148; *oblongifolius*, 55, 148, 157; *ontarionis*, 148; *patens*, 148; *pilosus*, 52, 149; *prenanthoides*, 149; *schreberi*, 149; *shortii*, 53, 59, 149; *tataricus*, 149
Astilbe biternata, 116
Astranthium integrifolium, 61, 149
Atherinidae, 167
Athyrium pycnocarpon, 82
Aureolaria virginica, 141
avens, 118
Aves, 176-201
Aythya affinis, 179; *americana*, 179; *collaris*, 179; *marila*, 179; *valisineria*, 179

baby's-breath, wild, 108
badger, 34, 35
balm, lemon, 138
balsam-apple, 147
Balsaminaceae, 127
baneberry, 110
Barbarea verna, 113; *vulgaris*, 58, 113
barley, 46; little, 88
Bartramia longicauda, 182
basil, 139
bass, 65; largemouth, 70, 167; rock, 168; smallmouth, 167; spotted, 167; striped, 167; white, 167
basswood, 52, 53, 54, 56, 61, 128
bats, 65, 70-71; big brown, 71, 72, 203; brown, 34, 35; eastern big-eared, 77; evening, 203; gray, 70, 71, 202; hoary, 203; Indiana, 71, 202; little brown, 72, 202; red, 203; silver-haired, 202
beadgrass, 90
bean, 46; wild, 122
bear, 33, 34, 35, 37, 77
beardgrass, 85
beard-tongue, 142
beaver, 34, 35, 65, 69, 77, 204
bedstraw, 144, 145
bee, 39
beech, 20, 26, 52, 53, 54, 103; blue, 102
beech-drops, 143
beggar's-lice, 137
beggar-ticks, 149
Belamcanda chinensis, 100, 156
bellflower, tall, 147
bellwort, 99
Berberidaceae, 112
bergamot, wild, 139
"Bettywood," 20
Betulaceae, 102
Bidens aristosa, 149; *bipinnata*, 149; *cernua*, 61, 149; *comosa*, 149; *connata*, 149; *discoidea*, 149; *frondosa*, 61, 149; *laevis*, 149; *polylepis*, 149; *tripartita*, 149; *vulgata*, 149
Bignonia capreolata, 143
Bignoniaceae, 143
bindweed, black, 105; hedge, 135; small, 135
birds, 69, 75-77, 159, 176-201
bird's rape, 114
bishop's-cap, 117
bison, 1, 32, 33, 35, 33, 36, 37, 38, 39, 48, 49, 60, 77, 208
bittercress, 114
bittern: American, 69, 176; least, 69, 176
bittersweet, 54, 126; nightshade, 141
blackberries, 57, 120
blackbird: Brewer's, 200; red-winged, 69, 199; rusty, 199; yellow-headed, 199
black-eyed Susan, 153
bladdernut, 53, 126
bladder-pod, 115
Blarina brevicauda kirtlandi, 35, 202
blazing star, 153
Blephilia ciliata, 137, 157; *hirsuta*, 137
bloodleaf, 107
bloodroot, 113
bluebells, Virginia, 137
bluebird, 63, 190
blue-eyed Mary, 141
bluegill, 70, 167
bluegrass, 2, 23, 26, 27, 48; annual, 90; Canada, 90; Kentucky, 90; rough, 90; woodland, 90
bluestem: big, 84; little, 91
blueweed, 137
bobcat, 77, 206
bobolink, 63, 199
bobwhite, 184
Boehmeria cylindrica, 104
Bombycilla cedrorum, 192
Bombycillidae, 192
Bonasa unbellus, 184
boneset, 149, 151
Boraginaceae, 136-37
Botaurus lentiginosus, 176
Botrychium dissectum var. *obliquum*, 81; *virginianum*, 57, 81
bouncingbet, 109
brachiopods, 33
Brachyelytrium erectum, 85
Branta canadensis, 178
Brassicaceae, 113-16
Brassica napus, 114; *nigra*, 114; *rapa*, 114
Brickellia eupatorioides, 149, 157; var. *corymbulosa*, 149
brome, 85

Bromus arvensis, 85; *catharticus*, 85; *ciliatus*, 85; *commutatus*, 85; *inermis*, 85; *japonicus*, 85; *purgans* forma *laevivaginatus*, 85; *purgans*, 85; *secalinus*, 85; *tectorum*, 86
broom-rape, 143
Broussonetia papyrifera, 104
bryozoa, 33
Bubo virginianus, 185
Bubulcus ibis, 177
Bucephala albeola, 179; *clangula*, 179
Buchloe, 26
buckberry, 57, 58, 146
buckeye, 19, 20, 23, 26, 54, 56; Ohio, 22, 29, 30, 52, 53, 58, 127; yellow, 22, 53, 127
buckhorn, 144
buckthorn, 58, 127
buckwheat, 106
buffalo. *See* bison
buffalo (fish), 162
buffalo-bur, 141
buffalo-nut, 105
bufflehead, 179
Bufo a. americanus, 172; *woodhousii fowleri*, 172
Bufonidae, 172
bugbane, 110
bugle-weed, 138
bullfrog, 65, 66, 68, 69, 172
bullhead, 70, 165
bulrush, 96
bunting: indigo, 64, 196-97; snow, 199
Bupleurum rotundifolium, 131
burbot, 66, 74, 166
bur-cucumber, 147
burdock, 148
bur-marigold, 149
Buteo jamaicensis, 183; *lagopus*, 184; *lineatus*, 183; *platypterus*, 183
Butorides striatus, 177
butter-and-eggs, 141
buttercup, 111, 112
butterfly-weed, 134
butternut, 52, 102
butterweed, 154
buttonbush, 144
buttonweed, 144, 145
Buxaceae, 125

Cacalia atriplicifolia, 150; *muhlenbergii*, 150
Cactaceae, 130
Cadidae, 166
Calcarius lapponicus, 199
Calidris alpina, 181; *fuscicollis*, 182; *himantopus*, 181; *mauri*, 181; *melanotos*, 182; *minutilla*, 181-82; *pusilla*, 181
Calystegia sepium, 135; *spithamaea*, 135
Camassia scilloides, 98, 156
Camelina microcarpa, 114
Campanula americana, 53, 59, 147
Campanulaceae, 147
campion: bladder, 109; red, 109; starry, 109; white, 109
Campostoma anomalum, 165
Campsis capreolata, 157; *radicans*, 57, 143
Camptosorus rhizophyllus, 82
cancer-root, 143
cane, 2, 20, 23, 24, 25, 26, 28, 32, 36, 37, 46, 52, 85
Canidae, 205-6
Canis dirus, 35; *latrans*, 205
Cannabinaceae, 104
Cannabis sativa, 104
canvasback, 179
Caprifoliaceae, 145-46
Caprimulgidae, 185-86
Caprimulgus carolinensis, 185; *vociferus*, 185-86
Capsella bursa-pastoris, 114
Carassius auratus, 163
Cardamine bulbosa, 56, 114; *douglassii*, 53, 114; *flexuosa*, 114; *hirsuta*, 114; *parviflora*, 114; *pensylvanica*, 114
cardinal, 196
cardinal flower, 147
Cardinalis cardinalis, 196
Carduelis flammea, 201; *pinus*, 201; *tristis*, 201
Carduus acanthoides, 150; *arvensis*, 150; *discolor*, 150; *lanceolatus*,150; *nutans*, 150
Carex aggregata, 156; *albursina*, 92; *amphibola*, 61, 92; *amphibola* var. *rigida*, 92; *amphibola* var. *turgida*, 92; *annectans*, 92; *artitecta*, 92; *blanda*, 61, 92; *bromoides*, 92; *careyana*, 92; *cephalophora*, 61, 92; *communis*, 92; *complanata*, 92; *conjuncta*, 61, 92; *cristatella*, 92; *davisii*, 92, 156; *eburnea*, 92, 156; *festucacea*, 92; *flaccosperma*, 93; *frankii*, 61, 93; *gracilescens*, 93; *granularis*, 93; *gravida*, 93; *grayii*, 93; *hirsutella*, 93; *hitchcockiana*, 93; *hyalinolepis*, 93; *jamesii*, 61, 93; *laevivaginata*, 93; *laxiculmis*, 93; *laxiflora*, 93; *leavenworthii*, 61, 93; *lupulina*, 61, 93; *lurida*, 61, 93; *mesochorea*, 93; *muhlenbergii*, 93, 156; *muhlenbergii* var. *enervis*, 94; *normalis*, 61, 94; *oligocarpa*, 94, 156; *pensylvanica*, 94; *picta*, 94; *plantaginea*, 94; *platyphylla*, 94; *prasina*, 94; *retroflexa*, 94; *rosea*, 94; *rostrata*, 94; *shortiana*, 61, 94; *sparganioides*, 94; *spicata*, 94; *squarrosa*, 94; *stipata*, 61, 94; *texensis*, 94; *tribuloides*, 94; *umbellata*, 95; *vulpinoidea*, 61, 95; *wildenowii*, 95; *woodii*, 95, 156
caribou, 33
carp, 163
carpet-weed, 108
Carphophis amoenus helenae, 174
Carpinus caroliniana var. *virginiana*, 53, 58, 102
Carpiodes carpio, 162; *cyprinus*, 162; *velifer*, 162
Carpodacus mexicanus frontalis, 201; *purpureus*, 201
carpsucker, 162
carrion-flower, 99
carrot, wild, 131
Carya cordiformis, 53, 54, 56, 58, 102; *glabra*, 53, 54, 55, 102; *laciniosa*, 22, 28, 52, 53, 54, 58, 60, 61, 102; *ovalis*, 53, 54, 55, 56, 102; *ovata*, 53, 55, 56, 60, 102; *tomentosa*, 102
Caryophyllaceae, 108-10
Casmerodius albus, 177
Cassia fasciculata, 120; *marilandica*, 120
Castor canadensis carolinensis, 204
Castoridae, 204
catalpa, 143
Catalpa bignonioides, 143; *speciosa*, 143
catbird, 191
catbrier, 99
catchfly, 109
catfish: blue, 165; channel, 70, 165; flathead, 165-66
Cathartes aura, 183
Cathartidae, 183
Catharus fuscescens, 191; *guttatus*, 191; *minimas*, 191; *ustulata*, 191
catnip, 139
Catostomidae, 162-63
Catostomus commersoni, 162
cattail, 83
cattle, 40, 49, 50
Caulophyllum thalictroides, 22, 112

Ceanothus americanus, 54, 127
cedar, 20, 51, 52, 53, 55, 56; red, 53, 57, 64, 83; Virginia, 20
celandine, 113
Celastraceae, 126
Celastrus scandens, 54, 126
Celtis laevigata, 103; *occidentalis*, 28, 52, 54, 55, 56, 57, 58, 60, 61, 103; *tenuifolia*, 57, 103; *tenuifolia* var. *georgiana*, 104
Centaurea maculosa, 150; *nigra*, 150; *solstitialis*, 150
Centrarchidae, 167-68
Cephalanthus occidentalis, 144
cephalopods, 33
Cerastium arvense, 108; *glomeratum*, 108; *nutans*, 109; *viscosum*, 108, 109; *vulgatum*, 109
Cerasus virginiana, 21
Cercis canadensis, 53, 54, 57, 58, 120
Certhia americana, 189
Certhiidae, 189
Cervidae, 206
Ceryle alcyon, 186
Chaenorrhinum minus, 141
Chaerophyllum procumbens, 131; *tainturieri*, 131
Chaetura pelagica, 186
Charadriidae, 180
Charadrius semipalmatus, 180; *vociferus*, 180
Chasmanthium latifolium, 86
chat, 64, 196
cheat, 85, 86
cheeses, 128
Chelidonium majus, 113
Chelone glabra, 61, 141
Chelydra s. serpentina, 173
Chelydridae, 173
Chen caerulescens, 178
Chenopodiaceae, 107
Chenopodium album, 107; *ambrosioides*, 107; *gigantospermum*, 107; *hybridum* var. *gigantospermum*, 107; *hybridum* var. *standleyanum*, 107; *missouriensis*, 107; *murale*, 107; *paganum*, 107; *standleyanum*, 107
cherry: black, 52, 119; choke, 119; perfumed, 119; wild, 19, 20, 21, 23, 25, 26, 27, 28, 31, 54, 55, 56, 57, 58, 59, 60, 119
chervil, 131
chickadee, 63, 64, 189
chickweed, 110; common, 109; field, 108; forked, 109; great, 110; jagged, 109; mouse-ear, 108, 109; nodding, 109
chicory, 150
Chimaphila maculata, 133
chipmunk, 65, 203
Chlidonias niger, 182
Chondestes grammacus, 197
Chordeiles minor, 186
Chrysanthemum leucanthemum, 153
Chrysemys picta marginata, 173
chub: bigeye, 163; creek, 163; hornyhead, 163; river, 163; silver, 164; speckled, 163; streamline, 163
chuck-will's-widow, 185
Cichorium intybus, 150
Ciconiidae, 177
Cicuta maculata, 61, 131
Cimicifuga racemosa, 110
Cinna arundinacea, 86
cinnamon vine, 100
cinquefoil, 118
Circaea lutetiana ssp. *canadensis*, 130; *quadrisulcata*, 130
Circus cyaneus, 183
Cirsium arvense, 150; *discolor*, 150; *vulgare*, 150
Cistothorus palustris, 190; *platensis*, 190
citronella, 138
Cladrastis kentukea, 53, 54, 55, 120, 156, 147; *lutea*, 120
Clangula hyemalis, 179
Claytonia caroliniana, 108; *virginica*, 58, 108, 156
clearweed, 105
cleavers, 144
Clematis dioscoreifolia, 110; *viorna*, 110; *virginiana*, 110
Clethrionomys gapperi, 35
cliffbrake, 81
clover, 23, 24, 25, 27, 48; alsike, 123; buffalo, 26, 123; bush-, 122; hop, 123; Japanese, 121; Korean, 121; low hop, 123; rabbit-foot, 123; red, 123; running buffalo, 123; white sweet, 122; white, 23, 48, 123; yellow sweet, 122
clubmosses, 81
Clupeidae, 161
Coccothraustes vespertinus, 201
Cocculus carolinus, 112
Coccyzus americanus, 185; *erythropthalmus*, 185
cocklebur, 155
coffee tree, Kentucky, 20, 21, 25, 28, 29, 30, 31, 52, 53, 54, 55, 58, 121
cohosh: black, 110; blue, 22, 112
Colaptes auratus, 186
Colinus virginianus, 184
Collinsia verna, 141
Collinsonia canadensis, 53, 138
Coluber constrictor priapus, 175; *c. constrictor*, 174-75
Colubridae, 174-75
Columba livia, 184
Columbidae, 184
columbine, 110
columbo, American, 134
Comandra umbellata, 105
comfrey, 136
Commelinaceae, 97
Commelina communis, 97; *diffusa*, 97; *virginica*, 97
composites, 80, 147-55
coneflower, 153; prairie, 153
Conium maculatum, 58, 131
Conobea multifida, 141
Conopholis americana, 143
Conringia orientalis, 114
Contopus borealis, 187; *virens*, 187
Convolvulaceae, 135-36
Convolvulus arvensis, 13; *pellitus* forma *anestius*, 135; *sepium*, 135; *spithamaeus*, 135
Conyza canadensis, 150
coot: American, 180
copperhead, 65, 75, 176
Coragyps atratus, 183
Corallorhiza odontorhiza, 100; *wisteriana*, 100
coral-root, 100
cormorant, 176
corn, broom, 46
corn, 91
Cornaceae, 132-33
corn cockle, 108
corn salad, 147
Cornus alternifolia, 132; *amomum*, 132; *drummondi*, 133, 157; *florida*, 53, 133; *obliqua*, 133
Coronilla varia, 120
Corvidae, 189
Corvus brachyrhynchos, 189
corydalis, 113
Corydalis flavula, 58, 59, 113
Corylus americana, 20, 22, 102
Cottidae, 169-70
cottontail, 63, 203
cottonwood, 101
Cottus bairdi, 169; *carolinae*, 170
cougar, 77
cowbird, 200
coyote, 205

crab apple, 22
crabgrass, 86
crane, 177-78
crane's-bill, 124
crappie, 70, 168
Crassulaceae, 116
Crataegus, 57, 58; *calpodendron*, 117; *crus-galli*, 117; *intricata*, 117; *margaretta*, 118; *mollis*, 118; *phaenopyrum*, 118; *pruinosa*, 118; *punctata* var. *microphylla*, 118; *rubella*, 118; *uniflora*, 118
crayfish, 66
creeper, brown, 189
creeper, Virginia, 127
Crepis capillaris, 150; *pulchra*, 150
cress: creeping yellow, 116; marsh, 115; mouse-ear, 113; purple, 114; spring, 114; yellow, 115
Cricetidae, 204-5
crinkle-root, 114
crinoids, 33
crossbill, 201
cross-vine, 143
Crotalus h. horridus, 75, 176
Croton capitatus, 125; *monanthogynus*, 125
Crotophaga sulcrostris, 184
crow, 62, 64, 76, 189
crowfoot, 111
crown-beard, 155
Cryptobranchidae, 170
Cryptobranchus a. alleganiensis, 170
Cryptotaenia canadensis, 131
Cryptotis parva parva, 202
cuckoo, 185
Cuculidae, 184-85
Cucurbitaceae, 147
cudweed, 152
cuphea, 130
Cuphea petiolata, 130; *viscosissima*, 130
Cupressaceae, 83
Cuscuta campestris, 135; *epithymum*, 135; *gronovii*, 135; *pentagona*, 135; *polygonorum*, 135
cutgrass, 88
Cyanocitta cristata, 189
Cymbalaria muralis, 141
Cynanchum laeve, 135
Cynodon dactylon, 86
Cynoglossum officinale, 136; *virginianum*, 136
Cyperaceae, 92-96
Cyperus aristatus, 95; *densicaespitosus*, 95; *diandrus*, 95; *esculentus*, 95; *flavescens* var. *poaeformis*, 95; *lancastriensis*, 95; *refractus*, 95; *rivularis*, 95; *strigosus*, 61, 95; *tenuifolius*, 95
cypress, bald, 157, 158
Cyprinidae, 163-65
Cyprinus carpio, 163
Cystopteris bulbifera, 56, 82, 83, 156; *fragilis*, 82, 83; *fragilis* var. *protrusa*, 82; *protrusa*, 53, 82; *tennesseense*, 156; X *tennesseensis*, 83

dace: black-nosed, 163; southern redbelly, 163
Dactylis glomerata, 86
daisy: oxeye, 153; Peruvian, 151; western, 149
dandelion, 155
Danthonia sericea, 86; *spicata*, 86
darter: banded, 169; blackside, 168; bluestripe, 168; channel, 168; dusky, 168; eastern sand, 168-69; emerald, 169; fantail, 169; gilt, 168; greenside, 169; johnny, 169; longhead, 168; orangethroat, 169; rainbow, 169; river, 168; slenderhead, 168; spotted, 169; Tippecanoe, 169; variegate, 169
Dasistoma macrophylla, 141
Datura stramonium, 140
Daucus carota, 131
dayflower, 97
day-lily, 98
dead-nettle, 138
deer, 1, 32, 33, 34, 35, 36, 37, 38, 39, 49, 62, 64, 77, 206
deerberry, 133
deermouse, 62, 63-64, 65, 70, 72, 204
Delphinium ajacis, 110; *tricorne*, 53, 59, 111
Dendroica caerulescens, 193; *castanea*, 194; *cerulea*, 194; *coronata*, 194; *discolor*, 194; *dominica*, 194; *fusca*, 194; *magnolia*, 194; *palmarum*, 195; *pensylvanica*, 194; *petechia*, 195; *pinus*, 195; *striata*, 194; *tigrina*, 194; *virens*, 194
Dentaria diphylla, 57, 114; *laciniata*, 53, 59, 114, 156
Deschampsia caespitosa var. *glauca*, 86; *flexuosa*, 86
Descurainia pinnata, 114; *sophia*, 114
Desmanthus illinoensis, 121
Desmodium cuspidatum, 121; *glabellum*, 121; *glutinosum*, 121; *laevigatum*, 121; *nudiflorum*, 121; *obtusum*, 121; *paniculatum*, 121; *pauciflorum*, 121; *perplexum*, 121; *rigidum*, 121; *rotundifolium*, 121
Desmognathus f. fuscus, 170
dewberries, 120
Diadophis punctatus edwardsii, 174
Dianthus armeria, 109
Diarrhena americana, 53, 86
Dicentra canadensis, 57, 113; *cucullaria*, 57, 113
Dichanthelium boscii, 26, 86; *clandestinum*, 26, 86; *commutatum*, 26, 86
dickcissel, 63, 199
Dicotyledoneae, 101-56
dicotyledons, 101-55; herbaceous, most significant, 157
Didelphidae, 202
Didelphis v. virginiana, 202
Digitaria ischaemum, 86; *sanguinalis*, 86
Diodia teres, 144; *virginiana*, 144
Dioscorea batatas, 100; *quaternata*, 100; *villosa*, 100
Dioscoreaceae, 100
Diospyros virginiana, 57, 133
Diplotaxis muralis, 114; *tenuifolia*, 115
Dipsacaceae, 147
Dipsacus fullonum, 147; *sylvestris*, 147
Dirca palustris, 130
dock, 106
dodder, 135
Dodecatheon meadia, 56, 133
dog, 34
dogbane, 134
dogberry, 117
dogfennel, 148
dogwood: alternate-leaf, 132; flowering, 20, 22, 53, 133; pale, 133; rough-leaf, 133; silky, 132
Dolichonyx oryzivorus, 199
Dorosoma cepedianum, 161; *petenense*, 161
dove, 63, 76; mourning, 184; rock, 77, 184
dowitcher, 181
Draba ramosissima, 115, 156; *verna*, 115
dragonhead, 139
dropseed, 91
drum, 169
Drycocopus pileatus, 187
Dryopteris marginalis, 57, 83
Duchesnea indica, 118
duck-potato, 84

ducks, 66, 69; American black, 178; ring-necked, 179; ruddy, 178; wood, 66, 69, 179
duckweed, 96
Dumatella caroliensis, 191
dunlin, 181
Dutchman's-breeches, 113

eagle: bald, 77, 183; golden, 77
Ebenaceae, 133
Echinacea purpurea, 150
Echinochloa crusgalli, 86; *muriata*, 87; *pungens*, 87
Echinocystis lobata, 147
Echium vulgare, 137
Eclipta alba, 150
eel, 166
egret: cattle, 177; great, 177; snowy, 177
Egretta caerulea, 177; *thula*, 177
Elaphe o. obsoleta, 175
elder, box, 19, 21, 31, 51, 52, 58, 59, 61, 126
elderberry, 51, 52, 146
elecampane, 152
Eleocharis calva, 95; *engelmanni*, 95; *erythropoda*, 95; *obtusa*, 61, 95; *palustris*, 61
Elephantopus carolinianus, 150
elephant's-foot, 150
Eleusine indica, 87
elk, 1, 32, 33, 34, 35, 36, 37, 38, 48, 49, 208
elm, 19, 20, 23, 25, 38, 51, 54, 55, 56; American, 29, 52, 53, 57, 58, 59, 60, 61, 104; cork, 104; red, 21; rock, 54, 104; September, 104; slippery, 20, 22, 53, 104; winged, 104
Elymus canadensis, 87; *glaucus*, 87; *riparius*, 87; *svensonii*, 87; *villosus*, 26, 87; *virginicus*, 26, 87
Emberizidae, I, 193-96; II, 196-99; III, 199-200
Empidonax flaviventris, 188; *minimus*, 188; *virescens*, 188
empress-tree, 142
Emydidae, 173
enchanter's nightshade, 130
Epifagus virginiana, 143
Epilobium coloratum, 61, 130; *hirsutum*, 130
Eptesicus f. fuscus, 203
Equisetaceae, 81
Equisetineae, 81
Equisetum arvense, 81; *hyemale* var. *affine*, 81
Equus, 35
Eragrostis capillaris, 87; *cilianensis*, 87; *frankii*, 87; *hypnoides*, 87; *pectinacea*, 87; *pilosa*, 87
Erectites hieracifolia, 151
Eremophila alpestris, 188
Ericaceae, 133
Ericymba buccata, 165
Erigenia bulbosa, 131
Erigeron annus, 151; *canadensis*, 150; *philadelphicus*, 151; *pulchellus*, 151; *strigosus*, 151
Erithizon dorsatum, 35
Erophila verna, 115
Erysimum aspera, 115; *repandum*, 115
Erythronium albidum, 53, 98, 156; *americanum*, 53, 98
Esocidae, 161
Esox americanus vermiculatus, 161; *lucius*, 161; *masquinongy*, 161-62
Etheostoma baileyi, 169; *blennioides*, 169; *caeruleum*, 169; *flabellare*, 169; *maculatum*, 169; *nigrum*, 169; *spectabile*, 169; *tippecanoe*, 169; *variatum*, 169; *zonale*, 169
eulalia, 88
Eulalia viminius, 88
Eumeces fasciatus, 174; *laticeps*, 174
euonymus, 126
Euonymus alatus, 126; *americanus*, 126; *atropurpureus*, 58, 59, 126; *fortunei*, 126; *kiautechovicus*, 59, 126; *obovatus*, 53, 126
Eupatorium altissimum, 151; *aromaticum*, 151; *coelestinum*, 52, 151; *fistulosum*, 151; *incarnatum*, 151, 157; *perfoliatum*, 61, 151; *purpureum*, 151; *rugosum*, 151; *serotinum*, 151; *sessilifolium*, 151
Euphagus carolinus, 199; *cyanocephalus*, 200
Euphorbiaceae, 124-25
Euphorbia chamaesyce, 125; *commutata*, 125; *corollata*, 125; *dentata*, 125; *heterophylla*, 125; *maculata*, 125; *marginata*, 125; *supina*, 125
Eurycea b. bislineata, 171; *l. longicauda*, 171; *lucifuga*, 171
everlasting, 151
excluded species, 157-58
eyebane, 125

Fabaceae, 120-23
Fagaceae, 103
Fagus grandifolia, 52, 53, 54, 103; var. *caroliniana*, 103
Falco columbarius, 184; *peregrinus*, 184; *sparverius*, 184
falcon, 65, 77, 184
Falconidae, 184
false mermaid, 125
fawn-lily, 98
Felidae, 206
ferns, 80, 81-83; most significant, 156; adder's-tongue, 81; bulblet, 82; Christmas, 83; fragile, 82; glade, 82; grape-, 81; maidenhair, 81; marginal shield-, 83; rattlesnake, 81; resurrection, 82; sensitive, 83; sweet, 148; walking, 82
fescue, 29; meadow, 88; nodding, 87; red, 88; sheep's, 87; six-weeks, 92; tall, 88
Festuca elatior, 88; *obtusa*, 87; *octoflora*, 92; *ovina*, 87; *paradoxa*, 87; *pratensis*, 29, 88; *rubra*, 88
figwort, 142
Filicineae, 81-83
Fimbristylis autumnalis, 95
finch, 77, 201
fire-on-the-mountain, 125
fire-pink, 109, 110
fireweed, 151
fishes, 69, 74, 159, 160-70
flax, 123; false, 114
fleabane, 151
flicker, 186
Floerkea proserpinacoides, 125
flycatcher: Acadian, 188; great crested, 187; least, 188; olive-sided, 187; scissor-tailed, 187; yellow-bellied, 188
flying squirrel, 64, 72, 204
foamflower, 117
fog-fruit, 137
forget-me-not, 137
fox, 65; gray, 63, 64, 70, 206; red, 63, 64, 205
foxglove: false, 141; mullein, 141
foxtail, 84, 91; meadow, 84
Fragaria virginiana, 118
Fraxinus, 28; *americana*, 28, 53, 54, 55, 56, 57, 58, 60, 61, 133; *americana* var. *biltmoreana*, 133; *nigra*, 19; *pennsylvanica*, 133; *pennsylvanica* var. *subintegerrima*, 61, 134; *quadrangulata*, 21, 53, 54, 55, 56, 58, 60, 134, 157; *sambucifolia*, 19
Fringillidae, 201
frogs, 64, 69, 74-75;

Blanchard's cricket, 172; bronze, 66, 68, 69, 172; bull-, 66, 68, 69, 172; chorus, 75, 159; Cope's gray tree, 65, 66, 172-73; mountain chorus, 75, 159; northern leopard, 172; northern spring peeper, 66, 68, 69, 75, 172-73; pickerel, 66, 69, 71, 172; southern leopard, 66, 68, 69; 172; tree, 172-73
Fulica americana, 180
Fumariaceae, 113
Fundulidae, 166
Fundulus catenatus, 166; *notatus*, 166

gadwall, 178
Galearis spectabilis, 100
Galinsoga ciliata, 151
Galium aparine, 58, 144; *circaezans*, 144; *concinnum*, 144; *lanceolatum*, 144; *obtusum*, 145; *pedemontanum*, 145; *pilosum*, 145; *tinctorium*, 145; *triflorum*, 145
Gallinago gallinago, 181
Gallinula chloropus, 180
gallinule, 180
Gambusia affinis, 166
gar, 161
garlic: false, 98; field, 98; wild, 97
Gaura biennis, 130
Gavia immer, 176
Gaviidae, 176
gentian, horse- 146
Gentianaceae, 134
Geomys sp., 35
Geothlypis trichas, 196
Geraniaceae, 124
geranium, wild, 124
Geranium carolinianum, 124; *carolinianum* var. *confertiflorum*, 124; *columbinum*, 124; *maculatum*, 124; *molle*, 124; *pusillum*, 124
gerardia, 141
Gerardia tenuifolia, 141
germander, 140
Geum canadense, 118; *vernum*, 118
ginger, wild, 105
ginseng, 131
Glaucomys v. volans, 204
Glechoma hederacea, 58, 138; var. *micrantha*, 138
Gleditsia triacanthos, 20, 21, 55, 57, 121
Glyceria melicaria, 88; *striata*, 61, 88
Gnaphalium obtusifolium, 151; *purpureum*, 152
gnatcatcher, 190
goat's-beard, 117, 155; false, 116
golden alexanders, 132
goldeneye, 179
golden-glow, 153
goldenrod, 154
goldenseal, 111
goldfinch, 201
goldfish, 163
Gonolobus gonocarpos, 135; *obliquus*, 135
Goodyera pubescens, 100
goose: Canada, 178; snow, 178
gooseberry, 59, 117
goosefoot, 107
goshawk, 183
grackle, 69, 76, 200
grape, 127, 128
grape-fern, 81
grape-hyacinth, 98
Graptemys geographica, 173
grasses, 23, 24, 28, 32, 47-48, 80; barnyard, 86, 87; bead-, 90; bent, 84; Bermuda, 86; blue-eyed, 100; bottlebrush, 88; buffalo, 23, 25, 26; canary, 90; crab-, 86; cut-, 88; English, 27; goat, 84; goose, 87; grease, 91; husk, 85; Indian, 91; Johnson, 91; love, 87; manna, 88; meadow, 27; melic, 88; munro, 90; oat-, 85, 86; orchard, 86; panic, 89, 90; poverty, 86; quack, 84; rescue, 85; rice, 89; rye, 88; stink, 87; sweet vernal, 85; switch, 90; triple-awn, 85; velvet, 88; wedge, 91; western wheat, 84; whitlow-, 115; witch, 88, 89; wool-, 96; yellow-eyed, 96
Gratiola neglecta, 141; *virginiana*, 141; *viscidula*, 141
grebe: horned, 176; pied-billed, 176; red-necked, 176
Greek valerian, 136
greenbrier, 99
green dragon, 96
gromwell, 137; corn, 137
grosbeak: blue, 196; evening, 201; rose-breasted, 196
ground cedar, 81
ground-cherry, 140
ground-ivy, 138
groundhog, 203
groundnut, 120
ground squirrel, 34, 35
grouse, 64, 77, 184
Gruidae, 177-78
Grus canadensis, 177-78
Guilandina dioica, 20
Guiraca caerulea, 196
gull, 69, 182
gum: black, 132; sour, 132
Gymnocladus canadensis, 21; *dioica*, 21, 28, 52, 53, 54, 55, 58, 60, 121, 157
Gymnospermae, 83
Gyrinophilus porphyriticus duryi, 171

hackberry, 19-20, 21, 26, 28, 29, 52, 54, 55, 56, 57, 58, 59, 60, 61, 103; dwarf, 103
Hackelia virginiana, 137
hairgrass, 86
Haliaeetus leucocephalus, 183
Hamamelidaceae, 117
Hamamelis virginiana, 117
harbinger-of-spring, 131
hare, 33, 35
hare's-ear, 131
harrier, 183
haw: black, 53, 146; southern black, 146
hawk, 62, 63, 64; broad-winged, 183; Cooper's, 183; red-shouldered, 183; red-tailed, 183; rough-legged, 184; sharp-shinned, 183
hawk-beard, 150
hawthorn, 29, 57, 58, 59, 117, 118
hazelnut, 22, 102
heal-all, 139
Hedeoma pulegioides, 138
Hedera helix, 131
Hedyotis longifolia, 145; *nigricans*, 145, 157; *nuttalliana*, 145; *purpurea*, 145; *purpurea* var. *calycosa*, 145
Helenium autumnale, 61, 152
Helianthus annus, 152; *decapetalus*, 152; *divaricatus*, 152; *grosseserratus*, 152; *hirsutus*, 152; *maximiliani*, 152; *microcephalus*, 152; *strumosus*, 152; *tuberosus*, 52, 152
Heliopsis helianthoides, 152
hellbender, 66, 170
Helmitheros vermivorus, 195
Hemerocallis fulva, 98
Hemicarpha micrantha, 96
hemlock: poison, 131; water, 131
hemp, 46, 47, 104; Indian, 134; water, 107
henbit, 138
hepatica, 111
Hepatica acutiloba, 57, 111

heron: black-crowned night, 177; great blue, 65, 177; green-backed, 177; little blue, 177; little green, 65, 69; yellow-crowned night, 177
Hesperis matronalis, 115
Heteranthera dubia, 97; *limosa*, 97
Heterodon platyrhinos, 174
Heuchera americana var. *brevipetala*, 116; *longiflora*, 116; *parviflora*, 116; *villosa*, 55, 116; *villosa* var. *intermedia*, 116; *villosa* var. *macrorhiza*, 116
Hibiscus moscheutos, 128; *oculiroseus*, 128; *palustris*, 128
hickory, 19, 20, 21, 23, 25, 26, 28, 51, 52, 53, 54, 55, 56; bitternut, 29, 31, 53, 54, 58, 102; great shellbark, 52; mockernut, 102; pignut, 29, 53, 102; shagbark, 20, 29, 30, 53, 59, 60, 102; shellbark, 19, 21, 22, 28, 29, 30, 31, 53, 58, 59, 60, 61, 102
Hiodon tergisus, 162
Hiodontidae, 162
Hippocastanaceae, 127
Hirundinidae, 188-89
Hirundo pyrrhonota, 188; *rustica*, 188-89
hog, 39
hog-peanut, 120
hogsucker, 162
hogweed, 150
Holcus lanatus, 88
Holosteum umbellatum, 109
honeysuckle: bush, 145, 146; grape, 145; Japanese, 58, 145; trumpet, 146; wild, 145
honeyvine, 135
hoop ash, 19-20
hoopwood, 19, 20, 23
hop-hornbeam, 102
hops, Japanese, 104
hop-tree, 124
Hordeum pusillum, 88
horehound, 138
hornbeam, 20, 53, 58, 102; hop, 54, 55, 58, 102
horses, 12, 33, 35, 40, 49, 50, 62; Kentucky Saddler, 49; Saddlebred, 209; Standardbred, 209; Thoroughbred, 2, 49, 209-10
horse gentian, 146
horsemint, 138
horsetail, 81
horseweed, 148, 150
hounds-tongue, 136
Houstonia canadensis, 145; *lanceolata*, 145; *nigricans*, 145; *purpurea*, 145; *tenuifolia*, 145
hummingbird, 186
Humulus japonicus, 104
hyacinth, wild, 98
Hybanthus concolor, 129
Hybopsis aestivalis, 163; *amblops*, 163; *dissimilis*, 163; *storeriana*, 164
hydrangea, 117
Hydrangea arborescens, 117
Hydrastis canadensis, 111, 156
Hydrophyllaceae, 136
Hydrophyllum appendiculatum, 136; *canadense*, 136; *macrophyllum*, 53, 58, 136; *virginianum*, 136
Hyla chrysoscelis, 173; *c. crucifer*, 172-73
Hylidae, 172-73
Hylocichla mustelina, 191
Hypentelium nigricans, 162
Hypericaceae, 128-29
Hypericum dolabriforme, 128, 157; *mutilum*, 128; *perforatum*, 128; *prolificum*, 129; *punctatum*, 129; *sphaerocarpum*, 129
Hypoxis hirsuta, 100
hyssop: giant, 137; hedge, 141
Hystrix patula, 88

Ichthyomyzon bdellium, 160; *greeleyi*, 160; *unicuspis*, 160
Ictaluridae, 165-66
Ictalurus furcatus, 165; *punctatus*, 165
Icteria virens, 196
Icterus glabula, 200; *spurius*, 200
Ictiobus bubalus, 162; *cyprinellus*, 162
Iguanidae, 174
Impatiens capensis, 52, 61, 127; *pallida*, 52, 61, 127
Indian-cup, 154
Indian-plantain, 150
Indian tobacco, 147
Inula helenium, 152
Iodanthus pinnatifidus, 56, 115
Ipomoea coccinea, 135; *hederacea*, 135; *lacunosa*, 135; *pandurata*, 136; *purpurea*, 136
Iresine rhizomatosa, 107
Iridaceae, 100
iris, 100
Iris cristata, 100, 156
ironweed, 155
ironwood, 19, 23, 105
Isanthus brachiatus, 138
Isopyrum biternatum, 57, 111, 157
Iva annua, 152; *ciliata*, 152; *xanthifolia*, 152
ivy: English, 131; Kenilworth, 141; poison, 126
Ixobrychus exilis, 176

jack-in-the-pulpit, 96
Jacob's-ladder, 136
jay, 189
Jeffersonia diphylla, 22, 53, 112, 157
Jerusalem artichoke, 152
jewelweed, 127
jimsonweed, 140
Joe-Pye-weed, 151
Juglandaceae, 102
Juglans cinerea, 52, 54, 56, 102; *nigra*, 21, 52, 53, 54, 55, 56, 57, 58, 60, 102, 156
jumpseed, 107
Juncaceae, 97
junco, 198
Junco hyemalis, 198
Juncus dudleyi, 97; *effusus*, 97; *tenuis*, 61, 97; *tenuis* forma anthelatus, 97; *tenuis* var. *uniflorus*, 97
Juniperus virginiana, 53, 55, 56, 57, 83, 157
Jussiaea decurrens, 130; *repens* var. *glabrescens*, 130
Justicia americana, 143

kestrel, 184
killdeer, 180
kingbird, 187
kingfisher, 65, 186
kinglet, 190
kingnut, 102
kingsnake, 64, 175
Kinosternidae, 173
Kinosternon s. subrubrum, 173
knapweed, 150
knotweed, 105; Japanese, 105; Virginia, 107
Kuhnia eupatorioides, 149
Kummerowia stipulacea, 121; *striata*, 121

Labiesthes sicculus, 167
Lactuca biennis, 152; *canadensis*, 152; *floridana*, 153; *saligna*, 153; *scariola*, 153
ladies'-tresses, 101
lamb's-quarters, 107
Lamiaceae, 137-40
Lamium amplexicaule, 138; *purpureum*, 58, 59, 138
Lampetra aepyptera, 160; *lamottei*, 160

lamprey: Allegheny brook, 160; American brook, 160; least brook, 160; Ohio, 160; silver, 160
Lampropeltis getulus niger, 175; *t. triangulum*, 175
Laniidae, 191
Lanius ludovicianus, 191
Laportea canadensis, 61, 104
Laridae, 182
lark, 188
larkspur, 110, 111
Larus argentatus, 182; *delawarensis*, 182; *hyperboreus*, 182; *philadelphia*, 182; *pipixcan*, 182
Lasionycteris noctivagans, 202
Lasiurus b. borealis, 203; *c. cinereus*, 203
Lathyrus latifolius, 122; *sylvestris*, 122
Lauraceae, 112
leaf-cup, 153
leather flower, 110
leatherwood, 130
leek, 98
Leersia oryzoides, 61, 88; *virginica*, 88
legumes, 28
Lemnaceae, 96
Lemna minor, 96
Leonurus cardiaca, 138
Lepidium campestre, 115; *densiflorum*, 115; *ramosissimum*, 115; *virginicum*, 115
Lepisosteidae, 161
Lepisosteus osseus, 161; *platostomus*, 161
Lepomis auritus, 167; *cyanellus*, 167; *gulosus*, 167; *humilis*, 167; *megalotis*, 167; *microlophus*, 167
Leporidae, 203
Leptochloa filiformis, 88
Leptoloma cognatum, 88
Lepus americanus, 35
lespedeza, 122
Lespedeza cuneata, 122; *intermedia*, 122; *procumbens*, 122; *repens*, 122; *stipulacea*, 121; *striata*, 121; *violacea*, 122
Lesquerella globosa, 115, 156
lettuce, 152, 153
Leucanthemum vulgare, 153
Liatris squarrosa, 153
licorice, wild, 144
Ligusticum canadense, 131
Ligustrum ibota, 134
Liliaceae, 97-99
Lilium canadense, 98
lily: blackberry-, 100; Canada, 98
Limnanthaceae, 125
Limnodromus griseus, 181
Linaceae, 123
Linaria vulgaris, 141
linden, 128
Lindera benzoin, 52, 53, 112
Lindernia anagallidea, 142; *dubia*, 61, 142
Linum usitatissimum, 123
Liparis lilifolia, 100
Lippia lanceolata, 137
Liriodendron tulipifera, 53, 56, 60, 112
Lithospermum arvense, 137; *latifolium*, 137
lizard, 64, 71, 72, 75, 174
lizard's-tail, 101
lobelia, 147
Lobelia cardinalis, 61, 147; *inflata*, 147; *siphilitica*, 52, 61, 147; *spicata*, 147
locust, 19, 21, 25, 26; black, 20, 22, 23, 25, 29, 30, 52, 57, 58, 59, 122; honey, 19, 20, 21, 23, 25, 26, 29, 55, 57, 59, 121; "pea," 19; sweet, 21
logperch, 168
Lolium multiflorum, 88; *perenne*, 88
longspur, 199
Lonicera dioica, 145; *dioica* var. *glaucescens*, 157; *japonica*, 58, 145; *maackii*, 59; *maackii* var. *podocarpa*, 145; *prolifera*, 145, 157; *sempervirens*, 146; *standishii*, 146
loon, 176
loosestrife, 130; fringed, 133; lance-leaf, 133
Lophodytes cucullatus, 179
Lophotocarpus calycinus, 84
lopseed, 144
Loranthaceae, 105
Lota lota, 166
Lotus corniculatus, 122
love grass, 87
Loxia curvirostra, 201; *leucoptera*, 201
Ludwigia alternifolia, 130; *decurrens*, 130; *palustris*, 61; *palustris* var. *americana*, 130; *peploides* ssp. *glabrescens*, 130
Luzula echinata, 97
Lychnis alba, 109; *dioica*, 109
Lycium halimifolium, 140
Lycopodiaceae, 81
Lycopodineae, 81
Lycopodium complanatum var. *flabelliforme*, 81; *digitatum*, 81
Lycopus americanus, 61, 138; *virginicus*, 61, 138
"lynn," 19, 20
Lynx rufus, 206
Lysimachia ciliata, 61, 133; *lanceolata*, 133; *nummularia*, 133; *quadrifolia*, 133
Lythraceae, 130
Lythrum salicaria, 130

Maclura pomifera, 57, 58, 104
madtom, 166
Magnoliaceae, 112
mallard, 178
mallow, 128; swamp rose, 128
Malvaceae, 128
Malva neglecta, 128; *rotundifolia*, 128; *sylvestris*, 128
Malvastrum angustrum, 128
Mammalia, 202-6
mammals, 77, 159, 202-6
mammoth, 33, 35
Mammuthus sp., 35
maple, 49, 52, 54, 55, 56; black sugar, 21, 52, 126; red, 61, 127; silver, 31, 127; sugar, 20, 21, 26, 28, 29, 31, 32, 46, 52, 53, 58, 127; water, 61, 51-52, 127
maple-oak-ash forests, 52
Marmota m. monax, 203
Marrubium vulgare, 138
marsh elder, 152
martin, 188
Martyniaceae, 143
mastodon, 33
Matelea gonocarpa, 135; *obliqua*, 135
matrimony vine, 140
may-apple, 112
meadowlark, 199
medic, 122
Medicago lupulina, 122; *sativa*, 122
Meehania cordata, 138
Melanerpes carolinus, 186; *erythrocephalus*, 186
Melica mutica, 88; *nitens*, 88
Melilotus alba, 122; *officinalis*, 122
Melissa officinalis, 138
melonette, 147
Melospiza georgiana, 199; *lincolnii*, 198; *melodi*, 197
Melothria pendula, 147
Menispermaceae, 112
Menispermum canadense, 112
Mentha longifolia, 138; *piperita*, 138; *rotundifolia*, 138; *spicata*, 138
Mephitis mephitis nigra, 206
mercury, 124-25

merganser: common, 179; hooded, 179; red-breasted, 179
Mergus merganser, 179; *serrator*, 179
merlin, 184
Mertensia virginica, 56, 58, 59, 137
Mexican tea, 107
Miami mist, 136
Micropterus dolomieui, 167; *punctulatus*, 167; *salmoides*, 167
Microsorex hoyi, 35
Microtus, 35; *ochrogaster*, 68, 204; *p. pennsylvanicus*, 68, 204; *pinetorum auricularis*, 35, 205; *xanthognathus*, 35
milfoil, 147
milkweed, 134
millet: broom-corn, 89; foxtail, 91
milo, 91
Mimidae, 191-92
mimosa, Illinois, 121
Mimulus alatus, 142; *ringens*, 142
Mimus polyglottos, 191
mink, 65, 69, 60, 206
minnows, 70, 71; bluntnose, 165; bullhead, 165; fathead, 70, 165; silverjaw, 165; suckermouth, 165
mint: hoary mountain-, 139; horse-, 138; pepper-, 138; round-leaved, 138; spear-, 138; wood-, 137
Minytrema melanops, 162
Mirabilis nictaginea, 108
Miscrostegium viminium, 88
mistflower, 151
mistletoe, 105
Mitella diphylla, 117
miterwort, 117
mockingbird, 191
mock-orange, 117
mole: eastern (prairie), 34, 35, 62, 202; hairy-tailed, 160
Mollugo verticillata, 108
molluscs, 33
Molothrus ater, 200
Monarda clinopodia, 139; *fistulosa*, 139; *fistulosa* var. *mollis*, 139
moneywort, 133
monkey-flower, 142
Monocotyledoneae, 83-101
monocotyledons, 83-101; most significant, 156
mooneye, 162
moonseed, 112
moorhen, 180
moose, 33
Moraceae, 104
morning-glory: common, 136; ivy-leaf, 135; red, 135; small white, 135
Morone chrysops, 167; *saxatilis*, 167
Morus alba, 104; *rubra*, 20, 52, 57, 60, 104
mosquitofish, 166
Motacillidae, 192
motherwort, 138
mouse: Bluegrass bog lemming, 63, 68, 205; eastern harvest, 63, 204; golden, 64, 77; house, 62, 72, 205; meadow jumping, 63, 68, 205; prairie deer, 62, 204; white-footed deer, 62, 63-64, 65, 70, 72, 204
Moxostoma anisurum, 162; *carinatum*, 162; *duquesnei*, 162; *erythrurum*, 162-63
mudpuppy, 66, 171
mugwort, 148
Muhlenbergia frondosa, 88; *schreberi*, 89; *sobolifera*, 89; *tenuifolia*, 89
muhly, 88, 89; slender, 89
mulberry, 19, 23; black, 25; paper, 104; red, 21, 52, 57, 104; white, 104
mule, 50
mullein, 142; moth, 142
Muridae, 205
muscadine, 128
Muscari botryoides, 98; *racemosum*, 98
Muscicapidae, 190-91
muskellunge, 66, 74, 161
muskrat, 34, 65, 69, 205
Mus musculus, 205
mustard: black, 114; garlic, 113; hare's-ear, 114; hedge, 116; tansy-, 114; treacle, 115; tumble-, 116
Mustela frenata noveboracensis, 206; *nivalis allegheniensis*, 35, 206; *v. vison*, 206
Mustelidae, 206
Mycteria americana, 177
Myiarchus crinitus, 187
Myiotilta varia, 193
Myosotis arvensis, 137; *macrosperma*, 137; *verna*, 137
Myotis, 35; *grisescens*, 202; *l. lucifugus*, 202; *sodalis*, 202
myrtle, 134

Najadaceae, 83
Najas flexilis, 83
Nasturtium officinale, 115
Necturus m. maculosus, 171
Nelumbo lutea, 110
Nelumbonaceae, 110
Neotoma floridana magister, 204
Nepeta cataria, 139
Nerodia s. sipedon, 175
nettle, 105; false, 104; hedge-, 140; horse-, 141; wood-, 104
New Jersey tea, 54, 127
newt, 64, 68, 171
Nicandra physalodes, 140
nighthawk, 186
nightshade, 141; bittersweet, 141
nimblewill, 89
ninebark, 118
Nocomis biguttatus, 163; *micropogon*, 163
Notemigonus crysoleucas, 163
Nothoscordum bivalve, 55, 98, 156
Notophthalmus v. viridescens, 171
Notorus eleutherus, 166; *flavus*, 66; *miurus*, 166; *nocturnus*, 166
Notropis ardens, 164; *ariommus*, 164; *atherinoides*, 164; *blennius*, 164; *boops*, 164; *buchanani*, 164; *chrysocephalus*, 164; *fumeus*, 164; *photogenis*, 164; *rubellus*, 164; *spilopterus*, 164; *stramineus*, 164; *umbratilis*, 164; *volucellus*, 164-65; *whipplei*, 165
nutgrass, 95
nuthatch, 64, 189
nut trees, 24
Nyctaginaceae, 108
Nyctea scandiaca, 185
Nycticeius h. humeralis, 203
Nycticorax nycticorax, 177; *violaceus*, 177
Nymphaea odorata, 110
Nymphaeaceae, 110
Nyssa sylvatica, 132
Nyssaceae, 132

oak, 19, 20, 23, 25, 26, 28, 31, 51, 52, 53, 54, 55, 56; black, 19, 22, 103; bur, 19, 20, 22, 24, 25, 28, 29, 30, 31, 32, 58, 59, 60, 103; chestnut white, 19, 22; chinquapin, 28, 29, 30, 31, 52, 53, 58-59, 103; overcup, 103; pin, 22; poison, 126; post, 103; quercitron, 19, 103; red, 20, 53, 103; shingle, 103; Shumard, 19, 28, 29, 52, 53, 59, 103; swamp white, 61, 103; white, 19, 20, 21, 22, 30, 53, 103
oak-ash forests, 53
oak-ash-maple forests, 52

oak-cedar forests, 53
oak-hickory forests, 51, 53
oak-hickory-cedar forests, 52
oatgrass, 85, 86
oats, 46
Obolaria virginica, 134
Ocrotomys nuttalli, 75
Odocoileus v. virginianis, 206
Oenothera biennis, 131; *speciosa*, 131
oldsquaw, 69, 179
Oleaceae, 133-34
Onagraceae, 130-31
Ondatra z. zibethicus, 205
onion, nodding wild, 97
Onoclea sensibilis, 83
Onopordum acanthium, 153
Onosmodium hispidissimum, 137, 156
Opheodrys aestivus, 174
Ophioglossaceae, 81
Ophioglossum engelmanii, 81; *pycnostichum*, 81; *vulgatum* var. *pynostichum*, 81
Oporornis agilis, 195; *formosus*, 195; *philadelphia*, 195
opossum, 64, 69, 70, 202
Opuntia humifusa, 130, 157
orchid, cranefly, 101
Orchidaceae, 100-101
orchis, showy, 22, 100
Orchis spectabilis, 22, 100
oriole, 200
Ornithogalum umbellatum, 98
Orobanchaceae, 143
Orobanche ludoviciana, 143; *ramosa*, 143; *uniflora*, 143
Oryzopsis racemosa, 89, 156
Osage orange, 57, 58
osier, 102
Osmorhiza claytoni, 131; *longistylis*, 132
osprey, 65, 184
Osteichthyes, 161-70
Ostrya virginiana, 54, 55, 58, 102
otter, 34, 35, 65, 77
otus asio, 185
ovenbird, 195-96
owl, 62; barred, 185; common barn, 72, 185; eastern screech, 64, 185; great horned, 34, 64, 185; short-eared, 62, 185; snowy, 185
ox, musk, 33
Oxalidaceae, 123-24
Oxalis dillenii, 123; *europea*, 124; *grandis*, 124; *stricta*, 123, 124; *violacea*, 124
Oxyura jamaicensis, 178

Pachysandra procumbens, 125, 157
Pachystoma canbyi, 126, 156
paddlefish, 66, 74, 161
painted leaf, 125
Panax quinquefolium, 131, 156
Pandion haliaetus, 184
Panicum, 26; *agrostoides*, 90; *anceps*, 89; *boscii*, 86; *capillare*, 89; *clandestinum*, 86; *commutatum*, 86; *dichotomiflorum*, 89; *dichotomum*, 89; *flexile*, 89; *gattingeri*, 89; *lanuginosum*, 89; *lanuginosum* var. *implicatum*, 89; *lanuginosum* var. *lindheimeri*, 89; *latifolium*, 89; *laxiflorum*, 89; *linearifolium*, 89; *microcarpon*, 89; *miliaceum*, 89; *philadelphicum*, 90; *rigidulum*, 90; *virgatum*, 90; *xalapense*, 89
pansy, 129
panther, 37, 38
Papaveraceae, 112-13
papaw, 20, 22, 52, 112
parakeet: Carolina, 39; monk, 77
Parascalops breweri, 160
Paridae, 189
Parietaria pensylvanica, 104
Paronychia canadensis, 109
parsley, fool's, 131; hedge-, 132
parsnip: meadow, 132; wild, 132
Parthenium integrifolium, 153
Parthenocissus quinquefolia, 127
partridge-pea, 120
parula, 193
Parula americana, 193
Parus bicolor, 189; *carolinensis*, 189
Paspalum ciliatifolium, 90; *laeve*, 90; *pubiforum* var. *glabrum*, 90
Passerculus sandwichensis, 197
Passer domesticus, 200-201
Passerella iliaca, 198
Passeridae, 200-201
Passerina cyanea, 196-97
Passifloraceae, 129-30
Passiflora incarnata, 129; *lutea* var. *glabriflora*, 130
passion-flower, 129, 130
Pastinaca sativa, 132
Paulonia tomentosa, 142
pea, perennial, 122
peach, 119
pear, 119
pearlwort, 109
peavine, 23, 26, 120
peccary, 35
Pedicularis canadensis, 142
peeper, 66, 68, 69, 75, 172-73
peewee, wood, 65, 187
Pelecanidae, 176
Pelecanus erythrorhynchos, 176
pelican, 176
Pellaea atropurpurea, 56, 81, 156; *glabella*, 81; *glabra*, 156
pellitory, 104
penny-cress, 116
pennyroyal, 138; false, 138
pennywort, 134
Penstemon calycosus, 142; *canescens*, 142; *digitalis*, 142; *hirsutus*, 142; *laevigatus*, 142; *pallidus*, 142
Penthorum sedoides, 61, 117
peppergrass, 115
peppermint, 138
pepper-vine, 127
perch, 169
Percichthyidae, 167
Percidae, 168-69
Percina caprodes, 168; *copelandi*, 168; *cymatotaenia*, 68; *evides*, 168; *macrocephala*, 168; *maculata*, 168; *phoxocephala*, 168; *sciera*, 168; *shumardi*, 168
Percopsidae, 166-67
Percopsis omiscomaycus, 166
Perideridia americana, 132, 156
Perilla frutescens, 139
periwinkle, 134
Peromyscus leucopus, 204; *maniculatus bairdii*, 204
persimmon, 57, 133
Petromyzones, 160
Petromyzontidae, 160
phacelia, 136
Phacelia bipinnatifida, 53, 136; *purshii*, 52, 58, 59, 136
Phalacrocoracidae, 176
Phalacrocorax auritus, 176
Phalaris canariensis, 90
phalarope, 181
Phalaropus fulicarius, 181; *tricolor*, 181
Phaseolus polystachios, 122
Phasianidae, 184
Phasianus colchicus, 184
pheasant, 184
Phenacobius mirabilis, 165
Phenacomys sp., 35
Pheucticus ludovicianus, 196
Philadelphus inodorus, 117
Philomachus pugnax, 182
Phleum pratense, 90
Phlox amplifolia, 136; *bifida*, 156; *bifida* var. *cedaria*, 136;

divaricata, 53, 136, 156; *paniculata*, 136
phlox, 136
phoebe, 65, 71, 187
Phoradendron flavescens, 105
Phoxinus erythrogaster, 163
Phragmites australis, 90; *communis*, 90
Phrymaceae, 144
Phryma leptostachya, 144
Phyllanthus caroliniensis, 125
Physalis angulata, 140; *heterophylla*, 140; *pubescens*, 140; *subglabrata*, 140; *virginiana*, 140
Physocarpus opulifolius, 118, 157
Physostegia virginiana, 139
Phytolacca americana, 108
Phytolaccaceae, 108
Picidae, 186-87
pickerel, 161
Picoides pubescens, 187; *villosus*, 187
Pidoceps grisegena, 176
pigeon, 63, 72, 76, 77 (*see also* dove, rock); passenger, 39, 77
pignut, 102
pigweed, 107
pike, 161
Pilea pumila, 105; var. *deamii*, 105
Pimephales notatus, 165; *promelas*, 165; *vigilax*, 165
pimpernel: false, 142; scarlet, 133; water, 133, 142; yellow, 132
pink: Deptford, 109; fire-, 110; wild, 109
pintail, 178
Pipilo erythrophthalmus, 197
pipistrelle, 34, 35, 70-71, 203
Pipistrellus s. subflavus, 34, 35, 203
pipit, 192
Piranga olivacea, 200; *rubra*, 200
"plane tree," 20
Plantaginaceae, 144
Plantago aristata, 144; *lanceolata*, 144; *major*, 144; *rugellii*, 144; *virginica*, 144
plantain, 144; rattlesnake-, 100; robin's-, 151; water, 83
Platanaceae, 117
Platanus occidentalis, 51, 52, 58, 60, 61, 117
Platygonus compressus, 35
Plecotus rafinesquii, 77
Plectrophenax nivalis, 199
Plethodon d. dorsalis, 170; *g. glutinosus*, 171; *richmondi*, 170
Plethodontidae, 170-71
plover: black-bellied, 180; lesser golden, 180; semipalmated, 180
plum, 26, 57, 119
Pluvialis dominica, 180; *squatarola*, 180
Poa alsodes, 90; *annua*, 90; *autumnalis*, 90; *compressa*, 90; *cuspidata*, 90; *pratensis*, 26-27, 90; *sylvestris*, 90; *trivialis*, 90
Poaceae, 84-92
pocket gopher, 34, 35
Podiceps auritus, 176
Podicipedidae, 176
Podilymbus podiceps, 176
Podophyllum peltatum, 112
Poeciliidae, 166
poison ivy, 126
poison oak, 126
pokeweed, 108
Polemoniaceae, 136
Polemonium reptans, 57, 136
Polioptila caerulea, 190
Polygalaceae, 124
Polygala senega var. *latifolia*, 124
Polygonaceae, 105-7
Polygonatum biflorum, 58, 59, 98; *canaliculatum*, 98; *commutatum*, 98; *pubescens*, 99
Polygonum aviculare, 105; *caespitosum* var. *longisetum*, 105; *convolvulus*, 105; *cuspidatum*, 105; *dubium*, 105; *erectum*, 106; *hydropiper*, 106; *hydropiperoides*, 106; *lapathifolium*, 106; *orientale*, 106; *pensylvanicum*, 106; *persicaria*, 106; *punctatum*, 106; *punctatum* var. *leptostachyum*, 106; *sagittatum*, 106; *scandens*, 106; *scandens* var. *cristatum*, 106
Polymnia canadensis, 53, 153; *uvedalia*, 153
Polyodon spathula, 161
Polyodontidae, 161
Polypodiaceae, 82
Polypodium polypodioides, 82; *virginianum*, 82
polypody, 82
Polystichum acrostichoides, 83
Pomoxis annularis, 168; *nigromaculatus*, 168
pondweed, 83
Pontederiaceae, 97
Pooecetes gramineus, 197
poplar, 20, 21, 25, 56; tulip, 22, 26, 53; white, 101
poppy: celandine, 113; white prickly, 112
Populus alba, 101; *deltoides*, 101
porcupine, 34, 35
Porphyrula martinica, 180
Portulacaceae, 108
Portulaca oleracea, 108
Porzana carolina, 80
Potamogetonaceae, 83
Potamogeton diversifolius, 83; *foliosus*, 83; *nodosus*, 83
potato, 46
potato-vine, wild, 136
Potentilla intermedia, 118; *norvegica*, 118; *recta*, 118; *simplex*, 118
prairie-tea, 125
Prenanthes altissima, 153
prickly ash, 25, 124
pirckly pear, 130
primrose, 131
primrose-willow, 130
Primulaceae, 133
prince's feather, 106
privet, 134
Proboscidea louisianica, 143
Procyonidae, 206
Procyon l. lotor, 206
Progne subis, 188
Proteidae, 171
Protonotaria citrea, 193
Prunella vulgaris, 139; var. *lanceolata*, 139
Prunus americana, 57, 119; *americana* var. *lanata*, 119; *angustifolia*, 119; *avium*, 119; *hortulana*, 119; *mahaleb*, 119; *munsoniana*, 119; *nigra*, 119; *persica*, 119; *serotina*, 21, 52, 54, 55, 56, 57, 58, 119; *virginiana*, 119
Pseudacris brachyphona, 159; *t. triseriata*, 159
Pseudotriton montanus diastictus, 171; *r. ruber*, 171
Ptelea trifoliata, 124
Pteridaceae, 81
pumpkin, 46
purple top, 91
purslane: common, 108; marsh, 130; milk-, 125
pussy-toes, 148
putty-root, 100
Pycnanthemum pycnanthemoides, 139
Pylodictis olivaris, 165-66
Pyrolaceae, 133
Pyrularia pubera, 105
Pyrus communis, 119; *malus*, 119

Queen Anne's-lace, 131
Quercus alba, 19, 53, 55 56, 103; *bicolor*, 61, 103; *borealis* var. *maxima*, 103; *coccinea*, 158; *imbricaria*, 103; *lyrata*, 103; *macrocarpa*, 28, 58, 60, 103, 157; *michauxii*, 158; *montana*, 158; *muehlenbergii*, 19, 22, 28, 52, 53, 54, 55, 56, 58, 59, 60, 103, 157, 158; *rubra*, 53, 54, 55, 56, 103; *shumardii*, 19, 22, 28, 53, 54, 55, 56, 59, 60, 103, 158; *stellata*, 103; *velutina*, 19, 22, 103
quillback, 162
quinine, wild, 153
Quiscalus quiscula, 200

rabbit, 34, 62, 63
raccoon, 34, 37, 62, 64, 65, 69, 70, 72, 106
racer, 62, 63, 65, 174-75
ragweed: common, 148; giant, 148
ragwort, 154
rail, 180
Rallidae, 180
Rallus elegans, 180; *limicola*, 180
Rana catesbeiana, 172; *c. clamitans*, 172; *palustris*, 172; *pipiens*, 172; *sphenocephala*, 172
Ranidae, 172
Ranunculaceae, 110-12
Ranunculus abortivus, 59, 111; *acris*, 111; *aquatilis*, 111; *fascicularis*, 111; *hispidus*, 111; *longirostris*, 111; *micranthus*, 59, 111; *parviflorus*, 111; *recurvatus*, 111; *repens*, 111; *septentrionalis*, 112; *trichophyllus*, 111
raspberries, 120
rat: Norway, 62, 65, 72, 205; eastern wood-, 65, 70, 204
Ratibida pinnata, 153
rattlesnake, 75, 160, 176
rattlesnake-plantain, 100
rattlesnake-root, 153
Rattus norvegicus, 205
raven, 39, 65, 77
redbud, 20, 22, 53, 54, 57, 58, 120
redhead, 179
redhorse, 162
redpoll, 201
redstart, 196
redtop, 84
reed: giant, 90; wood, 86
Regina septemvittata, 160, 175
Regulus calendula, 190; *satrapa, 190*
Reithrodontomys h. humulis, 63, 204
reptiles, 75, 159, 173-76
Reptilia, 173-76
Rhamnaceae, 127
Rhamnus caroliniana, 127; *caroliniana* var. *mollis*, 127; *lanceolata*, 58, 127
Rhinichythys atratulus, 163
Rhus aromatica, 54, 126, 157; *copallina* var. *latifolia*, 126; *glabra*, 57, 126; *radicans*, 126; *toxicodendron*, 126; *typhina*, 126
Rhynchospora capitellata, 96
Ribes cynosbati, 59, 117; *missouriense*, 117
Riparia riparia, 188
robin, 64, 191
Robinia pseudoacacia, 21, 52, 57, 58, 60, 122
robin's-plantain, 151
rockcress, 113
rocket: dame's, 115; purple, 115; sweet, 115; yellow, 113
rockfish, 167
Rorippa islandica var. *fernaldiana*, 115; *palustris* ssp. *fernaldiana*, 115; *sessilifolia*, 115; *sylvestris*, 116
Rosa canina, 119; *carolina*, 119; *eglanteria*, 119; *multiflora*, 119; *palustris*, 119; *setigera*, 120
Rosaceae, 117-20
rose, 119, 120
rose mallow, 128
rosinweed, 155
Rotala ramosior var. *interior*, 130
Rubiaceae, 144-45
Rubus, 57; subgenus *Eubatus*, 120; subgenus *Idaeobatus*, 120; *allegheniensis*, 120; *argutus*, 120; *congruus*, 120; *flagellaris*, 120; *louisianus*, 120; *occidentalis*, 120; *pensilvanicus*, 120; *praepes*, 120
Rudbeckia fulgida, 153; *hirta*, 153; *laciniata*, 52, 153; *triloba*, 153
rue, meadow, 112
Ruellia caroliniensis, 143; *caroliniensis* var. *membranacea*, 144; *humilis*, 144, 157; *strepens*, 144
ruff, 182
Rumex acetosella, 106; *altissimus*, 61, 106; *crispus*, 106; *mexicanus*, 106; *obtusifolius*, 106
running pine, 81
rush, 97; beak-, 96; path, 97; scouring, 81; spike-, 95; wood-, 97
Rutaceae, 124
rye, 24, 25, 26, 27, 48, 87
rye grass, 88

Sabatia angularis, 134
sage, lyre-leaved, 139
Sagina decumbens, 109
Sagittaria australis, 83; *calycina*, 84; *latifolia*, 84; *longirostra*, 84
salamanders, 66, 74-75; Bluegrass small-mouthed, 64, 67-68, 170; cave, 68, 71, 171; eastern zigzag, 64, 71, 170; four-toed, 75; Jefferson's, 68, 170; Kentucky spring, 171; longtail, 171; midland mud, 68, 171; northern dusky, 64, 71, 170; northern red, 68, 171; northern two-lined, 64, 67, 71, 171; ravine (Richmond's), 64, 71, 170; slimy, 64, 71, 171; spotted, 68, 170
Salamandridae, 171
Salicaceae, 101-2
Salix alba, 101; *caroliniana*, 101; *exigua*, 101; *fragilis*, 101; *humilis*, 101; *interior*, 101; *missouriensis*, 101; *nigra*, 59, 101; *purpurea*, 102; *rigida*, 102; *sericea*, 102
Salmo giardneri, 161
Salmonidae, 161
Salvia lyrata, 139
Sambucus canadensis, 51, 52, 146
Samolus parviflorus, 133
sandpiper, 181, 182
sandvine, 135
sandwort, 108
Sanguinarea canadensis, 113, 156
sanicle, 132
Sanicula canadensis, 132; *canadensis* var. *grandis*, 132; *gregaria*, 132; *trifoliata*, 132
Santalaceae, 105
Saponaria officinalis, 109
sapsucker, 186-87
sassafras, 57, 112
Sassafras albidum, 57, 112
Satureja glabella, 139, 157; *vulgaris*, 139
sauger, 168
Saururaceae, 101
Saururus cernuus, 61, 101
sawbrier, 99
Saxifragaceae, 116-17
Saxifraga virginiensis, 55, 58, 59, 117

saxifrage, 117
Sayornis phoebe, 187
Scalopus aquaticus machrinus, 35, 202
Scaphirhynchus platorhynchus, 161
scarlet pimpernel, 133
scaup, 179
Sceloporus undulatus hyacinthinus, 174
Schizachne purpurascens, 91
Schizachyrium scoparium, 91
Sciaenidae, 169
Scincella lateralis, 174
Scincidae, 174
Scirpus americanus, 96; *atrovirens,* 61, 96; *atrovirens* var. *georgianus,* 96; *georgianus,* 96; *lineatus,* 61, 96; *pendulus,* 96; *rubricosus,* 96; *validus,* 61; *validus* var. *creber,* 96
Sciuridae, 203-4
Sciurus c. carolinensis, 203; *niger rufiventer,* 203
Scolopacidae, 180-82
Scolopax minor, 181
Scrophulariaceae, 141-43
Scrophularia marilandica, 142
sculpin, 68, 71, 169, 170
Scutellaria elliptica, 139; *incana,* 139; *lateriflora,* 61, 139; *nervosa,* 139; *ovalifolia* ssp. *hirsuta,* 139; *ovata,* 140; *ovata* ssp. *calcarea,* 139; *ovata* ssp. *versicolor,* 140; *ovata* ssp. *pseudovenosa,* 140; *parvula,* 140, 157; *saxatilis,* 140
sedges, 61, 80; broom, 85; umbrella, 95
Sedum pulchellum, 55, 116, 157; *sarmentosum,* 116; *ternatum,* 55, 116
seedbox, 130
Seiurus aurocapillus, 195-96; *motacilla,* 196; *noveboracensis,* 196
self-heal, 139
Semotilus atromaculatus, 163
Senecio anonymus, 153; *glabellus,* 154; *obovatus,* 53, 154; *smallii,* 153
senna, 120
Serranidae, 167
serviceberry, 117
Setaria faberi, 91; *geniculata,* 91; *glauca,* 91; *italica,* 91; *lutescens,* 91; *verticillata,* 91; *viridis,* 91
Setophaga ruticilla, 196
shad, 161
sheep, 50
shepherd's purse, 114
shiner, 163-65
shooting star, 133
Shorthorn, 49
shoveler, 178
shrews, 64; least, 63, 202; pigmy, 34, 35; short-tailed, 34, 35, 63, 202; smoky, 202; southeastern, 77, 202; water, 33, 35
shrike, 191
shrubs, most significant, 157
Sialis sialis, 190
Sibara virginica, 116
sicklepod, 113
Sicyos angulatus, 147
Sida spinosa, 128
Silene alba, 109; *antirrhina,* 109; *caroliniana* var. *wherryi,* 55, 109; *cucubalus,* 109; *noctiflora,* 109; *rotundifolia,* 109; *stellata,* 109; *virginica,* 53, 110
Silphium perfoliatum, 61, 154; *trifoliatum,* 154
silverside, 167
Simaroubaceae, 124
siskin, 201
Sisymbrium altissimum, 116; *officinale,* 116
Sisyrinchium albidum, 100, 156; *angustifolium,* 100
Sitta canadensis, 189; *carolinensis,* 189
Sittidae, 189
skink: blue-tailed, 64, 72; broad-head, 174; five-lined, 71, 174; ground, 174
skullcap, 139, 140
skunk, 34, 65, 69, 70, 206
slider, 173
sloth, 33
smartweed, 105, 106
Smilacina racemosa, 58, 99
Smilax bona-nox, 99; *ecirrhata,* 99; *glauca,* 99; *herbacea,* 99; *hispida,* 99; *lasioneuron,* 99; *pulverulenta,* 99; *rotundifolia,* 99
snail, 66
snailseed, 112
snakeroot: seneca, 124; small white, 151; Virginia, 105; white, 151
snakes, 69, 75; black king-, 64, 175; black racer, 62, 63, 64, 65, 69, 174-75; black rat, 627, 63, 64, 65, 69, 71, 72, 73, 175; bull, 39; earth, 75; eastern ribbon, 75; eastern hognose, 174; eastern rough green, 65, 174; eastern milk, 62, 63, 64, 65, 69, 71, 72, 73, 175; eastern garter, 62, 68, 69, 71, 73, 175; horned, 39; midwest worm, 64, 71, 174; moccasin, 39; northern ringneck, 64, 71, 174; northern brown, 175; northern water, 66, 69, 175; queen water, 66, 160, 175; red-bellied, 75; timber rattle-, 75, 160, 176
snapdragon, 141
sneezeweed, 152
snipe, common (Wilson's), 68, 181
snow-on-the-mountain, 125
soapwort, 109
Solanaceae, 140-41
Solanum americanum, 141; *carolinense,* 141; *dulcamara,* 141; *nigrum,* 141; *rostratum,* 141
Solidago altissima, 154; *arguta,* 154; *bootii,* 154; *caesia,* 154; *canadensis,* 154; *flexicaulis,* 53, 154; *gigantea,* 154; *graminifolia,* 154; *nemoralis,* 154; *rugosa,* 154; *rupestris,* 154, 156; *sphacelata,* 55, 154, 157; *ulmifolia,* 53, 154
Solomon's-seal, 98, 99; false, 99
Sonchus asper, 154; *oleraceus,* 155
sora, 180
Sorex fumeus, 202; *longirostris,* 77, 202; *palustris,* 35
Sorghastrum nutans, 91
Sorghum bicolor, 91; *halepense,* 52, 91; *vulgare,* 91
Soricidae, 202
sorrel, 106
sow-thistle, 154, 155
spangletop, 88
Spanish needles, 149
sparrows, 63, 77; American tree, 198; chipping, 198; clay-colored, 198; field, 64, 198; fox, 198; grasshopper, 197; Harris's, 198; Henslow's, 63, 197; house (English), 62, 72, 77, 200-201; lark, 197; Leconte's, 197; Lincoln's, 198; savannah, 63, 197; song, 197; swamp, 199; vesper, 197; white-crowned, 198; white-throated, 198
spearmint, 138
Specularia perfoliata, 147
speedwell, 142, 143
Spergula arvensis, 110
Spermacoce glabra, 145
Spermophilus tridecemlineatus, 35
Sphaeralcea angusta, 128

Sphenopholis intermedia, 91; *nitida*, 91; *obtusata*, 91; *pallens*, 91
Sphyrapicus varnius, 186-87
spice bush, 52, 53, 112
spiderwort, 97
spikenard, 131
spike-rush, 95
Spiranthes cernua, 61, 101; *gracilis*, 101; *ovalis*, 101, 156; *tuberosa*, 101; *vernalis*, 101
Spirodela polyrhiza, 96
Spiza americana, 199
Spizella arborea, 198; *pallida*, 198; *passerina*, 198; *pusilla*, 198
spleenwort, 82
Sporobolus asper, 91
spring-beauty, 108
spring peeper, 66, 68, 69, 75, 172-73
spurge, 125
spurrey, 110
squawroot, 143
squaw-weed, 153
squirrel, 62; flying, 64, 72, 204; fox, 62, 203; gray, 34, 64, 72, 203; red, 33, 35
squirrel-corn, 113
Stachys riddellii, 140; *tenuifolia*, 140
Staphyleaceae, 126
Staphylea trifolia, 53, 126
stargrass: water, 97; yellow, 100
starling, 62, 76, 77, 192
star-of-Bethelehem, 98
Stelgidopteryx serripennis, 188
Stellaria corei, 110; *fontinalis*, 108; *media*, 58, 110; *pubera*, 110
Stenanthium gramineum, 99
Sterna antillarum, 182; *forsteri*, 182; *hirundo*, 182
Sternotherus odoratus, 173
stickseed, 137
stinkpot, 173
Stizostedion canadense, 168; *vitreum*, 168
St. John's-wort, 128, 129
stonecat, 166
stonecrop, 116, 117
stoneroller, 165
Storeria d. dekayi, 175; *occipitomaculata*, 75
stork, 177
strawberry: Indian, 118; mock, 118; wild, 118
strawberry-bush, 126
Strigidae, 185
Strix varia, 185
Strophostyles leiosperma, 122; *umbellata*, 122
studfish, 166
sturgeon: lake, 66, 74, 161; shovel-nosed, 66, 74, 161
Sturnella magna, 199
Sturnidae, 192
Sturnus vulgaris, 182
Stylophorum diphyllum, 53, 113
sucker: spotted, 162; white, 162
sugarberry, 103
sugar tree, 19, 20, 23, 25, 27
sumac, 54, 57, 126
sunfish, 167
sunflower, 152; false, 152 tickseed, 149
swallow: bank, 188; barn, 72, 188-89; cliff, 188; northern rough-winged, 188; tree, 188
swan, 34
sweetbrier, 119
sweet cicely, 131, 132
sweet fern, 148
sweet flag, 96
Swertia caroliniensis, 54, 134
swift, 186
sycamore, 19, 51, 52, 58, 6, 117
Sylvilagus floridanus mearnsii, 203
Symphoricarpos orbiculatus, 57, 58, 146
Synandra hispidula, 57, 140, 156
Synaptomys cooperi kentucki, 205

Tachycineata bicolor, 188
Taenidia integerrima, 132
Talpidae, 202
Tamiasciurus hudsonicus, 35
Tamias s. striatus, 203
Tanacetum vulgare, 55
tanager, 64, 200
tansy, 155
tapir, 33
Taraxacum erythrospermum, 155; *officinale*, 155
Taxidea taxus, 35
Taxodium distichum, 157-58
teal, 69, 178
teasel, 147
tern, 69, 182
Terrapene c. carolina, 173
Teucrium canadense, 140
Thalictrum dioicum, 59, 112; *polygamum*, 112; *pubescens*, 112; *thalictroides*, 53, 59, 112
Thamnophis sauritus, 75; *s. sirtalis*, 175
Thaspium barbinode, 53, 132; *trifoliatum*, 132; *trifoliatum* var. *flavum*, 132
thimbleweed, 110
thistle: bull, 150; Canada, 150; cotton, 153; field, 150; nodding, 150; St. Barnaby's, 150; star-, 150
Thlaspi arvense, 116; *perfoliatum*, 116
thorn, cockspur, 117
thoroughwort, 151
thrasher, 191-92
three-square, 96
thrush, 64; gray-cheeked, 191; hermit, 191; Swainson's, 191; wood, 64, 191
Thryomanes bewickii, 190
Thryothorus ludovicianus, 190
Thymelaeaceae, 130
Tiarella cordifolia, 117
tick-trefoil, 121
Tilia, 53, 54, 56; *americana*, 61, 128; *floridana*, 128; *heterophylla*, 52, 128; *neglecta*, 128
Tiliaceae, 128
timothy, 48, 90
Tipularia discolor, 101
titmouse, 63, 64, 189
toadflax, 105
toads, 62, 65, 66, 69, 71, 74-75, 172
tobacco, 46
tooth-cup, 130
toothwort, 114
topminnow, 166
Torilis arvensis, 132; *japonica*, 132
touch-me-not, 127
Tovara virginiana, 107
towhee, 64, 65, 197
Toxostoma rufum, 191-92
Trachemys scripta elegans, 173
Tradescantia subaspra, 53, 59, 97; *virginiana*, 97
Tragia cordata, 125
Tragopogon dubius, 155; *major*, 155; *pratensis*, 155
treefrogs, 65, 66, 172-73
tree-of-heaven, 124
trees, most significant, 157
trefoil, 122
Tridens flavus, 91
Trifolium arvense, 123; *campestre*, 123; *dubium*, 123; *hybridum*, 123; *pratense*, 123; *reflexum*, 26, 123; *repens*, 123; *stoloniferum*, 26, 123
trillium, 99
Trillium flexipes, 57, 99; *flexipes forma walpolei*, 99; *grandiflorum*, 99; *nivale*, 99, 156; *sessile*, 53, 99
Tringa flavipes, 180; *melanoleuca*, 180; *solitaria*, 181

Triodais perfoliata, 147
Triodia flava, 91
Trionychidae, 174
Trionyx spiniferus spiniferus, 174
Triosteum angustifolium, 146; *aurantiacum* var. *illinoense*, 146
Trochilidae, 186
Troglodytes aedon, 189-90; *troglodytes*, 190
Troglodytidae, 189-90
trout, 161
trout-lily, 98
troutperch, 166
trumpet vine, 57, 143
tulip poplar, 112
Turdus migratorius, 191
turkey, 34, 38, 77
turnip, 46, 114
turnstone, 181
turtlehead, 141
turtles, 68, 75; common snapping, 66, 69, 173; eastern box, 64, 65, 68, 71, 173; eastern mud, 173; eastern spiny softshell, 66, 174; map, 66, 173; midland painted, 66, 173
Tutonidae, 185
twayblade, 100
twinleaf, 22, 112
Typhaceae, 83
Typha latifolia, 83
Tyrannidae, 187
Tyrannus forficatas, 187; *tyrannus*, 187; *verticalis*, 187
Tyto alba, 185

Ulmaceae, 103-4
Ulmus alata, 104; *americana*, 51, 52, 53, 54, 56, 57, 58, 60, 61, 104; *rubra*, 53, 104; *serotina*, 104; *thomasi*, 54, 55, 104, 157; *viscosa*, 20
umbrella-wort, 108
unicorn-plant, 143
Uniola latifolia, 86
Urocyon c. cinereoargenteus, 206
Ursus arctos horribilus, 35
Urticaceae, 104
Urtica chamaedryoides, 105; *dioica*, 105; *procera*, 105
urus, 36
Uvularia grandiflora, 99; *perfoliata*, 99

Vaccinium stamineum, 133, 156
valerian, 146
Valerianaceae, 146-47
Valeriana pauciflora, 57, 146
Valerianella, 61; *chenopodifolia*, 147; *radiata*, 147; *umbilicata*, 56, 147
veery, 191
velvet-leaf, 128
Venus' looking-glass, 147
Veratrum woodii, 100
Verbascum blattaria, 142; *thapsus*, 142
Verbenaceae, 137
Verbena hastata, 137; *simplex*, 137; *urticifolia*, 137
Verbesina alternifolia, 52, 155; *helianthoides*, 155; *occidentalis*, 155; *virginica*, 155
Vermivora celata, 193; *chrysoptera*, 193; *peregrina*, 193; *pinus*, 193; *ruficapilla*, 193
Vernonia alissima, 155; *gigantea*, 155
Veronica agrestis, 142; *anagallis-aquatica* var. *anagalliformis*, 142; *arvensis*, 143; *hederaefolia*, 143; *officinalis*, 143; *peregrina*, 143; *serpyllifolia*, 143
vervain, 137
Vespertilionidae, 202-3
vetch, 123; crown, 120
viburnum, 146
Viburnum dentatum, 146; *dentatum* var. *deamii*, 146; *molle*, 146, 157; *prunifolium*, 53, 146; *rafinesquianum*, 146, 157; *rafinesquianum* var. *affine*, 146; *recognitum*, 146; *rufidulum*, 53, 146
Vicia caroliniana, 26, 53, 123; *dasycarpa*, 123; *grandiflora*, 123; *sativa*, 123; *villosa*, 123
Vinca minor, 134
vines, woody, most significant, 157
Viola arvensis, 129; *canadensis*, 129; *cucullata*, 129; *eriocarpa*, 129; *palmata*, 129; *papilionacea*, 52, 58, 59, 129; *pensylvanica*, 53, 129; *pubescens*, 129; *rafinesquii*, 129; *sororia*, 53, 129; *striata*, 52, 58, 129; *triloba*, 129; *triloba* var. *dilatata*, 129; *walteri*, 129, 156
Violaceae, 129
violets, 129; green, 129
Viperidae, 176
vireos, 64, 192-93
Vireo flavifrons, 192; *gilvus*, 192-93; *griseus*, 192; *olivaceus*, 192; *philadelphicus*, 193; *solitarius*, 192
Vireonidae, 192-93
Virginia valeriae, 75
virgin's-bower, 110
Vitaceae, 127-28
Vitis aestivalis, 127; *cinerea*, 128; *rotundifolia*,128; *vulpina*, 128
vole: meadow, 34, 35, 63, 68, 204; pine, 34, 35, 62, 63, 205; prairie, 204; red-backed, 34, 35; spruce, 33-34, 35; yellow-cheeked, 34, 35
Vulpes vulpes, 205
Vulpia octoflora, 92
vulture: black, 65, 183; turkey, 65, 183

wafer ash, 124
wahoo, 58, 59, 126
wake-robin, 99
Waldsteinia fragarioides, 120
walleye, 168
wallflower, 115
walnut, 20, 23, 25, 26, 27, 28, 31, 54, 55, 56; black, 19, 20, 21, 23, 25, 26, 28, 29, 30, 31, 52, 53, 57, 58, 59, 60, 120; white, 19, 20, 21, 26, 102
wall-rocket, 114, 115
wall-rue, 82
wapiti, 37
warbler, 64; bay-breasted, 194; black-and-white, 193; black-throated blue, 193; black-throated green, 194; blackburnian, 194; blackpoll, 194; blue-winged, 193; Canada, 195; Cape May, 194; cerulean, 194; chestnut-sided, 194; Connecticut, 195; golden-winged, 193; hooded, 195; Kentucky, 195; magnolia, 194; mourning, 195; Nashville, 193; orange-crowned, 193; palm, 195; pine, 195; prairie, 64, 194; prothonotary, 193; Tennessee, 193; Wilson's, 195; worm-eating, 195; yellow, 195; yellow-rumped, 194; yellow-throated, 194
warmouth, 167
watercress, 115
waterleaf, 136
water-lily, 110
water-meal, 96
water-pepper, 106
waterthrush, 196
water-willow, 143
waxwing, 192
weasels, 34, 35, 206
wheat, 46
whip-poor-will, 185-86
white-top, 151

whitlow-grass, 115
widgeon, 178
widow's-cross, 116
willow, 59, 101, 102
willow-herb, 130
Wilsonia canadensis, 195; *citrina,* 195; *pusilla,* 195
wingstem, 155
wintercreeper, 59, 126
wintercress, 113
wintergreen, spotted, 133
witch grass, 88, 89
witch-hazel, 117
wolf: gray, 37, 77; dire, 35
Wolffia punctata, 96
wood-betony, 142
woodchuck, 34, 62, 63, 64, 65, 203
wood-mint, 137
woodcock, 64, 68, 181
woodpecker, 62; downy, 187; hairy, 187; ivory-billed, 39, 77; pileated, 77, 187; red-bellied, 186; red-headed, 186
woodrat, 70, 204
woodsia, 83
Woodsia obtusa, 53, 83
wood-sorrel, 123, 124
wool-grass, 96
woolly croton, 125
wormwood, 148
wren, 63; Bewick's, 190; Carolina, 190; house, 189-90; marsh, 190; sedge, 190; winter, 190

Xanthium globosum, 155; *italicum,* 155; *pensylvanicum,* 155; *strumarium* var. *glabratum,* 155
Xanthocephalus xanthocephalus, 199
Xanthoxylum americanum, 25, 124
Xyridaceae, 96
Xyris caroliniana, 96

yam, wild, 100
yarrow, 147
yellowlegs, 180
yellowthroat, 196
yellowwood, 53, 54, 55
yerba de tago, 150

Zapodidae, 205
Zapus hudsonius, 205
Zenaidura macroura, 184
Zizia aptera, 53, 132; *aurea,* 132; *trifoliata,* 132
Zonotrichia albicollis, 198; *leucophrys,* 198; *querula,* 198

General Index

Adena people, 34
Allen, James Lane, 48
Allen, Samuel, 48
Alton swamp, 11
American Agriculturist, 48
American Farmer, 49
American Revolution, 42, 43
Anderson, W.A., 80
Anderson County, 11
Audubon, John James, 40, 46

Baltimore, Md., 49
Becket, Mary Ruth, 80
beech ridge, 20, 26
bentonite, 10
Berry, Wendell, 215, 221
Big Bone Lick, 33
Big Sink, 17
Blackburn, William, 80
Bluegrass, Outer, 8, 25, 33, 39, 47, 69, 77, 159
Bluegrass Area Development District, 223
Bluegrass Plain, 13, 20, 25, 27, 29, 43, 46, 48, 51, 58, 61
Blue Licks, 33, 36, 38
Boiling Springs, 41
Boone, Daniel, 1, 23, 24, 27, 36, 38, 39, 41, 43
Boone, Edward, 24, 27
Boone, Squire, 35, 38
Boone Creek (Fayette County), 13, 14, 15, 45
Boone's Creek (Bourbon County), 24
Boonesborough, 15, 23, 36, 38, 41, 49
Bourbon County, 15, 20, 24, 25, 26, 29, 38, 39, 47, 60, 80
Bourbon County Agricultural Society, 50
Bradbury, John, 26
Bradford, John, 24
Braun, E. Lucy, 1, 51, 80
Breckinridge, John, 45
Breeders' Cup races, 210
Bromfield, Louis, 12
Bryan, Hal, 80
Bryan's (or Bryant's) Station, 24, 43
Bryan Station Fault Zone, 8, 11, 26, *back endsheet*
Bryant, William S., 2, 60, 80
Bullitt, Capt. Thomas, 42

calciphiles, 156
Campbell, Julian J.N., 2, 80
Camp Nelson limestone, 9, 15
canebrake, 24, 25, 46
Cane Ridge, 24, 25
Cane Run, 216, 217
Carr, Elwood, 80
Castleman, Gen. John B., 26
cattle industry, 49, 50
caves, 70
Cave Spring, 7, 219
Cincinnati Arch, 5
Civil War, 46, 209
Clark, George Rogers, 41
Clark, Thomas D., 1
Clark County, 36, 41, 47
Clay, Green, 45
Clay, Henry, 45
Clay's Ferry formation, 8, 20, 158
Clean Air Act, 222
Clean Water Act, 222
Clear Creek, 15
Cleveland, Eli, 45
Clinkenbeard, William, 24, 25, 37, 38, 39, 46
Collins, Josiah, 24
Commerce Cabinet, Kentucky, 212, 221
Cranfill, Ray, 80
Cretaceous Period, 116, 228
Cross Plains, 38
Cynthiana, 17

David's Fork, 36
Davidson, Ursula, 2, 28, 31
Devil's Backbone, 11
Dix (Dick's) River, 15, 16, 20
Douglas, James, 42
drainage, 16-17, 18, 219-20
Drake, Daniel, 20
Draper, Lyman, 22
Dufour, Mr., 20
Duke Basil, 15, 17
Duncan Tavern, 39

Eden hills (Eden shale), 5, 8, 17, 20, 22, 47
Elkhorn Creek, Elkhorn lands, 15, 16, 18, 22, 23, 24, 25, 26, 57, 58, 216
Elk Lick Creek, 15, 56
endangered species, 156
Endangered Species Act, 222
English, Logan, 207
Environmental Impact Statement, 222
Eocene Epoch, 16, 228
Epsom Derby, 210
excluded species, 157-58

Falconer, Joice Craig, 36, 38
Farrar, Asa, 25
Fayette County, 2, 8, 17, 21, 22, 26, 28, 30, 31, 33, 36, 43, 47, 55, 56, 63, 75, 158, 210, 211, 226
Filson, John, 12, 25, 36, 39, 46, 57
Finley, James B., 24
Finley, John, 34, 41
Floyd, John, 42, 45
forest regions: Mixed Mesophytic, 51, 53; Western Mesophytic, 51
forest composition: maple-oak-ash, 52; oak-ash, 53; oak-ash-maple, 52; oak-cedar, 53; oak-hickory, 51, 53; oak-hickory-cedar, 52
Fort Ancient Culture, 32
Fort Harrod, 41
Frankfort, 15, 23, 37, 39, 218, 220
Franklin County, 11
French and Indian War, 40, 42
fur traders, 34, 41

Garrard County, 54, 55
Georgetown, 17, 24, 216-17

Georgetown College, 207
Gilbert Creek, 15
Gist, Chrisopher, 27, 40
Glenn's Creek, 24
Gluck, Maxwell H., Equine Research Center, 210
Graddy, Jesse, 24, 38
Grassy Lick, 27
Green Creek, 25
Guharja, Edi, 80

Hanson, Thomas, 23
Harrison County, 15, 29, 60
Harrodsburg, 17, 20, 24
Hedge, John, 38
Henderson, Col. Richard, 23, 38
Hickman Creek, 15, 25
Hickman Creek Fault Zone, 8, 11, 20, 26, *back endsheet*
High Bridge limestones, 9-10, 13
Hinkston Creek, 24, 26, 80
Hite, Isaac, 42
horse industry, 49, 209-14
Hutchens, Thomas, 25

Imlay, Gilbert, 25-26, 41, 46
Indians, 34-35, 45

January, Ephraim, 24
Jessamine County, 8, 13, 15, 18, 20, 45, 63, 219
Jessamine Creek, 15, 25
Jessamine Dome, 5
Jockey Club, 210

karst area, 16, 32, 215, 219
Kenton, Simon, 36-37
Kentucky, Commonwealth of, 220, 222
Kentucky Association for the Improvement of Breeds of Stock, 50
Kentucky Gazette, 24, 49, 50
Kentucky Horse Park, 211
Kentucky Land Office, 42
Kentucky River, 13, 15-17, 26, 45, 46, 66, 74, 77, *back endsheet*
Kentucky River Fault, 8, 15, 20, *back endsheet*
Kentucky River gorge and Palisades, 11, 13, 14, 20, 22, 51-58, 65, 213, 223-24
Kentucky River vicinity, 9, 20, 25, 47, 48-49, 57, 61, 64, 156
Knobs area, 69, 75, 77, 159

land: grants, 42-43, 45; surveys, 41, 42-45; use patterns, 221-22
Lee's Branch swamp, 18
Lemon's Mill Rd., 216
Lexington, 17, 18, 19, 22, 25, 30, 59, 67, 77, 209, 217
Lexington limestones, 10-11, 15-16
Licking River, 11, 15, 25, 26, 36, 47, 74
Long Hunters, 35

McAfee, James, 25, 53
McAfee, Robert, 25, 53
McComb, William, 157
McCoy, Thomas, 80
McFarland, James, 80
McMurtrie, Henry, 53
Madison County, 45, 54, 57
Martin, William H., 2, 60
Mason County, 25, 47
Mastin, Bettye Lee, 208
Maysville, 19, 37
Medley, Max, 80
Meijer, Willem, 80
Melish, John, 47
Mercer County, 54
Meredith, Col. Samuel, 42-43
Meredith, Samuel, 42-43
Michaux, André, 2, 31
Michaux, François, 2, 12, 19, 21, 49
microclimates, 55
mills, 48-49
Miocene Epoch, 13, 228
Mississippi River, 46
Montgomery County, 27, 36
Morse, Jedidiah, 25

Nashville, Tenn., 31
National Environmental Policy Act, 222
National Gazette, 38, 47
Nature Conservancy, 79
Nature Preserves Commission, 80
New Orleans, 46, 49
Nicholas County, 33, 80
Nicholasville, 17, 218
Nourse, James, 23

Ohio River, 25, 34, 42, 46
Ohio Valley, 32
Ordovician Period, 8-12
Oregon limestone, 9

Paris, 39
Parry, Needham, 26
peneplain, 12, 13, 17
Peter, Robert, 12
Philadelphia, Pa., 49
Pledge, John, 46
Pleistocene Epoch, 13, 33, 34, 228
Pliocene Epoch, 13, 17, 158, 228
Preston, Col. William, 42, 43
Prix de l'Arc de Triomphe, 210
Rafinesque, Constantine, 22
Raven Run, 15, 45, 223
Records, Spencer, 24
Rice, Steve, 80
Rogert, Joseph, 43
Royal Spring, 17, 216, 217
Russell, Henry, 43
Russell, Robert, 43
Russell, William, 43
Russell Cave Spring, 17, 43

St. Asaph's, 41
savanna, 25, 31, 32
savanna-woodland, 28-29, 32, 47-48, 59, 60
Scholl, Septimus, 27
Scott County, 33, 36, 37, 43, 47, 58, 60
Shakertown at Pleasant Hill, 223
Shane, John R., 22, 27
Shelby County, 47
Short, Charles Wilkins, 19, 21, 22, 32
Sierra Club, 224
Sinking Creek, 18, 219
sinks, 16, 17
Smith, Thomas, Jr., 49
soils: Huntington, Lowell, McAfee, 11; Maury, 11, 31
South Carolina, 49
springs, 17
Spring Station spring, 17
stamping grounds, 37
Stoner Creek, 15, 26, 38

Taylor, Hancock, 23, 42, 45
Teays drainage system, 15
Tennessee, 31
Todd, Levi, 23
Toulmin, 41
tourism, 210-11
Townsend Creek, 15
Trabue, Daniel, 38
Transportation Cabinet, Kentucky, 222
Transylvania University, 22
Trumbo Bottom, 11
Tyrone limestone, 9-10

University of Kentucky, 79-80, 157
U.S. Army Corps of Engineers, 218

Varner, Johnnie B., 2, 60, 79
Versailles, 17, 24, 218

Walker, Felix, 23, 36
Walker, Dr. Thomas, 40
Wall Street Journal, 212
Walnut Hill Church, 25

water: quality, 215; supply, 218
Welch Cave, 3, 33-35
Western Gazetteer, 48
Western Monthly Magazine, 48
Wharton, Mary E., 60, 79
Wilmore, 218
Wilson, Alexander, 39
Winchester, 24, 39
Wisconsin time, 32
Woodford County, 8, 13, 17, 18, 24, 33, 36, 41, 43, 47, 60
woodland pastures, 28-29, 47-48
Wymore, Martin, 24, 36, 63

xerothermic interval, 32

Yadkin Valley, 35

KENTUCKY RIVER AND WEST HICKMAN-BRYAN STATION FAULT ZONES

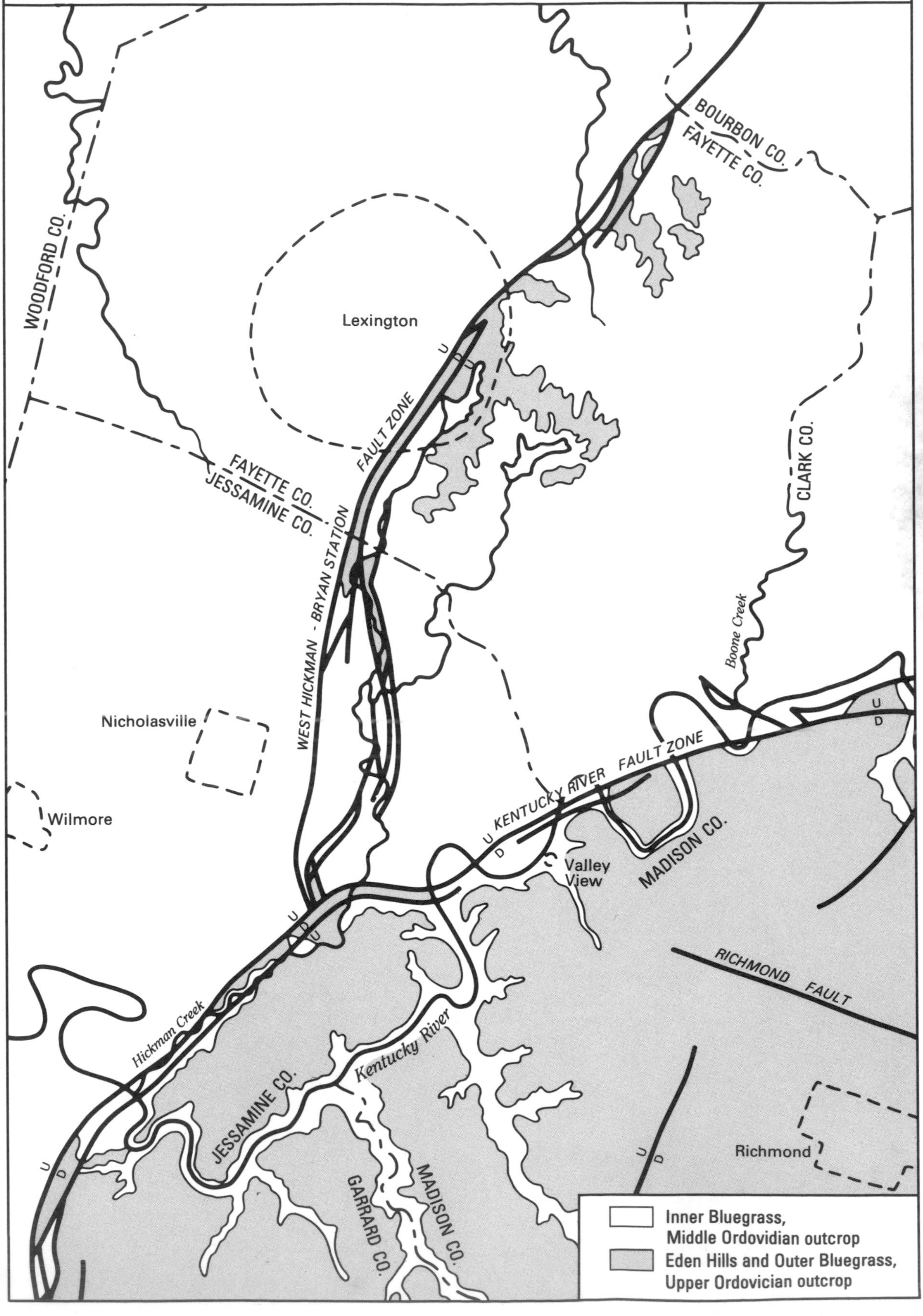